William Allen White

The Man from Emporia

William Allen White

William Allen White
The Man from Emporia

BY

EVERETT RICH

Illustrated with Photographs

FARRAR & RINEHART, INC.

NEW YORK   TORONTO

*What we want, and what we shall
have, is the royal American privilege
of living and dying in a country town,
running a country newspaper, saying
what we please when we please, how
we please and to whom we please.*

—Emporia *Gazette,*
December 6, 1911.

Preface

MY PURPOSE in the chapters that follow has been to portray in William Allen White's career the qualities of mind and heart that have impressed his community and nation. Mr. White achieved a national name in literature, journalism, and politics without leaving his home town—a midwestern village offering no advantages over thousands of others for influencing national thought; yet such is his reputation today "that few national enterprises of a public nature are launched without their projectors seeking at least his moral support." [1]

The story begins with his pioneer parents, who did much to shape his career. Before he was ten his mother had read the leading Victorian novels to him, and his father had acquainted him with politics and set him to work in a newspaper office. His public career has been an extension of these three interests.

Because all his writings bear the stamp of his personality, the generous quotations are not only to give authority to what I have written but also to portray his personality in his own words; and rather than clutter my pages with superfluous footnotes, I have followed the practice of footnoting the last quotation in a series from the same source.

I am indebted to many persons for much valuable assistance: to Professor DeLancey Ferguson, who worked with me personally on all my problems; to Dean E. J. Benton, who ushered me through the Progressive Era; to Professor Finley M. K. Foster, and Professor Harold A. Blaine, who read my manuscript and offered suggestions—all of Western Reserve

[1] Willis J. Abbot, *Watching the World Go By*, 51.

University; to Professor Theodore C. Owen, Emporia State Teachers College, who made numerous suggestions; to Mr. Ewing Herbert, editor of the Brown County *World,* for material relating to Mr. White's youth; to Mrs. Ralph Knouse, for typing the manuscript; to Professor George Phillips, Emporia State Teachers College, for copying numerous photographs; and to Mr. White, who freely answered all my questions. I am also obligated to four library staffs—Western Reserve University, Emporia State Teachers College, Emporia City, and Kansas State Historical Society—and to many members of the *Gazette* staff both present and past. Debts of a more fugitive kind have been acknowledged in the text.

I wish to state that all opinions and conclusions are my own. Mr. White read only the first two chapters of my manuscript, and offered but one opinion in all our conferences—something about his university education which I have now forgotten. As a writer, he has been giving his opinions about other men for fifty years and is determined that those who write about him will exercise the same privilege.

Lastly, I want to say a word in self-defense. If at times I am captious, I am trying only to be fair; and if at other times I am eulogistic—too much should not be expected from an Emporian who knows Mr. White and has read his writings daily for twenty years.

E. R.

Emporia, Kansas
April 7, 1941.

Table of Contents

Table of Contents

List of Illustrations

William Allen White
The Man from Emporia

CHAPTER I

The Stock from Which He Sprang

Kansas is the child of a race of pioneers, not a race of dreamers. The "dream state" we have erected is upon the visions of other minds, other generations, other seers. Kansas offers small encouragement to seers; she is no house of refuge for theorists, but if a two-fisted practical man with a workable plan to produce justice and good will comes ambling up the Kaw Valley he is met by a brass band. Nothing in Kansas is too good for him.[1]

IT WAS almost ten o'clock on Thursday night, January 19, 1865, when the Emporia stage went around to the hotel in Lawrence, Kansas, to take on its final passenger. That passenger, the new president of the Kansas State Normal School at Emporia, approached the driver and announced that he was Lyman B. Kellogg. The driver glanced at his waybill and nodded his approval, for this time the young president of the new school had made sure that he would not be left behind. This was Kellogg's first trip "West," and everywhere he was experiencing the unexpected. Especially was he not prepared for the activity going on all about him. Twice in the last forty-eight hours he had realized the harsh reality of that activity. Late the day before he had crossed the Missouri-Kansas line. At night when he sought a hotel room in Leavenworth, a city of thirty thousand people, he was told that every room was already occupied. The management, to relieve the over-taxed facilities of the hotel, had leased a near-by building. In this building, also, all the rooms were taken; but one was occupied by only one man, and into this room the night clerk put Kel-

[1] The footnotes will be found in the back of the book, beginning page 333.

logg, with the injunction that he would either have to leave his door unlocked or get up and let his roommate in when he returned. Kellogg went to bed leaving the door unlocked; and somewhat after midnight, when the other guest returned, he feigned sleep as he watched his bedfellow carefully remove a revolver from underneath his coat, inspect it, and put it under his pillow. Next morning Kellogg learned from the stranger that it was customary to carry a gun when away from home; and although one was not likely to need it, one never knew when one might, and "the occasion might come quickly." [2] Next morning he learned, also, that unless one registered for a stage in advance, one would be left behind when the stage was full. This oversight, however, did not occasion any great inconvenience; in a few hours an extra stage for which Kellogg had duly registered was on its way to Lawrence.

His first sight of the Emporia stage was not reassuring to Lyman B. Kellogg. The vehicle, neither large nor commodious, was a rather small two-horse affair known as a "jerky." Outside was the driver's seat; inside were two seats for two passengers each. Already nine persons were crowded into these three seats, and Kellogg was to make the tenth. As he tried to get in, a man's voice said, "You may come with us on the back seat. There are three of us here already, but you may sit on my lap, for a while anyway." [3] The speaker was Jonathan H. Hunt, the editor of the Emporia *News*. Kellogg climbed in, took his seat upon Hunt's knee, and began the last lap of his journey to Emporia.

That journey from Lawrence, now a ninety-mile trip which may be made easily in two hours by railroad or by automobile, lasted all that night and until after dark the next day. Between the two towns the country was practically uninhabited, with only here and there a village or a post where the stage stopped for meals or to change horses. At that time, when there was not a single railroad in Kansas, travel was entirely by stage, buckboard, horseback, or on foot. Roads were mere trails across the prairies, but even at this time of the year "smooth and dry, and to some extent dusty." This fact greatly impressed the new president from Illinois, where the winter roads "were always snow or frozen and hubby" or if thawed, "very muddy." No less strange to Kellogg was the mildness of the January weather, for it was "warm like October in Illinois." These aspects of the new country must have furnished many a topic for discussion for the passengers, and especially for Kellogg and the other passenger from Illinois— an Irish girl in her late thirties yet, even in that day, too youthful in spirit to be called old—as they jogged along in the stage or as they got out and walked up the hills to relieve their "cramped limbs" and "to lighten the load for the two horses." [4]

Next day the Emporia *News* printed the following local item:

Distinguished Arrivals

Arrived by last night's stage—Hon. J. R. Swallow, Prof. L. B. Kellogg, of the Illinois State Normal University; Mr. Buchanan, treasure[r] of Chase county; J. C. Fraker, treasure[r] of Lyon county; D. S. Gilmore, of the 11worth Times; R. S. Crampton, of Baltimore, and J. H. Hunt, of the "Emporia News." —All report favorable.[5]

From this "distinguished" group of editors, preachers, educators, and public officials, the name of the other Illinois passenger is missing. She was "coming out to Kansas" to go to college. Her name was Mary Ann Hatton, the Irish girl who became the mother of William Allen White.

It was in keeping with the circumstances of Mary Hatton's past life that she was now among strangers, enduring the hardships of a frontier civilization. Hers had always been a life of hardships, mostly among strangers. Her parents, Frank Hatton and Annie Kelly, had been married in Ireland without the knowledge and consent of their parents; and then, fearing parental opposition, had sailed for Canada. Near Quebec the young couple took up "land in the primeval forest," [6] where Mary Ann Hatton, the first of three children, was born in a log cabin on January 3, 1830. Her father, a stonemason, had little money after paying the passage to Canada and was compelled to find employment at his trade in Quebec. Consequently, the young wife and her baby were left alone much of the time in their forest home. In the woods about the log cabin lurked the wildcat and the bear, filling the mother's days and nights with terror. During the day the "friendly" Indians frequented her cabin to partake of her little store of food and to sit by her fireplace, frightening her hardly less than the wild beasts of the forest. The nearest neighbor lived a mile away; and when her husband was away from home, the mother was forced to walk to the neighbor's home for the baby's milk, leaving the baby behind alone in the log cabin. Never did the mother make this trip that she did not fear for her own and her baby's life, but so well did she hide her fears that the Indians "called her a brave squaw." [7]

After the birth of two more children, the Hatton family moved to Oswego, New York, where Frank Hatton became a contractor and prospered. But tragedy was to follow tragedy. First the father died, and then the mother; so that Mary Ann Hatton found herself an orphan at the age of sixteen with a younger brother and a younger sister to rear. She provided for them until her brother ran away to sea and her sister married. Then free of family responsibilities, she went to Chicago to live with a Mr. and Mrs. Wright, who had befriended her after the death of her parents. The Wrights were Congregationalists and were interested in Knox College at Galesburg, Illinois. Through them she became a student there.

Mary Ann Hatton evinced many of the characteristics attributed to the Irish; she was quick-witted, quick-tempered, and volatile. Her parents had been Catholics, but after their death she had become a Congregationalist. Environment had made her a "black" Republican and a militant Abolitionist. In Galesburg she heard Lincoln and Douglas debate, knew intimately Mother Bickerdyke, the Civil War nurse, went with the crowd to cheer "the boys" when they started for the Civil War, and wept because she had no one to send. She was, moreover, a person who had her own ideas and who wanted to make them prevail. She knew what she wanted, and could be bold in attaining it. At the age of seventy-nine she made a five-months' trip to Europe with her son and his family. In Ireland she saw the church in which her parents were married, and the house in which her mother was born. Because she wanted to see her father's birthplace, she rode an Irish jaunting cart from Dublin to the town in which he was born. Not easily was she dissuaded

from a course of action. Her school record at Knox shows that
from first to last she was in and out of school for a seven-
year period. She worked as a milliner, as a dressmaker, and as
a practical nurse to further her education. Then she became a
teacher, alternating teaching with going to school. At the age
of thirty-five, hearing about the new normal school at Emporia,
she set out to get more education.

The family story is that Mary Hatton was unable to find
a place to : m in Emporia; and the story may be true, for
Emporia had a population of only four hundred in 1865. For
several weeks, notices of the school's opening had been printed
in the weekly paper, and these notices called upon the citizens to make the necessary sacrifices to keep new students
from being turned away, noting at the same time that few people had extra rooms. It is just as likely, though, that her failure to remain in Emporia was due to her inability to find a
place "to work her way." And not having money enough to
pay for room and board, she turned again to teaching, securing
the spring term at Council Grove, a town thirty miles from
Emporia.

Mary Hatton found in Council Grove fewer amenities of
civilization than in Emporia. It was then the last important
outfitting post on the Santa Fe trail. Blacksmith shops, wagon
repair shops, livery stables, dance halls, and saloons lined its
streets. Everywhere were plainsmen, ox drivers, horsemen, and
Indians from a near-by reservation. Council Grove was pro-
slavery, and this fact got Mary Ann Hatton into trouble the
first Sunday she was there. She went to Sunday school with
the Wright family, who had preceded her in coming to Kansas;
and there she taught a Sunday school class of small girls.

One especially bright little dark-skinned girl attracted me, and it
did not occur to me that she was a colored child, though among
Congregationalists that would have made no difference. I told all
the little girls I hoped I would see them at school next day, and
added a special invitation to the little girl to whom I had been
attracted. . . .

News of my inviting a 'nigger' to come to school . . . spread,
and next morning when I went to the schoolhouse there was an air
of excitement among the children, and they stood around in groups,
whispering. The big bell had been taken away by a member of the

school board, but I called the children together with a little bell I carried with me . . . and I gave the little colored girl a seat. A pretty little white girl asked to sit by her, which I allowed her to do. Just then came a knock at the door. 'I want to talk to you—come outside,' a man said to me. 'No, come in,' I said. 'There's not much talking to do,' he said. 'I've come to put out that damned nigger—show her to me.' I refused, and he couldn't pick her out among the other children. He was chagrined when he found his own child was sitting by the 'nigger.' Other members of the board came, and several of the parents, and by the end of the first recess, my school of 70 pupils had dwindled down to 20, as ..ey took their children home. The primary teacher also declared she 'didn't come there to teach "niggers" ' so she, too, went home, after I told her she'd teach them if she taught with me. Her friends made up a purse for her, and she never came back. One of the larger girls taught the primary children.[8]

The next morning when she attempted to open the schoolhouse, she found the door locked and the windows nailed down. Wright opened the schoolhouse for her and school went on with a "light attendance." The pro-slavery people, again finding their will thwarted, held an indignation meeting that night. Wright asked to speak and introduced Sam Wood, who lived at Cottonwood Falls, a near-by town. Wood, a free-state adventurer, had once been a conductor of the Underground Railroad in Ohio. During the early territorial days he had come to Kansas to cast his lot with the free-state element. For two hours he staged a one-man filibuster. He joked, jollied, and entertained the pro-slavers, sometimes "kidding" them lightly about the "niggers," and at other times talking "about every thing under the sun," but always keeping them in a good humor. When Wood finally sat down, "it was time to go home, and the indignation meeting was a fizzle." [9]

Mary Hatton soon realized that the pro-slavery sentiment was too strong to insist that Negro children be permitted to attend her school; nonetheless, racial discrimination was to her so intolerable that she nagged at the members of the school board until they established a separate school for the Negro children. The victory which she thus won for the colored people was unqualified and complete, for to this day Council Grove maintains separate schools for colored children; but it was probably won at the cost of her job, for the next year she began to teach at Cottonwood Falls, where she lived with Sam Wood and his family.

Kansas, "a dreary and forsaken land," "far from the amenities of even the rough civilization in Illinois" [10] appalled Mary Ann Hatton. It was the negation of what she had struggled for in college. To escape its social poverty, she turned to whatever diversions her community had to offer. One night, while still teaching in Cottonwood Falls, she attended a dance at the Robinson House in Emporia. There she met Dr. Allen White—old Doc White, doctor, merchant, trader—for whom Emporia, with its four hundred people, its story-and-a-half frame hotel, its ten-year-old newspaper, and its newly-founded normal school, was already too crowded and too sophisticated.

The love affair of the ensuing months was probably "pretty mature and deliberate," she being in her late thirties and he in his late forties. That fall she again planned to attend Emporia Normal; but before she had completed her arrangements, she was summoned to her sister's home in Michigan, where "another baby was coming." [11] In the spring Allen White went to St. Louis to buy a new stock of goods; and four days after the marriage actually occurred, the local newspaper reported that "Madame Rumor has it that our friend and fellow-townsman, Dr. A. White, was married a few days ago in Michigan." [12] Two weeks later the arrival of the Doctor and his new wife confirmed the rumor.

On Monday evening a reception took place at the Doctor's residence, at which a large number of our citizens were present, including the members of the Silver Cornet Band. The Band entertained the company with some of their best music. A good supper was partaken of, which had been prepared by the Doctor's friends previous to his arrival, and all present enjoyed the occasion in the highest degree. None seemed to be happier than Dr. White and his estimable lady.[13]

In beliefs, in heritance, in temperament Dr. White and his wife were far apart. Both were Congregationalists, both were sentimental, and both were positive in their views; otherwise each traveled a separate road on most matters. He was an ardent Democrat; she a black Republican. She "fought, bled, and died" for the cause of abolition; and he, who all the while

believed in the South and its ways, said that his state had
denied her suffrage and had given it to the ex-slaves when the
Negro was enfranchised in Kansas. To her, life on the frontier
meant restriction, self-denial, and sacrifice; to him, it meant
activity, liberty, and success. She had struggled for two decades
at four trades to win an education and the bare necessaries of
life; he had come from a prosperous family, had been sent to
medical school, and after beginning his practice, being too
tender-hearted to collect doctor bills, had turned to storekeeping
and "dabbling" in real estate to find that everything he touched
turned to gold. Her opinion of money was, quite naturally,
high; and as for him, the only real economy he ever practiced
was that he "kept his high priced 'fine-cut' tobacco in a silver
case in his hip-pocket and carried plug tobacco in his coat
pocket for strangers." [14]

Their attitudes and habits, though in marked contrast,
differed no more than their ancestry. Allen White's American
forefathers dated back to Nicholas White, who was living at
Dorchester, Massachusetts, in 1643.[15] His descendants, car-
penters, surveyors, landholders, and town officials mostly, lived
in Raynham until after the Revolution. Allen's paternal grandfather was a sergeant in the Revolutionary Army, and his
father, John White, married into the Perry family, which contributed the American naval heroes of that name. In the early
years of the nineteenth century John White moved to New
York, where he established a foundry and followed his trade
as iron molder. The business eventually failed, and in the second decade of the century he loaded his family into a wagon
and moved west to Norwalk, Ohio. There Allen White was
born in 1819, the twelfth child in a family of thirteen children.

The prosperity John White had sought in New York he
found in Ohio. Thirteen stalwart sons and daughters guaranteed ample man power to clear and till the virgin soil. During
their teens the boys farmed the land, the girls did the work in
and around the house, and the father and mother saw that a
part of their prosperity went to educate their children. It fell
to Allen's lot to become a doctor; and after attending the Co-
lumbus Medical College, he practiced medicine and kept a store

in Delta, Ohio. There in an ill-advised union which ended in divorce, he married a woman so much older than himself that some of her children by a previous marriage were almost his contemporaries.

Allen White was born restless; he was fifty before he stopped moving from place to place. First, he went to Texas. Probably he chose a southern state because throughout his life he esteemed the South and southern ways of life; but once there he found that he could not abide the "South's fried food and hot bread." [16] His next move was to Americus, Kansas, in 1859. Then when the county seat was moved from Americus to Emporia, he went too. Next he took a two-year leave of absence from Emporia, practicing medicine, serving as county treasurer, and keeping the inevitable store in a near-by county. When this two-year sojourn was up, he returned to Emporia and married his second wife, Mary Ann Hatton. A year later on February 10, 1868, their only child to survive infancy, William Allen White, was born.

In 1868 the birth of a child was not news. The papers briefly noted marriages and deaths, but not births; consequently, the Emporia *News* does not record the birth of Emporia's most distinguished citizen. If the columns of the newspaper are a reliable index to their interests, Emporians in 1868 were concerned largely with their state's potentialities and the progress being made in developing them. Each weekly issue of the *News* contained a glowing report of some Kansas county which needed but men and money to blossom into an Eden. The week that William Allen White was born one such account appeared that must have stirred his father's pioneer spirit. Sixty miles southwest of Emporia was a county which eleven years before had been the "home of the Indian, buffalo, wolf," but which now boasted of twelve hundred people, nine schoolhouses, but as yet no churches or railroads. This region had "fine indications of coal but no developments," because of the abundance of wood. Its several needs were saw and grist mills, mechanics, schoolteachers, preachers, and laboring men of all classes; and its particular excellence lay in the assumption that its streams were unsurpassed. Within the year Allen White had packed up his earthly possession, his wife, and his "puny baby"

—whose mother all the first summer of his life had taken him
out for rides at four o'clock in the morning in order that he
might have fresh air and yet escape the intense Kansas heat—
and moved them to El Dorado, in Butler County, Kansas.

In or near El Dorado, Allen White lived the remaining
thirteen years of his life. There he found a congenial atmosphere, becoming a man of consequence in his community and
leaving behind him an honored name. He was a man of strong
convictions. One of his favorite, and original, sayings was, "It
is a good thing (for Smith or Jones) that there is no statute
against d——d fools." [17] But however strong his personal convictions, loyalty to his town took precedence over all personal
considerations. He had the reputation of being "the most public
spirited citizen in the new town." Whenever a subscription
paper was circulated to raise money for a local cause "the name
of Dr. White always headed the list with the largest contribution." [18] Above every other office he desired to be street com-
missioner that he might be the official as well as the unofficial
leader in the improvement of his town; and when El Dorado
set aside new land for a park, he, with his own hands, dug
holes and planted trees on the site. Whatever public improvement was proposed—be it a newspaper, a park, a hotel, or a
courthouse—old Doc White usually became its chief promoter.

Not only was he El Dorado's chief promoter; he was its
chief defender. Had it not been for Dr. Allen White, El
Dorado "would have been rubbed off the map." This account
depicts him in the role of chief defender of his town:

In the early '70's El Dorado was sitting pretty, near the center of
the big county into which a flood of immigration was pouring. But
stormy conditions soon gathered. A territory 20 miles wide on the
south end of the county had been ceded to settlers by the Osage
Indians. For the accommodation of this immigration a new land
office for filings was located at Augusta. That land office drew all
the settlers there to file on their claims. Land office attorneys and
real estate agents flocked there. Augusta boomed. It purposed to
divide the county and make for itself the county seat of the south
county, and from then on came the all-absorbing tug of a county
seat war.[19]

In order to maintain its advantage in holding the county
seat, El Dorado had to have a courthouse. A two thousand

dollar building was proposed, but the town lacked the popular
strength to vote taxation to build the structure. The building,
therefore, had to be erected by private contributions, and Dr.
Allen White's name headed the list of contributors with a do-
nation of $150.[20]

Fight after fight followed. Railroad bond propositions to give
[to] El Dorado or to Augusta an advantage were promulgated.
County seat elections and the choice of representatives in the legislature followed, wave upon wave.

Politics, and fitness for office, all things of public nature were
submerged beneath the all absorbing county seat fight. Nor did it
stop there: Private bitterness and personal animosities naturally
sprouted and grew. At one time and for quite a while both Augusta
and El Dorado had armed organizations to carry out their
purposes.[21]

. . . A battle almost occurred one summer night when Augusta
came armed to storm the courthouse by force and found El Dora-
doans, forewarned, packed inside the courthouse and over its roofs
with rifles sticking out of the windows and doors and bristling
from the roof like 'quills upon the fretful porcupine.' Augusta accepted the inevitable and retired, nursing its wrath. But 'old Doc.
White,' . . . a shining target in white nankeen pants, white pleated
shirt and white panama hat, paraded the streets around the courthouse, the only unarmed man in the town to greet the invaders
with gay and flippant persiflage. His wife begged him to put on
his black Sunday suit to be less conspicuous, but he was ribald
in his reply that if they hit him they wouldn't hit the courthouse!
And his wife was frightened to what now we know as the jitters.
Augusta stood around for an hour looking at the courthouse fortress and went home and burned Old Doc in effigy, head of 'the
Courthouse Ring!' It gave him delight to his dying days. For he
was so built that he loved better than the applause of the multitude,
the impotent cackling rage of his enemies. At that he could
chuckle.[22]

For all Allen White's public-spiritedness, his pioneer urge
did not surrender without a struggle to the oncoming tide of
civilization. If in his fifties he was not yet too old to move on,
matrimonial ties had firmly anchored him. One day an "awful
family row" started over a "fake farm adventure." The old
Doc, who had decided that he would be a gentleman farmer,
bought a big farm and built a log house on it, "with a big fireplace and all the foolish trappings of a pioneer farmer's place

in the early part of the last century—the kind of a place in which he was born and reared." [23] He could as well have had a decent board and plastered house, but he wanted to reproduce the good old days in so far as possible. The family lay down at night on log beds beneath dried pumpkin, sage, and other "smelly things" hung on the rafters above. He even built a trundle bed for his young son. The adventure, however, was short-lived. Allen White was too old to farm; men had to be hired to do the work, and hired men meant work—hard work for his wife. Then when she could get no hired girl to go to the farm, she "blew up" and the Whites moved back to town.

Allen White was soon in another characteristic role. El Dorado had no good hotel, and the old Doc, who had built a "whaling big house" after his return from the farm, decided to convert his new home into a hotel. By a simple method he gained a wide reputation as a model landlord. He served only the best food, "and that meant thick beefsteak and rare roast beef, . . . throwing away everything but the breasts from the prairie chickens, and real buckwheat cakes that you stir and leave on the reservoir of the stove to rise overnight to serve with real maple syrup in the morning. And all for $2 a day!" While Mrs. White "sweat in the kitchen" and complained that they were "headed straight for the poor house," he would "swank around the front porch in his nankeens, his white vest, and his white suspenders, talking politics. . . ." Then one day Mrs. White "blew up again." The hotel closed, breaking the old Doc's heart; for "keeping hotel and losing money at it, so that he could not accuse himself of capitalizing his hospitality, was the one proud period of his life." [24]

But for all Allen White's prodigality he was amassing a comfortable estate. He lived in the best house in El Dorado, owned rental properties in both town and country, had bonds, stocks, and a sizeable bank account. With him as with his son, William Allen, money always came easy, and went easy—but it always came. Like his son, he thought poorly of money and material things. Both violated every copybook maxim of success, and neither ever had to take thought of the morrow.

CHAPTER II

The Court of Boyville

. . . Behold El Dorado, Butler County, Kansas, in the early seventies: a frontier town, a dusty road crossing a prairie creek and making a grey streak up a long hill. Beside the road were dingy, unpainted wooden buildings, mostly of one story, a stone hotel facing a brick bank on the diagonal corner; a wood culvert crossing a ravine that ran from one side to the other of the street; a livery stable facing a saloon; shanties with false fronts stair-stepping in size down from the thick of the town out toward the sunflowers that lined the grey, dusty streak of a road as it topped the distant hill.

Beyond the shambling false fronts of the squatty town, set back from the street, rose the stone school house: two stories, four rooms, capped by a bell tower that clanged the first bell and the second bell twice a day, five days in the week, nine months in the year.

Beyond the school house, and up to its very door, stretched westward to the Rockies the illimitable prairie.[1]

WHEN the Whites moved from Emporia to El Dorado, they first lived in a native lumber house, which served both as their home and as a general store. It was a rambling, single-story structure with rusty sheet iron chimneys rising from every room. In the winter these chimneys spouted smoke and soot all over the roof till the neighbors christened the house the "foundry." Mrs. White had papered the rooms with old newspapers; and from the Emporia *News* that lined the kitchen, Will learned his letters. Here also he learned to love books, as night after night he sat in a chair looking up into his mother's face while she read to him and while the practical Yankee father growled that his son would never learn to read as long as his mother kept up this practice.

Will White was not an unusual student. "He was bright and quick in his studies," but not brilliant. Both in school and out he was "full of fun" and a "lover of all kinds of activity," though not "such a leader in sports as his own 'King of Boyville.'" As often as not he would "be seen sauntering off by himself, hands in his pockets, and whistling or humming the latest street catch." [2] "A thousand realities flooding his outer consciousness" were more real than singing the capitals and the multiplication tables, looking at pictures of wild beasts and naked men or musing over stories and poems. "His stub toes, his burning desire to whistle through his teeth, his deep consuming lust for a barlow knife, his magnificent adoration of the pink gods of the circus" [3] were far more real than anything that came out of books.

Distractions often played havoc with his school work, and all were not the harmless pranks related in *A Court of Boyville*. Once in an orchard within view of the school house, a posse surrounded a horse thief, and at recess Will White along with the other boys joined the mob while the men shot the outlaw to death.

The boys saw his lady friend come up from the covered wagon in the timber where she had been encamped, and throw herself, in the unbridled passion of her grief, upon the bloody form of her outlaw lover. So, alas! what the boys learned at school that day, and even during the week and perhaps in the months that followed, was precious little compared with what they learned in that tragic, bloody moment under the peach trees in the high grass when guilty death met guilty love.[4]

A prairie fire roaring up the far side of the hill from the little town was no unusual occurrence in those days. On such occasions the boys rushed from the school room, without waiting to be dismissed, to join the town in fighting the fire.

Sometimes they soaked their home made calico-lined coats in the rain barrels hauled to the scene on wagons and whacked the little blazes that ran before the flames like snakes in the dry grass; blistered their chubby faces, and returned to the school vain and tired boy heroes to boast of their achievements.[5]

Then there were the long, crawling caravans of covered wagons making their lazy way across the prairies, at which

Mrs. White grumbled because of the dust they made in the house and at which the little boy mused, dreaming the dreams of "Over the Hills and Far Away." Beside the tired looking horses walked the man with a long whip to prod up the lagging team, and after each snap he invariably squirted "a stream of tobacco juice between his teeth." In the front of the wagon sat "the sharp featured woman with the lusterless eyes and the bacon complexion," who, as the wagon passed through the town, craned "her neck out of the unfathomable conglomerated chaos inside" to see whatever sad sights the poverty-stricken little village had to offer. On the rear was tied the chicken coop "full of hybrid poultry with the irrepressible rooster"; and a few yards behind followed "the red faced, sullen barefooted boy, with his sister driving the half-starved long horned cows." [6]

Romance and politics also conspired to take the little boy's time from his uninteresting studies. Lila Heaton first came into Will White's life with her "faint perfume of romance" during the dramatic phase of his artistic development. She played the part of Mrs. Thumb while he played the part of the General in a tableau presented by the ladies of the Methodist Church. Then followed the political episode which awakened the eight-year-old boy to the knowledge of the watchful care of woman. Tilden and Hendricks were running against Hayes and Wheeler in the campaign of 1876, and Will White's father gave him a Democratic scarf with the names of the Democratic presidential candidates woven into the wool. Democrats then were almost as scarce as "rebels" in Kansas, and for most patriots the two terms were synonymous. To the young sons of the Civil War soldiers, "aged ten, or possibly middle-aged young patriots of twelve," the Democratic scarf was another challenge which threatened the permanency of the Union. One small boy grabbed one end of the scarf and a somewhat larger boy grabbed the other. "Lila Heaton ran up and by screams attracted the attention of still older and maturer statesmen possibly in their teens" who rescued him "from a martyr's death" with the able assistance of the teacher who dashed water into the little Democrat's face "to bring him to." [7]

After this heroic rescue the course of true love ran its

swift course. Will took the undeclared passion of his heart to the corn crib, where alone he breathed into a conch shell the sad songs of unrequited love. Soon, however, Lila's mother moved away to set up a millinery store in another town, and Will "acquired measles and scarlet fever and, by way of compensation, Robinson Crusoe and a little brass horn" upon which he learned to play "Go Tell Aunt Rhody," some gospel hymns, and other simple melodies.[8]

When all else failed to break the school-day monotony, the boy escaped into the world of day dreams. In Butler County in the seventies the cowboy was very real and very near to the schoolboy. About El Dorado thousands of cattle roamed the unfenced hills. The cowboy who herded these cattle, though he "wore no gun, no chaps, disported no broader brim to the shapeless rain-soaked hat than the farmer's hired man," was, nevertheless, a romantic figure to the imaginative boy, with his "rather fancy high-heeled boots and sometimes jingling spurs." And young Will White, like the other boys, in wild fancy would ride his prancing mustang right into Jim Thomas' saloon "and light a cigar with a five-dollar bill," or of a Saturday afternoon he would urge his rearing stallion over the dusty highway on the outskirts of the little village in the quarter-horse races where he had bet a king's ransom.[9]

The real curriculum of Will White's education was outdoors—the prairie, the woods, the streams, the farm, the barn, the alley, the church, and the singing school. What he learned in school was insignificant in comparison to what he learned from these. A boy's habitat in El Dorado ordinarily extended from the creek at the foot of the road to the schoolhouse at the top of the hill, but during vacations he wandered farther afield. Then he had as his companions "the coyotes in the rocks, the ground hogs near their holes, the prairie dogs on their mounds, the meadow larks in the buckrush along the road, and the lazy cows grazing in the lush grass of the ravines."[10] Ten years before the Indians had lived about El Dorado, and along the streams the boys found their fireplaces and picked up arrowheads. One of Will's companions was a little white boy who had been stolen and reared among the Indians until he was ten. "He was glum and silent," although he sometimes told Will "little odd things about his Indian infancy and childhood" when the two were together alone.[11]

Life in a Kansas village in the latter part of the nineteenth century differed little from life on a farm. Electric lights, telephones, municipal waterworks, steam and hot air furnaces, natural gas, modern plumbing, paved streets—all have come to the Kansas village since William Allen White was a boy. Dr. White, like the other leading citizens of El Dorado, had a barn, kept a horse, a cow, hogs, and chickens; and Will, like any farm boy, had chores to do. Each morning he filled the woodbox, cleaned the stable, fed the chickens, slopped the hogs, milked the cow, and curried the horse. After that he was his own master until night—to roam the alleys, the prairies, the woods, or to play in the barn with his gang.

In the barn and the barnyard the boy was liberally educated. There he played cards and read the rough romances of his day about the Indian killers. There he "practised the tricks of those shining, bespangled gods in pink tights who dazzled him at the circus." [12] Will learned to do a flip-flop, and Bill Betts learned to turn a double one over a stack of barrels. In the haymow he had a trapeze on which he could skin a cat, swing by his knees, and drop and catch by his heels, and a spring board from which he could do the "big drop." In the barnyard he went through a hoop, bent backward and touched the ground with his hands, and watched Bill Betts go through the same feat and touch his head. When the day was over he split wood, bedded down the cow, fed the pigs and chickens, sliced turnips for the calves, hoed the garden sometimes, "carried countless buckets of water from the pump to the straggling elm saplings along the weedy area where the parking one day would spread its cool green spaces from the sidewalk to the curb." [13] And after his outdoor work was done, if his mother thought his savage spirit needed further chastening, young Will White had a big apron tied around his neck and was put to washing and drying the dishes.

The inhabitants of El Dorado in the seventies were for the most part "young men and women in their twenties and thirties who had come out from the East and the Middle States to make their fame and fortune." They had neither time nor

money to give to any organized effort to help youth; consequently, the boys on the whole were "cut loose, and ran free
like unlariated stock," and the girls, in keeping with the Victorian attitudes of the day, "were tethered close to the little
houses, helping with the work." [14]

The boys and girls compensated for the lack of organized
social activity by turning their meeting places into sly courting
schools. They met in the various religious meetings, and across
the rows of benches, the boys on one side of the church, the
girls on the other, they "darted lightning-wise, electrically re-
freshing glances that renewed the joy of the week-day intimacy
after the long Saturday's absence of the lusty young males in
the woods, or alleys, or barns, far from the softening influences
of the gentler schoolmates." Religion in those "good old days"
was still full of hell-fire. At the revival the boy sat on the back
seat and sang "not without joy, but usually without much
conviction," and at the camp meetings he "roved in restless
herds in the timber about the torch-lighted circle where the
worshipers were gathered" and "what the devil lost under the
torches he gained out in the darkness of the woods." [15]

After the advent of Prohibition the Sunday school superintendent was frequently a man who ran a "whiskey drug
store," but this fact was in no wise disconcerting to the boy,
for the Sunday school was "a social rather than a religious
exercise." There he learned the Golden Text, and received cards
for good attendance, "cards which progressed in value as his
regularity increased" and which "came to have a fairly staple
market price. They were accepted in boy commerce without
haggling, as worth so many pins or marbles, so much chalk or
walnuts, fluctuating, of course, with the seasons." Three de-
nominations held Sunday school and each denomination at a
different time—"from nine o'clock in the morning, when the
Baptists met, through the noon hour, when the Presbyterians
assembled, until two-thirty, when the Methodists convened."
Three different meetings at three different times made it possible for the boy to attend all three, collect cards, "soak his
young hide full of Golden Texts," and see his girl three
times.[16] Probably no boy in El Dorado ever soaked his hide

fuller of texts than Will White. His writings abound in Biblical allusions, quotations, and paraphrases.

Both Will's parents thought their son "should be brought up," but their ideas of civilizing the young savage were somewhat dissimilar. Old Doc White's Yankee spirit had little sympathy for any "far-fetched" ideas about how "to raise a boy." What a boy needed was work to keep him out of mischief, and experience in the practical affairs of life. Thus it was that Will not only had to pick and dress the prairie chickens when his parents were running the hotel, but he had to accompany his father to the butcher shop to buy the steaks. Thus it was also that from the time Will White was large enough to accompany his father, he rode all over Butler County in the interests of the Democratic Party. Sometimes his father took him to Emporia, sixty miles away, and on rare occasions to Topeka, a hundred miles away. One trip to Topeka was memorable:

. . . The boy appears in a big, strange town, holding tightly to his father's hand, and it was a very fat, sweaty hand, and the boy lagged, and must have pulled, for the father prodded him with his cane. . . . The boy and his father are standing, looking at a long line of colored men—the first the boy has ever seen—and the father, seeing they are voting at some kind of a primary, snaps his silver tobacco box, after taking a big chew of fine cut, walking hurriedly off down the street, pulling the little boy after him, and the boy remembers that the father is very angry for a long time. And when some one in the convention says something about colored men voting, the father brought his cane down to applaud, and hit a little bare toe beside his. . . .[17]

One other trip to Topeka was hardly less memorable. On that occasion Doc White pointed out to his son a sputtering "purple white light" on a tall pole fifty feet above the ground —"the first electric light that shone in the street at Topeka." [18]

One day Dr. White took his son by the hand and led him to the office of the Butler County *Democrat*. Will was ten years old; and his father, who "didn't have any hallucinations about public welfare and child labor," thought when a boy reached the age of ten he should go to work. As the *Democrat* was more or less dependent upon Dr. White and two or three other Democrats of Butler County for the money to continue its publication, he had no difficulty in persuading the editor to give Will a job. For four or five days the new devil followed in the footsteps of Benjamin Franklin, and then one day he was sent down to the town pump to get a bucket of water, and again like Franklin, he ran off, but "with the boys who went swimming." [19] When he returned to resume his job as devil, almost ten years had passed.

After the "fake farm adventure," Dr. White tore down the old "foundry" and built the most pretentious house in El Dorado. The old Doc had become a man of affairs in the few years that he had lived in the little village. The general store had been succeeded by a profitable drug business, and the Yankee trading instinct had always enabled him to take care of himself in "a real estate deal." Now he was the vice-president of the Exchange Bank, and soon he was to retire from active business and devote his time to being a Democratic mayor in an overwhelmingly Republican town. Because of this prosperity the White home had "many comforts and luxuries that were all too few in Kansas homes of those days," and as a consequence, "Will . . . grew up under conditions more favorable for development" than fell to the lot of the ordinary western boy.[20]

Mrs. White was responsible for most of the wholesome influences in the White home. She had "spent ten years getting a college education when most women are having their love affairs and babies," and found "the shooting and drinking and sporting around were not what she had bargained for in life." [21] Long before she helped organize the city library, she brought books into her son's life, not children's books, but books for mature minds. Before Will was twelve she had read most of Dickens to him, a good part of George Eliot, one of George Sand's novels, and before his teens were well started, Scott, Charles Reade, and Wilkie Collins. So well had she implanted the love of good books that by the time Will was in his middle teens he was able to make his way "alone."

Music was quite as much a part of Mrs. White's existence as were her books; and from the time her son was large enough to carry a musical instrument, he had one by his side. In the singing school he learned to sing alto, and about this time he heard El Dorado's first band. The band often played at evening in a grove near the White home. "Silvery heavenly music" it seemed to the boy "who had never heard better." That he had to take up his "little ax and split kindling . . . did not make the experience less delicious." [22] Shortly thereafter, he became a leader of his gang in one of its numerous activities. The White barn was the general headquarters of the Court of Boyville band, and Will was its leader.

A boy's world is usually complete and sufficient to itself; the tragedies of adult life rest lightly upon the shoulders of the young. When out of nature came death and destruction to the pioneers of the seventies, Will White saw not the calamity of the grasshopper invasion, "but that men stood in the street looking at the sky;" and when he turned his face toward the sky, he saw also "the shimmering cloud of insects floating over him." Then followed "a time when boys caught grasshoppers by the bottleful and played with them, and made them 'spit tobacco juice.'" In a like manner the drought of 1874 impressed the little boy. At that time the White family was living on a farm north of El Dorado. The clouds "were high and big and white and feathery" and the sky "was bluer than ever, and the dirt in the road that passed before the house was warm to play in far after sundown." [23] The prairie chickens and quail "came up and ate with the tame chickens," the cattle had to be driven "twice a day from the upper pasture to the lower pasture where there was water," [24] and one day an antelope came up to eat with the cattle in the feed lot. The boneyard grew that year, and Will was not allowed to play there for a long time.

CHAPTER III

The "Devil" Editorializes

. . . Went swimming with Will White. Had a fine time.[1]
We took a boat, went up the Cottonwood fishing and hunting for walnuts. We found a few well frosted black paw-paws; we rowed until the morning sun made us tired and sweaty. Then we stripped to the skin and jumped in. It was a grand swim.[2]

AT THE age of sixteen "Dr. Allen White's boy" was gaily galloping through life, seizing lucky opportunities that have characterized his whole career. He had just been graduated from the El Dorado High School after steady but not unusually rapid progress through the grades. He stood second in his class, missing first place by the fraction of a point. He had shown no marked aptitude, however, for any particular subject, and at that time no one "would have thought of him as likely to become a writer." His graduation essay "cost him many a weary sigh," and on the May evening when he had to read it before the public, he had a "very nervous and perspiring time." [3]

A good student he unquestionably was, but Will White's fame lay in another direction; and the sandy-haired, freckle-faced, roly-poly, high-school boy was not without a local reputation. He and Dol Cowley, a fiddler "a bit weak as to eyes and chastely innocent of notes," [4] and George Younkman, a cornetist from the old Silver Cornet Band, had formed a musical triumvirate and played for such country dances in the environing county as would hire them for two dollars a night each. White long before this had ceased music lessons, finding it much easier to play by ear than to learn to play by note; and as he sat at the cabinet organ faking the accompaniment for Cowley's tunes, he sensed the first opportunity to sell his services at a higher price than his fellow workers could demand. Cowley's impaired eyesight would not permit him to prompt the square dancing, Younkman's prepossession with the cornet gave him a peculiar handicap, but White—with hands busy, lungs free, brain undisturbed, and eyes at liberty to roam at will—seized the chance to demand and to collect an extra fifty cents for the evening's performance for "calling off" the dances.

Two years before Will White's graduation from high school Dr. Allen White had died; and his will, characteristic of the Elder White's generosity and decision, provided that his son should be sent to Yale or to the University of Michigan to study for the law. A bank failure after the father's death, however, wiped out the thousand dollars that had been set aside for the law course. The mother, now "land poor," could not abide the idea that her son was not to go to college, nor could she bear the thought of his going from one to two thousand miles from home. She finally decided to send Will to Emporia, sixty miles away, to attend the College of Emporia. There he could pursue a classical course and at the same time be near enough to visit his home occasionally.

So far as her son's educational career was concerned, Mary White's decision to send him to the College of Emporia was not a happy one. This newly-founded Presbyterian school was ill-equipped and ill-manned. Its handful of students were crowded together on a single floor in a ramshackle old building, formerly a skating rink. Both the small enrollment and the school's poverty precluded the employment of a high-grade staff, and Will White, blissfully ignorant of what constituted an institution of higher learning, went through his first year intellectually undisturbed and wholly unconscious of how far the College of Emporia fell short of deserving its name. Yet two things which happened that year profoundly influenced White's subsequent career. He met Vernon L. Kellogg, son of the president of the Kansas State Normal School who had ridden in the same stagecoach from Lawrence to Emporia with

White's mother when the two came to Kansas. Vernon Kellogg, more studious and more serious than White, was to influence him more than any other single individual during their college years.[5] This year, also, as the second semester drew to a close, Will White, thinking it not "fitting and proper for a seventeen-year-old boy to let his mother keep boarders for him to go to college," [6] wrote to three El Dorado businessmen offering his services. One letter went to George Tolle, grocer; a second to Cass Friedburg, dry goods merchant; and a third to T. P. Fulton, editor. Tolle and Friedburg rejected White's proposals; but Fulton, who had been befriended by White's father, was receptive. In the El Dorado *Democrat,* on May 21, 1885, he announced White's entrance into the newspaper world:

Will A. White will take a
position on the Democrat on June 1st.

In 1885, printing had sunk to the lowest level in its more than four centuries of existence. As an art, it had practically ceased to be; as an industry, instead of ranking among the first half dozen in the country, as now, it was not important enough to be listed among the first twenty. Anyone with "a shirt-tail full of type" could start a newspaper, irrespective of financial credit, or moral or economic responsibility. Newspapers, for the most part, were political party organs, often springing up like mushrooms as campaigns approached and disappearing as quickly after the election. Every village and hamlet had its newspaper—sometimes two or three. A town which today cannot support a weekly paper could have kept one in steady circulation in 1885; for then a printer needed but a few hundred dollars to equip a country weekly. Today an editor must invest a thousand dollars for every hundred necessary before 1900. The change that has come over the newspaper business in the small town since William Allen White became a printer's devil can be attributed to no single cause, but a chief factor was the invention of the automatic typesetting machine. The year before White began to set type, the linotype was put into successful operation. Had it been as widely used in Kansas in 1885 as it is today, T. P. Fulton would not have needed Will

White to set type for the El Dorado *Democrat,* even had the *Democrat* been able to survive the newspaper revolution which the automatic typesetting machine was to bring about in the next fifty years.

The paper on which William Allen White began his career was not even as prosperous as the average newspaper of its time and place. Its editor, a capable and sometimes brilliant writer, was fonder of resting or fishing than he was of mending the editorial fences. He did not own a newspaper press; the forms were carried downstairs to the office of the El Dorado *Republican* to be printed on the *Republican* press. In a room where the walls were decorated with sale bills, theatrical notices, sheriff's sales, and fourth of July posters—in a room containing a few cases of type, a job press, and the pungent aroma of printer's ink well mixed with stale tobacco smoke, Will White learned to set type, to make up forms, feed presses, wash and distribute type, start fires, sweep out—do one and all of the sundry jobs of a printer's devil for the munificent sum of $1.50 a week.

This first summer of his devilship, White met a boy who was to become a lifelong friend. One noon as White was leaving the *Democrat* office he saw "a lithe, bony figure in a gray brown suit wrapped around the iron railing that enclosed the cellar way of the *Times* building," [7] and as the tall young man spoke to the other printers who hurried past him up the stairs, White recognized him as Ewing Herbert, the *Times'* new printer. Herbert was a mere boy of White's age, but he had been setting type longer and had now reached the stage of leaving home to try his hand as a journeyman printer. White already knew him, by reputation, as a very fine printer; and as White was only a devil in an office very inferior to the *Times,* he put as much importance into his gait as possible and walked across the street to look into his post-office box, which he knew to be empty. Returning from the post office, White fell in with another *Times* printer; and when the *Times* man stopped to exchange a word with Herbert, White also stopped. At that moment began an intermittent companionship which was to last for several years, and a mutual affection that ripened into a friendship and was never seriously threatened during the more than half-century of intimacy that followed.

National events had their influence on young White. In 1885 Cleveland became President, ending a long and particularly arduous fast for the faithful in Kansas democracy, who had tirelessly labored in the barren fields without opportunity to feed at the public troughs. Among those who thought the year of jubilee had arrived was T. P. Fulton, editor of the struggling El Dorado *Democrat*. Wearing his plug hat and his long-tailed Sunday coat adorned with a boutonniere, he appeared at the office one day and announced that he was "going down to Washington to get the post office." Beginning with his foreman, he gave directions to each of his workmen. To Will White, the devil, he turned last and said: "Willie, you go out on the street and pick up some locals. You know how to do that." [8] White replied that he did, although he had never written a line for print; and thereupon began a period during which White made notes about such local events as would interest the readers of the El Dorado *Democrat*. These notes he took directly to the printer's case where he put his stories into type without bothering to write them out.

Fulton's many absences were the signal for White and Herbert, who had joined the *Democrat* force, to cavort in unrestricted glee. Together they indulged in all printing office pranks. They showered their friends with dirty water while pretending to show them type lice, engaged in water fights, threw the soggy sponge at each other as long as it held together; and when it fell apart, continued the battle with the water-soaked office towel. Together they bought watermelons, ate what they liked, and then threw what was left from the upstairs window onto the heads of the printers from the other office as they passed through the alley below them. They divided between them what money they contrived to collect from the paper's advertisers and subscribers, and they slipped into the columns of the papers news items and jokes understood only by themselves. For all their escapades they had ample freedom and time. Both politics and fishing drew upon Fulton's time, and either was an excuse for absence from the cares of his paper. The post-office quest, especially, provided an uninterrupted period for hilarity; for the appointment proved more elusive than Fulton had imagined, and the ten days that were supposed to bring the spoils stretched into weeks.

When September came, Herbert left El Dorado to enroll in the College of Emporia, breaking the joyous companionship and leaving White behind to suffer long and lonely days. But the young printer was not cast for a life of dull monotony. A few doors down the hallway from the newspaper office, the town gambler periodically presided over a game of stud poker. The gambler, moreover, owned a red-wheeled buggy in which he "took out" a girl whose affections the young reporter desired to cultivate. This red-wheeled buggy gave White "a realizing sense of the wickedness of the gambler's life," [9] and thus it was White's first essay at reform got into print. The October 22, 1885, issue of the El Dorado *Democrat* bore a little editorial that the town marshal could not well ignore.

El Dorado has a few gambling holes that should receive the attention of the proper officers. We heard a man say, who we think is posted, that there are no less than a half dozen poker rooms in this place, and the most of them are being run in apparently open defiance of the laws. It is a blot on the fair name of our thriving city that should be rubbed out, and the guilty parties brought to justice.

The editorial failed. "That gambler sat up out of hours four long days trying to get a chance to kick our base of supplies into our subconsciousness, and only a fleet and earnest pair of young feet kept the gambler from achieving his end." [10] And the gambler married the girl.

By January, 1886, White had concluded that he had sufficiently mastered the printing trade to undertake college again. Accordingly, after a nine months' absence, he returned to Emporia to seek a job in a printing office and to reenroll in the College of Emporia.

. . . I walked into the office of a daily newspaper (the first I had ever seen where they didn't work by the week, where they worked by the piece, by the thousand ems) . . . I went in and lied—said I was a four-years man and wanted a sub case, and by the grace of God, I got it. . . . I didn't know anything about how to go to work. I had never set by the piece. I went over to the alley, hung up my coat, walked back to the foreman's desk and grabbed a piece of copy, a piece of flimsy Associated Press—[which was sent out] without being edited in those days; the "the's" and "and's" and most of the prepositions and conjunctions were left out. I took it over, pulled down the thing on the case that held the copy and looked at it. An old fellow next to me said, "You don't know anything about that, do you, boy?" I said, "No." He said, "Well, give it to me," and he took it and gave me a piece of reprint. Then he showed me how to dump under a slug. He showed me all the way around, and the next time I went to the copy desk, which was the foreman's desk, I drew a nice, beautiful piece of nonpareil.[11]

He said, "You don't know how to do that." I said "No." He said, "I will take it." He did, and I took another piece of reprint . . . and so by hand, he brought me up, and no one knew that I wasn't a full printer, and I got by with it.[12]

White's return to Emporia brought him and Herbert together as roommates. Herbert was relying upon newspaper work almost wholly to pay his college expenses, although he had traded an equity in a piece of land for a carload of buggies which were being sold for him by a hardware dealer. Both he and White were hard up most of the time. They pooled their money as it came in to buy "a meal ticket at a pie repository known to our bright lexicon of youth as the Star Beanery." Whatever was left over from the $3.50 required for the ticket, they "spent for porter-house steaks and buckwheat cakes at midnight for one or two nights at a club restaurant" and then lived on their meal ticket while it lasted. It was their custom to do without breakfast every day in the week; because it saved meals on the ticket and because they "could sleep an hour longer by skipping it." They "ate incredibly large dinners at the beanery and for supper tried to save 30 cents by buying a nickel's worth of cookies" to appease their hunger.[13]

Their boisterous pranks compelled them to move three or four times in the few months that they were together. Both held newspaper "comps" to the shows that came weekly to the town's opera house; and after each show they in turn attempted to imitate the actors in a harangue that ended all sleep for the other members of the household. Although enrolled in a Presbyterian school, they found the Episcopal practices more nearly consistent with their social inclinations, for at the Episcopal parish house they could dance free every Saturday night. Because neither had money enough to hire a hack to take his best girl for a ride, collectively they courted the pretty daughter of the town's leading banker, who owned the best carriage in town.[14]

Though White was a voracious reader, he was an indifferent student. He had little interest in the classical course, and less respect for his teachers. His Greek teacher "was half blind and half deaf," and his French teacher "was beautiful but dumb," [15] being the understudy of an older sister who had some competence in language. To prevent his teachers from ascertaining how little he knew, he used the trick of asking questions to keep them talking. Once when his Latin instructor asked him what he thought of Caesar, he replied that he thought "he had more Gaul than any man in his time." [16] On this flippant bit of repartee White was first quoted in print. Meanwhile, Vernon Kellogg was contributing materially to White's indifference to his studies. Kellogg, who had enrolled in the state university at Lawrence, had "found what a good school was like," [17] and was so enthusiastic about his studies at the university that he set White "on fire" to join him there.

Before the semester was half gone an incident occurred which marked White's advent as a reporter. Herbert, now a reporter on the Emporia News, was the college orator. Before going to Topeka to the state oratorical contest, he asked the city editor to let White substitute for him while he was away. Herbert had to go a few days before the contest, and White began chasing local items, but all the time knowing that he "would be scourged back" to his dungeon when Herbert came back.[18] But the gods were good to White, at Herbert's expense. On the night of March 12, 1886, Herbert, his mind full of "A Neglected Portion of Our History,"

walked on the stage at Topeka, struck an attitude, opened his mouth, spoke his first line, and stood there silent and beautiful. He kept standing there more silent, more beautiful before an audience aghast. Then he turned and walked off the stage, grand, gloomy and peculiar. He could not come back to face Emporia, and

so his printer student roommate got his first regular reportorial
job . . .[19]

In May, White returned to El Dorado to work on the
Republican, and almost immediately displayed his propensity
for getting into trouble. On the twentieth, the *Democrat* reported an irate cigar maker came near using him "as a mop
stick." That summer, he says,

. . . We were persuaded by a local advertiser to make a few sensible remarks about a lady peddling corsets in the town, who was
taking business from the merchant prince. The lady went to the
harness shop, bought a keen rawhide, and walked Main Street and
Sixth Avenue for two days and haunted the El Dorado Republican
office at all hours for the reporter. The boss and the foreman expressed virtuous indignation at the reporter, and he made his beat
from the alleys, meekly peering into a store from the back room to
see if she was there before entering it, and never getting far from
the alley door. We wrote our copy on the back stairs and sent it in
by the devil, who once, being eager for a foot race or Something
Equally Good, told the waiting and obdurate woman where we
were perched. Then that episode passed . . .[20]

Amid these fumbling reportorial days White had one lesson
about writing indelibly impressed upon his mind. The editor of
the *Democrat* being out of town, White was called upon to help
get out the paper. While he was preparing the issue for the
press, word came that Samuel J. Tilden was dead. Thereupon
White went to the case, and without copy put into type an
editorial obituary in the grandest and most turgid language at
his command. The editorial reads in part:

It is with feelings of mingled sorrow and unfitness that we
take up our pen to chronicle the death of another American hero
whose name has been familiarly dear to every American heart. We
refer to Samuel J. Tilden of New York. He was a hero without a
title, a man who by self-sacrificing acts and noble, fearless espousal
of the right, made his friends and followers love his very name
and caused his opponents to honor and respect him. . . . His
name will be enshrined in the hearts of his countrymen and carved
deep in the tablets of fame after the echo of other names heralded
with tocsin of war and bloody passion will have died away and are
lost forever. His life was gentle and the elements so mixed in him
that nature might stand up before all the world and say, "This was
a man." [21]

After the paper was out, White went into the *Republican* office to borrow some type, and there he found Mr. and Mrs. T. B. Murdock, the editor and his wife, reading his "grand piece."

Its grandiloquence must have been very amusing, for I remember they were laughing at it, and reading the vain, pompous phrases with great delight. I have never had the courage to read the piece since, but it taught me a lesson, and that was that Mr. Murdock's style, simple, direct, and above all, understandable, is the only kind of writing that really pays.[22]

CHAPTER IV

The Child Is Father of the Man

In the University I cut loose from classes, made an
average grade of "B" and a poor "B." [1] But I made
friends. . . . And when I left my University to go to
work, it was not with sadness at losing my degree but
with genuine sorrow at closing a lovely and glamorous
life with my friends who were more than friends and
have been dearly beloved to me all my life . . . [2]

WHEN William Allen White entered the University of
Kansas in the autumn of 1886, the university was
barely twenty years old. It was still so small that the
chancellor himself registered incoming students, enrollment on
the average scarcely exceeding four hundred. Faculty and students looked hopefully to the state legislature to provide needed
buildings and laboratory equipment, and were, on their own
initiative, attempting to make their institution a respectable
university. They had achieved most in the natural history department where, over a ten-year period, they had assembled
one hundred and fifty thousand specimens. Library facilities, in
terms of a modern university, were downright pitiable; nevertheless the catalog boasted that the books numbered eight thousand and thirty-five. The collection, it added, was "free from
frivolous trash," [3] a statement which fathers and mothers
would interpret to mean that novels would not corrupt their
sons and daughters at the University of Kansas. For at that
time novel reading was as "bad" as card playing and dancing;
two Kansas ministers, Charles M. Sheldon and Harold Bell
Wright, had not yet begun to write sermons in the guise of

novels, thus making it possible for millions of the "faithful" to read fiction with a clear conscience.

But irrespective of its size and youth, the University of Kansas was then one of the most extraordinary colleges in America. It was one of those rare moments when the institution was the meeting place of great personalities. A group of teachers assembled there during the late eighties and early nineties would have been an ornament to any university. About this faculty had gathered students capable of translating into action the knowledge and inspiration they derived from their instructors. The university had, in short, the "right" faculty and the "right" students, without either of which any system of education, regardless of the size or age of the institution, is nullified.

To White the university was a place of half a dozen teachers—all great personalities and all having distinguished careers. William Herbert Carruth, scholar and poet, was professor of German. Carruth wrote good poetry and made numerous scholarly contributions to his academic field. Later in life, he became professor of comparative literature at Leland Stanford University. David H. Robinson, whose renown as a classical scholar still survives, taught Latin. White, looking for a "snap" course, enrolled in Robinson's freshman Latin, although he had had a year of Latin at Emporia. To his consternation, he found that the class was to read Livy rather than Vergil or Cicero, which he had had; and to his amazement, he discovered that he "liked Latin so well that he took Horace the next year." [4] Arthur G. Canfield, "poet and inspiring teacher of good literature," [5] taught French. He later became professor of Romance languages at the University of Michigan. His brother, James H. Canfield, taught the social sciences. He was constantly puncturing the high tariff arguments of the sons and daughters of the Kansas Republican commonwealth and giving the editors of the state ample opportunity to editorialize. Canfield left Lawrence to become chancellor of the University of Nebraska, then he became president of Ohio State University, and finally, librarian at Columbia University. His daughter, Dorothy Canfield Fisher, has added further honor to the family name by her achievements in American letters. F. H.

Snow taught the physical sciences, and the scientists graduated during his years constitute one of the brightest pages in the University's history. And finally, among those personalities who influenced White was Arthur Richmond Marsh. Marsh was a young man in his middle twenties, newly arrived from Harvard to teach rhetoric and English literature. After a few years in Kansas, he returned to join the Harvard faculty. Still later, he had a successful financial career in Wall Street.

These half-dozen professors were the ones who inspired White most; next to them he was exalted chiefly by his associates in the Phi Delta Theta fraternity. Many of his companions had more illustrious careers than did their instructors. In his fraternity was Fred Funston whose colorful exploits made him a major-general in the United States army. Most influential of all, students or teachers, was Vernon L. Kellogg, distinguished zoologist who served as director of relief in Belgium and Northern France during the World War. After Kellogg came the two Franklin brothers, Edward C., the chemist, and William L., the physicist, both of whom became eminent American scientists. Lastly, of those who taught him affection, loyalty, and the joys of manly wrangling, was Walter Armstrong, the young man who, after devoting his college years to the study of Greek, started his career by carrying a surveyor's chain and ended as general manager of the western division of the Union Pacific Railroad.

Outside his fraternity White had numerous student friends who became national figures. Closest of these to him was Herbert S. Hadley, who in his multifarious career was first Republican governor of Missouri after the reconstruction period, chancellor of Washington University, college professor, attorney, and author. Another student, whose fame like White's became "greater than that foretold for him in the class prophesy," [6] was Edwin E. Slosson, a man of varied interests. He first became generally known to the public as literary editor of *The Independent*. Later, as director of Science Service at Washington, D. C., he attained singular distinction, being at the time of his death "easily the outstanding interpreter of science to the non-technical public." [7] A half century later when White was president of the American Society of Newspaper

Editors, Henry E. Riggs, another classmate, was likewise honored by election to the highest position in his profession—the presidency of the American Society of Civil Engineers. Finally, along with Hadley and Funston, White matched his wits with William E. Borah, later United States senator from Idaho and long time member of the Senate Foreign Relations Committee.

If the proper method of deriving the most from one's college years is to master the curriculum leading to a degree, then William Allen White bungled his education. Disgusted with his previous work, he wiped the slate clean when he went to Lawrence by enrolling as a freshman in the modern literature course. But though a freshman, authorities permitted White to take advanced subjects, since he had already completed some college work. This was his first undoing. More and more he pursued advanced courses in history, sociology, and economics. By the time he should have been a junior, he had so much senior work that he was beyond all classification. His second undoing was mathematics. At that time mathematics was a required course, and White never got beyond the freshman year. Three times he took the final examination in solid geometry, and three times he failed. After the third failure, Ephram Miller, the instructor, in the sadness of his heart said to him, "White, you just don't have a mathematical mind." [8] White always intended to make up the course, but never did.

Had White been honest with himself and taken the course which he really preferred, he would have become a music teacher. But music "was sissy," and he, therefore, avoided the music school. He did, however, join the orchestra, where he played the piano. He could not read music fast enough to keep up with the others, but a keen and receptive ear enabled him to fool the student director with his faked harmonies. For three or four weeks he had a gorgeous time playing in the orchestra. Then one day the head of the department came in; and as the orchestra went through a number, White, out of the corner of his eye, could see that he was watching him. Suddenly, he stopped the orchestra and asked White to play alone. White had to admit that he could not—that he could not read music. His curt orders were, "You get out of here." But White soon found his way back into the music department by another route.

One night when he heard a string quartet from Boston playing the chamber music of the masters, the door "opened into a new life." After that experience he "used to cut classes in study hours"[9] to sneak into the assembly room in Fraser Hall to listen to members of the music faculty lecture on music.

White's participation in extra-curricular activities directly sponsored by the faculty hardly extended beyond Professor Marsh's primary interests. Marsh carried his enthusiasm for literature beyond the classroom. During the summer he traveled throughout the state lecturing, and in the winter he sponsored student literary clubs and amateur theatricals. Into both literary and dramatic activities, White entered whole-heartedly. In the literary clubs, he learned to love the works of Emerson, whose poetry he read before various groups and on whose essays he lectured. In the amateur theatricals, he spread himself "and his kindly smile over the histrionic boards,"[10] and showed "both natural ability and careful work."[11]

In the social life of the campus, White followed the fashions; but social activities in the eighties were not the integral part of higher education that they are today. The students at the University of Kansas had little money to spend, and most of the boys "showed by gait and appearance the results of assiduously following the cultivator up and down the sweltering corn rows and wielding the pitchfork in haying time."[12] Fraternities had no advance rushing dates, and no fraternity had a house. Each fraternity had an eating club where the members gathered three times a day for their meals. For their chapter meetings and dances, the Greek organizations leased downtown halls, where once a week the students waltzed to airs from *The Mikado* and *The Gondoliers* and to "Over the Waves." Few of the men and not all the women could dance when they entered college, but they learned readily from their school fellows. White never learned to dance well; he enjoyed playing the piano more than he did dancing, with the result that his fraternity brothers kept him at the piano most of the time. Dances were not chaperoned. Nor had the dress suit become a requisite of a properly conducted party. "Sea-going hacks, carrying four, were a necessity for the big parties and in case of rain. Rubbers were de rigeur on the Hill,[13] for there were no pavements and Lawrence cross walks were deep in mud after every rain and thaw." [14]

Student life on the campus in the eighties seethed with politics. The yearbook, the oratorical association, and the student newspapers were all choice political plums. Annuals were published and discontinued because of political bickerings. Newspapers and magazines were started, and killed by political antagonists. Coalitions were formed to publish a single paper for the good of the university—only to fall apart and publish as many papers as there were factions, and advertisers to pay the printers' bills. Sometimes politicians were dirty; oftener they were matching their wits with relish. One night the Phi Delts got W. D. Ross, president of one of the literary societies, out of bed in the middle of the night and presented a petition asking for a meeting to be called the following morning at an "unholy" hour, long before the average student was out of bed. One of the Phi Delts had discovered that Ross was bound by the constitution to call a meeting upon petition of a certain percentage of the society's members, and that the Phi Delta Theta fraternity had that percentage within its own group. Ross called the meeting and in the early morning hours of the following day the Phi Delts took charge of the society and gleefully molded it according to their whims. White figured in every political skirmish, but he was often the front for a far more astute politician than he. Back of White, working secretly, quietly, and telling him what to do was Vernon Kellogg. Kellogg, by virtue of an official connection with the university, was forced to appear aloof from student politics, though actually he was using the information he secured through his office for his political coups.

White's prepossession with literature helped to wreck his academic career. All his life he had been a voracious reader; and before he could read for himself his mother had read to him hour upon hour. One day while working on the El Dorado papers, he picked up a copy of E. W. Howe's *The Story of a Country Town*. Howe had been unable to find a publisher for his novel; and in the hope of gaining some recognition, he had printed it himself and sent copies out for review. White read one of these copies and from it came his first desire to write a novel himself. Hitherto he "had read only the false and saccharine novels of the period which dealt not even remotely with life as he knew it." [15] But Howe's novel described people as he knew them. If a novel could be written about such people, then he could write one himself. From the day he finished *The Story of a Country Town,* Ed. Howe became White's major literary hero. And while White was still in his teens he made his first literary pilgrimage to Atchison "just to see the man who wrote *A Story of a Country Town.*" [16] After the appearance of this novel, Howe's locale naturally awakened interest in other books about Kansas people, with the result that when he was supposed to be making up his deficiency in solid geometry, he was reading books and reviewing them for the university's literary magazine.

During White's years at the Univeristy of Kansas, Mount Oread gave promise of becoming a Kansas Mount Parnassus. Arthur Canfield, Carruth, and Marsh were all writing poetry, and inspiring students to make "swallow flights." White fell under the poetic spell enveloping the campus, and for some years thereafter his chief literary ambition was to be a poet. He and a fellow-student, Thomas F. Doran, published an anthology of university poetry, "for the sake of preserving in a permanent from certain bits of poetical work which have truly interested a small circle of readers." [17] Modesty, however, forbade either of the young anthologists to include any of his own compositions. Nevertheless, White was devoting more time to the writing of poetry than he was to literary prose. As fraternity poet and class poet, he celebrated notable school anniversaries, and must have been very proud of himself when one of his poems was set to music and sung at the junior-senior banquet.

Most of his poems dealt with life as he knew it in El Dorado, the Willer Crick of his poems. Practically all of them were in dialect, then in vogue because of the popularity of James Whitcomb Riley, and through most of them ran a strain of pathos. "The Gradgerratun' o' Joe," though not published until after White left the university, is a typical example.

The Gradgerratun' o' Joe

Way down crost the medder an' cow lot,
  Thro' paths made by cattle an' sheep,
Where, cooled in the shade by the tall ellums made,
  The old crick has curled up to sleep;
Down there where the wind sighun' mingles
  I'th prattelun' waters at play,
An' the coo coo coo of the turtle dove too,
  Seeps in from the dim far away;
Down there by the banks of the Willer—
  In spring where the sweet-williams grow—
'Twas at this place 'at he, all the time used to be:
  The home of our little boy Joe.
        My Oh—
          How long ago.

Nope; none a' you couldn't 'a' know'd him,
  Way back there in seventy-four,
When Idy an' me concluded 'at we
  U'd edjicate Joe, rich or pore.
I mind how we skrimped, scraped an' worried,
  An' how our first Christmas was dim,
An' how mother cried when we had to decide,
  We couldn't send nothun' to him.
An' nobody else dreams the sorrow,
  'At Idy an' me'd undergo,
A livun' that way all alone ever' day
  A yearnun' an' longun' fer Joe.
        High Oh
          Long ago.

So Idy an' me went together
  To hear little Joe gradgerrate;
Little Joe did I say? meant big, anyway;
  He spoke on the subject of "Fate."
An' "my, but the effort was splendid."
  The folks said 'at set by my side,
But I never hyurd a sentence er word—
  An' mother jest broke down an' cried.
I hadn't the heart fer to ask her
  What was the matter, you know;
Fer I felt she'd a' said: "Our baby is dead,
  I want back my own little Joe:
        Our Joe
          Of long ago."

So foller me down thro' the cow lot—
Thro' paths worn by cattle an' sheep,
To where in the shade, by the tall ellums made,
The old crick is tucked in to sleep;
Where sighs of the tired breeze whisper
To quiet the waters at play;
An' the dreamy coo coo of the turtle dove true,
Frightens care phantoms away;
For I like to set hyur a thinkun!
An' astun' the waters 'at flow,
What's come o' the dear little boy 'at played here
In the days o' the long ago?
Our Joe;
High ho! [18]

In the summer of 1887, when White was reporting for the El Dorado *Republican,* the following prose poem appeared on June 28 in his column, "Saints and Sinners," which in the light of subsequent events, is significant:

O what shall we do on the Fourth of July, said the youth to the maiden fair. O we'll take down the hammock and quickly hie, to the home of the chigger and dark green fly, where through leafy bowers the breezes sigh, and dream of our love out there. O what shall we do on the Fourth of July said a youngster free from care. O we'll fill up our systems with green apple pie and purchase toy pistols and then we'll try to blow out our souls to their homes in the sky, to sing with the angels fair. O what shall we do on the Fourth of July the old codgers ask in despair. O we'll get a jug of Old Red Eye, and a gallon or two of rock and rye, and go out where there is nobody nigh, and get on a great old tare. O what shall we do on the glorious Fourth, said the editor weary and tired. We'll stay at home in this day of mirth, and boom the town for all 'tis worth. O we'll raise the price of our city's earth, although the boom's expired.

This "machine poem" was patterned after the poetic prose which Walt Mason, a printer-journalist of local reputation, was writing for various Kansas newspapers. Twenty years later Walt Mason, down and out because of drink, read a magazine article by White which seemed so kindly that he wrote him a letter asking for a job. White gave him work; and Mason, who had offered to write the *Gazette's* editorial column for six dollars a week, drove to Emporia, his sole worldly possessions

Mrs. Allen White, William Allen White's Mother

Student days in the Colorado Mountains—July 4, 1889

Reading from left to right:

Vernon Kellogg—died 1937—zoologist—director American Commission for Relief in Belgium, 1915-1916

Henry E. Riggs—civil engineer—honorary professor of civil engineering, University of Michigan

Frank Craig—died 1926—banker—former president of the Oklahoma Bankers Association

William Allen White

Herbert S. Hadley—died 1927—former Governor of Missouri—former chancellor of Washington University

William S. Franklin—died 1930—physicist—author—former professor of physics at Massachusetts Institute of Technology

Edward C. Franklin—died 1937—chemist—professor of chemistry at Stanford University—chief, Division of Chemistry U. S. Public Health Service—president American Chemical Society

Frederick Funston—died 1917—adventurer and soldier of fortune—Major General, U. S. Army

Schuyler Brewster—lawyer—former Attorney General of Oklahoma

being a rickety buckboard, a bay pony, and a battered typewriter. In his new environment he sobered up, and within two
years he was writing his rippling rhymes for millions of
readers.

In after years White's associates could look back on their
university years and say that he "gave promise of becoming the
man he turned out to be, although no one foresaw the fame
he would attain." [19] At that time, no one would have ever
imagined that White, Funston, the Franklin brothers, or
Hadley would have attained eminence. Borah was more mature
than the average student and knew that a university was a place
for work; Vernon Kellogg was always studious, but even he
was not above student frivolity. One Sunday afternoon he and
his brother Fred, White, Funston, Ed. Franklin, Paul Wilkinson and a half dozen others were gathered in Kellogg's and
Funston's room and with the aid of a mandolin in the hands
of Wilkinson "were making more noise than was seemly on
that particular day." [20] While they were thus engaged W. E.
Higgins, later a member of the university's faculty, dropped
in to urge them to attend a special meeting of the Y.M.C.A.
that afternoon and "was listened to somewhat disrespectfully."
At this juncture they heard steps on the stairway and realized
that the landlady was coming up to remonstrate with them for
their boisterous conduct. All except Higgins dashed through
the door into an unoccupied bedroom, locking the door after
them. Higgins was begged to save himself in like manner; but
bestowing a withering glance on them he replied, "I have done
no wrong. I scorn to fly," and remained to face the landlady
alone. She "was astonished that one of the pillars of the Young
Men's Christian Association would participate in revelries in
her house on the Sabbath"; and Higgins, strong and calm in
the knowledge of his own virtue, cleared his throat and started
out, "Madam, you do me a grave injustice. I assure you that—"
He got no farther. The indignant lady swept from the room,
while the real culprits who had been listening intently through
the door, howled with derision. For many years thereafter
Higgins was trying to live down the name, "Grave Injustice
Higgins."

Nor did the Phi Delts in their frivolity differ from the

general student body. One year a young college orator from
Ohio who was "not inclined to hide his light under a bushel,"
visited a relative in Lawrence. The young man made himself
known in university circles, and some of the students sized him
up as "easy game." A committee, headed by Hadley, waited
upon him, telling him that all had heard of his fame as an orator
and hoped to have the pleasure of hearing him while he was
in town. Each man introduced himself as the son of some powerful and rich man and invited him to be a guest in his home
while he was in Lawrence. The young man accepted the invita-
tions cordially as he did one to go on a "snipe hunt." That night
they took him to Blue Mound, seven miles south of town; and
as their honored guest he accepted the post of holding the sack
while the rest of them beat up the snipes and drove them
toward him. He was cautioned to stand perfectly noiseless and
to hold the lighted lantern in the mouth of the bag. Because the
night was damp, his hosts said, the birds might not enter the
trap until late, but when they did it would be sport for a king.
Then leaving the victim alone, they scattered presumably to
beat up the doomed birds in the surrounding fields but actually
to meet where they had hitched their horses, to drive back to
town. Just at daybreak the young man wandered into town
mildly wondering why he had seen nothing more of his fellow
sportsmen. He was told that their teams had been frightened,
broken loose, and that they had chased them back to town in
hope of overtaking them. The explanation was satisfactory, and
the young man was taken again that night; but this time the
tables were turned somewhat. Another group of students followed them on horseback; and as soon as his tormentors left
their teams, they drove their horses back to town, leaving them
all to walk the seven miles home. But the young man's gullibility
was endless. Two nights later the committee held a reception
for him in one of the city parks to which all the men students
were invited and directed to bring some musical instrument
"well concealed" about their clothing. William Harvey Brown
presided with dignity, and one of the Franklin boys delivered
an address of welcome in which he fairly covered the guest
"with glucose." As Franklin finished there was a wild yell for
the orator, who came forward and, lifting his right arm im-

pressively, began, "Fellow searchers in the fields of knowledge—" From several hundred throats arose cries of "Hear,
hear!" and "Magnificent!" He tried again but was "drowned in
the roar of applause punctured by the blowing of horns and the
vigorous beating of tin pans." A third attempt ended in like
manner and the committee explained to him that the boys "were
so overcome by enthusiasm over his presence that they could
not restrain themselves . . ." Then, though student parades
were forbidden by Lawrence authorities, they started to march
down Massachusetts Street in a column. At "the psychological
moment" the town marshal and his cohorts bore down upon
them. All escaped but the orator, who being unfamiliar with the
geography of the town, "was cut off and captured, but obtained his release on assuring the officers that he was a
stranger."

Student life, however, was not a one-sided affair, and
these harmless escapades were but evidences of excess energy.
Take the later career of William Harvey Brown, naturalist,
sportsman, and empire builder. After graduation, Brown
worked in Washington for the Smithsonian Institute and the
National Museum. In 1889, he was selected as one of an expedition party to Africa to observe an eclipse of the sun, and
there he remained to hunt big game for the Smithsonian Institute and to collect curios for the British Museum. He helped
found the city of Salisbury and became a member of the
Rhodesian Parliament. As an empire builder he was said to
have been "second only to Cecil Rhodes." [21] Most of the Kansas
University students in the eighties and nineties were sons and
daughters of pioneers and accustomed to hard work and few
luxuries. Even the most desultory student must have been inspired to greater efforts by the hard working faculty. The story
is told that Professor Snow could be seen on spring evenings
starting at sundown for the Wakarusa River "where he would
turn his pony out to graze until sunrise, light his bull's eye lantern, take a cyanide bottle and net, and -plunge into the
thicket." [22] For years he spent his spring and summer vacations
collecting entomological specimens, frequently in company of
students who "had been thrilled by his own enthusiasm"; and
it must have been this enthusiasm rather than the anticipation

of a student lark that induced White to drive a horse and buggy over Douglas County for two weeks selling subscriptions for a local paper in return for a railroad pass that enabled him to accompany an expedition to Colorado.

Only in journalism was White's work at the University of quality above that of the average happy-go-lucky, irresponsible student. From his freshman to his senior year, his newspaper work brought praise both on university hill and throughout the state. As early as February of his first year, the university paper was apologizing for one of its issues, because "White, one of our local chasers, has been very busy this week with his lessons, hence the general absence of 'goaks' in this week's issue." [23] The same year the Iola *Register* declared that he "has already done some of the brightest work the Lawrence papers have ever shown." [24] In a like manner the Kansas papers continued to speak of his newspaper work for the remainder of his college years.

Strangely enough White emerged from the ranks of cub reporters in the role of business manager. His second year he was business manager of the University *Review;* his third, of the University *Times.* As manager of the *Review* he perpetrated a bit of student blackmail that turned into a Kansas University journalistic classic. One afternoon he went downtown with the editor, Thomas F. Doran, to solicit advertising. The two called on a clothing merchant by the name of Urbansky and used their "most eloquent and persuasive powers" [25] to induce him to give them an advertisement, but he refused flatly. After they had left the store, White turned to Doran and said, "Tom, if you will publish what I write for the *Review,* we will get even with that — — — — — — — Israelite." Doran equivocated, but when White wrote out these lines, "the enthusiasm of youth" prevailed over his better judgment:

Urbansky Flashowhiski a Russian Jew, who keeps a junk shop in Messopotamia don't advertise in the Review and one of his clerks died from the effects of solitary confinement the other day. Ah there Isaac.[26]

Urbansky read the item and "was crazy." He rushed into the *Review* office, waved his hands, and tearfully exclaimed

that they "had ruined his business." Doran and White, seeing
the consternation of the poor merchant, told him frankly that
was exactly what they intended to do; that he had ruined their
business and that the students had patronized him and their
trade was not appreciated. Urbansky said he "would do anything to correct his mistake" and wanted to know if they would
write something to take the sting out of the original item. He
had some checked pants that he had been unable to sell, and
White wrote an advertisement about "all pants down, all pants
50% off at Urbansky's," which Doran thought was worse than
the original insult but which pleased Urbansky so well that he
gave them fifty dollars.

By the summer of 1888, White, just turned twenty, was a
figure in Lawrence journalism. Kellogg was editor of the *Daily
Journal* and White was city editor The titles meant little. Kellogg wrote the editorials on state and national affairs, and
White got up the local page. On this page he could editorialize
at will. For the first time, he was at liberty to write what he
thought, and for the first time he began meddling in other
people's affairs—a trait that marked his early editorial career.
Before the summer was well under way, White had a newspaper fight on his hands. Pete Foley, a Lawrence printer and
bookbinder, had started a daily Democratic paper, and prod-
ding the Democratic editor became the young Republican's pas-
time. Many of these paragraphs are neither clever nor witty.
Two retorts indicate the general standard. The first is an answer to Foley's charge that the *Journal* man cannot spell; the
second, to the suggestion that the *Journal* use a dictionary:

The brainless chumps whose impotent efforts to edit that
apology for a newspaper, which makes their half dozen readers
weary, can spell about as well as they can do anything.[27]
Possibly if he could be persuaded to come in and watch the
operation long enough to learn the motions, there would not be so
many errors of spelling and punctuation in that organ of the
illiterate democracy.[28]

When White took the initiative, he maintained about the
same standard:

It is said that the Democrat "Yoomerist" appreciates his own
jokes, and laughs heartily when he reads them to his friends. This

may be a good thing for the debilitated system of the Democrat's
Funny Fellow but it must be a severe strain on the silken ties of
friendship.[29]

While much of this bickering between the papers was
mere indulgence in personalities, White occasionally said things
that rankled. About one article appearing in the *Democrat,*
which he maintained was begun by another and finished by
Foley and the office devil, he wrote: "Out of respect to the intelligence of the 'devil' it is nothing more than fair to say that
the article reads as though Pete had done the big end of the
literary labor." [30]

In these controversies with Foley, White remained un-
perturbed until one night when Pete, stimulated by copious
Missouri "likker," called at the *Journal* office "with a large
feverish ball bat." [31] White, with reason, was scared; for the
drunken Foley "meant business," but "Vernon always said that
I talked him out of killing me, and so the incident passed." [32]

Another somewhat similar experience occurred in the fall
of 1889. Two disgruntled Republicans, having failed to win
majorities in the county convention, bolted the ticket and ran
for county offices as independents. To White, a bolter was the
direst of political sinners; and as city editor of the Republican
paper, he assumed the duty of denouncing the sin. Within
three weeks the campaign had developed to viciousness; charges
and countercharges were being hurled back and forth; and
White, now with a year or two of genuine newspaper experience back of him, was holding his own in the fight. So long
as he confined his charges to boodle, corruption, embezzlement,
and theft, neither the insurgents nor the town cared much. But
one day the following lines put the whole campaign in a new
light.

If Clarke [the bolters' candidate for sheriff] is elected Hank
[Hank Asher, a former sheriff] will be the deputy and allow some
more innocent colored men to be swung off the bridge and hung.
A man who hasn't nerve to protect the colored men can't ask for
their votes with very good grace.[33]

White, searching for an issue, had hit upon the idea of
associating the opposition with the most unsavory incident in

the history of the town. Seven years before, Sis Vinegar, a colored prostitute, enticed David Bausman, a Douglas County farmer, to the river bank. There three colored men fell upon Bausman and beat him to death with a hammer. The three fled, but were captured and brought back to Lawrence, where each confessed to his part in the crime. After the confession, the threatening mob became a reality. Under cover of darkness, fifty masked men appeared at the jail, where they "over-powered" Sheriff Hank Asher; and, after deciding by ballot not to hang the prostitute, took the three men to the middle pier of the river bridge, "three ropes over the wretches' heads, shoved them off and left them hanging." [34]

Lawrence had to bear both the shame of a brutal and un-savory murder and the stigma of a triple lynching in the very hotbed of the free-state movement. Consequently, when the young editorial upstart dragged the skeleton out of the closet and fastened the responsibility on the opposition, the campaign became one of the bitterest in county history. Members of the insurgent group told White that if he did not shut his — — — — — — — mouth they would kill him; and one, Jerry Glad-heart, a harness maker, sent word that he would shoot him on sight. The day after Gladheart's threat, White had to pass the harness shop. He bought two guns; and with one in each coat pocket he started down the opposite sidewalk. Gladheart was sitting in front of his shop reading; and when White saw him, he knew he had to cross the street. With every muscle of his body pushing the other way, he made his way to the other side. Gladheart, seeing fear written in every line of White's face as he passed him, banged the forelegs of his chair down on the sidewalk and let out a raucous laugh that might have been heard a block. The harness maker, now sober, had the sense to turn the affair into a joke. And White, realizing that the opposition was bluffing, continued the campaign with renewed vigor.

Had White displayed no more than a propensity for get-ting himself and others into trouble, his journalistic career would have been short; but in fact his work was often brilliant. He had been local editor of the *Journal* but three weeks when the *Tribune,* the *Journal's* competitor, declared that he "has put more sparkle into the Journal's local page than it has had since Prentis [35] left it." [36] The *Saturday Evening Post* tell this story about this period. As an editorial writer it was White's duty to disagree with every view put forth by the other daily. One day White's editorial antagonist fell ill and engaged White to take his place. For some weeks in the morning paper White assailed the position he had taken the night before in the evening paper, "ripping any ideas he may have put forward . . . to shreds and denouncing himself as a wretch deserving condign punishment for presuming to think that he had any ideas at all about anything." Then the editor of the weekly had to leave town and asked White to get up his editorials. To the disagreement between the dailies, White devoted an editorial, one paragraph of which reads:

We have been much amused, and some days not a little disgusted, by the recent bickerings indulged in by the editors of our two daily contemporaries. Precisely what the caterwauling is all about we will not presume to say, but the gist of it seems to be that each thinks the other is a mixture of fool and knave, equal parts. No doubt each has blundered on the truth; but as there is no novelty for the readers of either sheet in the discovery we cannot see the reason for devoting so much space to it. The better class of people are coming more and more to realize the shallowness of daily journalism in this city and turn to the . . . [weekly] for intelligent comment on current events.[37]

CHAPTER V

A Gay Young Blade

. . . How proud he was of his job!
He hired and fired the force, wrote the local items and most of the editorials. He had charge of the bank account, bought print paper and job stock—looked after the county printing—worked with the local statesmen —sat in the county conventions—wrote poetry and short stories on dark nights and rowed the girls down the Walnut on moonlight nights—hired a horse and buggy every Sunday afternoon from a livery stable—saved his money for a month—bought him a Prince Albert coat and gray pants, patent leather shoes, white spats and a broad black stetson hat—swanked around Topeka more or less—and was a sort of political editorial understudy for State Senator Bent Murdock, who was the glass of fashion, the mold of form and the clarion voice of the Murdock rebellion of 1890.

At times, being only 22, the youngster twittered a collegiate mandolin or twanged a guitar, sang tenor in a serenading club, took Charlie Curtis over Butler county fighting the Populists, fell desperately in love every six months and added the interest to his note every 90 days.

So by day he followed "the soul's invinsible surmise" and at night listened to his head swell and swell and swell—after the fashion of youth.[1]

THIS description of William Allen White at the time he became associate editor of the El Dorado *Republican* is typical of his references to himself. His foibles, faults, and idiosyncrasies are isolated and heightened; his virtues and merits are excluded. Every reader of the Emporia *Gazette* knows no one has ever been such a clown, a fool, or an ass as William Allen White has—when White tells the story. Nor does he stop with arraying himself in cap and bells. Any charge of personal dishonesty, hypocrisy, or charlatanry he answers with a self-indictment that makes the charge sound like a code of ethics. But, as every reader of the Emporia *Gazette* also knows, no editor who talked about himself at all ever said less than White about his serious activities. Few accounts of his worthwhile work ever make his paper, and his comings and goings are told in the fewest possible words. Two locals written nearly forty years apart are typical:

W. A. White, who went East last week, will probably not return for two weeks.[2]

W. A. White left Saturday for New York to attend a group of board meetings. He will return next week.[3]

The delay of White's return, implied in the first item, was caused by the assassination of President McKinley; White had gone to Washington with Theodore Roosevelt. Lincoln Steffens revealed that thirty years later when, in depicting Theodore Roosevelt's character, he told how Roosevelt, unable to conceal his joy at being president, grabbed Steffens with one hand and White with the other and rushed the two out of the White House into the streets, where he cavorted in unrestricted glee, attacking imaginary assassins by way of reducing the pressure of his bottled up emotions.[4] To the readers of the *Gazette*, however, the immediate results of the prolonged eastern trip was this:

A man who hustles for any public office is foolish. The same energy that the average politician puts into chasing office would make him rich. Generally speaking and with few exceptions, the man who has no resource of mind or heart or pocketbook—or either of these three—outside of politics is mighty unhappy. There is more fun in a small business that is paying than in a big game of politics.[5]

In the case of the second item what the subscribers of the *Gazette* got as a result of the trip was a two-column editorial on the economic situation in New York, the prospects of the two major political parties, the current Broadway plays, and the latest styles in women's hats. Never a word about what William Allen White did or said—but a complete record of his thinking in so far as he felt himself permitted to take his subscribers into his confidence. In general, readers of the Emporia *Gazette* know less than do the readers of the New York *Times* about what William Allen White is doing; but when it comes to their editor's thinking, no group of readers since the days of the giants in personal journalism—Greeley, Dana, Watterson, and their kind—has ever known better what was going on in their editor's mind.

Because of White's reluctance to talk about himself in his own newspaper except in retrospect as a freak that has barely escaped locking up, his description of the *Republican's* new editor must be taken as the surface picture of a young journalist already well on his way toward success in the newspaper field. Had he been otherwise, as good an editor as Bent Murdock would never have entrusted his paper to him.

White left the University of Kansas in December, 1889, and assumed charge of the El Dorado *Republican* in January, 1890. T. B. Murdock, the editor, who was also a state senator, needed someone to oversee the paper while he attended the sessions of the legislature. He had known White from the time when, as a little boy, he was the office pest; had been, in fact, a sort of foster father to him, and during two summers had employed him. Murdock, who wanted to devote his time to politics, offered White eighteen dollars a week to take active control of the paper. White had never been paid more than eight dollars a week, and Murdock's fabulous offer, together with the ever present knowledge of his deficiency in mathematics, was enough argument to make him leave the university without taking a degree.

Murdock's faith in White's ability was not misplaced; he made a good editor. In 1890, the Farmers' Alliance was in flower. Hard-pressed Kansas farmers had rushed into this organization in the hope that through it they could regulate the railroads and trusts, lower interest rates, and ease the mortgage burden. When their pressure on the Democratic and Republican parties failed to achieve satisfactory results, they went into politics as an organization, putting their own ticket in the field. White, in his fervent moments, attempted to paralyze the Farmers' Alliance and was ridden through the streets in effigy and his paper boycotted, thus proving beyond all doubt that what he wrote was being read. Nor was the young editor less known or less read because of his political screeds. When the candidate for county attorney on the Alliance ticket bought a gun to answer his charges, he made additional grist for his editorial mill. Since the town was already hopelessly divided over politics, White's contribution to the strife had little effect on the local well-being. All reason had departed from politics, and the more White said about the Alliance people and the later Populists the more they wanted to read his paper. In the meantime, he was editing a good small-town weekly. Typographically it was a delight to the eye; and in the matter of news it was "fresh, bright, and breezy." Personally, the editor was active in civic affairs and unofficial spokesman for all organizations that had the good of his community at heart.

His greatest weakness was his vanity in his language. He could not resist the temptation to display his vocabulary or his ability to put words together in startling arrangements. As a result, his propensity for "fine writing" often destroyed his effectiveness. His readers read him for his style rather than for his thought. At times, he quite obviously wrote for the pleasure of fine rhetoric. One pretext for such writing arose when the advance agent of a circus gave White only eight complimentary tickets. For thus insulting the young editor with such stinginess, the circus had to endure an onslaught which reads in part:

We are also vicariously informed that "there will be a grand street parade" that will make the noonday sun crawl under the barn and use the fiery comets of the heavens only as black punctuation points for the glittering line of march; seven noble $3 knights with tin foil and gilt paper clothing will ride on spavined, ring boned horses, and five squinted eyed beauties from Fourth street and the West bottoms of Kansas City will add considerably to the radiant lustre of the Oriental rip snorting, crimson pageant. Huge lousy camels, led by tent hands in yellow and red callico; and dens and vans containing two sleepy coyotes; a real live lion stuffed with straw and cotton batting and a dead hyena barking at him; a den of garter snakes and toothless rattlers; a box of well mounted birds and bats will startle the gaping crowd as the procession moves majestically along. At the show grounds the same side show with the fat woman and the flaxen haired circassian and the hand organ will be on deck.[6]

During his year and a half on the El Dorado *Republican* White experimented with many types of writing. Besides writing the regular run of news and editorial assignments, at odd times he wrote a column, paragraphs, poetry, short stories, and essays. His subject matter was first and last El Dorado, its people, and its interests. Most of his compositions appeared under the pen name of Elder Twiggs, an imaginary character and something of a wood stove philosopher. The nature of his philosophizing is indicated by the titles of the essays: "The Demon Rum," "Dudes," "Holiness and the End of the World," "Platonic Love Attachments," "Old Maid in Love," and "Temporary Status of One in Society." Not a few of these essays have the eighteenth century manner of holding a mirror up to society for the purpose of castigating its freaks and foibles; and one, on hell, faintly indicates that White might have descried even at that early date that he was living in a changing world—if only in the field of religion.

You don't hear so much about Hell as you used to. Is it getting old-fashioned too? I can remember when I went to church and sat on the back seat with the young folks that a little weak voiced woman always got up in the middle of the church to ask folks to pray for her boy who was going to Hell. And I remember an old red whiskered man who used to kneel down and begin praying in a very low voice and gradually get louder and louder till I wanted to run away somewhere and hide, being very young at that time. The old man prayed so often that his voice would crack and creak and sound quite terrible. He never asked for anything but grace and forgiveness for sins, (he was a good man and I used to think that he asked for forgiveness in the same spirit that people now fish for compliments by disparaging themselves); although he would often be at a loss for an idea he would never falter but fill up the pause with "and ah Oh Lord" and continue with his request. I wonder what kind of a figure this old man who used to start all the hymns with his enthusiastic but wavering voice would cut in one of our modern churches, where the choir leads and where there are carpets and cushioned seats and an organ. How he would be lost at the quiet earnest pleading prayer meeting in our churches today. He would be stared at when he shouted and told people to flee from the wrath and talked of the burning fiery pit of Hell. He has a brother now in the Salvation army; and if the old man were living today, he would doubtless be working with the Army. Yet the old man was orthodox in his day. I wonder

what our present orthodox people will be called in the middle of
the twentieth century.[7]

William Allen White's twenty-one months under Bent
Murdock were one of the most profitable periods of his life.
Murdock was not only a good newspaper publisher; he was a
good writer. His style was in many respects remarkable:
"simple, strong, built upon the commonest words of the language, put together with short, direct sentences."[8] He went
straight to the point without rhetorical flourishes, and he was
always understandable. He had, moreover, the unusual talent
of being able to write with both vigor and charm. Nearly forty
years after leaving Murdock's paper, White, as a member of
the most distinguished group of editors in America, told his
colleagues that this country editor was the best editorial writer
he had ever known."[9] White's writing inclinations were largely
in the opposite directions, but he consciously attempted editorials like Murdock's. He studied his style, and knowing in a
general way his attitude on specific issues, wrote editorials in
imitation of his master. So apt a pupil was he that he fooled the
editors who were reprinting editorials from the *Republican;*
many of the quotations were credited to Murdock, though
White had written them.

Above all White wanted to succeed, and to this ambition
was linked a young man's natural yearnings for praise. Having his editorials credited to Murdock, whose writings were
held in the highest esteem by Kansas editors, gave White moments of unalloyed joy. Murdock, however, was judicious in
his praise; his encouragement offered little inducement for the
young man's head to "swell and swell and swell." When White
threw himself unreservedly into the legislative rebellion headed
by Murdock and had his editorials credited to him, his disciple's
ardor probably amused the Senator. He would go to the *Republican* office, rummage about among the exchanges, and
finding an editorial of White's credited to him, he would square
up to White, squint out of his glasses and say, "You seem
to be risin' hell, I notice." If a paper contained a dig at him
because of an editorial by White, he would take it over to
White's desk, "put his finger on it and grunt, chuckle and toddle

back to his desk." [10] However proud he was of White's work, he conveyed only enough of his approval to indicate that he was doing all right.

One September day in 1891 Murdock sidled up to White's desk and said, "Well, Mistofer, you think you have done it, don't you?" Then he grunted and added, "Old Plumb says you are all right. He says your piece is a daisy. Thinks it is like your father." Looking at White a minute over his glasses as though he were trying to think of a day long past, he said, "Old—Doc—White, Old—Doc—White"; [11] then he turned on his heel and went back to his desk. Years later White learned that Murdock was immensely proud of his "piece."

White had published in the September 4 issue of the El Dorado *Republican* "The Regeneration of Colonel Hucks," [12] a political short story. The story was a portent of what was to happen five years later, for within the state it brought White the same type of recognition that "What's the Matter With Kansas?" brought to him nationally. Senator Preston B. Plumb, seeing the value of the story as campaign material, had the Republican state central committee circulate it throughout Kansas.

As political propaganda, "The Regeneration of Colonel Hucks" had merits. The chief character is an old Union soldier who, after two years of wandering in the wilderness of the Alliance Party, returns to the Republican fold. He is made a delegate to the Republican state convention at Topeka, but is reluctant and ashamed to face his former Alliance companions. As his regeneration continues, his courage returns; and he experiences a kind of religious exaltation in his rebirth. Being once again in the Republican Party after the two-year defection, he not only has a more intelligent appreciation of the merits of the party but receives greater personal recognition than ever before. The story was a standing invitation to all Populists to depart from the error of their ways and partake of the joys of being back among the elect. It also glorified the Republican Party, its leaders, and subtly hinted that in the matter of patronage the Republican Party was the one on which to rely.

To its author, the story brought offers from both the

Kansas City *Journal* and the Kansas City *Star* to write editorials at twenty-five dollars a week. White wanted to know something of the ways of Babylon, and the increase in salary seemed to indicate that he could realize his ambition to own a typewriter, an evening suit, and a leather couch; consequently, he accepted the *Journal's* offer in preference to the *Star's* "because it was a Republican paper." [13]

CHAPTER VI

End of the Apprenticeship

Mr. Nelson's reporters were really lieutenants, emis-
saries, and proconsuls rather than mere writers. They
made the news as they went, and like a general in his
tent, the big white-haired, ruddy-faced, bull-voiced old
soldier of righteousness sat and swore sweetly in mellow
joy at the news from the front.[1]

WILLIAM ALLEN WHITE's choice of the Kansas City
Journal in preference to the *Star* was a mistake for
the moment, but only for the moment. No older
and no wiser than he was in the newspaper business, he soon
discovered the difference between a free and a controlled press;
and the lesson coming early and coming forcibly was worth the
cost at which it was bought. Fresh from a country daily where
he had been accustomed to writing what he thought without
fear or favor, he found the limitations imposed by the *Journal*
peculiarly exacting. For the *Journal* was a paper that sold advertising by favor, exploited real estate deals, and formulated
its editorial policy in accordance with the welfare of "special"
interests. Instead of being free and vigorous, it was restrained
and timid; and Will White, the unsophisticated crusading country bumpkin, was ill constituted either by training or by temperament to conform to the policy of a paper controlled by
special interests. The fact that Charles Gleed, both a member of
the *Journal's* staff and an official of the Santa Fe railroad, had
secured his position for him seemed not to have sobered him
to his obligations; consequently, when White asked to be
transferred to Topeka as the *Journal's* Kansas reporter, the
change came as a relief to both White and the *Journal's* staff.

White had served the *Journal* five months as editorial
writer when in March, 1892, he became its Kansas correspondent. His six months at Topeka were invaluable in providing a
background for his future career. "No one has ever known
more about the outward customs and behaviors of an American
state than Mr. White," [2] and not a little of the basis of this
knowledge was gained in the Populist upheaval of 1892. This
campaign was no drab affair. Everywhere seasoned politicians
were using all the resources at their command to outwit those
colorful characters who were capitalizing on the dissatisfaction
of the masses and threatening to reduce to impotency the
traditional power of the old parties. Every type of office holder
he came to know, from justice-of-the-peace to presidents and
future presidents. Every type of personality he studied individually and en masse, under every sort of political condition.
The experience acquainted him with political leaders, trained
him in political reporting, and furnished a wealth of material
for fiction.

The immediate cause of White's leaving the *Journal* was
a row with the telegraph editor. White was sent to Wichita
to cover the state convention of the Populist Party. On a tip
from Jerry Simpson, a leading Populist, he learned that the
convention would nominate L. D. Lewelling for governor at
about half-past eleven in the morning. Lewelling was an unknown dark horse, and White and Tom Norton, another *Journal* reporter who was afterwards general counsel for the Santa
Fe, undertook to scoop the other newspaper men.

. . . We proceeded to file all we could think of about Lewelling
and his record, and long before the balloting had come off we had
a good story, a column and a half,[3] and everything but the balloting. When the ballot came along, we had the wire into the convention hall and we got the ballot and the whole story. Lord! but we
were proud of ourselves, because Arthur [Senator Arthur Capper,
then a reporter for the Topeka *Capital*] and Dick Lindsay of the
Star had to wait for it and they didn't get it into the first edition.
They caught the city edition.

When we got to the train to go up to Kansas City, I bought a
Journal at Newton and started down to show Arthur how I had
got it on him and the story wasn't on the first page. Then I looked
on the second page. It wasn't on the second page, and then [I]

turned over to the society page and it wasn't there. I skipped over
to the editorial page and on through, and on the market page that
telegraph editor had put our beat. Tom and I went into the [Jour-
nal] office . . . walked up to the telegraph editor's room. . . . At
about seven o'clock, we locked the door, called him every kind of
a name we could lay our tongues on, told him that if he would fight
either of us, the other would leave the room, did everything in the
world we could to make him fight, and then, of course, we didn't
have any job.[4]

From September, 1892, to June, 1895, White wrote editorials for the Kansas City *Star,* working in as congenial an
atmosphere as was possible for such an individualist. He had
as associates T. W. Johnston, Ralph Stout, Alexander Butts,
Roswell Fields, Noble Prentis—all newspaper men of outstanding caliber—and the master of them all, William Rockhill
Nelson, whom White regarded as an editor without a flaw.

Nelson had established the Kansas City *Evening Star* in
1880, and thereafter until his death thirty-five years later no
American editor of a comparable paper ever surpassed him in
the personal direction he gave to his organization.[5] To achieve
the ends the *Star* was seeking, he believed that every person
who had a hand in the paper's production

should clearly understand those purposes and have them constantly
in mind, so that no news or information or influence bearing upon
any of them shall be overlooked or disregarded. . . . And, in
general, every one should strive to furnish ideas and suggestions;
to find new opportunities for the paper's active service; new
features of interest; new ways of doing things.[6]

This attitude toward his staff welded it into a harmonious unit,
and brought about a spirit of co-operation wherein each member met the other members, including Nelson himself, on terms
of greatest familiarity. Each man was an integral part of the
organization, making his contribution to a paper that came to
be regarded as an institution, like a great university.

White admired many qualities in Nelson, but those that
appealed to him most were his independence, his courage, and
his enterprise. Nelson was a fighter, and the greater the odds
the harder he fought. To protect his community from the de-
signs of unscrupulous men and organization, to secure for it

all the public services at a fair and reasonable rate, to promote all the agencies and activities that added to human welfare, to work for the beautification of homes, parks, and streets—in short, to make Kansas City the best possible place in which to live—was the sacred trust of the Kansas City *Star*. Nelson was often a pioneer, and he was often in the minority. More often, perhaps, he was courageously fighting some private interest for the public good. So well did Nelson succeed that his paper is credited with surpassing all other American newspapers in continuous and efficient service to its community.[7]

White participated in one of the *Star's* most notable achievements. One day Nelson asked him if he knew anything about gas and gas rates. White did not; until he went to Kansas City he had never lived in a house "with anything better than a kerosene lamp," and he confessed his ignorance.

"All right," said the Colonel,[8] "you have an open mind. Go out and study the gas problem in Kansas City; take your time. Take a month or two before you write a line, longer if you want to. But tell me, when you are ready, what you think about dollar gas for Kansas City." [9]

For several months White devoted all his available time to study the gas problem. Kansas City was paying $1.60 for a thousand cubic feet of gas, a rate much higher than that of other cities; and when White finally concluded that the gas company could sell gas at a dollar a thousand, he discovered that a lawyer whom Nelson had engaged to study the situation had reached the same conclusion. As a result of their agreement —arrived at independently—the *Star,* with White writing most of the editorials, waged a successful fight for dollar gas.

Not infrequently Nelson maintained his position at great personal risk. The single humorous anecdote that White tells of his *Star* days grew out of Nelson's opposition to a political boss.

I remember one day we were all sitting there at work. The telegraph editor's office and the editorial writers and the Colonel and the managing editor were all on one floor. I was hitting it up at my typewriter along about half past nine or ten in the morning when I heard an uproar across the hall in the Colonel's room. Then

I heard the unmistakable bang bang and a fall, and we all ran and there was a fellow in to lick the editor, and there was the dear old Colonel on the floor. So I got there just as the managing editor, Tommy Johnston, who was about six feet two, and the telegraph editor, who was a little taller than I, and the city editor, Ralph Stout, who weighed about 240 pounds, arrived, and we gathered up the man, a fellow named Joe Davenport. Each took a handle. I remember I had an arm and Stout had a leg and Tommy Johnston had a leg, and Pipsey had another arm. We carried him down the hall to one of those double stairways and one, two, three, and down he went. I, being the youngest, being twenty-three at the time, scrambled down, met him on the landing and as he gathered himself up, he pulled out a large gun. I was in the War and saw some large guns, but I never saw such as gun as that. . . . He poked it under my nose and I was on the landing, leading down into the main office. . . . I first thought I would crawl into the gun. But I had another thought and I put my hand on the railing and jumped over it, and as I jumped over it, I said, "Excuse me, Mr. Davenport," and as I looked over I saw old Campbell, the live stock editor in the city desk. He had a gun and had a bead on Davenport, so if Davenport had killed me, I knew that my redeemer lived and that I would be avenged, which didn't do me much good. But I landed right in the midst of a white-headed boy, not Gus, but one of Gus's brothers in the circulation department, who didn't know much about the show. I landed right on his desk and he was the only fellow who had any real trouble out of the thing, for they had to bring him to.[10]

White's indebtedness to Nelson is great. The two men were wholly unlike in actions and temperament, even though both made their papers the direct expression of their personalities. White had participated largely and actively in public organizations; Nelson seldom took part even in those organizations most directly concerned with the movements which vitally interested him. Nevertheless, despite differences in personalities and in methods of work, many policies that made the Kansas City *Star* the paper it was under Nelson have been White's guides in his direction of the Emporia *Gazette*. White's refusal to limit his sphere of action by taking political office resulted from his association with Nelson. White drew the line on remunerative offices; Nelson went the whole distance by including every office. Both men departed from their principles once. Nelson to serve as temporary national committeeman from Missouri for the Progressive Party and White to become an independent candidate for the governorship of Kansas. White's oft repeated words, "Every young man entering the newspaper business should take monastic vows against office holding," [11] came originally from Nelson.

Whether White learned from Emerson that consistency is the hobgoblin of little minds or whether he got it from Nelson or someone else matters little. In Nelson he saw an exemplification of the idea and its practical results. White has carried the principle much farther than Nelson did. Nelson applied it to the policies of the *Star*, whereas White has never hesitated to reverse himself on any statement when changed conditions or additional information made his original statement untenable. The list of identical editorial policies might be extended. They range from the theory that a newspaper never loses in an honest, courageous fight to a mutual opposition to the comic strips.

When White joined the staff, the *Star* had already taken its place among the leading papers in America. The weekly had been founded; the daily had passed the 50,000 mark in circulation. Aside from the crusading policies, the circulation had been built up by conscious avoidance of sensationalism and by eschewing the so-called popular features appearing in other papers. From the beginning Nelson's ideal in the choice of non-news features had been "a family journal . . . strictly first class." As a consequence, the paper had a strong literary flavor. White as a school boy first discovered Kipling and Stevenson in the *Star!* Nelson, however, did not stop with contemporary writers. "Noble thoughts were news," [12] and such a poem as Milton's "Il Penseroso" [13] was as likely to be found in the *Star* as one by a recognized contemporary poet.

With the founding of the Sunday *Star* in 1894 the demand for feature articles increased; and Nelson, believing that the men working for him were as capable feature writers as those whose wares were peddled by the syndicates, assigned each member of his staff a local color story for each Sunday edition. White soon discovered that his Sunday stuff was full of dynamite. One of his first features, about the Kansas City stockyards, "all but lost a big advertising contract for the paper"; and another, about a poor quarter of the town, "made the real estate owners in that section of the village march in serried ranks into the *Star* office and lift up their voices in woeful lamentations." The frequency and the violence of these explosions prompted Tom Johnston, the managing editor, to remark "in sorrow, not in anger," "Billy, you can raise more hell in three innocent-looking lines imbedded in a 1000-word story than any man I have ever known. You will drive me to drink." [14]

These explosions confirmed White still further in the opinion that he wanted a paper of his own where he could be his "owned damned fool in his own way." To avoid a recurrence of the unpleasantness that arose from his feature articles, he turned to fiction. Short stories he found both safer and easier to write than features, and in lieu of local color articles he contributed short stories for the rest of his time with the *Star*. A number of these were later collected in *The Real Issue*.

Meanwhile, White was still the aspiring poet. He was regularly contributing poems to the *Star;* and an invitation to read his poetry before the East Side Literary Society, with Ewing Herbert making the critical remarks, brought such enthusiastic commendations that the two embarked upon a series of lectures in the vicinity of Kansas City. Engagements were made through friends and former schoolmates, Herbert giving the lecture and White reading from his poems. The two had hoped to make some money, but were not greatly disappointed when it turned out otherwise, since they were having a good time enjoying the hospitality of friends.

At the very time the entertainments promised to pay, they ended abruptly and prosaically. Every ticket to the hall at Belton, Missouri, had been sold, but when the two arrived to fill their engagement, it was raining so hard that not more than a half dozen persons appeared for their show. The promoter told White and Herbert that he dared not pay them for the engagement with so few present, and asked them to return at a later date. This was agreed to, and White in his expansive manner refused to ask for expense money. Then they found that the only way White could get back to Kansas City by the time he was due was to board a freight train at a watering station. They waded mud for three-quarters of a mile and were no sooner aboard the caboose than they found themselves out in the mud again. Both, being newspaper men, flashed railroad passes, but for another road. On the strength of these passes, the conductor consented to carry them to the next station. There in the darkness they made their way alongside the freight to a flat car carrying sections of a tile culvert. In these sections they rode to Olathe, Kansas, where a policeman picked them up. With their passes and other evidences of newspaper connections deftly woven into a tall tale, they talked the officer into buying their breakfasts, after which they boarded the Santa Fe, for which their passes were good, and rode in state to Kansas City. But the illustrative lectures on fancy and the imagination were finished.

White's second poetical adventure with Albert Bigelow Paine, Mark Twain's biographer, ended in disappointment for all concerned. In issuing *Rhymes by Two Friends,* White and Paine had a dual purpose in mind: to give a selection of their verses permanent form and to bring their work to the attention of the eastern press. M. L. Izor, a printer at Fort Scott, Kansas, where Paine was living, undertook to act as publisher. Five hundred copies were to be issued, White and Paine to receive a hundred each. Before the printing was finished, Izor became financially hard-pressed, and Paine, being in Fort Scott, advanced the necessary money to finish the job. When the book came off the press, Paine blundered in sending out for review all his own and nearly all White's copies, thereby temporarily straining their friendly relations. Izor, who had hoped for a profit from the printing, found that the volume would scarcely sell, and eventually turned over the unsold copies to Paine to repay his loan. The book, now a collector's item, was later regarded by both men as a mistake; and White is credited with saying that he would buy them up at five dollars a copy to get them out of circulation.

The unproclaimed but most important event in White's life occurred when he was married to Sallie Lindsay, a Kansas City school teacher. Miss Lindsay's parents, Fannie and Joseph M. Lindsay, were Kentuckians and typical southerners in both thought and appearance. The father was tall and blond, the mother small and dark. Fannie, after the time-honored fashion of her class, attended a boarding school; and Joe, who at the outbreak of the Civil War owned a plantation and from seventy-five to a hundred slaves, served under John Morgan with "Morgan's Raiders," a group of volunteer cavalrymen famed for their daring. Lindsay was captured with Morgan, served eighteen months in a northern prison, and endured the hard lot of all Civil War prisoners. He, like his wife, remained a more or less unreconstructed rebel throughout life. When the war ended, he did not take the oath of allegiance; and she was proud of being a Daughter of the Confederacy and an old-fashioned, uncompromising Democrat.

After the birth of her fifth child and fourth son, Fannie Lindsay decided that Kentucky with its liquor was no place to bring up boys; and the family moved to Atchison, Kansas, where there were no saloons. Later they moved to Kansas City where Sallie graduated from high school, and at sixteen became one of the youngest teachers ever to serve in the Kansas City system. In the course of time the Lindsay girls became teachers and the boys engineers. As a family they were highly loyal to each other, and to this day are proud that they "always pulled together."

Walter Armstrong, White's old university schoolmate, introduced White to his future wife. The two were at a party, and Sallie maintains that the minute she set eyes on White she said to herself, "There's my man." White says he thought he pursued her, but she was there and ought to know. After an uneventful, average-length courtship, they became engaged. Since Sallie did not care for jewelry, they put their money together and bought a rug instead of a diamond. On April 27, 1893, they were quietly married in her parents' home in the presence of only the immediate relatives; and, after the wedding breakfast, started on a three-weeks' honeymoon trip to the Rocky Mountains. They spent two weeks in New Mexico near Las Vegas, then went to Santa Fe, Manitou, and finally Estes Park where they lived in a one-room cabin not far from the one where they have been spending their vacations for a quarter century.

Estes Park in 1893 was not the commercialized resort it

is today. Cabins did not have electric lights, running water, and innerspring mattresses. One rustled the fuel from the mountain side, carried the water from a near-by stream, cooked the food over an open fire, and slept on a bed of pine boughs cut with his own hands. But life must have been delicious for the young married couple. When White's leave-of-absence from the *Star* was up, they decided they wanted to stay longer—and stay they did. Then came the midsummer panic, closing the bank at Manitou and sweeping away every cent they had to their names. In the week that followed, while they were attempting to salvage something from the crash, the *Star* fired its absentee reporter. But all was not lost. The same panic that swept away their money drove one of the *Star's* reporters to a nervous breakdown. White got the reporter's job and the two went back to Kansas City on a railroad pass to live in their own home and dream of the day when they would own their own paper.

Sallie Lindsay was the wife for White. She did not try to make over the somewhat irresponsible, erratic country youth; she recognized his potential genius and set about to develop it. In the long years that lay ahead of them, she, by her devotion and practical sense, steered him in his course. White has reaped the worldly fame; but his work is her work, her work his. She has always entered into the spirit of his activities as if they were her own; indeed, she thinks of them as her own. They make every decision together. She goes over all his writings for magazines and books, she reads his proofs, and helps him in a thousand important and unknown ways. When they were married, she was probably ahead of him intellectually; certainly she was a better writer. One who examines an original White manuscript need be no great critic to recognize Sallie White's interlinings as definite stylistic improvements.

Socially, she was many miles ahead of her husband, for Sallie had been brought up to be a lady. Her kindness, refinement, and graciousness did not come accidentally. First, there were nine other children who had to be lived with; then there were her slave-holding parents who trained her to cook, dress, and entertain after a lady's fashion of the old South. The essential qualities of her personality, her husband lacked conspicuously; and she, who thought of herself as shepherd to her brothers and sisters, became shepherd to William Allen White. All this White realized in later years, and it explains not only his devotion to his wife but many of his attitudes in public affairs. He will not, for example, support a candidate for the presidency until he has met the candidate's wife.

CHAPTER VII

Hustler

It is reported that W. A. White has purchased the Gazette, a paper published in this city, and will take charge the 1st of June. Next.[1]

ELEVEN days after the insolent "Next" appeared in Emporia's leading newspaper, as the Santa Fe Kansas City plug train deposited its passengers in Emporia, a young man hesitated on the platform. He had just descended from a chair car, and standing on the platform, suitcase in hand, he did not cut a very smart figure. In his late twenties, he showed a marked tendency toward obesity, which made him appear shorter than he actually was. His trousers bagged at the knees, and both trousers and coat looked as if he had slept in them. His dress, however, was not his most striking feature. The innocent-looking, moonlike face easily overshadowed all else, though part of its conspicuousness was due to the hat that encircled the back of his head like a halo. There was discernible in his entire make-up a devil-may-care attitude; but that attitude, for the moment, had been dropped. If he were now to make a favorable impression on the folk of Emporia, it would augur well for the future; but the creation of such an impression was a problem of some magnitude. In one pocket of the baggy trousers was a dollar and a quarter—his total assets. Should he carry his grip and walk to the boarding house? Should he spend the quarter for a hack and ride in state and style? That was the first momentous decision the new editor of the *Gazette* had to make. And in keeping with a life of prodigality, he spent the quarter.

William Allen White bought the Emporia *Gazette* on sheer nerve. Every cent of the purchase price he borrowed—a thousand dollars from Governor E. N. Morrill, another thousand from Major Calvin Hood, and a third from the Preston B. Plum estate. With this $3,000 W. Y. Morgan, his predecessor, had bought the Hutchinson *News.* The *News* was a more valuable newspaper property than the *Gazette,* but one White would not have had "at the same price" he paid for the Emporia paper. White "wanted to be in a college town." [2] Already he had tried unsuccessfully to buy papers in three other Kansas college towns—Manhattan, Ottawa, and Lawrence. And so long had he bargained for the *Gazette* that when the sale was finally completed the announcement was not "very startling news" [3] to either the newspapers or the people of Emporia. Furthermore, White wanted a paper that would give him a living and leisure to write. Some day he hoped to reach the kingly estate where his income would be $3,000 a year.

The physical assets of the paper were nothing for the new editor to wax enthusiastic over. The plant occupied a floor space of 25 by 60 feet. There were a Cranston cylinder press with a water motor, four or five cases of type, a couple of make-up stones, and some miscellaneous printing material. All the equipment could have been bought for a thousand dollars. The other two thousand of the purchase price had gone for good will. This good will consisted mainly in a subscription list. While the boys folded the papers the first night, White stood at the end of the press and counted the names on the list. There were 485. One other asset—little dreamed of at the time—went with the property, Walter Hughes.

The day White bought the *Gazette* he first saw Walter Hughes. He, a lad of seventeen, was feeding the cylinder press. White was ten years his senior. Until Hughes' death thirty-seven years later, the two "walked shoulder to shoulder," "from boyhood through youth to manhood and maturity." [4] In many ways the one was the complement of the other. Hughes was a born conservative, always cautious, always practical, always businesslike. As the years went by, White more and more relinquished to him the management of his business interests, knowing well whether at home or abroad that from first to last Walt Hughes held closest to his heart the welfare of William Allen White. Not a few of White's ever widening interests were made possible by the man who relieved him from the responsibility of attending to the multiplicity of minor details connected with a newspaper office.

On June, 3 the new editor's salutatory editorial appeared. Specifically, it has that one quality which more than any other differentiates the editorials of William Allen White: the intensity with which it reflects a unique personality. Its remarkableness, however, lies in its revelation of a young man whose editorial aims and aspirations have remained essentially unchanged, even though his attitudes toward the world and its institutions have undergone a revolution.

In the first place, the new editor hopes to live here until he is the old editor, until some of the visions which rise before him as dreams shall have come true. He hopes always to sign "from Emporia" after his name, when he is abroad, and he trusts that he may so endear himself to the people, that they will be as proud of the first words of the signature as he is of the last words. He expects to perform all the kind offices of the country editor in this community for a generation to come. It is likely that he will write the wedding notices of the boys and girls in the schools; that he will announce the birth of the children who will some day honor Emporia, and that he will say the final words over those of the middle age of life who read these lines. His relations with the people of this town and county are to be close and personal. He hopes that they may be kindly and just.

Recognizing his youth and inexperience, he calls on "the good, honest, upright, God fearing, law abiding people" of the community to guide him by making known their private opinion that it may become public opinion, to be his friends, to counsel with him, and to stand by him. This is the young pharisee speaking: Humanity falls into two static groups—in one group is the sheep; in the other, the goats. The sheep *a priori* know and live by the true, the beautiful, and the good; the goats in their perversity and ignorance choose to remain blind and indifferent. Forty years later White was to write, "I know now that there is no group of best people. Facing every question and in every crisis, a new group, a different group of best people emerges; those who see the truth about it and have courage to follow it." [5]

About politics, soon to figure so prominently in the new editor's future, White says, "He is a Republican and shall support Republican nominees first, last, and all the time. There will be no bolting, no sulking, no 'holier than thou' business about his politics . . ." Strange words these from the man who has been accused of doing more to wreck the Republican Party than any other man alive, who has bolted the Republican Party three times, and who, from the point of view of the regulars, has sulked not once but many times. But he wrote these words before the Theodore Roosevelt era. White lived up to them for a half dozen years. Yet he unconsciously wrote his political Declaration of Independence with the same ink that affirmed his unwavering party allegiance, when he declared that "If he could get an office he wouldn't have it." White needed but a Messiah to lead him out of intellectual thralldom; otherwise he was free.

Lastly, and very significantly, he writes, "I shall hustle advertising, job work and subscriptions, write locals, editorials and 'telegraph' twelve hours a day in spite of my high ideals. The path of glory is barred hog tight for the man who does not labor while he waits." And hustle he did. Cronus from the heights of the Emporia *Republican* must have known as he watched this Zeus among the mortals below that he himself was "Next." Here was a young man who believed that if one were kind, honest, and just, success was in the divine order of things provided he had average intelligence and worked sixteen hours a day. Ignoring the bleaching journalistic bones of those who had been vanquished by the *Republican,* White set about to make the *Gazette* a permanent part of Emporia. By the end of his first year, he knew that he had succeeded.[6]

A half dozen years passed before the *Gazette* took on its present appearance and character. In the meantime, White was experimenting. Never did he show greater energy and resourcefulness than during his first year. Instead of filling his columns with state national news, he sought news of local interest. As soon as carfare was available, Mrs. White came from Kansas City to write locals, and to introduce a society column. Every

Monday White printed an interesting column of church news. He captured the interest of the school children by running once a week a column of locals written by them. Every item printed carried the author's name, and the child writing the best one was given a dollar. Instructions for writing an interesting local were printed, so that every child's item would be in usable form. Before Thanksgiving a series of articles showing why Emporia should be thankful was solicited from representatives of such diverse groups as ministers, lawyers, landowners, school teachers, and football players. Special editions of the *Gazette* featuring Emporia's industries, Emporia's homes, and Emporia's tradesmen—from horse traders up—were common.

White's literary training was invaluable to his success. His first Saturday night's issue was obviously copied after the Sunday edition of the Kansas City *Star*. For that number, in addition to an editorial, he wrote a poem, and one of his best stories, "The King of Boyville." In the same paper he warned his subscribers that they would "have to put up with home made stories" until "this paper pays a little more." [7] Evidently the money was forthcoming. Before his first year was up, he had printed serially, *A Study in Scarlet, The Medal of Brigadier Gerard,* and *The Sign of the Four,* by A. Conan Doyle; *The Undertakers,* by Rudyard Kipling; *Young Robin Grey,* by Bret Harte; and *The Spectre of the Real,* by Thomas Hardy. White himself contributed a series of sketches of the life and manners of a country town. The first, a character sketch unfavorably drawn, presented a fictitious John Bigsby, who inclined toward atheism.[8] The following day "A Sympathizing Neighbor" came to Bigsby's defense, by contributing a study of his wife, who spent all her time in church activities to the neglect of her husband and home. Then followed in quick succession the "three town crowds," as seen through the eyes of "Jack Robertson's Baby"; the woman who flits from fad to fad, as seen by a doctor; and the hired girl who gossips about the families she has worked for. As long as the *Gazette* was an obscure country paper, these sketches went unnoticed. But the first time one appeared after White became nationally known, he was asked to write a series of such thousand-word sketches for a hundred dollars each.

As a part of the plan to make himself an Emporia fixture, White kept his readers informed of the development of his paper. Two weeks after he took charge, he announced that the news stories had been cut to essentials, that the advertising had been segregated from the news, that a half column of advertising had been refused on that date, and that sixty-three new subscribers had been secured since June 1. He printed such information regularly; and in June, 1896, as a summary of his first year's achievements, he pointed to three hundred new subscribers and the installation of a $600 job department wholly paid for. He stated that he had no outstanding bills more than thirty days old, that his receipts for the preceding month were $987.32, and that during the month he paid off $214 in notes. "This office," he concludes, "is a paying institution. It is here to stay. If you want to get in the band wagon, bring your work here." [9]

Within sixty days after taking over the *Gazette,* White had an old-fashioned newspaper fight on his hands. The cause of the friction was twofold. The *Gazette* had been made the official city paper, and the *Republican* had contested the award in court. The other point of contention was the result of White's hustling. He was ambitious to secure the Associated Press franchise for his paper; and to lay the ground work for a regular telegraphic service, he was spending around fifty dollars a month for bona fide telegraphic reports. At the same time the *Republican* was printing two or three columns daily under the heading, "Telegraphic News." These stories had already appeared in the Kansas City papers. They had been set up there, then stereotyped and shipped by express to the *Republican.* White did not hesitate to point out these facts. He printed signed statements by the manager of the Postal Telegraph Company stating that the *Gazette* was the only Emporia paper that printed genuine telegraphic news. Almost daily the *Gazette* carried an item of this character.

Tomorrow all the telegraph which appears in this paper today will appear in the other paper. This is absolutely the only paper in Emporia that gets one solitary word by wire. The Gazette is willing to give $100 to charity if it is not the only paper in Emporia that receives all of its telegraphic reports by wire.[10]

The *Republican,* goaded incessantly by the *Gazette,* retaliated by belittling the *Gazette* and attacking its editor :

The Gazette is not a newspaper. In representing itself as such it could be prosecuted for obtaining money under false pretenses. It has no excuse for living. Those who have money to shove down a rat hole can take all the comfort they can get out of the reflection that the Gazette is, after all, a newspaper. But such a reflection is only another instance going to show that fakers still find a field in which to work their humbugs.[11]

The next day White answered the *Republican,* deftly turning the attack to his advantage :

A long array of shimmering dancing gems of thought about the editor of the Gazette gleamed forth from the first column of the Republican's "choice reading" page last evening. The subject is an interesting one but the chances are that the subscribers of that paper would much prefer the welcome news that the military board decided yesterday afternoon to hold the state militia encampment at Emporia this year. That piece of news was published exclusively in the Gazette last evening.

So the fight continued, sinking more and more into personalities. By the end of August, White was calling ex-Governor Eskridge, the *Republican* editor, "liar"; and Eskridge was calling White "lunatic" and "silly Willie." A final specimen from the pen of Eskridge clearly indicates the level of the controversy :

Hot bricks to his feet to create a proper circulation of the blood and a wet rag pinned around his head to reduce the swelling might be beneficial for a time but there is no hope for a permanent cure.[12]

The controversy divided the town into two hostile camps, and flared up periodically until the *Gazette* finally squeezed the *Republican* to death. Its most disgraceful episode occurred in 1899. An old character of the town, L. Severy, disgruntled at his failure to secure the Republican nomination for mayor, bolted the ticket and became an independent candidate. White, still an unwavering adherent to the theory of party regularity, devoted a long editorial to Severy's defection, maintaining that men of his type were the greatest enemies of organized parties, devoid of character, and inimical to the well-being of society. The upshot of the editorial as reported by White was this:

> This noon, as W. A. White was crossing between the Emporia National bank and the Star Clothing house, he passed L. Severy. Mr. White spoke pleasantly to Mr. Severy. After Mr. White had passed Mr. Severy, Mr. Severy whirled and struck Mr. White on the back of the head with a heavy walnut cane, felling him. While Mr. White was unconscious for a few seconds, Mr. Severy struck him a second blow on the back of the head, breaking his cane. Recovering from his daze, Mr. White started on his way toward the Star Clothing house, when Mr. Severy drew back and started as if to pull a gun from his overcoat pocket. Whereat Mr. White told Mr. Severy he was too old a man for a gentleman to touch. Mr. Severy used vile and obscene language. A little later, Mr. White went to the Creamery restaurant.[13]

The immediate extent of the episode is not wholly recounted here. As White arose from the blow, Ed Reese, a bystander, called White a coward. White struck him in the face, and a fight was averted only by the interference of the crowd that had assembled.

Both White and Severy were brought into court on a warrant charging them "with quarreling and fighting and using abusive language, indecent and insulting language on the streets of Emporia." Severy pleaded guilty and his fine and court costs were paid from a subscription that had been circulated on his behalf. White pleaded "not guilty" and was acquitted. Severy offered affidavits from witnesses showing that White was facing him when he struck, to which White replied through the columns of his paper:

> Without desiring to question the veracity of the two gentlemen who swore that Severy was standing in front of W. A. White when he struck the blow that felled him, the Gazette desires to offer in evidence, as exhibit "A," one head, size $7\frac{3}{8}$ with a large lump directly on the back, and one $35 suit of clothes with mud down the front and not a spot behind, as exhibit "B." When a man is slugged from the back, he falls forward. The lump and the clothes are better than a stack of affidavits miles high.[14]

Newspapers throughout the state generally sympathized with White, but the *Republican* assumed a holier-than-thou attitude:

The Gazette has always been too free in its criticism of persons and things, even young ladies in the city, and, sometimes, has come near calling down on its head the vengeance of different parties. Even the churches have not escaped its vituperation. That kind of journalism is pernicious, being circulated to keep up strife and do great mischief in the community, verging on the commission of crime, or being the instigation of it from blackmail to murder. There is no telling what may follow its continuance.[15]

What did "follow" was a gold-headed cane presented a week later to Severy "by his friends" to replace the one broken over White's head. The presentation took place in the *Republican* office.

Meanwhile, lesser Emporia papers were finding the *Gazette* a more and more formidable foe, much of their inability to cope with the paper being due to its editor's facility with a pen. Here is his account of the demise of the *Democrat:*

Editor Phillips, late editor, owner and publisher of the Emporia Daily and Weekly Democrat, has left for parts unknown, probably to the horror and consternation of the parts, and certainly for the general betterment of this community. Far be it from this paper to say aught that would cast an unwarranted aspersion upon an earnest though unfortunate gentleman. It is not the purpose of the Gazette to be sensational nor to exaggerate interesting facts. But as a matter of news and stated in the precise terms of scientific description, without coloring the statement by loose vernacular, the simple, homely truth demands that it be said of Phillips that he was, is and will be while he lives on this easy old earth, the most picturesque, unique, original, shameless, deliberate, conscienceless, malicious and indefatigable dead beat that ever pressed the sidewalk of Commercial street with his velvety feline feet. It is but just to him to add that he was not a harsh and irascible man. He did not exact tribute with either club or gun or buzz saw. He had the soft, self-deprecatory, insinuating voice of a cooing dove; and he glided into his machinations with the gentle, noiseless, hypnotic sinuosity of a rubber-tired rattlesnake. He was as bland as a sunrise and as deadly as a pestilence.

Not only did he have the face to charge for a total circulation of 150 copies, advertising rates that would make reputable editors blush whose papers circulated by the thousand; but Editor Phillips actually got those rates. Earth was a wilderness of suckers for him. He put the marks of his easy touch all over the town and when advertisers were coy he cut their advertisements from other papers, charged up the account, waited till the store keeper was out and traded out the amount of his account and twice as much besides. Rebuffs and insult rebounded from him without denting his pachyderm complacency, nor rubbing the creamed and mantled waters of his stagnant moral sense.

Poor old Phillips, he has left us. We may never look upon his like again—thank Heaven—until the sulphurous blazes of perdition illuminate the job lot in the deepest part of the seventh pit.[16]

The same energy that White put into boosting the *Gazette* he also put into boosting Emporia. He worked untiringly for all projects that would improve the appearance of the town, he advertised home industries and attempted to secure new ones, he labored long and patiently to secure additional railroads, he promoted street fairs, he demanded better music for the bands, and ardently advocated patronizing home industries. His editorials would have warmed the heart of the most exacting, selfish, hypocritical businessman who ever attempted to drum up trade by preaching local patriotism. Speaking of the new spirit of co-operation which seems to be coming over Emporia, he says:

And while the change is on we should first of all get in a habit of keeping what little money we have at home and the way to do that is to patronize home industries. Begin in the morning. Eat nothing but biscuits made from Emporia flour. It is the best in the world. It sells well everywhere. It should sell in Emporia. Eat nothing but Emporia bacon and ham, and Lyon county eggs, and Emporia creamery butter. They are as good as the world produces. Put on an Emporia overcoat over an Emporia suit of clothes. If the money spent in Kansas City for cheap tailoring were spent here thirty tailors would find work here who are now living in the big city. At lunch, eat Emporia canned goods when the factory opens, as it will this season. Save freight and help to keep the men at work here at home. Eat Emporia killed and cured beef. Use Emporia iron foundry products in building and in business. Work for home, talk for home, patronize home. That is the way to win.[17]

The excessive boosting was in part a reaction to the calamity howling of the Populists. For every economic affliction White had but one cure: Shut up and go to work. Where there was trouble, the community or the individual was at fault. The economic principles as embodied in the laws of the land were as immutable as the Ten Commandments. The suggestion

that these laws might operate to the advantage of a privileged
few was heresy, socialism, or anarchy. To the Republican
Party the Tablets of Stone had been delivered; and the revelation, as put into operation by that party, guaranteed to every
man an equal opportunity so long as men stayed "within the
law."

White's boosting was nicely balanced with an equal amount
of castigation. Not for a half dozen years did he cease from
being up early and late to war on some aspect of Emporia life
that he thought inimical to the general welfare. Everything
from immorality to improper diction ran the gauntlet of his
editorial page. Loafers, gamblers, mothers, students, preachers
—all were drubbed in turn. Even the lowly college paper did
not escape his crusading zeal. It was labeled a parasite, accused of living off the town and taking advertising away from
legitimate mediums. He told mothers when their daughters
might properly appear on the streets, and carried his campaign
to the point where he printed the names of girls who disobeyed
his edicts; he requested Emporians to call a bull a bull, but
when they saw a cow to "call him a cow." [18] Preacher that he
was, the ministers were the targets of many a shaft.

Does any Emporia minister dare to investigate the facts as the
Gazette has done and say from his pulpit that there has been an
O. M. B. joint for some time running over Ed. Atyeo's meat
market, one near the middle of the block on the east side of Commercial street between Third and Fourth, and another a few doors
south of it. Or will we have a brave outspoken attack on the Sultan
of Turkey for his nefarious butchery of the Greek! [19]

When the ministers talked back, White surfeited them
with praise, damned himself to perdition, and left the public to
find the truth for itself. He honored the Reverend Sellers
doubly, with a report of his sermon and with an editorial. The
news story states that the revival at the Christian Church is
doing well, that a hundred or more were turned away from the
services, and that "the *Gazette* came in for a share of the general shakeup."

. . . Reverend Sellers said that the editor of the Gazette had never
been in the Christian church and from competent authority the
preacher had learned that the editor had not attended any church

very much. Reverend Sellers wanted to know how he knew what
the preachers were talking about. A good point. . . .

The audience was satisfied with the scorching given the
editor of the Gazette and were with the preacher. It was a good
sermon to a good audience about the old sinners of Emporia.[20]

As a reporter White sensed that a personal attack was
choice news. To the disinterested it was the editor's best argument; to others it gave immense satisfaction because the editor
had at last got his deserved skinning. Such attacks White never
answers directly. He has never gone farther than to hint that
he is not a part of the issue. Oftener, an editorial provides a
few moments of merriment for the "gentle reader." "Brave
Parson Sellers'" is typical:

By turning to the local page of the Gazette the gentle reader
may discover that Parson Sellers had the courage to read a piece
from the Gazette and hold its editor by name up to public scorn.
That is the kind of courage that the Gazette admires. If the Parson will put the same kind of nerve into a sermon paying his
respects to Emporia people who dance, and play cards, and rent
rooms to poker clubs, and charge illegal interest, and lie about
their neighbors, and dodge their church dues, and cheat in business, the Gazette will give him a double column six inch advertisement of his business every Saturday, and he can furnish the copy.

It takes nerve to run a meeting house, and the Gazette has
reason to believe Parson Sellers has plenty of it. That makes two
preachers in town that are not afraid to say what they think. Now
that the Gazette has been disposed of by the Parson, it being
honored as the greatest sinner in town by the first skinning, there
is reason to hope that a number of other hard boiled unregenerate
old devils hereabouts will get a few whiffs of sulphur up their
noses next Sunday night when Parson Sellers gives out his promised polemic diatribe against Emporia iniquity.[21]

At the end of his first year, White reported his first
national convention. With fewer than a thousand subscribers
to write for, he covered the Republican National Convention.
To help defray expenses, he also reported the convention for
the Kansas City *World*. In company with Ed. Howe, he went
to St. Louis to see how the city and the convention looked to a
citizen of Emporia. His reporting was based on the theory that
what interested him would also interest the average reader of

the *Gazette*. His reports are, therefore, markedly candid and
strongly colored with human interest.

St. Louis stinks. There is a peculiar sour smell about the
place that goes through everything. It is the smell you find in hotels
after they have been running a number of years. It is a cooking
smell, and it makes the head ache. Ed. Howe, who has been across
the ocean, says it is like the smell that comes from the steam
kitchen when you are sea sick.[22]

Despite the odor, he was having a good time. The next
day he wrote that he and Howe had been out to the Union
Market, where "the meat looks good and the vegetables are
clean." The two of them "took an arm load of it into a restaurant nearby and made them serve it." That greatly amused
the people in the restaurant, but "there were two of us and we
could laugh back." Actually, though, what they were laughing
about "was the way the waiter girl had her necktie tied." Regardless of dress "all the girls and women in this town are
ugly," but the men "are unusually handsome and are very
polite," much more so than in Chicago. Music seems to be
about "the best thing" in the town, and "the amount of beer
consumed . . . is amazing. Yet no one seems to be drunk."

What the people of Emporia saw, in addition to the
Union Market, were the fashions, the tastes, and the manners
of the people of St. Louis, as they went to breakfast with their
editor.[23] The convention reports are similarly flavored:

[Chauncey Depew] is not so big nor so handsome as he looks in
the tailors' plates, but he has a wonderfully sensitive face, with
mobile lines about the eyes, and a woman's mouth.

Quay is a little fellow. He looks like a poker dealer with a
reddish brown face and dirty hair. His eyelids were made for a
pair of eyes two sizes larger than he wears.[24]

[Fairbanks, the temporary chairman,] in a cold, mechanical
voice, ill timed gesticulations, enunciation deficient, . . . made a
speech that was long, tiresome and worrying.[25]

On the average, the "human interest" took up about a third
of the reports. The other two thirds were given to an analysis
of the serious activities of the convention. He was hustling as
well as seeing the big show. The third day of the convention
his paper printed three and one-half columns from his pen.

CHAPTER VIII

Heckled to Fame

He was a young man then, in his late twenties, much smarter than he is now, brash, cocksure, vigorous and proud of his language. But he was in a terrible minority in Lyon County, which didn't bother him as he has always had a seven-devil lust for minority positions which 30 years have not quenched.[1]

T HE KANSAS political campaign of 1896 was the last spasm of a dying revolution. The genesis of the political turmoil lay in the economic predicament of the farmer. In 1890 three fourths of Kansas farms were mortgaged, and on these mortgages the farmer was struggling to pay an average annual interest of 9 per cent. In many cases, the face of the mortgage was as much as the value of the land. Lyon County, regarded as one of the most prosperous in the state, had a total mortgage indebtedness of $5,588,600 against a valuation of $6,493,491. From 1880 to 1890 approximately 450,000 mortgages were written on Kansas property, and about one-third of these "were foreclosed or the property deeded to the holder of the mortgage without legal proceedings." In the first six months of 1890 more than 10,000 farms were either foreclosed or transferred to the mortgage holder to save the expense of foreclosure. In Reno County foreclosures reached the staggering figure of 426 in a single term of court. Farmers, attempting "to hang on" and ever looking forward to higher prices, had plunged farther and farther into debt. To pay interest and taxes, they had had to borrow on their chattels at an annual rate of from 40 per cent to 375 per cent. At the same time, they were burning their corn because they could not exchange it for coal except at a loss, and burying their eggs because they were not worth hauling to market.[2]

Suffering from these and a hundred other ills, real or imaginary, farmers, laborers, and merchants were in the right psychological state to listen to any Messiah who promised to lead them out of their economic wilderness. And saviors, both men and women, arose by the score. Mary Elizabeth Lease electrified her listeners by telling them that they should "raise less corn and more Hell"; Jerry Simpson rode to national fame by championing the "single-tax," attacking the "grain gamblers," railroads, and kindred groups and organizations; and the names of a half-dozen others became household words throughout the nation. Under the inspiration of these leaders the discontent solidified itself in the form of the Populist Party, and the campaign of 1890 had all the earmarks of a religious reawakening. Tens of thousands flocked to the party gatherings where every man under the influence of a political revivalist became his own authority on the railroads, trusts, finance, taxation, and other topics of the hour.

Attended as it was by religious hysteria, the Populist movement attracted to its ranks the lunatic fringe in politics. On this aspect of the movement, the Republican Party centered its major attack. Without seriously attempting to answer the arguments of the Populists, the Republicans reviled and ridiculed the party by picturing it as a conglomeration of ignoramuses, half-wits and crackpots. The nation at large, out of sympathy with the movement, accepted the vilification at face value. "Sockless" Jerry Simpson is a case in point. Simpson, far from being the clod-hopper of popular imagination, was a cultured gentleman and "of more than usual sense for an American congressman."[3] He was not only a serious student of economics, but widely read in both American and English literature. He had come to Kansas with fifteen thousand dollars; and after seven years of farming, his money was gone and he was city marshal of Medicine Lodge at forty dollars a month. Throwing over his marshal job, he became the farmers' candidate for Congress against James P. Hollowell, a Civil War colonel, a successful lawyer, a congenial spirit, and an eloquent speaker, "known among his friends as 'Prince

Hal.' " Simpson, in attacking Hallowell, compared his own
lowly estate with that of his opponent's and asserted that
Hallowell wore silk underwear. "I can't represent you in Congress in silk underwear," he said; "I can't afford to wear it."
Victor Murdock, then a young reporter, substituted "socks"
for "underwear" and in reporting the speech quoted Simpson
as saying, "Prince Hal wears silk socks: I don't wear any." [4]
Murdock's story was accepted as true, and within a week everywhere Simpson was spoken of as "Sockless" Jerry or "Sockless" Simpson. Later, William Allen White added Socrates,
and Simpson "came to be known throughout the length and
breadth of the land as the 'Sockless Socrates from Kansas.' " [5]

By 1894, Kansas Populism was definitely on the decline.
The Populist Party, which had swept the Republicans from
office, had failed to alleviate the general economic suffering. As
a consequence, its leaders had fallen out, and were calling each
other names. But because the economic situation remained
essentially unaltered, the forces of discontent needed but one
clear strong voice to rally them. In 1896 the magnificent voice
of William Jennings Bryan captured the remnants of this once
powerful organization as he earnestly pleaded for the free
coinage of silver, and every man became an authority on the
currency.

Day by day as the McKinley-Bryan campaign progressed,
the young editor of the Emporia *Gazette* laid his offering on
the Republican altar. By every rule of self-interest he should
have been writing editorials extolling Bryan and denouncing
the Republican McKinley. But for some indefinable reason, he
thought of himself as a member of the privileged class. When
the Populists marched up and down Emporia streets waving
banners, "Abolish Interest and You Will Abolish Poverty," he
did not see his newspaper profits going to pay the interest on a
mortgage—he saw red. Preaching that sort of thing was
"lunacy"; it was "anarchy." In unqualified terms he told his
readers just that; and for his pains the Populists taunted him
with "Silly Willy" and drew a picture of the *Gazette* as a jackass and put it into their procession.

For White the silver issue in the 1896 campaign was but
ostensibly the question at stake. The real issue was, "Shall

American institutions, as they have been since the beginning, stand, or shall they be changed?" [6] The cardinal principle on which the American government had been founded was that "the state should give every man protection in his right to enjoy 'life, liberty, and the pursuit of happiness.'" Beyond the protection of the citizen "in his enjoyment of peace" the state had no right to interfere. The American way was "hands off," taking the part of neither the weak nor the strong. What had grown up in the West in recent years was the "un-American doctrine of state paternalism."

It is claimed by these doctors that when one man is weak, when he fails to get on in the world, when he finds himself at the bottom of the heap, the state should help him up. The believers in the new creed hold that it is the duty of the state to check the accumulation of one man's wealth and to end another man's poverty. They say that the man with the large fortune and the man who commits a crime are both subjects for state interference. They say that the man who is without means is the nation's ward, that he should be protected against the "oppression of wealth."

To White such a theory of government was neither American nor democratic; it was European and socialistic. The true American theory, as conceived by "the fathers" and as embraced by the Republican Party, says to the weak man:

. . . "Be strong or go under." It says to the strong: "Only be fair and keep within the law." It says to the poor: "There is no way on earth to get rich except by frugality, good management, and industry." The Republican party, speaking for the old-fashioned, sturdy Americanism, says to the man who asks that the state shall step in and relieve him of his burden: "You had an equal opportunity with your fellows. You had as good an education, as good a body, as fair a start; if you are behind and the other man is ahead, the thing for you to do is to catch up. We can't stop him. He is running his own race; if he is violating no law we shall let him go ahead—the faster he goes the better."

Furthermore, the Populists and their whole infernal lot, who were now attacking the foundations of the government, were the same party "which sympathized with treason in '61," . . . "abused Lincoln for upholding the government by continuing the war," and "defied the troops of the United States in Chicago." It now "silver plates a revolution, and calls to its aid all the forces of failure, of jealousy, of malice and sectional hatred to accomplish its dangerous scheme. It rallies state's rights under Altgeld, revolution under Tillman, despair under Peffer, anarchy under Debs, greed of office under Gorman, and all the wild, remorseful emotions of men who have failed in life under Bryan."

But though the young editor was writing as if the fate of the nation were in the balance, he planned to go on a vacation in the very midst of the conflict. Regardless of the threat to the nation, the intensity of a political campaign has never interfered with William Allen White's chucking the whole thing if he decided to do something else. Thus it was that while he was opposing the Fusion Party [7] most vigorously, he set August 15 as the date of his departure for Colorado, where he was to join Mrs. White for a short vacation. Early that Saturday afternoon as he was returning from the post office with an arm load of letters and exchanges, a Populist stepped up to him and began to ply him with questions on a silver argument which he thought White could not answer. White, annoyed at the interruption, was further irritated when a crowd gathered, which applauded everything his opponent said and jeered all his responses.

Any Saturday afternoon crowd in Emporia in August is largely made up of farmers and "town men of leisure," whether it be in 1896 or at the present time. And in August, 1896, in the midst of a prolonged drought with the thermometer standing at 107 degrees, wheat selling at 40 cents, corn 16, butter 10, chickens 8 if dressed, eggs 6, steers 3, hogs 2½, and the city without a street force because of no money—their political sympathies emphatically did not coincide with those of the editor of the *Gazette*.

They were naturally for Bryan and the vigor of the campaign in the Gazette together with the easy, innocent looking face of its youthful editor, gave them a notion that it would be a lot of fun to play horse with him on the street, which they proceeded to do. A crowd of them, 15 or 20, surrounded him and played froggy-in-the-meadow politically with the young smarty, guying him and reviling him and provoking him to language. But somehow his language got jammed. The madder he got the more he sputtered and the less he spoke, and his face lost all expression except its

color. He looked as featureless and as mad as a freshly spanked
baby in the combat area, and finally, with his arm full of mail,
stalked proudly down the street with a number of thoughts corked
up in him.[8]

When White did reach the *Gazette*, he found the printer
"howling for more copy for the editorial page." Glancing at
his watch to see how much time he had left to catch the train,
he plunged into writing, all hot and angry. Sentences "simply
rolled off" his pen; and as the pages were completed, the printer
took them one by one "hot off the griddle." [9] That evening
Democrats and Populists were treated to "What's the Matter
With Kansas?" another tirade of "Silly Willy's":

Today the Kansas department of agriculture sent out a statement which indicates that Kansas has gained less than two thousand people in the past year. There are about two hundred and
twenty-five thousand families in the state, and there were about
ten thousand babies born in Kansas, and yet so many people have
left the state that the natural increase is cut down to less than two
thousand net.

This has been going on for eight years.

If there had been a high brick wall around the state eight
years ago, and not a soul had been admitted or permitted to leave,
Kansas would be a half million souls better off than she is today.
And yet the nation has increased in population. In five years ten
million people have been added to the national population, yet
instead of gaining a share of this—say, half a million—Kansas has
apparently been a plague spot, and in the very garden of the world,
has lost population by ten thousands every year.

Not only has she lost population, but she has lost money.
Every moneyed man in the state who could get out without loss
has gone. Every month in every community sees some one who has
a little money pack up and leave the state. This has been going on
for eight years. Money has been drained out all the time. In towns
where ten years ago there were three or four or half a dozen
money lending concerns stimulating industry by furnishing capital,
there is now none, or one or two that are looking after the interests
and principal already outstanding.

No one brings any money into Kansas any more. What community knows over one or two men who have moved in with more
than $5,000 in the past three years? And what community cannot
count half a score of men in that time who have left, taking all
the money they could scrape together?

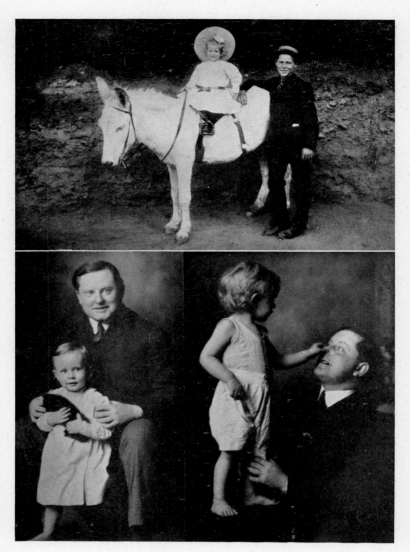

Top—Mary and young Bill
Bottom—William Allen White and young Bill

Mary White, taken when she was fifteen years old

Yet the nation has grown rich, other states have increased in population and wealth—other neighboring states. Missouri has gained over two million, while Kansas has been losing half a million. Nebraska has gained in wealth and population while Kansas has gone down hill. Colorado has gained every way, while Kansas has lost every way since 1888.

What's the matter with Kansas?

There is no substantial city in the state. Every big town save one has lost in population. Yet Kansas City, Omaha, Lincoln, St. Louis, Denver, Colorado Springs, Sedalia, the cities of the Dakotas, St. Paul and Minneapolis and Des Moines—all cities and towns in the West have steadily grown.

Take up the government blue book and you will see that Kansas is virtually off the map. Two or three little scrubby consular places in yellow-fever-stricken communities that do not aggregate ten thousand dollars a year is all the recognition that Kansas has. Nebraska draws about one hundred thousand dollars; little old North Dakota draws about fifty thousand dollars; Oklahome doubles Kansas; Missouri leaves her a thousand miles behind; Colorado is almost seven times greater than Kansas—the whole West is ahead of Kansas.

Take it by any standard you please, Kansas is not in it.

Go east and you hear them laugh at Kansas, go west and they sneer at her, go south and they "cuss" her, go north and they have forgotten her. Go into any crowd of intelligent people gathered anywhere on the globe, and you will find the Kansas man on the defensive. The newspaper columns and magazines once devoted to praise of her, to boastful facts and startling figures concerning her resources, are now filled with cartoons, jibes and Pefferian speeches. Kansas just naturally isn't in it. She has traded places with Arkansas and Timbuctoo.

What's the matter with Kansas?

We all know; yet here we are at it again. We have an old moss-back Jacksonian who snorts and howls because there is a bathtub in the statehouse; we are running that old jay for governor. We have another shabby, wild-eyed, rattle-brained fanatic who has said openly in a dozen speeches that "the rights of the user are paramount to the rights of the owner"; we are running him for chief justice, so that capital will come tumbling over itself to get into the state. We have raked the old ash heap of failure in the state and found an old human hoop skirt who has failed as a business man, who has failed as an editor, who has failed as a preacher, and we are going to run him for congressman-at-large. He will help the looks of the Kansas delegation at Washington. Then we have discovered a kid without a law practice and have decided to run him for attorney-general. Then for fear some hint that the state had become respectable might percolate through the civilized portions of the nation, we have decided to send three or four harpies out lecturing, telling the people that Kansas is raising hell and letting the corn go to weeds.

Oh, this is a state to be proud of! We are a people who can hold up our heads! What we need is not more money, but less capital, fewer white shirts and brains, fewer men with business judgment, and more of those fellows who boast that they are "just ordinary clodhoppers, but they know more in a minute about finance than John Sherman"; we need more men who are "posted," who can bellow about the crime of '73, who hate prosperity, and who think because a man believes in national honor, he is a tool of Wall Street. We have had a few of them—some hundred and fifty thousand, but we need more.

We need several thousand gibbering idiots to scream about the "Great Red Dragon" of Lombard Street. We don't need population, we don't need wealth, we don't need well-dressed men on the streets, we don't need cities on the fertile prairies; you bet we don't! What we are after is the money power. Because we have become poorer and ornier and meaner than a spavined, distempered mule, we, the people of Kansas, propose to kick; we don't care to build up, we wish to tear down.

"There are two ideas of government," said our noble Bryan at Chicago. "There are those who believe that if you just legislate to make the well-to-do prosperous, this prosperity will leak through on those below. The Democratic idea has been that if you legislate to make the masses prosperous their prosperity will find its way up and through every class and rest upon us."

That's the stuff! Give the prosperous man the dickens! Legislate the thriftless man into ease, whack the stuffing out of the creditors and tell the debtors who borrowed the money five years ago when money "per capita" was greater than it is now that the contraction of the currency gives him a right to repudiate.

Whoop it up for the ragged trousers; put the lazy, greasy fizzle who can't pay his debts on the altar, and bow down and worship him. Let the state ideal be high. What we need is not the respect of our fellow men, but the chance to get something for nothing.

Oh, yes, Kansas is a great state. Here are people fleeing from it by the score every day, capital going out of the state by the hundreds of dollars; and every industry but farming paralyzed, and that crippled, because its products have to go across the ocean before they can find a laboring man to work who can afford to buy them. Let's don't stop this year. Let's drive all the decent, self-respecting men out of the state. Let's keep the old clodhoppers who know it all. Let's encourage the man who is "posted." He can talk, and what we need is not mill hands to eat our meat, nor factory hands to eat our wheat, nor cities to oppress the farmer by consuming his butter and eggs and chickens and produce. What Kansas needs is men who can talk, who have large leisure to argue the currency question while their wives wait at home for that nickel's worth of bluing.

What's the matter with Kansas?

Nothing under the shining sun. She is losing wealth, population, and standing. She has got her statesmen, and the money power is afraid of her. Kansas is all right. She has started in to raise hell, as Mrs. Lease advised, and she seems to have an overproduction. But that doesn't matter. Kansas never did believe in diversified crops. Kansas is all right. There is absolutely nothing wrong with Kansas. "Every prospect pleases and only man is vile." [10]

In the meantime, William Allen White had boarded the Santa Fe and was proudly bearing the proofs of a little collection of short stories to Mrs. White that they might read them together. So completely had he forgotten the incidents of the afternoon that not even the name of the Populist who provoked the editorial remained in his memory. His temperature, like that of his state which by Monday had broken to 71 degrees in Emporia, had burned itself out. Thus closed the first chapter of "What's the Matter With Kansas?"

The second chapter opens in Chicago. Paul Morton, vice-president of the Santa Fe, "happening to meet Herman Kohlsaat, publisher of the Chicago *Times-Herald,* told him he had just read an editorial in a little Kansas paper giving a striking picture of conditions which, Morton said, Chicago and the East ought to know about." [11] Kohlsaat asked Morton to send him the paper, and he reprinted the editorial in both the *Times-Herald* and *Evening Post.* By way of Chicago the piece reached New York, where the *Sun* reprinted it. Then the Republican national committee began turning copies out in 100,000 lots, as the Republican press throughout the country broadcast the editorial to their countless readers. White, vacationing in the Colorado mountains, was totally unaware that he had caught the popular imagination. By the twenty-seventh of August, he, back in Emporia, had learned that Mark Hanna was using his "wail of woe" as a campaign document, and banteringly asked his readers if that ought to "be good for the post office." [12] A month later, although the Republican national committee was to distribute a million copies during the campaign, White had not yet seen a single reprint from that source.

Yet long before this date White knew he was standing on the threshold of fame. Kohlsaat wrote him that "the article has attracted more attention than anything that had been published during the campaign." Tom Reed, Speaker of the House of Representatives, wrote that he had "not seen as much sense in one column in a dozen years." [13] Every reputable Republican paper in towns of 50,000 or more had reprinted the editorial. Exchanges were pouring in; letters from individuals and McKinley clubs were sending money and asking for thousands of copies. Edition after edition had to be printed. Eight years later with McKinley in his grave, with Roosevelt in the White House, and with White totally reversed in his political attitudes, on the average from two to three letters a week were still dribbling in asking for copies.[14]

The popularity of "What's The Matter With Kansas?" was as much accidental as merited. White called it a "scratch shot," [15] "the angry after-thought of a man who was unable to hold his own in a crowd of hecklers." [16] The Chicago *Evening Post* called it "the utterance of a wit in whom the bitterness of reality cannot wholly suppress mirth over the utter imbecility that had caused it." [17] The *Post's* words were equally applicable to a dozen other editorials White wrote in the same campaign. "What's the Matter With Kansas?" read in the sober light of another day, when the conditions that brought it forth have passed, seems no more vigorous, no more impassioned, and far less convincing than a half dozen other philippics from White's pen at that time. Its thesis in so far as it had a thesis was "that if Kansas fought the money power, the money power would fight back." [18] The slight statistical matter contained in it White got from a talk with Eugene Ware, the Kansas poet. But these statistics are but the prelude to the main theme. Not until White gets by the figures does he strike that ironical sweep that rises to a breath-taking swell. And herein lies its first distinction. The longer White wrote the more ironical he became, and irony is a literary form which White almost never employs. Its second distinction lies in that accidental appreciation which has again and again in subsequent years lifted editorials from the limited circulation of the Emporia *Gazette* and given them national dissemination. Its third distinction lies in the fact that it gave a composite picture of the maniacal ravings of a group of people who, the country at large believed, had gone completely mad. One extract from a single letter goes a long way toward explaining the avidity with which the editorial was snatched up:

How strange it is to find a strong defender of common sense in Kansas. The popular idea of a citizen of Kansas is a man with one gallus, and that fastened with a nail, sitting in his shirt sleeves on a dry goods box spitting tobacco juice out of the door onto a plank sidewalk which is edged with dog-fennel, and as he whittles a piece of a shingle, giving his views on finance, which are about as sensible as the views of a Zulu savage on some question of ethical culture. It is a relief to hear from out of the midst of a Populist ridden community not only soaked with ignorance but proud of its asininity, the clear, strong, ringing notes of your bugle blast.[19]

Fortunately for White, "What's the Matter With Kansas?" was no flash in the pan. Had he lacked the substance within him to live up to the reputation the editorial brought, he would have disappeared as quickly from the national arena as did Arthur Guy Empey. But being what he was, the editorial was the turning point in his career. It meant a political career outside the realm of office holding; it meant that royalties from his books would retire the *Gazette's* indebtedness, build a new home for the paper and another for its editor; it meant that by one mighty leap his short stories landed in *McClure's Magazine* alongside those of Stevenson, Kipling, and Hamlin Garland; it meant a commission to write feature articles for the McClure Syndicate; it meant that metropolitan newspapers thereafter quoted William Allen White; it meant, most of all, that William Allen White was accepted with respect in three distinct fields of endeavor—journalism, politics, and literature.

The afterglow of White's editorial was first reflected in the public's recognition of *The Real Issue*, his first volume of short stories. This little book was a selection from the stories that had earlier appeared in the *Gazette*, the Kansas City *Star*, and the El Dorado *Republican*. None had appeared in a magazine of general circulation, for magazine editors had declined

his stories. But after the appearance of "What's the Matter
With Kansas?" the stories took on new importance. When
The Real Issue appeared in late November, it was reviewed,
praised, and sold out of all proportion to its merits. Within two
weeks, it was standing third in sales at Chicago, and S. S.
McClure had arranged with the publishers to use two of the
stories in *McClure's Magazine*. By January the volume had
reached its second edition and by the middle of February its
fourth. One advertisement in the *Gazette* reprinted reviews
from Buffalo, St. Louis, Boston, Chicago, Philadelphia, New
York, Scranton, and Hartford.

The immediate success of the book brought to its author
an invitation from Way and Williams, the publishers, to come
to Chicago and bask in the light of popularity. In Chicago,
White met and was feted by the literary lights and bigwigs
of that day. As the guest of Mr. and Mrs. Irving Way, he
met Hamlin Garland, George Ade, Mrs. Ella W. Peatie, Carl
Smith, Herbert Stone, Melville Stone, R. M. Field, and Robert
Todd Lincoln. In the whirlwind of receptions that followed he
was a guest in turn of all but two of these.

As a result of "What's the Matter With Kansas?" Mark
Hanna made White one of the principal speakers at the Lincoln Day banquet of the Ohio Republican League, at Zanesville, Ohio. White dubbed the gathering a "national feast of
Belshazzar"—a title not inappropriate when one considers
those who attended and the contemporary descriptions of the
banquet. From Cleveland alone a special train carried three
hundred delegates to the League's convention. Notables at the
banquet included, in addition to Hanna and White, Asa S.
Bushnell, governor of Ohio; John M. Thurston, United States
senator from Nebraska; James S. McCleary, congressman from
Minnesota; and Booker T. Washington, Negro educator. As
to the banquet itself, it began "to the perfume of flowers and
the music of an orchestra stationed in the hall that floated
through the open door." At 12 midnight, the last course was
served and not until "well towards morning" did "the last
speaker's voice reach the close of his remarks and the attend-
ants sought sleep long deferred but much needed." [20]

White's response to "What's the Matter With Kansas?"

"elicited roars of laughter and repeated rounds of applause." [21] He declared that Kansas was all right, that Kansas Republicans "had learned courage," and some day would give the country a patriot like John Sherman, Foraker, Hanna, or McKinley. To the Populists he paid a characteristic tribute:

Cain was the first Populist. When he saw that his brother's gift was acceptable to God and that his own gift was not acceptable, Cain did what every Kansas Populist would do, and what every Ohio Populist would do, and what the Nebraska Populist would justify in glowing rhetoric. Instead of getting out and hustling for a better offering, Cain got a club and went after his most diligent and successful brother—just what the Populist today is doing. Gentlemen, from the tree that grew the club of Cain, has come every plank in the Chicago platform.[22]

On Hanna's insistence, White went to Canton to see McKinley, who because of illness had been unable to attend the Zanesville meetings. Hanna's proposal was the result of White's flatly declaring that he wanted no office. White accepted the proposal reluctantly. He had met McKinley before, did not greatly care for him, and wanted no political rewards. Only after repeated urgings did he go, and then he carried a letter of introduction from Hanna stating "He wants no office."

The meeting was hardly a success. McKinley, ill, distracted by office seekers, and probably doubting the genuineness of "He wants no office," [23] received White so coldly that his reception amounted to a snub. White, tickled at the outcome, in company with his publisher, Chauncey Williams, rushed in boyish glee to the first photographer's shop where he "to perpetuate his expression" [24] had a quarter's worth of tintypes made of himself with Williams. These he mailed to his friends in Cleveland with this bit of doggerel:

Canton and Cleveland

These faces young and comely are not smiling
    they are bent
In those uncanny postures by a frigid President.
His heart is ice, his hand is stone, his meditations
    grow

In forms of grotesque hoar frost and his dreams
    are drifted snow
And when these two lads struck the blast of his
    cold storage cheer
They took the train for Cleveland and they got
    the glad hand here.

W. A. White.[25]

The immediate result of the Ohio trip was to confirm White still further in his opinions. He wrote of it as "a wonderful discovery." For the first time in his life he saw men "regularly at work." The industrial development "was wonderful." In his twenty odd years in Kansas he had "never actually seen a factory in operation," and he concluded that the reason Kansas was laughed at was that it would rather vote for government aid than develop its natural resources.[26]

CHAPTER IX

Consolidating His Gain

I have never had a bored hour in my life. I get up every morning now wondering what new, strange, gorgeous thing is going to happen and it always happens at fairly reasonable intervals. And generally, and this is a part of the unbending curve of my life, adventure comes from afar, from the outside, from things over which I have no control. Lady Luck has been good to me. I fancy she is good to everyone only some people are dour and when she gives them the come hither with her eyes they look down or turn away and lift an eyebrow. But me, I give her the wink and away we go.[1]

POLITICS put White's name before the public; fiction kept it there until his political knowledge caught up with his fame. The author of "What's the Matter With Kansas?" schooled primarily in state issues, attained a national reputation without a national breadth of view. During the McKinley-Bryan campaign, the issues at stake in Kansas became matters of national concern; hence the national interest in White's editorial. Its author, however, had no opinions on issues not directly affecting the welfare of his state; and White's thinking remained so circumscribed until the achievements of such personal friends as Fred Funston, Joseph L. Bristow, and Theodore Roosevelt enlarged his mental horizon. But he had observed human nature accurately, and human nature is universal. These observations expressed in the prevailing literary forms kept his name in the national magazines while he was groping his way toward a more intelligent understanding of political problems.

The Real Issue, though miscellaneous in content, reveals White's two favorite themes, politics and boys. The second theme dominated his first magazine sketches, later collected in *The Court of Boyville.* The volume's chief merit lies in the author's sympathetic understanding of boy nature, but a part of its charm is due to his wistful longing for the freedom of childhood and his vivid portrayal of incidents vaguely and romantically remembered by the average adult. All his boys are healthy young animals, "with the Divine right of boys to eat what they please, to believe what they please, and, under loyalty to the monarchy of the world, to do what they please . . ." [2] His heroes, the sovereigns of the vacant lot, the swimming hole, and the mud fight, are unhampered in their natural bents; his martyrs, the primly-clothed, shoe-wearing weaklings, are condemned to conform to parental notions. Thus the picture is realistic rather than moralistic. In the boy world, goodness and obedience carry their own retribution. Mamma's boy suffers a double agony. Inwardly, his own weakness shames him; outwardly, his companions crucify him; for "boys have an ugly name for one of their kind who discovers suddenly, in a crisis of his own making, that he is not allowed to fight." White, therefore, held "it were better to see a boy with a dozen claw-marks down his face than to see him eat that name in peace." [3] Because of this attitude, his stories met a mixed reception. Realists praised them for their fidelity to boy nature; moralists condemned them for their lack of sermons on proper conduct.

While *The Court of Boyville* was still appearing in *Mc-Clure's,* White began a series of political stories in *Scribner's.* He knew his stuff. He had attended his first state convention at the age of eight. At eighteen he was reporting county conventions for his home paper, and riding the town hack on election day to round up recalcitrant voters. Before he could vote, he sat as a delegate in a county convention. His political fiction, however, differs from the earlier sketches. White, feeling his way toward the novel, was writing more deliberately. Five stories appeared in three years. These stories, equal to the average novel in length, were published under the title *Stratagems and Spoils.*

Stratagems and Spoils portrays human nature against a political background. The characters are actuated by lust for power, greed for money, hunger for fame, and kindred passions. White, who knew what motivated men in politics and the methods whereby they attained their ends, brought his accumulated knowledge to these stories. The result was the first body of substantial political fiction in American literature. William Dean Howells, attracted by the authoritative ring of the stories, wrote:

If he has held his hand anywhere the reader does not suspect it, for it seems, with its relentless power of realization, to be laid upon the whole political life of Kansas, which it keeps in a clutch so penetrating, so comprehensive, that the reader does not quite feel his own vitals free from it.[4]

Though Howells declared that *Stratagems and Spoils* showed the "inwardness as well as the outwardness of men," its graphic picture of how the political machine was manipulated accounted for much of its contemporary interest. In his preface White asserts that politicians are as honest as storekeepers, lawyers, bankers, farmers, teachers, or preachers, but in his stories he depicts them as crooked, helpless, or weak-kneed, submitting to the ruthless machinations of financiers and corporation attorneys. Whenever an issue involving the welfare of the masses is at stake, the will of the people is powerless. Popular opinion seldom prevails; when it does, it is the result of chance. Four of the five stories cry out for political reform; and appearing on the eve of a reform period, they attracted the attention of the rising political figures. Roosevelt praised "The Mercy of Death," and Albert J. Beveridge, after reading the collection wrote to George Horace Lorimer, editor of the *Saturday Evening Post:*

"I was so captivated . . . that I immediately sat down and wrote him a letter of appreciation." Why should not White displace Senator Harris, the Populist, the next year? Why should not Lorimer take it up personally with White, and push it? "If I ever get to know him in a personal way, I shall jab him fuller of this with the hypodermic syringe of suggestion than the cocaine fiend fills himself with dope."[5]

To such pleas White was deaf. He advanced many reasons for not seeking a political career, but what chiefly determined his course now was a belief that he could be more influential as a writer than as a legislator. He saw no necessity for legislative reform. Readers who in the light of White's later career see *Stratagems and Spoils* as propaganda for legislative change are mistaken. The volume is intended to be a transcription of life; and in the one story where political reformers play a part, the author shows himself entirely out of sympathy with them. Any proposal to change a political organization which permitted men of ill will to exploit a helpless people, White would have dismissed as a nostrum. "Human nature which is at the bottom of our ills can't be changed at the next meeting of the legislature." [6] As he saw the situation, the problem resolved itself into getting good men into office; and an editor and magazine writer, free from the entangling alliances of office holding, who threw his influence to candidates of impeccable character was far more powerful than one well-intentioned man in the legislative halls.

At this time, also, White was more interested in making a place for himself in American literature than in politics. Gratified as he was by proposals that he become a senator, he cherished far more such tributes as Howells' to "The Man on Horseback," that the story "seemed to me so perfect in its way that I should not have known how to better it." [7] The month this story appeared Howells lectured in Emporia, and White's advance publicity in the *Gazette* brought him his largest audience. The young editor and his wife gave a dinner in his honor, and White's reverence for "the great man" is pleasantly recalled thirty-eight years later.

So the White family put the big pot on the little one, started them all to boiling and gave a dinner; the first rather formal and elaborate dinner given by them at 927 Exchange. Someone . . . sent in a dozen quails which were the big feature of the dinner. The whole neighborhood was excited about the dinner to the great man. Neighbors came in during the afternoon to see how things were going; people from as far west as State street wanted to know about it. Mr. and Mrs. Victor Murdock of Wichita and Alexander Butts of the Kansas City Star, and Miss M. Louise Jones, head of the English Department at the Normal, and Miss Martha Wooster, her assistant, were the guests.

A brand new spic and span hired girl had come that day for the occasion. It was her first town job. She lived over by Reading and probably her folks had to tie her to get shoes on her. The idea was to serve the dinner in courses, soup, the quail, a salad mixed at the table, and a mince pie—it being in November; then coffee and candy, raisins, nuts and things. The new girl stood by and batted her eyes and said "Yes," as she listened to the instructions. The quails went into the oven just before the guests were called, so all hands sat down and the soup came on all right.

The talk was pretty good. Victor Murdock and Alex Butts were good single-handed dinner table talkers and never let chattery cross talk break up the dinner. Mr. Howells also was putting out his line—a good one! Then suddenly, in the door with the quails came Mrs. J. M. McCown, who lived nearby and unbeknownst to the hostess had poked her nose in the kitchen to see how things were going, as two or three other neighbors had just before dinner. Mrs. "Mac" found the new girl with her hat on and her bundle in her hand, just about ready to jump. Answering an inquiry the new girl said "My God, I can't do it. I have got it all mixed up. I don't know which goes when." So Mrs. McCown took a look in the oven and assumed command of the regiment. When she appeared with the quail she gave the hostess a wink and the host a dirty look, indicating he should keep his mouth shut, and the dinner went on.

After the mince pie was served with the cheese, Mrs. McCown was invited to sit down and from that minute all went merry as a marriage bell. Whereupon Mrs. "Mac" explained what had happened in the kitchen, and that final course was the best of the evening. And how Howells enjoyed it! How Alex Butts threw his head back and laughed, and Victor had to be told three times, he enjoyed the story so much.

Since that day men who were to be president and men who had been president have sat around that oval table. Major generals, cabinet officers, powerful politicians, literary pundits and J. P. Morgan's family have poked their pink toes under it. But no one ever sat there of whom the host and hostess stood in such awe then and since, the greatest man of them all.[8]

In Our Town, White's next volume, marks the apex of his interest in short fiction; thereafter short stories were incidental to his other interests. As a literary type, *In Our Town* is local color fiction. Some stories are wholly without plot; in all, the interest in the descriptive element and in the characters' peculiarities is as important as the interest in the plot. White's locale is the middle western village. In the center of the village stands the country daily, touching all phases of the town's life.

From this vantage point, the editor gives a composite picture of the villagers. As editor, he knows intimately the town characters, the merchant prince, the local statesman, the social matron, the town drunkard, the country banker, the delivery boy. His subscribers differ little from the metropolitans in their reading interests. When the reigning social belle marries, they want to know the prospects of the bridegroom, how the bride was dressed, who were the guests, and all about the ensuing honeymoon. The daily flow of small town life, White depicts kindly and tolerantly. Accepting human nature as it is, he makes many allowances for human weaknesses.

To the outsider, the country editor has always remained something of a mystery. Mark Twain once warned William Dean Howells that if he wrote a projected novel with a country editor for its hero, he would be misunderstood. It was to be expected, therefore, that *In Our Town* would lead literary historians astray. On the misinterpretations of the single phrase, White has been labeled "a provincial with a provincial's prejudices and a provincial's qualms."

. . . For instance, he tells of a girl named Maybelle who came to him in Emporia, saying that she would "accept a position" on the *Gazette*. Just from his way of describing her in the opening sentences, we realize how little she, with her aspiration, could fit into his scheme of things—and how little Bernhardt would have fitted into it—or Duse—or Shaw's Great Catherine—or Meredith's Diana —or any one of the great women of the world. Not that Maybelle was great, but that she was in revolt against Kansas and Mr. White is Kansas. He is Kansas City and Dubuque, points east, points west and most of the people in between. His are the virtues and vices of common men; his the common man's distrust of vanity. . . .[9]

The interpretation of the story [10] is quite mistaken. Maybelle was no more in revolt against Kansas than against London; she would have been as much out of place in the editorial office of the New York *Times* as in the Emporia *Gazette*. She had not the faintest idea of what was of interest to newspaper readers, and a complete incapacity to learn. Her original ambition was to write about Shakespeare; and when told that "we didn't care for editorial matter," she brought in a local story in which the facts were so submerged in rhetorical flourishes that no one knew what she was writing about. Because her ability could never equal her ambition, she remains from first to last a pitiable figure.

Yet in many ways, Maybelle was the typical product of her environment. Pretense was still a major aspect of village life. Presidents of defunct banks rode to their offices wearing silk top hats, frock coats, and carrying gold-headed canes. Against one form of pretense the new generation of country editors was in revolt—the high sounding phrases employed to cover up the simple facts. To the old-fashioned, turgid rhetoric, shallow-minded Maybelle subscribed heart and soul, and "when she said she would like 'to accept a position' with our paper . . . we knew that she was at least highly improbable if not entirely impossible." From the beginning of his editorship, White had been proud that his news stories were forthright, simple, and clear.

. . . The Gazette never speaks of a dying person as "lying at death's door"; it never lets a boy who has rustled for a job on a grocery delivery wagon "accept a position." It has sworn off speaking of the groom as "a rising young business man," and the bride as "the beautiful and accomplished daughter." Also a funeral is not spoken of as "the last sad rites" in the Gazette, where "a large concourse of friends" came "to pay their last tokens of respect." An "elaborate luncheon" is never "served in courses" by the society editor of this paper, and a country town like Emporia is not called "this city." [11]

Very early in his career, White became a controversial figure. All his public life he has been praised indiscriminately and abused excessively. Controversy about his personality usually centers about his political activities, and is usually based on honest difference of opinion rather than on ignorance of facts. In the literary histories, the reverse is true. Literary historians invariably go astray when they turn from the writings to the man. They assume that White's interests and activities are to be found in his fiction, which is strongly regional. This assumption has inspired statements even farther apart than those written in the heat of a political campaign. In 1930, these two statements appeared, the first by a literary critic familiar with White's fiction; the second by a magazine writer familiar with his public activities.

Like his activities, White's major interests have been bounded by a relatively small portion of middle America.[12]

He is more at home in Washington than the average Congressman; he belongs to leading clubs in New York, where he is decidedly more versed in metropolitan ways than those of us who grub in that city at our daily pursuits; while in London and Paris, and even in Russia, he belongs to the type of cosmopolitan American publicist like Dwight Morrow, or Tom Lamont, or the Herbert Hoover of fifteen years ago.[13]

For ten years after White broke into national magazines, he averaged a story or an article a month. That curiosity about sectional life that made local color fiction possible gave him his first opportunity to write feature articles. At first he confined his articles to Kansas; then he gradually enlarged his territory until he was covering significant industrial developments as far west as the Pacific coast. Politics took him east, and magazine assignments west. He early developed into a rover. When he was away, Mrs. White was in charge of the *Gazette;* and long-time residents of Emporia still talk about how their son, William L., spent his infancy in the *Gazette's* wastepaper basket. As her husband's full partner in the direction of the paper, Mrs. White was more than his equal in business matters. More than once White came home to find that important improvements had been made in the mechanical department.

While White was struggling for a place in American letters, a political article again put his name in the headlines. At the request of S. S. McClure, he undertook short biographies of Roosevelt, Cleveland, Folk, Hanna, Platt, and other outstanding political leaders. All these studies proved harmless, except the one on Senator Platt, which pricked the New York boss to the quick. He charged that the "so-called biography" "was made of a tissue of lies," that there was "malice in every line" of it, and that it was designed to make him appear "a contemptible object in the eyes of the world." [14] He threatened to sue both White and *McClure's,* but directed most of his resentment at White. Day by day he gave out angry interviews, usually terminating with some such statement as "I'll get this man's scalp if it is the last act of my life."

Platt's wrath made White a seven-day wonder. The article was widely reprinted and widely commented upon. Editorial writers called it scorching: White had depicted Platt as a "slimy reptile of politics," "wholly base, without a particle of patriotism or public spirit, dragging down friends and foes alike to perpetuate his political power." Wherever White went, he was hailed as the man who made Platt mad. Speculation and rumor followed facts. Would the suit be tried in Kansas or New York? Was White liable to arrest in New York? If the suit ever came to trial, it would be one of the most interesting of its kind ever heard in the United States. It was rumored one of Platt's sons would call White personally to account if he ever went to New York.

When newspapers stated that White was "not only an intimate friend of the President and his biographer, but, also, the court of final appeal in all matters of patronage in Kansas," the enraged Platt had a pretext to see Roosevelt. He wanted to know if these things were true. "No man who is White's friend, after what he has written, can be my friend." Roosevelt's answers were wary. He knew White "but not to the intimate degree that had been suggested"; he had not given him "carte blanche to settle Kansas patronage disputes for him or authority to lead others to think that he had been favored"; he had not read the article, but "promised to do so at once and give an opinion" the next time the Senator called at the White House. When Platt emerged from the President's office, he told reporters that "this man White will never again darken the doors of the White House." In New York, a few days later, he was still raging. "I intend to use all my money, all my power, to bring about the punishment of this man who has so maliciously attacked me."

White's article was but ostensibly the cause of Platt's anger; his vow to sue both the magazine and author for libel and set damages so high that professional defamers would let him alone in the future was a bid in a game where Platt momentarily believed he held the aces. When Roosevelt was governor of New York, Platt found him a challenge to his political authority. To shelve him, so Roosevelt believed, Platt had conspired to make him Vice-President. White's article related the contest between the two, with the boss coming out second best. "The governor had smiled toothfully and accepted the situation. The boss got up to go. He got nearly to the door; then turned back, and surrendered, body and breeches." [15] Platt suspected the hand of Roosevelt in the article; and rightly so, for Roosevelt had materially aided in its preparation. Roosevelt was Vice-President when the article was written and had nothing to lose in the repercussions; but before it appeared, he had become President. If the article then, which defamed the political boss and glorified the President, could be made the basis for a successful libel suit, the verdict would not only be for Platt but against Roosevelt. Platt's victory would erase the exposures of the article, and leave Roosevelt in an embarrassing situation.

Platt's reasons for backing down have never been revealed. From White he had nothing to fear. White was a poor country editor, unable to employ competent legal talent. But his fight was *McClure's* fight, and *McClure's* began to gird itself for battle. The prospective scale of the contest may have scared Platt. "Someone" [16] whispered to him that *McClure's* would welcome the suit. White had not told all; the magazine had still more damaging information that it thought should be made public. At any rate, this seems the most plausible explanation for Platt's failure to make good his threats.

The final chapter of the episode was writtten a few months after the article appeared. White, in Washington, received an invitation to the White House. After breakfast, Roosevelt grinned and said, "When you were writing that article, did you ever talk to Platt?" White's reply was, "Yes, for half an hour or so." Thereupon Roosevelt blinked and said, "Well, he won't remember you. Let's take a chance."

And so, scared out of four years growth, [White] . . . walked with the President into the Presidential office and sat by the President's desk. The first caller, by appointment, was none other than Thomas Platt. The young friend of the President was introduced as "Mr. Um Um." Platt paid no attention to him and went on with a rather intimate conference with the President, scarcely looking at the wax figure seated near the desk. When Platt went out, the President had a conniption fit of laughter.[17]

A few minutes later, White walked out of the executive office, through the row of newspaper reporters who had taken Platt's story that White was barred from the White House. He answered no questions—just grinned, but made sure that all the reporters saw him.

CHAPTER X

On the Home Front

W. A. White lunched with the President's family a day or two ago. He says they had oyster soup, broiled chicken, mashed potatoes, string beans, (boiled with salt pork in the old fashioned way) and baked apples. That sounds like it might have been served in Emporia.[1]

PROBABLY an anecdote best illustrates the unimpressive appearance of the *Gazette* in the late 90's and early 1900's. White, ill from overwork and threatened with a nervous breakdown, consulted a nerve specialist in California. The specialist told him his condition was rather serious and asked him what he did. White replied that he was the editor of a daily newspaper. At once the specialist's face grew serious. "You will have to change work," he said. "No man in your condition could ever think of following newspaper work. It will kill you." Next day White proudly showed the specialist a copy of the *Gazette*. He looked at it a moment, then said, "Well, I suppose editing this paper won't hurt you."

Any small town daily of that period is a sorry sight by the side of its modern descendant; mechanical development in the printing industry as a whole had been at a standstill for half a century, and in readability, interest, and appearance the country paper was much closer to the first papers in America than to those after 1920. The *Gazette,* like its contemporaries, had two or three printers who did job work, made up the forms, and ran the presses. Body type was all set by hand, usually by girls who were paid four dollars a week after a three-months' apprenticeship. Each day the girls set the type—local news and editorials which were scattered throughout the paper. Printers assembled the type into page forms, then ran them on an old, rattle-bang, hand-fed cylinder press which printed around five hundred copies an hour. Then the papers were folded by hand and distributed by newsboys. The printing finished, the printers carried the forms outside, scrubbed them with lye to wash off the ink, and the girls distributed the type to have it for the next edition. Everyone worked long and irregular hours; but employment was steady, though wages were low.

Reporters wrote all their copy in longhand, and that which the country correspondents sent in was often illegible and sometimes illiterate. Any typesetter who could take country correspondence and put it into readable form was at a premium. Local display advertising was almost nonexistent, and the little there was ran daily for months without any change in text. White, or one of his two helpers, solicited the local advertising; and they, with Mrs. White writing locals and the society column, kept the books, wrote the stories, and completed the reportorial staff. Not until 1904 was local advertising important enough to be assigned to one man. Walt Hughes then took it over, but it was not of sufficient importance to interfere with his duties as mechanical foreman and supervisor of job printing.

The *Gazette,* as were all papers of comparable size, was filled with quack doctor and patent medicine advertising. The latter in many cases was no more than liquor advertising under the guise of cure-alls. Next to patent medicine advertising, stereotype filled its columns. "Boiler plate," as it was called, was the space fillers for country papers. Stories of every sort and length were set up in cities, then stereotyped, and shipped in column-length plates to country papers far and near. If an editor ran short of home copy, he could fill a column in a half minute by slipping one of these plates on a patent base. Stories were arranged in various lengths to meet every emergency, so that the editor could saw the plates and fill any space from an inch to a column. Because of the cheapness of boiler plate, editors ran column after column daily. It was their only means of printing state, national, and international news, for a small paper could neither pay for press dispatches nor afford to set them by hand. And because the country daily pretended to print

all the news, it usually filled most of its front page with these
stale reports. White, who believed a holiday was a holiday,
filled his entire paper with boiler plate on such days and told
his readers they knew what they could do if they did not like
the way he was running his paper; but as long as he was editor
of the *Gazette*, his employees were going to observe the holi-
days.

Methods of production, advertising, and news, as regards
the *Gazette*, began to change with the turn of the century.
White was concentrating more and more on local news, so that
he was printing the best paper in Emporia; but best or not,
Emporia would have read him anyway. No local editor could
compete with another who told his readers what he had for dinner when he dined with the president. Merchants were learning
that intelligent advertising paid them well. White, who in those
days spent most of his time on the street chasing stories and
advertising, once talked Emporia's leading merchant into running a page advertisement. The merchant thought he could not
afford the extravagance, and White had to write the advertisement to get it; but so well did it pay that the merchant said he
could not afford thereafter not to take a page advertisement
once a week.

What contributed most to the *Gazette's* mechanical development was the money White was making from his books and
magazine articles. He paid off the $3,000 mortgage and built
and moved his paper into a new building in 1900. By 1903 his
circulation, which had grown to 1,500, warranted buying the
exclusive Associated Press service and installing a linotype.
This move made the *Gazette*, and it began to take on its later
character. No other Emporia paper could compete with it. The
linotype, which sets type as fast as three or four hand com-
positors, enabled him to print the same dispatches as the Kansas
City papers. The result was that his circulation doubled in
three years, forcing him to enlarge his building and buy a new
press.

The installation of the new press was a red-letter day in
the *Gazette's* history; White announced his paper had crossed
the Rubicon. Now it was possible to put all the forms on the
press, print the papers from a roll, and have them come out

folded at the rate of 5,800 an hour. Of more importance was
the fact that his new linotype and Associated Press service
had whipped all challengers. His last two competitors had died
in 1905, and all but seventy-five Emporia homes were taking
his paper. The Kansas City papers had lost a thousand Emporia
subscribers, had a smaller circulation in Emporia than in any
other Kansas town of like size, and the *Gazette* was adding
around seventy-five new subscribers a month. The new press,
like the other equipment, was made possible by the royalties
from White's magazine articles and books. The "In Our
Town" sketches in the *Saturday Evening Post* paid for it; and
in justice to Mrs. White and Walter Hughes, it should be said
that they had as much to do with its purchase as White did.
The three of them always worked hand in hand in developing
the *Gazette;* and Mrs. White and Hughes remodeled the building and installed the press while White was in California on a
writing assignment.

Linotypes and presses had to have operators; and while
the Whites were building their paper into a permanent and
growing institution, they were assembling a little group of
printers who became as much a part of their printing plant as
they. Sam Rice was brought in to run their new press, and since
that day he has pulled a lever or pressed a button every week-
day afternoon to provide evening papers for thousands of Emporians. Rice and his associates had so little to do in their early
days that they played checkers to pass the time. Roe Collins
came the next year and George Caspari the next and both became linotype operators. Con Jones and John Schottler were
already old employees. Jones had been with the Whites seven
years and Schottler six. Jones, small, quiet, and scholarly-look-
ing, as make-up man has handled more words and used fewer
than any other man in Kansas. Schottler worked up from a
typesetter to foreman and has never had a disagreement with
White; but the credit is not White's. The welfare of the
Gazette is his prime thought in every decision affecting the
paper.

In these years, also, were formulated most of those editorial policies which have guided the *Gazette* through the years.
When White was a boy setting type on the El Dorado *Demo-*

crat, the country paper was an organ of a local political organization; when he came to Emporia, it was the mouthpiece of the country banker, who held its mortgage; when about 1900 as newspaper advertising increased and it threw off the shackles of the politician or the banker, it gave signs of passing into the control of advertisers. And in each period there were the clamors of subscribers. White dealt with all pressure groups alike. It was "a cold-blooded proposition," not only a matter of doing "good in the world" but of making money.

No newspaper can make money . . . till it convinces its readers that their sentiments and views and opinions will not influence the attitude of the paper against what its owner thinks is right. A paper that truckles to its constituency, that does not dare to stand for the right, when its whole subscription list is wrong, will never make much money.[2]

Few editors have been more enterprising in educating their readers to their journalistic ideals. In this period, however, White was more aggressive in stating his policies than in later years. He had competitors and the town was split into factions. He set as his task the establishment of the integrity of his paper and the elimination of these factions. Since he was a man who is first on one side of the fence then on the other, factions could not survive after he had eliminated the papers that represented them. In 1903, he defined his standard for judging a newspaper.

A newspaper is like a man—because generally it reflects some man—and it should be judged as a man should be judged; largely and on the whole. No man lives a perfect life; no editor prints a perfect paper. If an editor is honest he is bound to offend someone every day of his life; if he doesn't offend someone, the editor is namby-pamby and flabby. The same thing is true of the average man. A newspaper is bound to make mistakes; in getting news it must necessarily take hear-say. But if, in the long run and in the main, day after day and year after year, a paper stands for decency, for honest thinking and clean living, if it speaks fair for those who are trying to do good, and condemns sneaks and cheats and low persons, that is a good paper.[3]

By 1905, the flagrant boosting of Emporia had dropped out of the *Gazette*. In his attitude toward industrial expansion,

White had made an about face. He had concluded that the booster who screamed in headlines about the glories of the town got nowhere. Only the editor who by his own practice as well as his own preaching, who stood for decent things and glorified giving rather than taking, had a constructive attitude which was sure to help his town. Such an editor might not bring in more people, but he certainly would make life better and happier and broader and more comfortable for those who lived there. It is better, he thought, to have 10,000 people living equitably and happy than to have 10,000 people growing fat upon the toil of 90,000 who lived lean and sordid lives.

One of the first decisions White had to make was what types of news to exclude from his paper. An experience with a divorce scandal taught him to confine his reports to "the names of the parties, the causes briefly stated, and the disposition of the children, if any."[4] News, he concluded, was "what the newspapers play up," and a newspaper which truckles to details of murders, hangings, suicides, sex crimes, highway robberies, burglaries, and crimes of violence is a public nuisance.[5] In 1903, resolutions of respect were dropped in characteristic fashion:

> No more cards of thanks will be printed in this paper for any price. They are in wretched taste. . . . You needn't bring any more to the Gazette office. Only jays do so, and you don't want to be thought a jay . . . don't advertise your gratitude and sorrow. Only cheap things are advertised.[6]

Patent medicine advertising, the names of first offenders in police court, unless under unusual circumstances, quack doctors and unlisted mining and promotion stock dropped out in these years. Patent medicine hastened its own demise because White was careful to read his advertising contracts. When patent medicine firms began slipping in clauses aimed to control legislation, out went the advertising. Later Mark Sullivan exposed the practices of these firms by securing documentary evidence "by various devices and by co-operation of a few newspapers which would not accept contracts limiting their freedom, especially William Allen White and his Emporia, Kansas, *Gazette* . . ."[7]

Shrewdest decision White ever made, so far as personal

publicity is concerned, was when he decided to print a story about himself. It set Emporia and the editors of the Middle West rollicking in laughter. Done in the style of the Elder Bennett of the New York *Herald,* it represents White's most famous scoop.

Last evening at dusk as the editor of the Gazette was starting for home, a few yards from the office door he met Mrs. Delta Meffert, divorced wife of William Meffert, of whom mention was made in these columns recently. She was accompanied by a lady friend, and as the Gazette man started to pass, Mrs. Meffert pulled from her cloak a small but effective looking whip. The editor of the paper side-stepped and did what every true gent would do; ran forty yards like a whitehead back to the office by the back door.

That calm dispassionate communion which a man holds with a situation in the sixteenth part of a second convinced the man in question that when a lady challenges a gent to an athletic contest of any kind, he cannot win a sparring match with any grace, nor be the victor in a wrestling match with a lady with any credit at all; but that a foot-race is the one event in the sporting calendar in which any gent may vie his prowess with any lady. And how he did run! Shooting the chutes, leaping the gap, or looping the loop are clumsy, dilatory tactics, compared with the way that fat old codger hiked the hike around to the back door of his office.[8]

The first years of this century were in many ways the Whites' most difficult years. Money was not of so much concern as when they first came to Emporia, for the books and magazine articles had put them on the road to prosperity; but money did not come easy. White did his writing at night after a full day's work at the *Gazette.* The inevitable result was a nervous breakdown. In 1902, he was in California several months for a rest, and friends who saw him go away never expected him to return alive. The next year he was again forced to take time off, and not until after a European trip in 1909 did White appear to be "rested."

Then there were the children. Their first child, born in 1900 and christened William Lindsay White, immediately became "Young Bill" and Young Bill or Bill he remains to this day. Mary was born four years later, a sickly baby. The physician had given Mrs. White a stimulant to strengthen her heart which poisoned Mary's system. For the first three or four years of her life, she was a frail child; and this meant doctor bills, nurses, hired girls, and worry. One nurse was suspected of giving Mary "something" to keep her ill in order to hold her job. Anyway, that was Grandma Lindsay's interpretation of what was going on. Grandma was sent with the nurse and Mary to Galveston for Mary's health. She, who had brought ten children into the world, fired the nurse and took charge of Mary herself. Both Grandma Lindsay and Grandma White played important roles in bringing the two children up, for Mrs. White's health was poor and she frequently accompanied her husband on his trips. No doubt the two grandmas contributed their share toward spoiling the children; but in fairness to them, it must be added that the Whites never had "in-law" trouble and both grandmas were fast friends.[9]

In their childhood Mary and Bill were as unlike as two children could be. Bill was quiet and timid. Mary active and daring. Both liked blood-curdling ghost stories, and they sometimes made life miserable for the hired girls. One girl returned one Sunday night to find a man standing on the porch. She spoke to the stranger, then let out a scream when she saw that he was pointing a gun at her. Mary and Bill watched the show from the shrubs; and it took the whole family to convince the girl, who had run across to Grandma White's, that the murderer was a dummy with a toy pistol. Both children seldom agreed on anything and enjoyed arguing. One thing they had in common. They liked to read and were far ahead of their years in the books they read.

The *Gazette* was only one of the evidences of the Whites' growing prosperity. They had bought one of the finest homes in Emporia, built partly of brick and partly of stone from The Garden of the Gods in Colorado. It had belonged to a wealthy lawyer and cattleman who had fallen on evil days financially and had lost his home to a mortgage company. The Whites paid $6000 for it and were said to have got it for a song. They still live in the same building, though after a fire in the early 1920's, it was done over for them by Frank Lloyd Wright. Today, it is one of Emporia's showplaces. White announced the year he bought his new press that his family had "reached a point in social prominence and affluence" where they felt they could "afford to drive out of a summer evening and look at other people's porch boxes, and admire other people's flower gardens." [10] In short they wanted to buy a horse; and Old Tom and his equipage—a canopy-topped phaeton with a fringe around it and cut under front wheels—became a familiar Emporia sight. Old Tom, however, was no more famous than his master's driving. Emporians said that Old Tom always reached his destination in spite of his master, and had he been left to himself he would have covered the distance more quickly and more safely. He seems to have been mostly a luxury, one of those marks of estate which distinguished the bankers and merchants from those who worked for them. White continued to walk to work each morning accompanied by Mrs. White to Seventh and Union, about four blocks, where she stopped and waved at him as long as he was in sight.

Socially, the Whites' were not yet among Emporia's "four hundred," and their failure to make the grade was due to a number of reasons. Just ten years before White had been so poor that he and Ewing Herbert had one dress suit between them and took turns going to parties. Dances in those days were held in an old skating rink, and White wanted to go to one masquerade so badly that he would have given part of his life to attend. But it was Herbert's turn, and the best he could do was to stand on a box on the north side of the building and watch the party through a lookout which he had discovered. Herbert knew he was there, and, at White's request, took a girl friend out to see him; for White was never ashamed of his poverty. Later, when he was working for Bent Murdock, he brought Murdock's daughter, Alice, to Emporia to a dance. As he was dancing the "Boston Dip" with an Emporia girl, he dipped so far that the tail of his coat touched the floor with every dip. She told him not to dip so much, that she would step on his coat. Then she learned that the oversized Prince Albert belonged to Murdock. Such frankness did not set too well with Emporia's stuffed shirts.

When the Whites came to Emporia, the town was split into two factions. Part of the division was over politics, part was over small-town bickering and gossip. A contributing factor to the split was a story that one tycoon's wife had gone to another man's house and tried to get their best hired girl away

from them. The town had its self-designated "four hundred,"
a few of whom were bank clerks and very small small-town
merchants. Some of them had put up the cash for White to
buy the *Gazette,* but lending him money and accepting him and
his wife into their social group were two different matters.
Furthermore, the newspaper business was a precarious occupa-
tion. When White bought the *Gazette,* he became its third
editor in five years; and there are reasons to think that those
who lent him the money thought they were getting a hired man
to represent their political faction. The Whites were, therefore,
accepted into Emporia's society as much as any young couple
without money—which meant they were not accepted at all.

The town's exclusiveness began to disappear as some of
the "four hundred's" money vanished. The Whites, meanwhile,
had made friends in the East, and these easterners began to
stop off to see them. Edna Ferber made the natives' eyes pop
as she, in her white fox furs, walked downtown with White;
and a little later Emporia's moneyed crowd gave up the ghost
when the Morgans came to town to pay their respects to the
Whites. Then the "four hundred" were ready to admit a family
who did not care for dancing and cards and whose social life
consisted of dinners and sparkling conversation.

All the while the Whites were growing in the social graces.
Some things White learned readily; others took him a lifetime.
When White was working in Kansas City, he watched Alexander Butts, one of Kansas City's social ornaments, mix a
salad; thereafter White knew how to mix a salad. In matters
of dress the story is different. A contemporary said his clothes
looked "as if they had been planned and cut out by the town
tinner." [11] Yet White wanted to look well. One day he walked
into George Jones's clothing store and said, "George, I have
been summoned to the White House to see Roosevelt. What
kind of hat should I wear?" Jones, looking at White's hat
jammed down at right angles, answered, "Bill, I don't think it
makes any difference what kind you wear?" White was immensely pleased at the compliment, but Jones had not intended
it as such. When Mrs. White was invited to dine at the White
House, she did not know whether or not to wear a hat. She
asked her husband to ask the President, but Roosevelt had never

noticed whether the women left their hats on or took them off
and he did not see that it made any blankety blank difference
either way. Mrs. White decided to wear her hat and when they
called ask Ike Hoover what to do. When the question was put
to him he answered, "Mrs. White, your hat is very becoming.
I would wear it if I were you." Both were amused at the
diplomacy; nevertheless twenty years were to pass before people
began to tell White his clothes were becoming. In 1928 Burton
Rascoe, noting the change in White's appearance, was sure that
he had a New York tailor.[12] Rascoe was wrong; Emporia's
E. E. Anderson had been making White's clothes for years,
but he had not always been able to get White to stand still long
enough to stick pins in the cloth.

Fact of the matter is that nothing but sheer stupidity could
have kept the Whites from growing socially and intellectually.
Both of them read the best that was coming from the American press; and both knew the intellectual leaders in American
life, for Mrs. White usually accompanied her husband wherever
he went and White seemed to know everybody. Just how far
he had to travel intellectually may be seen by taking a look at
his thinking around the turn of the century.

CHAPTER XI

From What He Grew

America proposed to civilize the Indians here at home.
Was one ever civilized? Of course not. They lie around
the reservations and eat government rations and drink
surreptitious whiskey and die of scrofula. The Indian
schools do no good. The graduates go back to the blanket.
Civilization can no more be decreed by teaching than it
can be by proclamation. It is a matter of heredity. The
Filipinos will be a burden on America. They will have to
be murdered off just as the Indians were. The most humane solution of the Philippine question, now that we
have them on our hands, is to give them lots of American whiskey and let them drink themselves to a speedy
and hilarious death. . . . The question which now faces
the American people is not how to civilize the Filipinos.
That cannot be done. The question is what is the most
humane way to murder them or reduce them to docile
slavery. . . . Shall we lubricate . . . with whiskey and
scrofula, or rapid firing guns and the blood of our young
men.[1]

UNTIL 1901 and 1902 White's editorials had the flavor
of those in mediums which make their appeal to the
moronic mob. They were brash, cocksure, provincial,
illiberal, and intolerant. White's point of view resembled the
klansman's of the 1920's. Had the 100 per cent Americans
flowered during the last five years of the nineteenth century,
they would have found the Emporia editor a sympathetic lis-
tener. White was as narrow, nationalistic, and uncharitable as
the average klansman. That such a man should so completely
shed the mantle of his youth was little short of a miracle.

During this chapter in White's life, his thinking grew
from his training. He came to Emporia just six years out of
college. He had studied the classical economists, conspicuous

among whom was Francis Walker, and in common with most
young college men of that day, believed "that this was the best
possible world." [2] The law of supply and demand was as in-
exorable as the law of gravitation; wealth was an evidence of
virtue; poverty an evidence of sin or weakness. Those who
championed the poor were worse than the poor, for they pan-
dered to poverty to profit by it. None but the righteous inherited
the earth; the acquisitive faculty alone had survival value.

To one holding such an economic philosophy William Mc-
Kinley's fitness for the presidency was questionable. McKinley
had trifled with free silver, and the gold standard was as immutable as the Ten Commandments. After McKinley's nomination White supported him as the lesser of two evils. Bryan was
"a trimmer, a fire brand, shallow, unlettered, ignorant, tricky
in his oratory, a cringer to the mob, emotional, crazed by his
own demagoguery, vain, fanatical, unreasoning, domineering
when in power, shivering in terror when alone, impractical, in-
efficient, incapable . . ." [3]

The many ramifications of White's illiberality were generally grounded in his economic beliefs. A quarter of a century
later he zealously guarded freedom of speech and press, but in
1899 he granted few privileges to the critics of the American
system. When a commencement speaker at the Kansas State
Agricultural College asserted that "the salvation of a Chicago
man's soul may depend on his attitude toward the subject of
municipal franchises, or toward the tax assessment of railroad
property; while his church and his prayers may literally have no
more to do with his soul than the geology of the moon," White
retorted with all the fanaticism of a witch burner. This address
"teaches the doctrines of pessimism and destruction. It calls for
the overthrow of everything in civilization. It denounces the
Christian religion and almost every civic and social habit which
the world is now practicing." [4]

White's attitude toward the address was based on sheer
ignorance. However much the Chicago professor may have
overstated the truth when he said "that the national government and the government of every state was controlled by corporations," this much is sure: The Emporia editor had no
knowledge of what was happening in certain sections of the

country. Robert M. La Follette's name had never appeared in
the *Gazette* either for praise or condemnation. In five years
White was beating the drum of the professor; but in 1899, this
"sort of stuff" was heresy.

These are the doctrines which the Christian fathers and mothers of
Kansas are sending their children to imbibe. The graduate from
such a curriculum would be little better than a moral and social
outcast, unfit to associate with respectable men. If Kansas is bound
to put up with this sort of education she had far better stay in
ignorance and burn her colleges to the ground.[5]

Just how far the editor traveled in matters of academic
freedom is exemplified by a situation twenty-nine years later.
During the Spanish revolution a University of Kansas student
enlisted with the loyalist forces and lost his life. This gave the
red-baiters their opportunity and they attempted to force a bill
through the legislature to investigate alleged Communistic activities at the school. The committee which would have investigated was already convinced that the university was guilty;
and the daily press of the state, incensed at the injustice of
the proceedings, turned on the legislature and defeated the bill.
White, entirely out of sympathy with Communistic teachings,
asserted time and again the teacher's duty was to acquaint his
students with all theories of government.

The boy who died in Spain had a right to go there if he wanted to,
and no one but his parents could have headed him off. If the teachers of K.U. taught him that this world is not the best possible
world and that it should be improved and that many solutions were
offered to the troubled world for its wrongs—Fascism, Communism, democracy and anarchy—and if the professors explained
carefully each of these offerings, they were within their individual
rights and they were doing their exact duty as teachers—no more,
no less.[6]

Early subscribers to the *Gazette* often wished that White
would write more fiction and do less preaching. Their attitude
is understandable. Kansas had been a plague state. She had
suffered man-made booms and panics; she had endured every
caprice of nature. In the early days, pioneers were forever
pushing into the western half of Kansas to burn out or blow
out. Every two or three years covered wagons trekked back

and forth across the prairies in hope or in despair. By 1900, the truth was generally recognized that in the then present state of agricultural knowledge farming was out of question in the western portion. Nevertheless, the futile attempts at settlement, the plagues of nature, and the hard circumstances of life still lingered in memory.

White knew the droughts and floods of the past, and during his first years in Emporia they recurred in their severest forms. But in nature's plenteousness or scarcity, he stoutly maintained that if a man did not prosper he was lazy or incompetent. "Old pluck and hard work" was the unfailing receipt for success. "All it takes to be a plutocrat is an active brain and industry." [7] A privileged class existed, to be sure, but it sprang from superior intelligence and industry. Both nature and man had established a system wherein all were on an equal footing. If one man prospered more than another, both got their just deserts. The laggard had no one but himself to blame.

His old schoolmate, Walter Armstrong, was a case in point. Armstrong started his career as a schoolmaster at twenty-five dollars a month. Later he abandoned the schoolhouse for the railroad, and by 1898 had risen to a division superintendency. His road to success had been "the simple, old-fashioned, inevitable way," and like every other successful man he would have to suffer the calumny and hate of the mob he had left behind.

In a few years this man Armstrong will be riding up and down the earth in a private car oppressing the poor, while his friends and companions, who have been wearing high collars and cussing the government will be standing on the depot platform bewailing the social conditions that make opportunities scarce.

Ten years from now young Armstrong will be hated for his success. Fairy tales will grow up among people who are too lazy to amount to anything, telling about what an old thief he is; how he ground people to death; robbed widows; gutted estates and committed burglary and mayhem to get his start. They will be lies of course . . . but ornery people will believe the lies and will look at Armstrong in his private car and think of dynamite.[8]

Prior to the World War few country editors ever ventured outside America in their editorials. The *Gazette's* editor was no exception. For the first five years he confined his editorials to his state and community; with the rise of the progressive movement he enlarged his field to national problems; with the World War he threw off his geographic limitations and roamed the world. In his early *Gazette* years he scarcely noticed the news on his front page. Only in the face of a crisis did he ever comment on an international situation.

In 1885, the Cleveland administration demanded a settlement of the dispute over the boundary between British Guiana and Venezuela under authority conferred upon the United States by the Monroe Doctrine. When the British refused to arbitrate on the terms laid down by the State Department, Cleveland asked Congress for authority to determine and maintain the legal boundary. His action, which amounted to a flat defiance of Great Britain, caused great excitement in both America and England and many feared that it might involve the two countries in war. White's reaction is typical of his racial attitude. The Anglo-Saxons were the chosen people of God; all others he treated with contempt.

Suppose that the United States bluff England out of the Venezuela row. Concede that Venezuela is right in this row. Then before two months some little yellow legged dictator in a little South American fly up the creek Republic will feel brave because of the Yankee backing he has, and slap some country like Russia in the face. Russia will fight. Then Uncle Sam must get his gun and fight. The Monroe Doctrine must be vindicated. The logical consequence of the enforcement of the Monroe Doctrine is to be in a continual row, because some strutting little dago politician in South America loses his temper. What does the United States get out of this Monroe Doctrine? Why wouldn't it be better to let the Anglo Saxons civilize South America under England than to keep a lot of hot tamale governments on their feet by backing them up in their red shirted quarrels with their elders and betters? An English colony wouldn't be so bad. Canada is a better neighbor than Mexico.[9]

Again, in Roosevelt's first administration the British, German, and Italian governments acted jointly to force Venezuela to settle claims for defaulted debts. They established a formal blockade, seized several Venezuelan gunboats, and bombarded Venezuelan coastal fortifications; and though the controversy threatened to involve the United States, White saw nothing to get excited about. Presumably, matters of war and peace could be left to Washington and Emporians would do well to interest themselves in their own affairs.

A man hurried breathlessly into the Gazette office early this morning with an awful story about the wrongs of Venezuela. His story is probably true. He is earnest about it and desires something done. The Gazette is willing to agree with him to save time in arguing the question, but it insists that if he wants anything done he should go and do it himself and not bother others with it. There is enough for the Gazette force to do getting out this paper. It isn't much of a paper, but it keeps the force busy. The reporters who desired to help the man, went into all the stores in Emporia this morning to see if there was anyone who had time to help Venezuela, but no employer could spare a clerk. Every one in this town is busy and is earning money and saving it. Everyone is engaged in honest work and is looking after his own family. The Gazette contends that this is better than bothering with Venezuela. Venezuela can wait, till there are men and women in Emporia who don't need attention.[10]

White's lack of interest in international problems did not include the Spanish-American War and its aftermath. This is largely explained by the name of one man, Fred Funston. The friendship of the two men, and Funston's dramatic experience made him a perpetual source of news to the Emporia editor. Funston, after a rough and tumble career as a Santa Fe train collector in the Southwest, got a place as a botanist in the government service and was the lone member of the Death Valley expedition to survive death or insanity. In Alaska, he and a missionary spent the arctic winter at an abandoned Hudson Bay Company trading post. Losing their way one evening, he and an Indian joined a party of Indians on their way to a whaling fleet in the Arctic Ocean. The nine hundred mile return journey, he made in the night of an arctic winter. Quitting the post, he traveled a thousand miles down the Porcupine and Yukon in an open boat, reported to the government and resigned from the service.

Funston next turned up in Central America, where he attempted to establish a coffee plantation and failed. He then

joined the Cuban army, enlisting as a private, and came out as
a lieutenant colonel and chief of artillery under the division
led by Garcia. His rank was higher than that of any other
American officer in the Cuban revolution. Three times he was
wounded, once through the lungs, once through the arm, and
once in the thigh.

Such were some of the high lights of Funston's career
before he began making the daily headlines with his exploits
in the Philippines. For Kansas newspapers he made news. For
William Allen White he made new interests.

White's editorials on the Spanish-American War do not
indicate any knowledge of the issues. Before war was declared
he was unalterably opposed to intervention; after the war began he blew alternately hot and cold. One day he would write
a rabble rousing editorial; the next he would as strongly condemn the whole affair. One of his editorials, "The Gaiety of
War," he later regarded as one of the most "terrible" things
from his pen.

Everywhere over this good fair land of ours, flags are flying,
for war is here. Trains carrying soldiers are hurrying from the
North, from the East, from the West, to the Southland, and as
they fly over the green prairies and the brown mountains, little
children on fences greet the soldiers with flapping scarfs and handkerchiefs and flags; at the stations, crowds gather to hurrah for
the soldiers and to throw hats into the air and unfurl flags. Everywhere it is flags, little flags, poor, starchless, faded flags, big flags,
tattered smoke-grimed flags in engine cabs, flags in button holes,
flags on proud poles, flags fluttering everywhere. . . .
So let them flutter, the brave, beautiful flags; as for the
cheering, it comes from bonny hearts, and the handkerchiefs of
the women should dance in the breezes and be gay now—now, for
tomorrow they will be heavy with tears. But tears are good. They
make the world better. Sorrow is a great lever in prying the world
upward. War is good for the sorrow that it brings. Whom the Lord
loveth He chasteneth. And war, that tears women's hearts and
men's limbs, war, that feeds on the flesh of the young men, war,
with its tragic gaiety, is good; it is one of God's weapons for
fighting the devil in man." [11]

A month later he was still supporting the war with religious fervor.

The war came in the nick of time. Its fortunes have guided
the Nation in a course no one could know of—least of all those

who were wildest in their rage for war.[12] Some great sentient power, destiny, evolution or the Lord of Hosts—is guiding the course of this war. It remains "in the name of humanity"—but in a wider meaning than he knew who coined the phrase, when he took it from the mint.[13]

Yet within ten days he asserted that the *Gazette* stood exactly where it was six months ago. "One American soldier's death is unjustifiable to give all the yellow-legged, dagger-sticking, garlic-eating Cubans in the world freedom they are not capable of appreciating or of holding." [14] Then six months later, "By the lever that ignited the fuse that blew up the Maine God lifted twenty million people a little nearer the light." [15]

White's wavering was largely due to his belief in racial superiority. At one moment he thought it possible to give the Cubans independence; the next, he was sure they were incapable of it. Had intervention been left up to him the United States would never have entered the war. The Cubans were a "lazy, yellow-legged outfit," "not worth fighting for." If the Spanish oppressed them, they were "a treacherous, mangey, lick-spittle lot" or they would not have stood for it. "People who deserve liberty get it themselves." Liberty can't be boxed up in cartridge boxes and shipped across the sea." [16] On the other hand, the Anglo-Saxons were the "chosen people." It is their "manifest destiny to go forth as a world conqueror." They "will take possession of all the islands of the sea"; they "will exterminate the people" they cannot subjugate. "It is so written. Those who would protest will find their objections overruled. It is to be." [17]

White's range of interests during his political orthodox days was as narrow as his point of view. Outside of literary and local matters, he wrote almost wholly about partisan politics. On all occasions he preached the doctrine of party regularity. The "best sort of Republican doesn't bolt the ticket. He takes his medicine like a little man, knowing that the man who submits is ten times stronger to help good government than the man who bolts." Though at times the machine may be dirty, it can best be cleaned by the regular after an election, better than by the man who puts a rock into it and "tries to break it when it is going at full speed." [18] Before 1900 there is but a single criticism of the Republican Party and its leaders. When McKinley proposed to cut down the civil service list, White could not agree. "Public service should be put upon the merit system—not upon the basis of party affiliation." [19]

In late 1901 and early 1902 the *Gazette,* more conservative than some other stalwart Republican papers, carried on a protracted debate on the boss system. White argued that it was "the best system of government there is." It changes its name frequently, but it "has worked with the same machinery for a long time." The mainspring of the system was force— "brute force, mental force, spiritual force." Moreover, the people "like it." The only alternative was mob rule, and from his editorial sanctum he thanked heaven that "the boss system prevails, and the government at Washington still lives." [20]

The boss system was good, White contended, because it enabled a man who desired a law to buy it, if the law were "not too bad," whether the people had "ever thought about the law one way or another." One could

even buy immunity from the foolishness of the people by contributing money to the state central committee, which controls the party caucus in the state legislature. For in Kansas and in every other state in the Union, railroads have bought immunity from popular folly dozens of times, and from both parties. They have bought it without bribing a legislature or violating a statute. They have done so without "an understanding" with the chairman of either committee—depending commonly upon simple gratitude for past favors to get the future ones.[21]

White had little faith in democracy. Parties existed not for the purpose of enabling the majority to express their will, but to control the unthinking mob. Having no faith in the masses to act wisely, he opposed every move for greater self-government. The election of United States senators by direct vote would be a mistake. "The people will elevate men to the senate who are as cheap as the men elected governors." [22] The boss system was immune from reformers and amenable to financial interests. And financial interests represented the highest intelligence. His thinking was not wholly without reason. For years he had watched reform movements sweep fanatical messiahs into power, to be turned out later, by the very people who put them there, because they had miserably failed.

CHAPTER XII

The Damascus Road

Ten years ago this great organ of reform wrote a piece entitled "What's the Matter With Kansas." In it great sport was made of a perfectly honest gentleman of unusual legal ability who happened to be running for chief justice of the supreme court of this state, because he said in effect that "the rights of the user are paramount to the rights of the owner." Those were paleozoic times; how far the world has moved since then! If Andrew Carnegie in the campaign of 1896 had said what he is quoted as saying today, [people are partners in every great fortune and there is no private ownership of anything] he would have precipitated a panic or a riot, or both. . . . The Gazette and Andrew were wrong in those days and Judge Doster was right. But he was out too early in the season and his views got frost bitten.[1]

IN WILLIAM ALLEN WHITE'S writings one can trace a growing faith in the innate decency of the common man, in the virtues of tolerance and an open mind, and in the ability of government by the people to survive and surmount and correct its own mistakes. Human life is noble in its kindness, its self-denial, and its service. The brash, cocksure youth mellows into the kindly, peace-loving middle-aged man, who in the hour of trial stands solid and unflinching.

The changes in White's point of view cover about the first decade of this century. They affect his entire outlook, but are most obvious in his social, economic, and political thinking. During the McKinley-Bryan campaign he was proud to be in the ranks of those fighting for "the principle of individual responsibility for individual failure or success." The "existing conditions, which have prevailed in America and in the world for two generations, are satisfactory conditions." The *laissez faire* theory of government was just; the *status quo* should be maintained at all costs. Prosperity was an end in itself, and "every man should be protected in his accumulations, whether they be large or small." The rich man's wealth cannot be cut off "without curtailing the poor man's income," and "a law which will slash the man with a million," cannot be enacted and "leave unscathed a man with a hundred." The law was for every one and no respecter of persons. "Vested rights," and he bound the loathed Populist term to himself as a badge of honor, should and must be protected.[2] Any proposal for change was unpatriotic, socialistic, anarchistic, or worse.

In ten years his cry of paternalism fades. The ideal government administers justice, promotes human welfare, and frowns on the accumulation of wealth at the expense of the masses. If, then, education, justice, care of the poor, and control of business are functions of government, and he believed them to be, "old age pensions should be a government duty." [3] In his advocacy of old-age pensions he had outdistanced his party a quarter of a century. But the proposal does not mean that he had arrived at later characteristic attitudes in all matters. Two years after he came out for old-age pensions the deliberate attempt "to kill the chief of police of Chicago" shows that 'the danger menacing this country is a condition rather than a theory. For years the anarchists have been preaching their doctrines in this country, practically without molestation." America, by permitting this sort of thing, "has been sowing the wind, and she is now in a fair way to reap the whirlwind." [4] He was far short of his later belief that in freedom of utterance "folly will die of its own poison, and the wisdom will survive."[5]

Writers have advanced many theories for White's switch from the conservative to the liberal wing of the Republican Party: his relationships with Lincoln Steffens, Ida Tarbell, Ray Stannard Baker, and other members of the *McClure* staff, his association with Theodore Roosevelt, the rise of progressivism in his section of the country, and finally, an insight which enabled him to see greater material rewards from the enactment of progressive measures. Every theory contains some element of truth, except the last; and it, too, is true if an exception is made of White's personal affairs. Many progressive laws, both early and late, worked to the profit of Kansas; but when White switched from the defense to the prosecution of "vested rights," he had passed from the debtor to the privileged class; when he cried out against the evils of the railroad pass, he "had a book of passes in his hip pocket that stuck out like a dromedary's hump." [6] All White's life railroads had issued passes to editors, partly in exchange for printing the local time table but mainly in hope of getting the "right" publicity. White's traveling had been done on passes. They made possible his first trip out of the state, his honeymoon journey, his first vacation from Emporia, his first attendance at an eastern political gathering, and his first visit to the White House. When he worked to abolish the pass system, he was biting the hand that helped feed him.

In the decay of White's conservatism, the greatest single factor was Theodore Roosevelt. Through their writings both men knew each other before they met. Roosevelt's first acquaintance with the *Gazette* came from the fact that White's paper was the only one in Kansas that supported Thomas B. Reed for the 1896 presidential nominee. White did not meet Roosevelt at the Republican convention in St. Louis, but saw him carrying, in characteristic dramatic fashion, a "Tom Reed Is for Gold" banner. In a few months, Roosevelt became a regular reader of the *Gazette,* and when White published *The Real Issue,* the two exchanged books. Then White went to Washington to persuade McKinley not to appoint him Emporia postmaster, and Charles Curtis introduced him to the Assistant Secretary of the Navy. It was love at first sight. White was captivated by Roosevelt's personality. He began telling his readers that Roosevelt would be president some day. In June, 1899, Roosevelt went through Emporia to attend a reunion of the Rough Riders. The *Gazette* printed editorials daily to get the people out, and White met Roosevelt in Kansas City to accompany him in his journey across the state. For two years they had been fast friends.

White respected Roosevelt first and foremost as a man. What he did for the country—the laws he pushed through

The Country Editor at his desk

W A White   Theodore Roosevelt
gazette Exchange Print   September 1913 Emporia
                              Kans

Congress, the policies of administration he inaugurated, the righteousness he made public morals—formed a "unique career in our history." But they did not form the most important part of the heritage that he gave to the people.

The chief thing he has given is himself. He went into office a strong, virile, frank, honest, fearless man—full of youth, full of faith in man and God, full of ideals. And for seven years and a half he has lived and worked before the people, and has come out— not a broken, jaded, wornout, disillusioned man—but the same high, clean, unbending, youthful man that he went in. . . . He has given an example of what a decent man may do.[7]

Roosevelt uniquely inspired White. Under ordinary circumstances the Emporia editor would not interrupt his day's work to walk across the street to see the kings of the earth, but once when writing the Thunder Mountain articles in Idaho for the *Saturday Evening Post,* he rode one hundred and fifty miles on horseback to meet Roosevelt.

Relations between the two were close and personal—so much so that the press often assumed that White was speaking for Roosevelt when he was speaking for himself. Again and again White had to deny that he was speaking on information furnished him by the President or necessarily representing his views. Sometimes Roosevelt praised White publicly, as when he stated in his comments on the postal scandals that White laid before him information "tending to show corruption by or under Tyner, assistant attorney general for the post office department." [8] But usually White's influence on the Roosevelt administration was private. Once Roosevelt was prepared to appoint a Democrat to a federal judgeship. The bar associations found the man for him and the two senators from his state gave their endorsements. White knew the man to be a railroad lobbyist, who had not practiced law or been in court for twenty years. He went to Washington, told Roosevelt the facts and gave him names of men who could produce the candidate's record. Roosevelt investigated, and in amazement and indignation said that had he made the appointment it would have been a lasting stain on his administration.[9] White was not the final word on Kansas patronage, but Roosevelt had ample occasion to respect his recommendations.

Their common point of interest lay in their progressive principles. There they saw alike, believing that social reform had to evolve gradually and that it was better to yield and get half a loaf than to stand uncompromisingly and get no bread at all. The *Gazette* took no note of Roosevelt's foreign policies and ignored the building of the Panama Canal completely. When Roosevelt advocated the strenuous life, White felt the urge to relax. Trophies from the Colonel's hunting expeditions grace the White home; but White never saw Roosevelt with a gun in his hand, nor did White himself ever hunt or fish after he passed the playground age. What the boxing gloves were to Roosevelt the piano was to White; while one shot lions the other mixed salads. The Colonel was "Daniel Boone" and the Editor was "Old Boulevardier," from his habit of holding the "knife edge of his balance" so perfectly in his magazine articles that his readers could not see his bias.[10] Yet for all their marked dissimilarity White admired Roosevelt to the point that all his writings on him are eulogies.

The incident that elevated Roosevelt to the presidency revealed to White that all was not perfect in American life. On the assassination of President McKinley, he let out a blast against "the great captains of industry" that would have done him credit in later years. Money makers had filled America "with human vermin." "Millions of Polaks and Hunkies and Italians, the very scum of European civilization, have been shipped into America to fill mines and furnaces and replace honest, well-paid, intelligent, conscientious American labor." "Greed, selfishness, wickedness—whether corporate or incorporate, whether national or individual—find their natural punishment though the victim stricken is innocent—as in the case of William McKinley." His wrath at the practices of industrialists nicely balances with his contempt for foreigners. "The Polak who shot McKinley is as incapable of understanding American liberty as a tiger is of understanding the Beatitudes." "Liberty is not in laws; it is in men, in their traditions, in their breeding, in their blood." [11] The Anglo-Saxon is still the chosen race, but the Emporia knight was off on a crusade to give business a conscience.

During Roosevelt's first term, reform centered about making business deal justly and getting honest men into office. The first objective started White toward insurgency; the second broke his standpattism. Anarchists, the bugaboos of the 100 per cent Americans of this time, had upset White; but by 1903 he was showing an understanding sympathy. They were utterly wrong, but the product of conditions under which they lived and worked. Labor agitators who broke their word were bad; they hurt all honest unions. "But the trust makers who laugh when his dupes call for justice, the 'smooth' party in business are patterns for dishonest labor leaders." "There is anarchy in high places as well as in low places. Neither justifies the other, but the rich man has less reason for his lawlessness than the poor man." [12] Socialism, once a flaming red flag, had faded to a pale pink, and no longer blinded. "The day is coming and that right soon, when the business interests of the country will be as closely under government control as the banks and the post office department. . . . If this is treason—what are you going to do about it?" [13] The Roosevelt policies had "put into polite Harvardian terms the barbaric yawp of Bryan and his predecessors." [14]

The *Gazette's* echo of Roosevelt's policy of policing big business was its advocacy of railroad legislation. That railroad legislation should have been the chief objective in the Kansas movement for industrial reform was inevitable. Regulations of railroads was one of the nation's chief problems; and in Kansas, except for oil, railroads were the only large corporate industry. Kansas, being an agricultural state, was almost free of "big business." White, reflecting Rooseveltian phraseology, showed his first interest in the railroad problem when the Supreme Court in the Northern Securities Case declared the merger of the Northern Pacific, the Great Northern, and the Chicago, Burlington and Quincy railroads illegal and forbade holding companies such as the one under which the roads were being operated. The decision, he said, "should teach the railroads one thing: That aggrandizement is the most dangerous position for a corporation to take." Railroads' mixing in politics becomes conditional. They "should be in politics for defense and defense only, and not to control politics." In Kansas just now they "control more thoroughly than they ever did before." The

people of Kansas "demand of the executive that it stand as
Roosevelt stands, for the people, and against railroad aggrandizement." [15] By early winter he was advocating new laws:
Railroads should be compelled to furnish cars to shippers under
certain conditions or submit to a fine, the railroad commission
should be delegated more power, the commission's power to fix
rates should carry the authority to compel the roads to adhere
to them or show why the rates are unjust, the commission's
rates should be operative while the roads are "lawing." In the
years to come he was to advocate other legislation—chiefly, a
physical valuation of the roads and taxation on the same basis
as other real property, the equality of freight rates, and the
abolition of passes.

As the desirability of getting honest men into office became more apparent, White's rigid Republican allegiance began
to waver. In this Roosevelt had a hand. Once when White
boasted to Roosevelt that he had never scratched a ticket, the
President asked him if he were apologizing or confessing, then
convinced him that party regularity was not the highest of virtues. More convincing evidence came later. The Republican
Party of Kansas had the distinction of sending Joseph R.
Burton to the United States Senate, whom Roosevelt put into
jail. Behind Burton was a twenty-year record of corruption,
treachery, bribery, and forgery, and White had helped to elect
him. In the same period, Joseph W. Folk, of Missouri, "an
honest Democrat," emerged as one of the nation's chief reformers. White knew him well and appealed to all good citizens
of Missouri, irrespective of party, to elect him governor. Nor
did all honest Democrats live in Missouri. "The old-fashioned
idea that a man should be drawn and quartered who did not
vote the entire ticket—Democratic or Republican—of his party,
yellow dogs and all, has departed." No one is more liberal than
President Roosevelt "with the man who believes it his duty to
refuse to vote for a dishonest or incapable man merely because
that man is nominated by a party." [16] Roosevelt had scratched
the ticket a dozen times and expected to scratch it a dozen times
more if he lived. White, himself, had been voting the Republican ticket "for upwards of fifteen years without a scratch,"
but that "is nothing to be proud of—for a man." The best

party service "is that which serves the country best," [17] and
the voter who helps "partisans stay in office or get into offices
they might want" is not rendering the highest service to his
country or his party.[18] Just five years before White had been
knocked cold on the street by a man whom he had berated for
bolting the ticket.

White was moving rapidly from his earlier position, but
he was going no faster than the rank and file of Kansas people.
In the election of 1904 the Republicans were split into two factions. Contestants were either aligned with the "Boss-busters"
or the "Machine." The "Boss-busters" won [19] and the state
legislature began enacting progressive measures. A contest with
the Standard Oil Company was the feature of the new administration and equal rights for all became legislative objectives.
Pipe lines were made common carriers and maximum rates
were fixed for the transportation of crude oil by railroads. A
bill, later declared unconstitutional, provided for the construction of a state oil refinery. Railroad legislation established uniform freight rates, prohibited such special privileges as rebates,
made obligatory the furnishing of cars without discrimination
for shipping purposes, and regulated employees' hours of labor.
Juvenile legislation included a child labor law. In the next session the legislature enacted as many similar measures, and a
special session in 1908 created the first state-wide primary
system.

The primary law was an attempt to end the political machinations of the railroads and to put the choice of candidates
into the hands of the people. White had been advocating such
a law for four years. Two years before its enactment he had
declared that the people of the West did not need two parties.
"All the people hold about the same views on the dominant
issues before the people." [20] The most imperative legislation,
then, was an act that would enable voters to choose candidates
who represented their views. At this time he was attacking conservative Republicans with all the old-time anti-Populist vigor.
Here is how the Topeka *Capital* sized him up:

Old Bill White is taking the fire of the standpat, mole-eyed
party organs and not batting an eye under their broadsides. It is
such men as Old Bill and such papers as the Emporia Gazette that

make a party worth its salt as a representative of honest, faithful government. If the Republican party pulls away from its unconscionable tricksters and fixers and bosses, it will be due to the Emporia Gazette style of truth-telling Republicanism.[21]

The first election under the primary law over-shadowed all else in the 1908 Kansas campaign, and the spotlight focused on the nomination of the Republican candidate for United States senator. Never in the history of the state has a senatorial contest been more vigorously waged; and White, as unofficial manager for Joseph L. Bristow, was ringmaster for the liberal wing. He had known Bristow from his college days. When White was a student at the University of Kansas, Bristow was district clerk in that county. Later Bristow bought a Kansas paper; and through editorials in his Salina *Journal*, Robert La Follette's name first appeared in the *Gazette's* editorial columns. At this time, Bristow had probably had more influence on White's thinking than any other man except Roosevelt. White had implicit faith in his integrity. As fourth assistant postmaster general under McKinley, Bristow had been sent to Cuba to make a postal investigation. So thoroughly did he do his work that a number of men were convicted of fraud and sent to jail. In 1903 White recommended him to Roosevelt to conduct an investigation in the postoffice department. Again he pushed his investigation with the same relentlessness. Later he was instrumental in convicting Senator Burton of Kansas. To White, he was the honest, fearless public servant, the epitome of the good man in office. Conversely, Chester I. Long, the senatorial incumbent, was the reactionary, the machine man, the friend of special privilege, the enemy of the people.

As Long's prosecutor, White was as prominent in the eyes of the public as either of the candidates. He wrote reams of material for his own paper and the Kansas City *Star*. On the basis of Long's record he brought thirty-five charges against him, showing that he was the friend of special interests, out of step with the Roosevelt administration, and, in general, an enemy and traitor to the people of his state. The local railroad attorney arranged to bring Long to Emporia to convince White that he was mistaken. Long, in a public meeting, explained his record and attacked White's character. White dismissed the attack with the statement that he was not an issue in the campaign and the fat, old rascal of the *Gazette* could take care of himself. He then launched into a five-column analysis of Long's defense, admitting that he was wrong in three of his accusations but contending that his other thirty-two charges stood unaltered. The Long supporters then flooded the state with a pamphlet, "What Happened at Emporia," quoting White's charges and retractions, thereby adding to White's reputation for inconsistency. The intensity of the contest attracted wide interest. Norman Hapgood, editor of *Collier's,* charged Long with attempting "to make Kansas a great conservative stronghold—a sort of Western Rhode Island." [22] When the votes were counted Bristow had won—with far-reaching effects. He went to the Senate, became an insurgent, being one of the ten who voted against the final draft of the Payne-Aldrich bill and helped to precipitate the split in the Republican Party.

CHAPTER XIII

Not Without Honor in Emporia

Heaven knows the town had bought uniforms and new horns for the band often enough for it to do something public-spirited once in a while without being paid for it. So the band did not come to the town as a shock in and of itself. Neither for that matter did the hack—the new glistening silver-mounted hack, with the bright spick-and-span hearse harness on the horses; in those bustling days a quarter was nothing, and you can ride all over the Ridge for a quarter; so when the comrades at the depot, in their blue soldiers' clothes, their campaign hats, and their delegates' badges, saw the band followed by the hack, they were of course interested, but that was all. And when some of the far-sighted ones observed that the top of the hack was spread back royally, they commented upon the display of pomp, but the comment was not extraordinary. But when from the street, as the band stopped, there came cheers from the people, the boys at the station felt that something unusual was about to come to them. So they watched the band march down the long sheet-iron-covered station walk, and the hack move along beside the band boys; and the poet's comrades-in-arms saw him sitting beside the poet's wife. . . .[1]

ERNON PARRINGTON aptly points out that the years from 1903 to 1917 form a distinctive period in American history—"a time of extraordinary ferment, when America was seeking to readjust her ideals and institutions to a revolutionary economic order that had come upon her."[2] The discovery of gold in California and oil in Pennsylvania, the coming of the railroad, and the stimulating effect of the Civil War had wrought far-reaching changes in American life. In the decades immediately following the war newly discovered processes and inventions made possible the development of petroleum, electricity, and steel. Quite as important as these was the discovery of the limited liability corporation. After the war partnerships declined; corporations emerged, then the pool and the trust. Such changes in the world of finance and industry enabled men to seize the opportunity to develop and exploit a nation fabulously rich in raw materials and natural resources.

The industrial revolution changed America from an agricultural to an industrial nation. In thirty years while the rural population and its products trebled manufacturing increased twelvefold. By 1880, manufactured products had passed farm products in importance. By 1890 the United States had passed Great Britain in the production of pig iron and steel; by 1899 she had exceeded her in coal, and by 1908 in cotton goods. This phenomenal industrial advancement wrought a remarkable change in the distribution of the nation's population. In 1860, sixteen per cent of the people lived in cities, in 1900, thirty-three per cent.[3]

America's industrialization developed without regulation and without direction, condoned in its vicious practices by those in public trust in order that the job might be done. Rapacity and graft were the order of the day; business, politics, and sometimes vice allied to operate for the profit of the few at the expense of the many. With the turn of the century, the country became genuinely alarmed. Business had got out of hand, and the trusts especially were a perplexing problem. Political protest swelled into a social movement, which overflowed into literature.

In the study of American life, the so-called muckrakers attained the greatest popularity. Lincoln Steffens, editor of *McClure's,* was the first of the lot. In cities where reform was under way, he undertook to take the "confused, local, serial news of the newspapers and report it all together in one long short story for the whole country." [4] What he actually did was to ferret out facts showing that a political-economic-vice combination was exploiting the masses. His exposures were sensational and his name became a household word over night as did those of Ray Stannard Baker, Ida Tarbell, Upton Sinclair, and others who followed in his train. The movement spread to other fields of study as well as to other magazines, and the muckrake articles tended to show that the political corruption resulted from beneficiaries of special privileges who bribed officeholders for the right to plunder the people.

William Allen White barely missed being a muckraker. His early fiction revealed the close connection between economics and politics, but all his stories were written as an end in themselves. Two of his political biographies had the muckrake flavor. Both "Platt" and "Croker" depicted the unscrupulous man in politics, the domination of the political machine, and a certain connection between business and government. It was, however, the moral character of the men and their political machinations that he emphasized. Again, when Lincoln Steffens launched his series of articles on the cities, he hoped that White would expose the states, feeling that he was the best equipped man for the purpose. Steffens was probably wrong. To White, man's nobility, rather than his baseness, was a congenial subject. In *A Certain Rich Man*, his literary contribution to the reform movement, it was in keeping with his nature that his hero-villain should ultimately divest himself of his ill-gotten wealth and sacrifice his life in the name of humanity.

A Certain Rich Man starts at the very roots of middle western life and shows the beginnings and growth of the social and industrial problems agitating the American people in the first decade of the nineteenth century. The story opens in 1857 when John Barclay, the chief character, was a boy of seven. Four years before, when his family was on its way West, his father was shot at Westport Landing for preaching an abolition sermon. His mother, a cultured woman, takes in washings to support herself and her son after the father's death. The Civil War begins when John is eleven. When the local company joins the army, John and his boyhood friend, Bob Hendricks, hide under a load of saddles and are carried away to the scene of hostilities. Before they are sent home, they go through a battle; and John is shot in the foot and is lamed for life. Under his mother's direction he reads widely and develops a passion for music. He and Bob continue their early intimacy, and their closest playmates are Ellen and Molly Culpepper. When they go to the state university, Molly is engaged to Bob; and Ellen promises to wait for John. In college, John's earlier capacity for sharp trading further asserts itself, and with the death of Ellen the "joy of sacrifice" departs from his life.

In 1872, the two return home. Barclay becomes the law partner of General Ward, dreamer and idealist; and Bob begins work in his father's bank. From the beginning John prospers. The panic of 1873 enables him to capitalize on the misfortunes of the farmers; the Hendricks' bank is closed temporarily, and John sends Bob East to manage the sale of stock in a gigantic wheat land scheme. John's operations become more and more extensive and one by one he sacrifices his friends in his insatiable desire for wealth. To protect his interests, he keeps Bob in New York for several years. Under the pretext of saving Bob and his father and Molly's father from ruin, he persuades Molly to marry the local editor. Bob's father is forced to commit a forgery to cover John's overdrafts and dies of a broken heart. Bob returns home, learns the truth about Barclay, and enters the struggle for good government and clean politics.

The years pass and Barclay emerges as one of the wealthiest and most powerful men in the nation. In 1903, he is indicted by the government, but escapes prison because the judge is an accomplice in his crimes. A realization of his moral failure, nevertheless, begins to dawn on him. The death of his wife, caused by the polluted water supply, and the unhappiness of his daughter from a broken engagement, forced by the father because her fiance reveals his corrupt practices, works his regeneration. He disposes of his ill-gotten wealth and loses his life a few years later in an effort to save an unfortunate woman from drowning.

A Certain Rich Man was written under the influence of Theodore Roosevelt's efforts to make ancient concepts of morality prevail in the business world. It represents White's mite in the cause of honest business practices. John Barclay was the son who went into the far country and lived upon husks, and in the end, weary and broken, rose and returned to his father's house. It presupposes the existence of a moral order in the universe, the transgression of which brings its own retribution to the individual or to the nation.

Righteousness, . . . [Barclay] knew, was not piety—not wearing your Sunday clothes to church and praying and singing psalms; it was living honestly and kindly and charitably and dealing decently with every one in every transaction; and sin . . . was the cheating, the deceiving, and the malicious greed that had built up his company and scores of others like it all over the land. That, he knew—that bribery and corruption and vicarious stealing which he had learned to know as business—that was a reproach to any people, and as it came to him that he was a miserable offender and that the other life, the decent life, was the right life, he was filled with a joy that he could not express. . . .[5]

The novel is more than an indictment of malicious greed, more than a preachment of commonplace morality. It depicts the development of Kansas from a raw frontier to a fruitful state, the character of its people and their struggle to make certain economic and moral concepts prevail; and lastly and foremost, it reveals the methods of men who used the people and their government to serve their selfish ends.

But behind Bemis was the sinister figure of young John Barclay working for his Elevator Company. He needed Bemis in politics, and Bemis needed Barclay in business. And there the alliance between Barclay and Bemis was cemented, to last for a quarter of a century. Barclay and Bemis went into the campaign together and asked the people to rally to the support of the party that had put down the rebellion, that had freed four million slaves, and had put the names of Lincoln and of Grant and Garfield as stars in the world's firmament of heroes. And the people of Garrison County responded, and State Senator Elijah Westlake Bemis did for Barclay in the legislature the things that Barclay would have preferred not to do for himself, and the Golden Belt Elevator Company throve and waxed fat. And Lige Bemis, its attorney, put himself in the way of becoming a "general counsel," with his name on an opaque glass door. For as Barclay rose in the world, he found the need of Bemis more and more pressing every year. In politics the favors a man does for others are his capital, and Barclay's deposit grew large. He was forever helping some one. His standing with the powers in the state was good. He was a local railroad attorney, and knew the men who had passes to give, and who were responsible for the direction which legislation took during the session. Barclay saw that they put Bemis on the judiciary committee, and by manipulating the judiciary committee he controlled a dozen votes through Bemis. He changed a railroad assessment law, secured the passage of a law permitting his Elevator Company to cheat the farmers by falsely grading their wheat, and prevented the passage of half a dozen laws restricting the powers of railroads. So at the close of the legislative session his name appeared under a wood-cut picture in the *Commonwealth* newspaper, and in the article thereunto appended Barclay was referred to as one of the "money kings of our young state." That summer he turned his wheat into his elevator early and at a low price, and borrowed money on it, and bought five new elevators and strained his credit to the limit, and before the fall closed he had ten more, and controlled the wheat in twenty counties. Strangers riding through the state on the Corn Belt Railroad saw the words, "The Golden Belt Elevator Company" on elevators all along the line. But few people knew then that the "Company" had become a partnership between John Barclay of Sycamore Ridge and less than half a dozen railroad men, with Barclay owning seventy-five per cent of the partnership and with State Senator Bemis the attorney for the company.[6]

White's moralizing, his protruding his own personality between the reader and the story, his stopping to talk about the characters—all done in the manner of the Victorian novelists—have drawn the fire of later critics. His hearty bubbling energy, his courageous convictions, his sentiments, all his laughter, and all his tears still carry the same high endorsement that they did when his book appeared. Its epic quality, the writer's exact knowledge of his material, and its slow, deliberate composition make it an important part of the social history of an era. Originally, its author had planned to call it *John Barclay and His Times,* and as such it makes its greatest appeal to present-day readers.

A Certain Rich Man first took form in its author's mind in 1906. White's duties in Emporia being too heavy to permit any progress in writing, he and his family went to Colorado, where in the summer and autumn of 1907 he spent five months writing the book through. That his work might not be disturbed, he pitched a tent some distance from the log cabin, and from nine-thirty or ten each morning until late afternoon he pounded the typewriter each day or sat staring into space in search of the elusive words. Each night he read to Mrs. White what he had written during the day and she criticised it. While his writing was red-hot, he says, he could not get any perspective on it. Each day's output seemed the finest literature he had ever read. Mrs. White did not always agree with him and when she disapproved, he threw away what he had written and did the assignment over. The book written through, he and Mrs. White during the next eighteen months revised and recopied it three times, cutting it down a half. Then in March, 1909, White turned the manuscript over to the publishers, and the *Gazette* announced in a little local on the back page that he, Mrs. White and their children, Mary and Bill, and his mother, Mrs. Mary White, would sail for Naples to be gone six weeks or six months.

When the Whites sailed for Europe, they left the *Gazette* in the care of the most competent force it had ever had. Three of them warrant especial mention.

Two years before Walter Hughes had been made business manager, which meant that he was final authority when White was away. Though but thirty-one years of age, he had already spent nineteen years in printing. August 1, 1890, Hughes delivered the first issue of the *Gazette;* then served a full printer's apprenticeship. Some time after his apprenticeship, he went on his travels as a journeyman printer, working mostly on the West Coast; but the Whites soon called him back to be foreman. As foreman he began buying supplies and figuring job work; then in 1904 he took over local advertising, so that he was actually business manager before he had the title. In many respects he was already a unique printing executive. When the *Gazette* bought its first linotype, Hughes went to Brooklyn where he worked in the linotype assembly plant. The linotype is an intricate machine, and Hughes, to make sure that the *Gazette* could keep its new machine in order, worked in the factory to master its mechanism. Again, in 1905 when the *Gazette* bought its new Duplex press, he went to Battle Creek where he helped assemble the press, and later he was able to take it down and reset it himself. All the paper's machinery he had bought and set up. His thorough ways, his cautious manner, and his balanced judgment would have satisfied the requirements of a far more exacting man than White.

Laura French was managing editor. Three months after White bought the *Gazette,* she came in from the farm, a product of Lyon County schools, to learn the printer's trade. What she had missed in formal schooling, she had more than compensated for by her reading. She knew Dickens, Thackeray, Scott, and other classical novelists, and could quote poetry by the yard. Her exact knowledge of grammatical construction and her ability to spell were the marvel of her fellow workers. After she became a member of the force, no grammarians or spellers appeared at the office. It was said that she had already "cleaned up the stock" but had enough for all so that they were not missed. When she became the paper's best printer, the state plant at Topeka lured her away; but White, needing a city editor two years later, induced her to return. Her greatest value to him was that she could reflect "the absolute color and shade" of his opinion. She often disagreed with him violently, thought him crazy and told him so. Nevertheless, she could "carry the exact shade of the lunacy in the *Gazette* for months." [7]

Walt Mason, last of the trio, was already on his way to fame and fortune. Twenty-two years earlier when White was in the University of Kansas, he had first read Mason's rhymes in the Atchison *Globe*. Mason then was a roving reporter who had graduated from the tramp printer estate. All the old tramp printers loved to soak themselves in alcohol, and Mason had caught the habit from them. Three times he took the Keeley cure and three times fell off the water wagon. Mason would get a job on a paper and in a few weeks or months work himself to the top; and then his alcoholism, being periodic, would get the better of him and he would pull out. For twenty years he followed that pattern; and in 1907, down and out, he wrote White asking for a job and offering to write his editorial page for six dollars a week. White was in Colorado writing *A Certain Rich Man;* and although he had never seen Mason, he was familiar with his life and work. He told Mason to go to Emporia and wrote Hughes to get him a room, a meal ticket, a suit of good clothes, give him some cigar money, and see that he did not get in with Emporia's drinking crowd. Two months later when White returned, Hughes' first words were: "We have got to do something about this man, Mason. . . . He's chocking us full of copy. He writes all over the place—locals, editorials. He even sits down at the telegraph desk and writes funny heads. We are two days back on his copy now. Someone's got to shut him off. I don't tackle him for fear he will take to drink."

Then White saw Mason for the first time—a middle-aged man with a head as large as a water bucket, a hay shock of hair, and a face freshly shaved and having that peculiar sheen bespeaking its unfamiliarity with the razor. He was down on the world, and the world was down on him. Over his desk he had printed crudely in large, red letters, "There Ain't No Other Hell." Sometimes he would jump up from his chair, rush out of the office, get aboard a little buckboard, and drive his little pinto pony crazily down the street out in the country. After an absence of an hour, a half day, or day, he would return quietly and take up his work where he had left off. No one ever mentioned drink to him, and gradually the spasmodic seizures became further and further apart. One day, years later, he said to White, "The dreams have quit!"

"What dreams?" White asked. "Oh," Mason replied, "you don't know, do you? I mean dreams about liquor. God, they're awful! I hope to get nothing worse than that in hell!" [8]

One dull Saturday afternoon the *Gazette* was needing copy, and Mason wrote a few verses, printed as prose, urging people to go to church the next day. The verses caught on and Mason wrote another little poem the next day and the next. Papers began copying him, and White, who had concluded there was no end to the torrent of words, sent some of them to George Matthew Adams, who was running a syndicate in New York. In a few months, Mason's name was on its way to becoming a household word in America and abroad. Eventually two hundred newspapers printed his daily poem; and Uncle Walt, as the *Gazette* force affectionately called him, was writing for a score of magazines, a daily short story for the Chicago *Daily News,* a book review page for the Kansas City *Star,* and two or three thousand words a day for the *Gazette.* His income had grown to around twenty thousand a year, and he was indulging his childlike delight first in fine horses and then in fine automobiles.

Such, in brief, was the character of the three persons to whom White had entrusted the destinies of the *Gazette* while he was away; and as a matter of precise fact, the Whites' going abroad was the best thing that could have happened to the *Gazette*. The first rule a reporter learns at the *Gazette* is that he stands in peril of his life if he prints its owner's name. When White went away he told his force to run the paper as if it were their own; and that was exactly what they did. When he became the biggest piece of local news the town had had in ten years, they chuckled to themselves and made the most of it, knowing well that if White took them to task they could confront him with his own words.

While the Whites were getting their first view of Europe, he wrote a series of newspaper articles for Kansas papers somewhat after the fashion of *Innocents Abroad*. *A Certain Rich Man* appeared before their return, and the initial edition sold out the day of publication. It was hailed as "the great American novel" and praised in superlative terms. The New York *Times'* comment is typical: It "holds the mirror up to more that is truly native and characteristic in American life than has been reflected by any other story teller who has essayed the task." [9] White, in Europe, had no knowledge of his book's reception. The news of its success, coming suddenly and unexpectedly, was the supreme moment of his life.

. . . The editor of the Gazette and his family took passage upon the Celtic from Queenstown to America. It was a big ship for those days—a fair fine ship to see, and we all mounted the ladder in pride. After she pulled out of Queenstown we went on deck. There the deck crowd was sprawled about in chairs, and one man was reading a copy of the New York Times. Looking over his shoulder two Emporians saw in the Times a half page advertisement that made their eyes bug out. It was a proclamation declaring that A Certain Rich Man was in its "fourth large printing"—and it had been out but three weeks. We had left the manuscript with the publishers when we sailed, read the proof in Europe and in the joy of our first European journey had all but forgotten the book. And there it jumped out of the advertisement at us—a success. That we knew. Hand in hand, two youngsters, one in his first forties, the other in her late thirties, went to the cabin, and without a word burst into tears. And the two little children could not understand what the sobbing was about.

For eight days we read and reread that advertisement, and gloated. The children played on the deck and won prizes and even grandma—aged seventy-nine, and a captain of a woman—realized what the advertisement meant. The Celtic has carried many a cargo since then of rich cargo and precious freight. But never before nor since has the fair fine old ship . . . carried so much joy as she bore out of Queenstown that August passage long ago.[10]

In Emporia the people were all aglow. Local bookstore sales ran to more than twenty-five hundred copies before Christmas—about a copy for every person in four in the town. Walt Mason, not hesitant about advertising himself or anybody else, pushed White's fame with all the power of his prolific pen. When the train brought White and his family home, the town turned out to give him a hero's welcome. The band greeted them with "The Conquering Hero Comes"; banners waved "In Our Town Once Again," "The Real Issue," "The Homecoming of Colonel Hucks," and "What's the Matter With Kansas, Hey Bill?" and a special edition of the Joplin *News-Herald,* published by a former White employee, was handed to White as he got off the train. The entire front page, printed in two colors, was given over to White. To the left of his picture bold type proclaimed "First in war, first in peace, first in the hearts of his countrymen," to the right, "Back to Empory in all her glory. Back to the busted garden hose." The family was hurried to low-neck hacks, and, headed by the band and followed by a procession of townspeople, borne to Humboldt Park. Then followed a program built on the novel. W. Y. Morgan of Hutchinson and Victor Murdock of Wichita were there, and they and old citizens of the community, in the roles of the various characters, welcomed them home. A quartet sang "Home Again from a Foreign Shore" and "Ever of Thee I Am Fondly Dreaming," the air which Barclay's mother liked to have sung. The reception ended by the family riding home behind Old Tom, the family horse, which in his day, to the shame of automobile owning citizens, pulled Mrs. J. Pierpont Morgan, Anne Morgan, Theodore Roosevelt, and other notables from and to the Santa Fe station.

In the meantime, the evening *Gazette* appeared. White had written for his first book "The Homecoming of Colonel Hucks," a story of two pioneers who visited the Ohio home of their youth after living a generation in Kansas. The dream spots of their childhood turned out to be disappointing; they cut their vacation short to get back to Kansas, and as the Colonel drew nearer and nearer home, he talked louder and louder about the glories of his state. The *Gazette* printed a sparkling paraphrase of this story with White in the role of the Colonel.

When the train reached Lawrence, the Colonel could restrain himself no longer, and bursting from the Pullman he ran out and grabbed the hand of the cabman who had hauled him many a night as a serenader, when he was a student, and who always carried him to and from the Hill, when in later years he made regular visits to attend the meetings of the regents. And again the Colonel's wife had to come to the rescue and pull him aboard as the train pulled out.

As he settled in his seat, he breathed, ecstatically, "Is there any sound on earth like it, Sallie, in Italy, or in France, or in Ireland? the Kansas language, Sallie, the Kansas language!" And for a brief pause he closed his eyes in contentment, and then fell to devouring the landscape again.

At Topeka, he was out in the platform, shouting "Hello Ross," "Howdy Joe," and holding an informal reception with half the statehouse and the newspaper men. "Can we call you lieutenant governor?" asked one, and the Colonel threw up his hands in horror.[11]

From Topeka to Emporia the miles began to drag with ever-increasing slowness, so that by the time the junction was reached, the Colonel had arranged the baggage for the fiftieth time. At Exchange Street he noticed that the pavers had only reached Fifth Avenue, and that there would be plenty of time to change the service pipes before the paving reached Red Rocks.[12] It seemed to him that Freemont park, with its playing fountain and well arranged flower beds, was the most beautiful garden he had ever seen. "Sallie," he said, "did the Champs Elysées compare with that? And say," he remarked a few seconds later, as the train whizzed by the elevator of the City Roller mills, "that thing looks twice as high as the Eiffel tower."[13]

That night the *Gazette,* also, bade farewell to William Allen White and *A Certain Rich Man.* No more reviews of the novel appeared in its columns, and twenty years passed before it was referred to again in its editorial page.

CHAPTER XIV

Evidences of Things Unseen

I am a progressive because I believe in the continuous orderly growth of human institutions; that the world is not bundled up for immediate delivery into the millennium; and that only as we give of our lives in the effort to replace human wrongs by human rights do our institutions grow. I am a progressive because I believe that institutions grow only as they develop greater depths of fellowship among men in our laws and in our customs; that fellowship deepens only as those who enjoy life more abundantly than their brethren surrender their special privileges in the joy of service. There is no danger of life coming to a common level of mediocrity; the qualities of men will make differences in men forever. I am a progressive because I have seen men of high qualities give and give, and grow in giving, while the world waxed better for the gifts it got.[1]

To WILLIAM ALLEN WHITE the twofold struggle of the first decade of this century which attempted to regulate corporate industry more drastically and to put greater powers of government in the hands of the people became a contest of the rights of man against the rights of property. Ultimately, in his thinking this struggle resolved itself into the belief that the contest was for a return of an older, but vastly enlarged, democratic form of government. By 1909, he had sufficiently pondered the problem to write a series of articles on American government, past and present, which he published in book form as *The Old Order Changeth*.

The industrial forces released by the power of steam, as he saw the past twenty-five years in retrospect, created an extra-constitutional government, which in many matters was superior to the constitutional one.[2] The nation maintained its government, "punishing crimes committed by individuals"; and capital maintained its government to protect itself in its crimes against the public. Those "who in the name of the industrial and commercial progress of the land took what was not their own from the public, or those who assumed to add to the national production and accumulation of wealth" came under the jurisdiction of the extraconstitutional government and too frequently "were immune from the constitutional government." Court decisions were finally colored in favor of those who enjoyed special privileges until special privileges became vested rights, and "thus specially privileged classes captured the constitution," and merged the two governments. Laws were enacted, interpreted, and administered for those who enjoyed special privileges, and the two governments "were cemented in the customs and traditions of the people."

This alliance between business and politics, between capital and democracy, he believed, had not been "projected deliberately and with malice prepense." Ignorance and prejudice, produced by demagogues in the days following the Civil War, had forced business into politics in self-defense. But once in politics it "found that a dollar invested in a campaign fund brought on the whole more direct results that any other dollar that might be invested—up to a certain maximum of investment."

Money had got into politics in this way. During the eighties and nineties, the party system "had built a machine made for the uses of corruption." Candidates for all offices got their election and appointments from party organizations. The apathy of the voters "made party success more or less dependent upon getting all the voters to the polls, and money became necessary to hire carriages and workers" to get out the voters, presumably to vote for the organization that brought them to the polls. Campaign speakers had to travel, and literature "had to be distributed to convince the voters of the justice of a party's claims to the voter's support." From these honest uses of money in politics grew the dishonest uses. "Hiring a man to work at the polls shaded gently into hiring him to vote for the party that paid him for his work." Campaign speakers'

expense grew to include pay for personal influence. Printing
funds were diverted to newspapers for the purpose of coloring
the news.

The upshot of money in politics was the purchase of party
organizations. Buying a party became "so brazen that men
thought it was clean."

Did a street railway desire a city franchise, it gave money to the
dominant party in the city, or if there was any doubt about the
election, the franchise seeker contributed money to both parties in
the city where he desired to loot. After the election had been won
with the would-be looter's money, the granting of the franchise to
the benevolent looter became an administration policy.

Corruption was possible because of the machine and its
bosses. Delegates to local conventions were elected from precincts or wards or townships. At the bottom, in these smallest
political units was the precinct boss.

The party convention in a county, town, or city was made up
of from two to four hundred . . . delegates. They nominated the
local county, township, ward or city candidates for the offices that
composed the local government. . . . The precinct boss at the bottom of the system generally said who should go to the county, town,
or city convention as delegates. And in any precinct of two hundred votes on such a matter, not over fifty people in either party
paid serious attention to politics. And year after year the same
men represented each precinct in the local convention. They were
the men who obeyed the dominant precinct boss at the base of
things. He was not an officer of the government, but he controlled
delegates to local conventions which nominated candidates for all
the offices of the local government, so he became an actual part of
the local government of every community. Half a dozen precinct
bosses controlled the average county or small city. And the indomitable man among them controlled them.

This indomitable local boss had relations with the group of
bosses that controlled the district or the great city. He was one of
them. He controlled the larger group if he was strong enough.
And he had relations with the still more powerful group of bosses
that controlled the state conventions and state legislatures of his
party. If he was one of the larger groups, he was powerful enough
to say who should be nominated for the legislature in his county,
who should have the judicial and congressional nominations in his
district, and who should attend the state convention as delegates to
name the candidates for state office. . . . Sometimes he was a
member of the actual organization of his party; at other times he

preferred to name those who should be members. But always he controlled; and the fifty men in either party in each precinct who paid intelligent attention to politics, together with the fifty men in each of a score of other precincts in the town or city, knew this high-grade boss, went to him for favors, considered him as the vicegerent between them and the big boss who controlled the group of bosses in the inner temple that controlled the state.

The extra-constitutional place of the boss in government was as the extra-constitutional guardian of business. If a telephone company desired to put its poles in the street, and the city council objected, straightway went the owner of the telephone stock to the boss. He straightened matters out. . . . Always business was considered. And in some exceptional cases, vice was considered business. That was because vice paid rent, and property interests could not be disturbed. . . . He merely reflected his environment. Otherwise more than fifty people would consider the little precinct boss obnoxious, and he would lose control, and a different group would conduct the public business of the precinct. So the secondary boss —the town or county boss—saw that local business was not hampered . . . business big and little paid money into the party committees; and as the bosses controlled the committees the sale of special privilege was simple, legal, and unquestioned. Money in politics was there for the purpose of protecting the rights of property under the law, as against the rights of man. So prosperity dwelt among the people. The greed of capital was rampant, the force of democracy was dormant. . . .

For the corruption, White blamed the people themselves. Politics "was no worse than business; and business was no better than the people who did the trading." The panic of 1893 had made prosperity the chief end of men, and "every man was willing to yield just a little bit for the larger good of a prosperous nation." Before 1894 evils "were sporadic, local, and not of first importance." There were clean cities, clean states, a clean federal government. But with the rise of Mark Hanna "business in politics became chronic in the politics of the nation." In him "were united the greedy forces of business and the greedy forces of politics"; with him the folly of business in politics grew national. But to him also, "for putting America thoroughly upon a business basis," the country owed "whatever gratitude is due a man who brings out the rash, makes the impurities plain, and aids diagnosis." White did not believe that all business and all politics were corrupt. Relatively, the area of dishonesty in the two was not wide. But it was important. Sometime in 1901 he began dedicating whatever power he had to the task of cleaning house.

White's remedy for the existing evils was the overthrow of the boss system and the regulation and control of capital. From 1901 on he identified himself with the rising progressive movement. Originally he advocated getting honest men into the political machine and giving business a conscience. During the early progressive or insurgent period, he stood for regulation of public service corporations, retention and operation of mineral lands under lease for the people, reduction of the tariff, and liability of manufacturers for industrial accidents. In politics, he advocated in turn corrupt practice acts, secret ballots, direct primaries, direct legislation which gave voters authority to propose laws through petition and have them voted upon in the general elections and which prevented most acts of the legislature from becoming immediately effective so that the voters might petition to have a legislative act referred to the people at the next general election, and the recall, or granting voters authority to recall a public official from office by a special election. As the movement widened, he saw further economic changes, providing for the support of dependent mothers, taxing of incomes, safeguarding bank deposits and establishing flexible credits, readjusting the tariff under a restatement of the principle of protection, taxing inheritances, shortening the hours of labor by legal recognition of the eight-hour day, preventing child labor and enforcing juvenile education, making public sanitation a public responsibility, abolishing the saloon, regulating competition under the Sherman Anti-Trust Act, and conserving the sources of water, coal, timber, and minerals for public use and benefit. In its economic and political changes— the referendum, initiative, recall, secret ballot, direct primary, and direct election of United States senators—he envisioned a new world, a world worth taking his coat off and fighting for.

The whole movement, as he saw it, was a turning from representative to democratic government. The tendency to make money, capital, property, or financial distinction count for nothing in politics, save as an indirect influence on the ballot box, was a step toward democracy. The secret ballot, the primary, and the reformed party were a move "toward the Declaration of Independence and away from the Constitution, which so feared majority rule that the majority was hedged about with checks and balances at every possible point." [3]

But though White was wedded to the program heart and soul, he never saw the millennium around the corner.

. . . Between Eden and Utopia there is a solid ground for sub-stantial advancement—not far, but safe to take and to hold. . . . When we have moved from ideals and traditions and customs that have dominated this nation for a quarter of a century, we shall not be a changed people. We shall be somewhat kinder in our view of the working man, and shall see to it that capital and not labor bears the loss of wear and tear of men in the workshops; we shall be more generous in our view of the average man's stake in the coun-try, granting him a share in the mines and waterways and forests that he has never had before. We shall realize a little more clearly that capital is the secretion of our civilization, and no one will claim that our civilization is the increment of capital; so we shall control capital more largely for the common good than we control it now. But . . . there will be sorrow in the world, and poverty and crime and meanness and injustice. . . . All that will happen is that we shall have organized into law and custom somewhat more of the altruism growing slowly in our hearts.[4]

That actual progress was being made, he was sure. Men were running up and down the earth, "getting out the vote and saving the country to little purpose, still in the long run the surest fact in history is progress."

Life is easier for the average man than ever it was before. There is less difference between the man at the top and the man at the bottom, and the going is easier toward the top. There are lifts and moving stairways and free schools, and hand rails, and blazed trails and modern plumbing and a thousand first aids to the wounded in the struggle for the top that the ancient world or the medieval world or the feudal world never knew.[5]

The Emporia editor was then, as ever after, the patient reformer. Stop the channels of governmental change and you would have a blowup. Resort to force to create a new world, and you would have the excesses of a French Revolution. The English way was immeasurably the better way. During the nine-teenth century, after much floundering and wallowing in the muck and mire, England had by slow and peaceful methods brought greater justice to the poor and down-trodden. To the English method, he was committed; in the long run the English had accomplished more than the French, and at far less cost. Any reform, moreover, did exactly what it was primarily expected to do—no more, no less. "Establish the primary and you give the people potential power; but you don't endow them incidentally with sense and independence and leadership. Tax incomes and you tax incomes; you don't stop big incomes or make their recipients honest or patriotic." A reform pays, but it does not "return usury." [6] This business of saving the country was a "long and tedious, yet always for the man of faith, a joyful job."

For always, just as he gets his Indians whipped, or his Boston tea party over, or his immortal Declaration written, or his Constitution adopted, or his bill of rights accepted, or his slaves freed, or his Union cemented, or his specie payment resumed, or his railroads controlled, or his social and industrial justice in the hearts of the people, and his country all baled up tightly in its perfection —bang! comes a new calamity (and a very real one it always is), hitting the precious country between the aurora borealis and the Gatun dam, breaking the bales and leaving a man's-sized job for the youth of the next "jocund day" that "stands tiptoe on the misty mountain-tops." [7]

White's faith in the progressive movement was basically his growing faith in the innate decency of the average man, his confidence that the average man would act wisely and justly if given the facts. He had seen in the popularity of the muck-rakers "a demand for men who will tell the facts." Americans at bottom were "a moral people, even though they are a busy people, and when they know what is good and true and worthy in government they will have it, though they may not hasten to it." [8] The first obligation, then, of reformers "should be to go to the bottom and make men and women who can think and feel and act justly and unselfishly." [9] The salvation of a people depends upon education "that teaches men to do their best and live their wisest, education that gives man a love of industry, justice, and sincerity." [10] The most vital question in the reform movement was "what will our schools do for us." The secret ballot, direct primary, direct legislation, and all other measures looking toward self-government were but means to an end, and "as sure as there is a just God, the more we make laws unleashing the power of the people without widening the vision of the people, those laws, those very laws that release the people from political bondage, will be 'vessels of wrath, fitted unto destruction.' " [11]

Americans had been asleep. Their minds had been so occupied with the creation of wealth that they had unknowingly permitted and condoned practices in politics, government, and industry leading to unforseen evils. "It was the inevitable trend that affairs must take when the heart of an intelligent democracy turns from spiritual to material things." [12] With the turn of the century a new sense of justice awoke in the hearts of men. There was a quickening of the moral perception; a new force was abroad in the land.

It moves toward truth and decency in the relations of men and women; it moves toward fairness in business; it moves toward clean family relations. It moves toward temperance and sobriety. Whether one believes in God or not, whether one goes to church or not, whether one is religious at all or not, if he has any eyes in his head he must see that this moving force toward good conduct and honest living is the biggest force in the world. It is the mainspring of all the latent energy for the good of all that we call civilization. It is the force that holds society together, keeps down anarchy, and enforces law. [13]

White saw the progressive movement as an expression of this force, and as such, it commanded his allegiance.

Ultimately White viewed the movement as a by-product of an eternal contest. It was not a contest between the "have's" and "have not's." Greed was greed—whether it voted for discriminatory railroad legislation or the "full dinner pail." In every man two spirits wrestled for control. One, "the altruistic spirit," embodied justice, generosity, kindness, service, and faith; the other, "the egoistic spirit," embodied greed, avarice, ruthlessness, selfishness, and cynicism. Extension of self-government was good only in so far as it unleashed the altruistic spirit; regulation of capital was good only in so far as it curbed the egoistic spirit and protected the helpless. The vital issue was the world-old fight for the establishment of ideal justice between men; and it was "the problem of this generation and the next and the next to civilize the conscienceless devil of malicious greed out of the hearts of men." [14] Out of this thinking he saw man's duty to himself and his fellowman—out of this thinking came his philosophy of life.

Only by service to one's fellows can one call up from his soul the latent sense of duty to humanity which moves through this life of ours, and works among us for the promotion of eternal righteousness. He who serves for the joy of service, whether he be inventing a dynamo or digging a ditch in the street to carry away fever-breeding filth, is releasing the instinct of growth in his heart which God planted within life when He made this world. And only by giving full play to the instinct of growth in his being which impels him to help his fellows, may a man work out the divine purpose within him. And conversely, if he does not serve his fellows in a real way, if he does not give them that service which comes from the altruistic instinct of growth within him, he has failed in life, and no matter how much money he has accumulated, no matter how much apparent power he may command, still that man has failed. For success in this life is service to one's fellows.[15]

By 1910, the Emporia editor could have written his later definition of democracy. With changed times and changed conditions, the spirit of democracy manifested itself in various forms, but its underlying principles remained unaltered.

Democracy is the institutionalized expression of the Christian philosophy in ordinary life—whether in social habit or commercial practice, in industrial organization or governmental administration. Of course man is not able in his present state of moral and intellectual progress to achieve really more than thirty or forty per cent of his Christian aspiration. So democracy is carrying even less than that small per cent of everyday human altruism in government or in business or in the social life of the American people.

But in so far as governments have curbed greed, they have established some approximate of democracy. In so far as we have brought the common man into the enjoyment of many of the benefits of our civilization, giving him a high standard of living, educating his children, looking after his health, providing highways for his journeys, giving him police protection against the larcenous fellows armed with lethal weapons or with a corporation charter—in those things we have set up democracy.

In so far as we are shortening the hours of labor of the common man and bringing to him amusements and diversions, books, music and drama which he can afford—spiritual blessings like those that once were the playthings of kings—in that much, or that little we are true to the democratic ideal.

In so far as we are giving the average citizen opportunity and power through government to redress his wrongs, we are following the democratic vision. In so far as we are using our government as an intelligent agency for human welfare and at the same time leaving to the man of ten talents full leeway for the highest possible development of those talents commensurate with honest, neighborly, social conduct, in that far democracy is a success.

And with all these material achievements, in so far as we have made man a free spirit—free to aspire, to protest, to follow any vision in his heart or mind and which leaves his neighbor equally free—in that realm have we planted democracy upon a firm foundation.

Democracy at base is an attitude of mind. Its failures are obvious. But even our small and often futile democratic endeavor is worth the cost. Moreover the democratic order has upon the whole, admitting its faults, made more people happy, useful and decent than any other institutionalized system ever established by man.[16]

CHAPTER XV

Bull Mooser

We may as well be entirely frank. This is a waiting game. So long as the Democratic party continues under its present progressive leadership there is no chance for the Progressives, and so far as that goes, we don't care for the offices while the Democrats carry out the principles of the Progressive platform. On the other hand, when the Democratic patronage gives out, probably the progressive leadership of the Democratic party will begin to crumble. The Democratic standpatters will begin to appear. Then when the progressive leadership of the Democracy fails, the Progressive party will be in a position to offer a decent home to the progressive Democrats.[1]

WHEN Kansas Republicans nominated Joseph L. Bristow for the senate in 1908, White's interest in the campaign began to lag. The nomination was equivalent to election, and White had no other vital interest in the campaign. His conclusion on the national situation, after covering both national conventions for a newspaper syndicate, was that both parties stood about the same on issues. The only question involved was the fitness of the two presidential nominees. Taft was competent, Bryan incompetent. His support of Taft, however, was tepid. Throughout the campaign, he maintained an attitude in keeping with his earlier estimate. Judge Taft represented "the progressive policies of the President—law enforcement without favor, and further legislation where it is necessary to promote public and private honesty." Any man who pretended to be a supporter of President Roosevelt "should throw all the weight of his influence to Taft." [2] Yet before Taft took office, White must have had some misgivings about his zeal for Roosevelt's program. Roosevelt, fearing that the conservative element of the Republican party would capture Taft, had written White asking him to lay before the new president, clearly and forcefully, the attitude of the Middle West.

William Howard Taft had been made president by the grace of Theodore Roosevelt. His early career as a federal judge revealed pronounced conservative tendencies, but his consistent support of Roosevelt's policies led the President to choose him to continue his program. Roosevelt, through personal influence, management of federal patronage, and manipulation of southern delegates, succeeded in having Taft named on the first roll call at the party convention. The Republican platform lauded Roosevelt's record, called for increased regulation of trusts, restrictions on granting of injunctions in labor disputes, and a revision of the tariff based on the difference between "the cost of production at home and abroad, . . . with a reasonable profit to American industries." [3] Both the new President and the platform on which he was elected seemed to point to a continuation of reform legislation. Taft, however, was ill equipped to succeed Roosevelt. When Roosevelt left for a hunting trip in Africa, Taft reverted to a more conservative point of view on public questions and was disposed to let the country enjoy a period of rest after seven years of agitation. Moreover, he was inclined to conciliate the powerful conservative leaders whom Roosevelt had antagonized, and soon displayed a positive genius for political ineptitude.

Soon after taking office, Taft convened Congress to revise the tariff, a thankless and dangerous task for any party; and while the Republican platform did not specifically call for a reduction in rates, it had been so interpreted and Taft had made clear in numerous speeches that he favored a downward revision. The House of Representatives, in accordance with his recommendations, passed a bill reducing rate; but when the bill went to the upper house, the Senate under the leadership of Aldrich, an arch-conservative, amended it 847 times, increasing duties mostly, so that the new Payne-Aldrich law actually represented an increase over the former one. During the long and bitter senate fight, the insurgent Republicans, Senators Cummins and Dolliver of Iowa, La Follette of Wisconsin, Beveridge of Indiana, and Bristow of Kansas, tried to block the increases at every point; and not getting the expected support from Taft, they felt that the President had deserted their cause. After the passage of the bill, Taft undertook to defend it in a series of speeches and by the Winona, Minnesota, address, in which he declared the tariff the best the country ever had, he further antagonized the progressives.

Again, the Ballinger affair put Taft in the worst possible light. The conservation movement was the pride and joy of the progressives; Roosevelt's zeal in conserving the natural resources added immensely to his popularity, and his achievements so far out-distanced his predecessors that they stood nowhere. One phase of conservation attempted to prevent private exploitation of minerals, forest, and water-power sites. Roosevelt had zealously guarded the nation's interests in making contracts with private firms and had in numerous cases cancelled outstanding contracts which he construed as inimical to national welfare. When, therefore, Gifford Pinchot, the chief forester and a Roosevelt holdover, accused his chief, Taft's Secretary of the Interior R. A. Ballinger, of favoring certain large corporations seeking land grants, he raised a heated controversy that further confirmed the progressive's suspicions of Taft's conservatism. Although Taft probably had no choice but to dismiss Pinchot for insubordination, the dismissal in nowise lessened the growing impression that Taft was the friend of special interests. Public resentment was so great that Ballinger was shortly forced to resign.

Finally, the breach between Taft and the progressives was further widened by their fight to reduce the powers of Joseph G. Cannon, Speaker of the House and ultraconservative. Cannon appointed all Republican members on all committees and had the power to demote or could refuse to reappoint any member who did not act according to his wishes. As the dominating figure on the House Rules Committee, he could arbitrarily direct the whole course of lawmaking. When the Republican progressives ultimately rebelled and, with the help of the Democrats, sheared Cannon of his dictatorial powers, Taft threw in his lot with Cannon.

During the Senate fight over the Payne-Aldrich tariff bill, White was in Europe. He sailed before the fight got under way; and when he returned, it was over. Had he been in America, he would have supported the insurgent Republicans. After his return, he printed editorial excerpts from papers on how Taft's defense of the bill was being received; and when, in the next election, the Republicans lost their majority in the House, he interpreted the results as a rebuke to "that kind of tariff making" and a condemnation of the materialism of the Taft administration. "The people knew that the law was unrighteously passed." They "felt that it was by log-rolling, and that duties were fixed, not because they were just, but because they were based upon campaign contributions of great manufacturing interests. Granted that fact, the more revenue the bill made the angrier the people grew." [4]

Two months later it was obvious to White that "insofar as President Roosevelt had been the voice of the people, President Taft refuses to follow Roosevelt." Taft proposes "to be an administrator and nothing more." He "takes no leadership; he frames no program; he makes no demands; he argues no brief for the people against those who are despoiling them; if the people can't send men to Congress to look after those things, clearly President Taft considers it their business, not his." [5] By early January he saw a political crisis facing the Republicans. The only way to save the party "is for Republicans of the rank and file to save it themselves, and turn out of nomination and out of public life the Republican congressmen who are known to be Cannon men, whose past allegiance has been so thick and thin that Cannon and the party have become inseparable." It was not congressmen and senators who were in revolt; it was the people.[6] Though White was putting himself in line to go out of the party two years later, when the break came, he then believed that a third party would be unwise. Talk of a third party was "of all the fool things under the sun . . . the foolest thing. . . . The old barnacles that had loaded down the ship will be scraped off. . . . Those who talk of a new party are not the best friends of progress." [7]

In 1910, Kansas was a hot bed of insurgency. Victor Murdock, a ringleader in shearing Speaker Cannon's power in the

House, W. R. Stubbs, later to be one of the seven governors to sign the petition giving Roosevelt an excuse to enter the race against Taft, and Senator Bristow, an insurgent from the word go, had all contributed to the spirit of revolt. Moreover, a sizable portion of the daily press promoted the insurgent cause. Arthur Capper's Topeka *Capital*, Henry J. Allen's Wichita *Beacon*, Murdock's Wichita *Eagle*, Bristow's Salina *Journal*, White's *Gazette*, and the Kansas City *Star*, which has a tremendous Kansas circulation, were all definitely inclined to the insurgent wing. When Roosevelt made his midwestern tour late in the summer, his trip across Kansas was a triumphal procession. Probably it was not by accident that the ex-President chose Osawatomie from which to announce his "new nationalism"; he was in the heart of the progressive territory.

It is safe to say that few, if any, who heard Roosevelt deliver the Osawatomie speech had any inkling that they were hearing more than a typical Roosevelt speech. The occasion was in every respect an over-grown country fair. Farmers loaded their families into carriages, buggies, and spring wagons to drive ten to thirty miles to see the man they had heard so much about; railroads ran special trains for two hundred miles to handle the sightseers. And Roosevelt, standing on a table placed on a platform, "towered high above the dense crowd" [8] speaking slowly in a high-pitched voice. Everyone cheered, forcing Roosevelt to hold up his hand time and again in protest; but few of the cheering thousands heard what he said. Either they were too far from the speaker or his voice was unable to rise above the barkers running sideshows or selling peanuts, popcorn, pink lemonade, and hot dogs in the booths lining the outskirts of the grove where the ceremony was taking place. But everyone was happy and Roosevelt "looked on with great enjoyment," as he charted the Progressive party platform for 1912.

As for the Kansas progressives—Bristow, Stubbs, Allen, White, and their lot—they had all but captured the Colonel. The day before they had adopted the state platform embodying advanced progressive principles, and the question uppermost in their minds was whether or not Rooosevelt would go along with them. Two days before in Denver, Roosevelt had partially fulfilled their hopes so that they were in a happy mood, and each jubilantly entertained the crowd as a prelude to the main show, White smiling "expansively till the crowd laughed."

The occasion was perfect for a new nationalism. Roosevelt was dedicating a new park on the site of the battlefield where John Brown had fought the Missourians on August 30, 1865; and he aptly paralleled the Civil War days to his own time. Specifically, the measures he recommended differed little from the policies he had previously advocated. He wanted the rules of the game "changed so as to work for a more substantial equality of opportunity and of reward for equally good service." Special interests had to be driven out of politics and out of government. It was necessary for the government to supervise the capitalization of all corporations doing interstate business. An expert tariff commission, "wholly removed from the possibility of political pressure or of unproper business influence," was the answer to the tariff problem. The time had come for direct primaries, corrupt practice acts, inheritance and income taxes. The welfare of the laborer should be protected by workman's compensation acts and by laws regulating sanitation, safety devices, and conditions under which children and women worked; the farmer should be aided through the Department of Agriculture, agricultural colleges, and experiment stations; and the natural resources should be used for all the people. Also, the authority of the state and national governments should be clearly defined.

At one or two points, however, Roosevelt seemed dangerously close to socialism. "The man," he says, "who wrongly holds that every human right is secondary to his profit must now give way to the advocate of human welfare, who rightly maintains that every man holds his property subject to the general right of the community to regulate its use to whatever degree the public welfare may require it."

This statement and one or two similar ones aroused widespread criticism in some sections of the country, and Roosevelt confessed "that it had been 'a blunder of some gravity' to express himself in such a manner that his remarks could be considered apart from their context and misunderstood." [9] But in

Kansas his socialism created not a ripple. As for White, Roosevelt's brand of progressivism was growing stale. He was the "Progressive Hen" that mothered the "Insurgent Ducklings." He had brought them into being, but he was not one of them.[10] A year later when Governor Stubbs announced that he would support Roosevelt rather than Taft for the Republican nomination, the *Gazette* came out for La Follette, "believing that he will represent progressive ideas better in the presidency than Colonel Roosevelt . . ."[11]

Roosevelt, meanwhile, had broken completely with the man whom he had made president and had entered the race for the presidential nomination on the theory that Taft had betrayed him, the Republican party, and the country. La Follette's prospects then faded, and White, returning to the Roosevelt camp, plunged into the Taft-Roosevelt controversy. The details of this controversy, each man's responsibility in bringing it about, and his subsequent role would fill a volume. Here we must be content to say that the passions engendered set brother against brother, and for once White did not hold the knife.edge of his balance so perfectly that his readers could not see his bias. "Taft acknowledged that he was nominated by a party pledged to continue the so-called Roosevelt policies." He had not carried out the pledge. It was understood that Taft would retain such members of Roosevelt's cabinet "as desired to stay." Again he had not kept faith. After Taft's election, he listened to Roosevelt's enemies and while Congress was buffeting Roosevelt, he "gave no sign of displeasure" when a word from him would have silenced them. Taft had told Roosevelt that he "expected to retain the old cabinet as far as it could be retained," then consulted Roosevelt no further, leaving Roosevelt to learn "from the newspapers who the new cabinet members were to be." In the tariff fight Taft discredited Roosevelt's friends and honored "those men whom his predecessor had found it wise to distrust." Taft wilfully remained away from Roosevelt's reception on his return from Africa. Taft did not invite Roosevelt to the White House. Taft made it impossible for Roosevelt to get his convictions before the President "except by impudently forcing his way unasked into the White House."[12]

Later writers have uncovered information showing some of White's charges to be wrong, but he wrote with so much positiveness that his article indicated inside information. His publisher, admitting his closeness to Roosevelt, still held the opinion that Taft had "appeared the more dignified figure in some of the events alluded to." [13] In view of White's mistaken assumptions, it seems reasonable to believe that he had been misinformed. Possibly some of his charges were a result of Roosevelt's power of hypnotizing himself into believing things that never were.[14]

The Emporia editor was one of a group that drafted a platform for the Roosevelt delegates. His summary of the progressive objectives at this time represents in his judgment the problems they had to cope with.

We are struggling to get these weapons of democracy, direct legislation, the control of elected officials, the final word, as to constitutionality of our laws—not as ends in themselves, but as means to an end. That end is economic. . . . This century seems to be ready to witness the rise of the man at the bench, at the desk, in the workshop, in the ditch, at the counter, on the farm, on the railroad, in the mine, in the factory. He now is demanding his share of the fruits of the civilization which he toils to maintain. . . .

The problem as it comes to us is largely a problem of equitable distribution of the state, county, city and federal taxes, and therefore, a question of what political activities we shall engage in. The problem of the hours and wages of labor; the problem of transportation, and communication; the problem of ownership of our national resources; the problem of society's liability for the waste of industry in accident, age and disease; the problem of housing the poor—in short, all the problems that come to a civilization as the result of sordid environment reacting upon character and making for chronic poverty, that may be relieved by changing the sordid environment. . . .

We can answer them, not by taking the judgment of the few, however wise, but by taking the wisdom of the many. For we believe in the people may be found the judgment to solve the problems of the people.[15]

The phrase, "final word as to the constitutionality of our laws," refers to the mooted recall of judicial decisions. White never advocated the judicial recall. In lieu of it he proposed "a constitutional provision to prevent courts from declaring legislative acts unconstitutional excepting by a three-fourths

majority of superior courts; and barring courts of lower jurisdiction from having any power whatever to declare legislative
acts unconstitutional." [16]

The Roosevelt platform was abortive. An hour before
the Republicans renominated Taft, White resigned as national
committeeman and bolted the party to stand with Roosevelt
at Armageddon. There was no question in his mind about the
nature of Taft's nomination. By disqualifying duly elected
Roosevelt delegates and seating Tafts', the national committee
had stolen the nomination. But the theft of the nomination was
not his sole grievance. The committee had acted to perpetuate
its "present color indefinitely." On the day preceding the nomination, it ruled that any member "who did not give such support to the party candidate as the committee deemed necessary
could be removed at once by the committee," and when a man
is removed from membership, his successor "shall be appointed
by the committee." [17] The second ruling irked White. Hereto-
fore, vacancies had been filled by the state central committee,
and taking that power from its hands meant the indefinite
domination of the national committee by those then in control.
However, White would have bolted the party despite the committee's ruling. Roosevelt, he thought, was the honest choice of
the party, and Taft's nomination "was accomplished by fraud
so gross that to call him the nominee of the Republican party
is to be guilty of a grotesque joke." [18]

It was easy for White to follow Roosevelt into a new
party. The two saw eye to eye on political questions, and the
personal attachment was strong. With White personal loyalty
counts for much; he once supported a dyed-in-the-wool conservative for the Republican presidential nomination in gratitude for his services to Kansas and as an old personal friend.
Yet despite the attachment of the White family to Theodore
Roosevelt, there never was a White who had much in common
with his personality save Mary. There the likeness was strong.
Mary had the Roosevelt joy in life, his zest for living, his un-
bounded energy, his love for the outdoors. She lived her own
life and wanted the respect of others because she was Mary
White, not William Allen White's daughter. She defied the
conventions of her own social group and made a friend of every

yellow dog in Emporia. Her exhaustless energy, her ceaseless activity, her unaffected independence disclosed a personality as distinct as Roosevelt's.

The birth of the Progressive party was White's occasion for rejoicing. At last America had a "radical party." Roosevelt was but "an episode in this contest." Long after Roosevelt is gone, "the party will continue." It "is pledged at the beginning to definite social and industrial reforms. It is not pledged to prosperity, but to justice. It is pledged to so change the environment of chronic poverty that whatever the changed environment can do to ameliorate or remove chronic poverty will be done." Its platform "is much more important than either of the candidates on the head of the ticket.[19]

But the Democrats' nomination of Woodrow Wilson had made a Progressive victory difficult. A year before White had noted Wilson's talks as "full of dynamite," [20] and from time to time printed extracts from his speeches in his editorial column. The Democratic convention, however, further confirmed his opinion of the party's inherent reactionarism. A party "that hesitates five days in nominating a man like Wilson is not to be trusted to carry out the progressive policies that he stands for." "By all the rules of common sense and political wisdom Wilson should have been nominated on the first ballot." [21] Bryan had forced Wilson's nomination "to eliminate Roosevelt and make the Democratic party definitely progressive, as the Republican party had declared itself to be definitely reactionary." The problem, then, facing the Progressives was "to prove to the country that a party which in its local organizations in the various states is reactionary, as the Democratic party is in all the Southern states, and in many of the Northern states, is not made progressive by the mere nomination of a progressive national ticket upon a progressive platform." Southern states, White thought, had little in common with Wilson; the Middle West little in common with Taft. "It would seem to be highly proper for perplexed gentlemen of both [old] parties who desire to see things clearly to go out and take a large cooling drink of buttermilk—that cheers but not inebriates. . . ." [22]

White proposed to do his part toward showing the

Kansas voters the wisdom of supporting the new party. During
its life he served as national committeeman; in its two campaigns, he raised the state war chest, accepting no money from
the national committee. At no time, before or since, has he got
so much fun from politics. He established the Roosevelt headquarters at the *Gazette,* and enjoyed the campaign as much as
a three-ring circus. For four years he fought for the Lord,
not in grimness, but in joy. The new dispensation was at hand,
and his spirits bubbled over. When Progressives proposed him
for governor, he declined in accelerated animation.

To which the Gazette says no—a thousand times no. For we are
on to that man White, and without wishing to speak disrespectfully
of a fellow townsman, who, so far as we know, may be at least
outwardly decent in the simpler relations of life—perhaps he pays
his debts when it is convenient, and he may be kind to his family,
though that's not to his credit, for who wouldn't be—and he may
have kept out of jail, one way or another, for some time; without
as we say, desiring to speak disrespectfully of this man, we know
that he's not the man either to run for governor or, if such a grotesque thing could be imagined, to serve as governor.

He can't make a speech. He has a lot of radical convictions
which he sometimes comes into the Gazette office and exploits, and
which are dangerous. He has been jawing politicians for twenty
years until he is a common scold, and he has set up his so-called
ideals so high that the Angel Gabriel himself couldn't give the performance that this man White would have to advertise on the
bills.

So, in the words of the poet, nix on Willyum Allen. The
Gazette's nose is hard and cold on the proposition to make him
governor. He is a four-flusher, a ring-tailed, rip-snorting hellraiser,
and a grandstander. He makes a big noise. He yips and kyoodles
around a good deal, but he is everlasting and pre-eminently N. G.
as gubernatorial timber—full of knots, warts, woodpecker holes,
and rotten spots. He would have the enmity of more men who have
walked the plank politically than any other man in Kansas, and his
candidacy would issue an irrevocable charter in Kansas for the
Progressive party to be the official minority report world without
end. Men and women would be trampled to death at seven o'clock
election mornings, trying to get at the polls to cast the first vote
against him, and at night perfectly good citizens, kind fathers and
indulgent husbands, would risk a jail sentence to get in at least ten
votes against him as repeaters. It may be that the Progressive party
needs a goat, but the demand doesn't require a Billy-goat! Now is
the time for all good men to come to the aid of the party. But this

man White is a shoulder-galled, sore-backed, hamstrung, wind-broken, string-halted, stump-sucking old stager who, in addition to being no good for draft and general purposes, has the political bots, blind-staggers, heaves, pink eye, and epizootic. Moreover, he is locoed and has other defects.

People in the state may be fooled by the doped gait and fancy steps of this man White, but we know him. If he is a candidate for governor or for any other office, we propose to tell the truth about him—how he robbed the county with a padded printing bill, how he offered to trade off his support to a congressman for a government building, how he has blackmailed good citizens, and has run a bull-dozing, disreputable newspaper in this town for twenty years, and has grafted off business men, and sold fake mining stock, and advocated anarchy and assassination.[23] These are but a few preliminary things that occur to us as the moment passes. But if his fool friends insist on playing up this self-advertising game for him any longer, we propose to abandon twenty years of guarded innuendo and prattling subterfuge, and come out with the real facts. We shall speak plainly hereafter.

A word to the wise should gather no moss![24]

The Emporia editor believed that Roosevelt would win the three-sided contest, but a Roosevelt victory would not be of major importance. "Taft is eliminated," and the race is between the other two. "Each of these men is honest, conscientious and inherently progressive." "So far as candidates for the presidency are concerned it is easy sleeping these nights for all Progressive citizens."[25] The day preceding the election, he wrote an editorial stating the fight was won "for a more equitable condition of affairs in America, as outlined by the Progressive national platform."

The result of the election is an incident. The progressive principles, control of trusts, a scientific protective tariff, conservation of American resources for all the people, old age pensions, short hours for workers, a minimum wage for women, the right of labor to organize, the workingman's compensation—these measures have come before the American people; they are in the hearts of the people, and soon they will be upon American statute books. That is the chief thing. It is not important whether Roosevelt is elected or defeated.[26]

Election night White remained in the *Gazette* office until the returns from Americus township were brought to him.

He had Samuel Blythe's forecast and early returns from the East. When he had scanned the Americus figures, he turned to the election party and said, "Fellows, the Colonel is beaten. When the most typical American township in America goes for Wilson, that's the way the country's going—as goes Americus, so goes the West." [27]

White's faith in Wilson was not so great as his pre-election pronouncements indicate. His ideal administrator is a man like Theodore Roosevelt or Alfred E. Smith—one long-schooled in politics who knows when to stand firm and when to compromise, one who has learned by experience how to manage politicians. Wilson, practically as newcomer in politics, lacked that experience; and was, moreover, in White's opinion, the head of a reactionary party. White feared Wilson would be unable to push his measures through Congress. When Wilson, with promptness and dispatch, succeeded in enacting his program, White viewed the performance with amazement.

As a political curiosity it would be unbelievable if it were not in evidence. Here is a mild-mannered, rather soft-voiced man, who has a supercilious and sometimes highty-tighty way with him—an exalted schoolmaster, with but two years of political experience, moving gently down on Washington and taking the leadership of a great party—notoriously untamed and turbulent—and, by his sheer intellectual force we see him playing upon office hunger and patriotism with impartial skill, making that rampant Democracy "mild and lovely, gentle as the summer breeze."

Men take his orders; old stagers in politics, men past masters in the art of dissembling, men rooted in traditioins of the three branches of government, men standing for a life time upon certain convictions about economic theories, have at the wave of this man's hand, dropped their convictions, abandoned their political faith and given over their very ideas about the constitution of this republic. . . . Woodrow Wilson—too shrewd to say it, but not too wise to realize it, is the Government of these United States as no other President has been since the republic was founded.[28]

At the end of Wilson's first year, White noted that "his advent marked the end of an era in American politics . . . The dynasty that fell might be called the business dynasty, to distinguish it from the political dynasty of the first period of American life, and from the slave holding dynasty that fell with the rise of Lincoln." The year following March 3, 1913,

The Editorial Room at the *Gazette* Office

The White home on East Tenth Avenue, Emporia, Kansas

"is more than a year of Wilson's administration; it is the first year under the new regime." He then summarizes Wilson's accomplishments: ratification and use of the income tax, direct election of senators, "redemption of a rather foolish tariff pledge without scandal," passage of a currency bill which is "a step firmly in the right direction," victory "of the idea of a government owned and constructed railroad in Alaska," adoption of a number of great peace treaties, continuation of the same policy of non-interference in Mexico, and the beginning of a trust policy by a national administration, having at least the germs of a "constructive policy." These are great times, he concludes, "but only the beginning of greater times." Wilson "has lived up to his opportunity; he is a leader worthy of his times . . ." [29]

His admiration grew as the Wilson administration progressed. Except Theodore Roosevelt, Wilson commanded more of White's respect than any other of the ten presidents he has known; he commanded more of his charity than any president. When his enemies made political capital out of his appointment of a railroad lobbyist and a political machine manipulator, White came to his defense.

That President Wilson will appoint some bad men is unfortunately true. That he will appoint some bad men, knowing they are bad, is sadly true also. That he will be doing wrong in doing this is unquestioned. . . . But human nature is human nature. . . . The best of us makes a fool of himself now and then. Wilson will get out of line and drawing with the truth, will fail to see himself in perspective, will cut such capers before high heaven as will make the angels weep—and still, on the whole, be a pretty square man who is trying, one day with another, to do the decent thing.

There is a fairly safe though not an original rule to follow in such cases. Wilson is wrong. He deserves the scorn of all men—who have not made about the same mistake.[30]

White's personal acquaintance with Wilson was less than that with any other president he knew, except, possibly, Harrison. A few personal meetings, a letter now and then from the President commending him for something that he had written, some routine official correspondence, and the Russian appointment at the Peace Conference measured White's association with him. White's regard was based on Wilson's accomplishments and ideals. When Wilson in the League of Nations struggle with the Senate, stood adamant, White, in anguish, saw him fumble the opportunity of putting America into the League. White would have compromised for the "half loaf."

Wilson's success in enacting progressive measures, his hold on the Democratic Party, were, nevertheless, giving the Emporia editor qualms about the new party's future. Before Wilson's election, he predicted that his election would split the Democratic party wide open, and the united progressives would "come into power at the next election." [31] As the 1916 campaign approached, the Democratic split seemed farther away, and White was consoling himself with the thought that "if the Bull Moose should happen to get pink-eye, hollow horn, pip or the bots and turn his pretty pink toes to the daisies, he would have lived a short life and a happy one at that!" [32] It was White's belief, though, that the Democratic split would ultimately come; then one of the old parties would disappear, and America would have a liberal and a conservative party. With this thought in mind he fought in the 1916 convention to save the Progressive party.

Both the Republicans and the Progressives convened in Chicago on Wednesday, June 7, 1916. To White, all the Progressive proceedings were a bitter disappointment. He was a member of the committee on resolutions and one of the seven men who drafted the tentative platform. He spent an entire night with the platform committee, losing a fight for an emphatic declaration of principles. In his judgment the platform said "almost nothing and is probably less drastic than that of the Republicans." [33] The platform, however, could have been overlooked. The fate of the party hinged on the convention's nominee; and with White it was Roosevelt or nothing. The Progressives were now split into two factions. The Perkins group hoped to compromise with the Republicans on a candidate acceptable to both parties. The radical group wanted an early nomination of Roosevelt. The radicals believed that if the nomination of Roosevelt "could be brought about Thursday that there could be no reason or excuse for Colonel Roosevelt's refusal to accept it." One of two things would then happen in the Republican convention. They "would nominate

Hughes, who, seeing Colonel Roosevelt on the Progressive ticket, would refuse to run," or they "would nominate a favorite son—a weak creature who would make the presidential race a three cornered race, giving Roosevelt a change at the election, or who in the conference between the two national committees could be easily pulled down, by popular clamor for Colonel Roosevelt as a fusion nominee."

The radicals' strategy was to nominate Roosevelt the second day of the convention, and White worked toward that goal. He voted against the motion to send the harmony delegation to the Republicans, and on Thursday afternoon he tried to get John Parker [34] on the platform to put Roosevelt's name in nomination. But his efforts, and those of the other radicals, were in vain. Perkins did not want to nominate until after the Republicans, hoping they "would nominate Roosevelt" or Hughes "who would make such a radical statement as would satisfy the Colonel and the conservative group of the Progressive party, that third party action was unwise." Perkins was in control of the convention, and the nomination was delayed. On Saturday the Republicans nominated Hughes on the third ballot, and while they were balloting the Progressives stampeded to Roosevelt. In the weeks that followed, Roosevelt, after numerous conferences, endorsed Hughes and thereby ended the Progressive party.

White's view of the aftermath was that we now "have the picture of the dear tender hearted Colonel, cutting off the tail of the dog an inch at a time, to save the feelings of the dog." Because the Perkins group could not see, as the radicals saw, the Progressive party as "a definitely radical party" whose "first aim was to present intelligently and in their most attractive form the advanced ideas of the world's soundest political thinkers, for the consideration of the American people, looking to the final acceptance of those ideas, and their adoption in the American institutions," they had by their actions left the radicals "all dressed up in their fighting clothes, with nowhere to go."

White found his place in the Republican fold, but his enthusiasm had temporarily departed. He compared the rallies of both parties to "a compromise between a memorial service and directors' meeting." [35] When Hughes criticised the eight-hour law, he condemned him; and not once did he mention the Democratic slogan "He Kept Us Out of War." Probably Wilson's re-election did not greatly disappoint him.

CHAPTER XVI

A New Heaven and a New Earth

It will advertise the cheap and develop the brave; it will draw us together in a common purpose and reveal a vast amount of grafting and venality; it will sell newspapers by the ton, and make a few real heroes. Mothers will weep and states will be remade, while the tide of progress in the world rests in its forward movement. God save us all from war, but when it comes make us worthy of the best that it breeds in us.[1]

HOWEVER laudable the achievements of the progressive movement, it had centered the American mind exclusively on domestic issues. When Europe suddenly, and to Americans surprisingly, burst into flames in August, 1914, the American mind was wholly unprepared for the war. No one wondered whether we could keep out, no one said, "It's our war"—for the thought never occurred to the average American that his country might become involved or that he had a vital interest at stake.[2] True, when Germany invaded neutral Belgium to dispose of France before Russia could get into action, her ruthlessness shocked the entire world. But it was not our job to protect the weak; it was not our duty to resist aggression. Six weeks after the war began and when the "rape" of Belgium was complete, Theodore Roosevelt gave his blessing to President Wilson's proclamation of neutrality and said we had "not the smallest responsibility" for what had happened in Belgium.[3]

White was on vacation in Colorado when the World War began. He, like all other country editors in the Middle West, had given little thought to foreign affairs. When hostilities began, his major concern was with the fate of the Progressive

Party; but to him, as to his regional contemporaries, the war ultimately brought the realization that a pistol shot in a far away Sarajevo might disrupt the normal modes of life far more than the defeat of a favorite party. In his attitude toward the invasion of Belgium, he was the perfect neutral. The Germans "are no worse than the rest of us." When a people "go the limit, the limit is bad, and war is the everlasting lust limit of humanity. War brings men down to the brutes quicker than whiskey, surer than women, and deadlier than even the love of money." [4]

From the outbreak of the war to Wilson's fight with the Senate over the peace treaty, White supported the President unconditionally. A month after the war began, when Wilson asked for a war tax to cover a probable treasury deficit, White lashed out at the "cheap partisans of all parties" who were trying to make political capital out of Wilson's request. "The deficit," he said, "came as the direct result of the war." Imports had been shut off, "and trade generally disorganized." It is "to the credit of Wilson's courageous statesmanship that he has asked for this tax, and asked for it in advance of the deficit." Then he pays him a typical tribute.

A fine, fair, brave, wise man is this man Wilson. His party is not up to his own level of intelligence and courage. But he has displayed fine common sense and infinite tact in dealing with his inferiors in many things. He has been handicapped as no President since Lincoln was handicapped, by wars and rumors of wars, a greedy party, and an unscrupulous group of reactionaries in the country—in his party and out of it. Yet he has shown in every crisis and every important decision the heart of a Christian gentleman and the mind of a scholar. The people are with Wilson irrespective of party, and the politicians may rage, but the people will not imagine a vain thing about him.[5]

For several months White practically ignored the conflict. He wrote a few articles on Belgian relief, but his editorial interests lay in noting the enactment of progressive legislation. Meanwhile, the war was touching America in numerous ways which in later years would have been topics for daily discussions in the *Gazette's* editorial columns. Both sides in the conflict were bidding for American support; both were actively engaged in propaganda. France and Britain more subtly and less offensively than Germany. German agents tried to frighten Congress with the eight million German-American vote. Her spokesmen demanded that the government prohibit exporting munitions and, failing in the demand, began sabotaging Allied war supplies. Britain also was giving offense, chiefly to seizing American shipping. Her navy had cut off German foreign trade; and when Germany began to import through neutral Holland, Denmark, Norway, and Sweden, Britain seized American shipping destined for these countries on the theory that she had the right to seize goods going through a neutral nation into enemy territory. America protested but the issue was never settled because German violations of American neutrality more and more aligned America on the Allied side.

Not until submarines began taking the lives of neutrals did White show any partiality in the conflict. Germany, relying on the submarine to effect a counterblockade, had announced British merchantmen would be destroyed in the war zone even though it were not possible always to save their crews and passengers. She also declared that since British vessels used neutral flags to disguise themselves, neutral ships would not be safe in the war zone. The results of this policy was that a number of American citizens lost their lives in American and British ships. One incident stirred the nation. On May 7, 1915, without warning a German submarine destroyed the *Lusitania* off the Irish coast. The ship sank in eighteen minutes taking down 1,153 men, women, children, 114 of them American citizens. Because of the enormity of the act and the prominence of some of the persons lost, a wave of deep indignation swept the country and for the first time White put into words the thought that Germany was in the camp of the unrighteous.

To Germany, the great leader of science and the world's torchbearer in literature and art, everyone must give honor. But to the military caste that is waging this war, mad with the belief that material force and not spiritual force must win, scant honor comes from the world, and even if the tide of battles should turn toward Germany, she would still have the world's conscience against her, and her victory would turn to ashes.[6]

Ultimately, White was to view the conflict as a war of material force against spiritual force, but not yet. Certainly he was not ready to resist force with force. The sinking of the *Lusitania* was no excuse for America "running amuck." On one side was "German barbarism"; on the other, "English Philistinism." Not Germany but the war itself threatened the foundation of civilization.

Some high devil in the forces of hell seems to have found a lever that has turned into the street all the madness of humanity that is pent up in human hearts. The world's highways are filled with homicides. Let all sane men go in and shut their doors. To go out means contagion and death. Americans—South Americans and North Americans—hold the ark of the covenant of civilization. In a world war mad, we have the peace that passeth understanding. By God's grace we should keep it.[7]

Then five days later:

The essence of civilization is communal kindness. The essence of savagery is communal cruelty. War always is bestial, cruel, insane.

There is no such thing as civilized warfare, and may God help us to keep peace.[8]

President Wilson through a series of diplomatic notes wrung from the German government à promise of greater respect for the rights of neutrals; and the *Lusitania* incident passed, but not the question of America's policy. White was unconsciously abandoning his theory of isolation, and with its abandonment came a period of perplexity. "The foundations of our experience have been shaken," he wrote. The impossible "has happened," and we "cannot say what may not happen." Convictions cannot be formed "upon evidence that is so contradictory." [9] Allied propaganda, nevertheless, was having its effect. White was still holding that both sides were more or less wrong, but when the war was a year old, "Germany and Germany alone" had committed the inhuman atrocities. Germany and Germany alone had "murdered defenseless men and women on the high seas." She alone had backed "women prisoners against the wall" and shot them as spies; and she alone allied herself "with the unspeakable Turk and is standing for the massacre of the Christians in Armenia solely because they are Christians." She alone "makes a continuous military policy of slaughtering defenseless people in city streets with bombs dropped from the sky." [10]

Yet the war was not a major topic in the *Gazette's* editorial column. Never had his space been more absorbed by local and domestic matters. Woodrow Wilson's wedding was a matter of more comment than any European event. White still more or less subscribed to the theory that a mad dog was loose in the world and that all sane men should shut themselves within their houses. He loathed the war prosperity. As a nation the United States was "rich with blood money." It had "come from the suffering and tragedy of other nations." We had "built up our own wealth by making things to destroy the wealth and lives of others"; and quoting, "Vengeance is mine saith the Lord; I will repay," he asserted that the Lord had "a neat little bill against this United States." [11]

By early 1917, White had concluded that America could not stay out. Wilson had been re-elected president on the slogan, "He Kept Us Out of War," and the Germans interpreted the election a guarantee of American neutrality. Unrestricted submarine warfare and American involvement were but a few weeks away and White in common with most Americans was advocating preparedness though he did not believe war with Germany would entail the use of United States troops. He saw America waging a war of sympathy, carrying food and war supplies to the Allies. Troops, he thought, could not be trained in less than two years and by that time the war would be over.

As America's entrance approached, he lashed out against the Kaiser.

With William, treaties are scraps of paper, and America's entrance into the war should be the death knell of the ruling dynasty in the German Empire. With the Hohenzollerns, not with the German people, is our war. And it should be pushed to an everlasting defeat for that proud house.[12]

Three days later, he thinks the Kaiser after all is not "a bad Deutcher."

He is better than the average crowned head. He is the best of the European rulers—the ablest, the wisest and by far the most demo-

cratic, if not in his instincts, at least in his premonitions. He has
seen social democracy coming, and has met it more than half way.
. . . He has led German economic thought, and has made advantageous compromises with the socialists wherever they would let
him compromise. But the war devil took possession of the time-
spirit of his country, and overcame him.[13]

White was running true to form. He was judging the
news as he saw it day by day, with little thought of what he
had already written. Such editorials have brought letters time
and again from his subscribers asking why he did not make up
his mind. His answer has always been that the *Gazette's* subscribers paid him for his honest opinion on passing events and
what they got was as unbiased and honest as the times permitted. The *Gazette* may praise a man today and condemn him
tomorrow, it may condemn him today and praise him tomorrow; it may even praise and condemn him in two different
articles the same day. The *Gazette* tries to judge a man by the
rightness or wrongness of his position. It seems glaringly in-
consistent "to the mind that wears labels and sends out its
thinking to be done by party, by church, or by groups or
cliques or clans or crowds and factions." [14]

April the third, White wrote a panegyric on Wilson. All
along he had supported the President's diplomatic efforts to
keep the country out of war, the policy of watchful waiting.
Roosevelt, on the other hand, had clamored for action. This
was the one time in the long friendship of the two men that
they did not see alike on major policies. White never mentioned Roosevelt by name, but he talked about "America's hard-
headed believers in action, and action, and always still more
action in crises," [15] chafing and fuming under the Wilson
leadership. On the eve of the war, in a characteristic tribute
to Wilson, he said that the President would have been justified
in going to war three times, on the invasion of Belgium, the
sinking of the *Lusitania,* or the subsequent slaughter of Americans on the high seas. Instead, Wilson had waited until the
country was united, and now we are "fighting not a war of
vengeance, not a war of defense, but a war for democracy, a
war for Christian civilization." [16] White, nonetheless, greeted
a court decision a few days later many times more enthusias-

tically than he did the war declaration. When the Supreme Court upheld the Oregon minimum wage law for women and a maximum ten-hour day for men, he shouted "Glory be!" Not yet had he conceived of the war as a world conflict embracing the progressive principles.

To the war hysteria, White never completely surrendered. He wrote many things to make him blush after the war, but his writings at their worst were sensible compared to the war mania in his state. Kansas had many naturalized Germans and native-born citizens of German extraction. Most of these were thrifty, law-abiding, patriotic farmers. For their nationality they suffered the fruits of fanaticism. Many a German was forced to contribute more than his share to the Liberty Loans and to the Red Cross; many awoke to find their houses or barns smeared with yellow paint. If an oil tank burst, the Germans did it; if a building burned, it was German sabotage. Some one in the next county had adopted Belgian orphans; their hands or their feet had been cut off by the barbarous Huns—but they always lived in the next county. When America entered the war, men like Henry Van Dyke heard "the cry of anguish from the victims of the Hun" and added a stanza to "The Battle Hymn of the Republic," "for God is marching on"; papers like the Kansas City *Star* held German music to be the product of a race of uncivilized monsters; and great orchestra conductors like Walter Damrosch, in deference to public opinion, omitted Wagner. By the end of the war, White had mildly succumbed to the hate propaganda, but only mildly. He cautioned his readers against questioning the loyalty of a German citizen, he gave thanks that the reported attempts to assassinate the Kaiser had failed, he called the spy scares silly, he pleaded for "no coddling" on German music and literature, he resented the throttled press, and he despised the malicious liar. All a liar has to do, he wrote, "is to think about some German, man or woman, that he dislikes, then to tromp on the juice of his lying machine and cut her wide open and wriz." [17]

A few months after America entered the war, the Red Cross Commission sent White and Henry J. Allen to Europe to study conditions on "effectual means of American co-ordination and co-operation in war relief work." White was in Eu-

rope three months, visiting France, Italy, and England. Out
of the observations in these countries came *The Martial Adventures of Henry and Me*.

The book is part novel, part travologue. It was hurriedly
written, almost thrown together. Its purpose made immediate
publication imperative, for the author's object was to give a
preview of the war and an interpretation from the standpoint
of Emporia. Not a line was devoted to the horrors of war, few
to arousing German hatred. Read today, it would appear to
contain not few but many "lines that churn the bile of hate
through the human heart"; read in its time and place, it contained no charges that Americans at large did not accept as
facts.

The Martial Adventures of Henry and Me is a blithe and
guileless story, characteristic of the surface light-heartedness
in which America sent her soldiers abroad to hang the Kaiser.
Its chief characters are two fat, middle-aged, middle-western
Americans, amused at the war show, a bit scared, and conscious of cutting a ridiculous figure. Broad humor character-
izes its pages. A typical example is White's account of their
experiences with their uniforms.

The two buy $17.93 Red Cross uniforms in New York.
In Paris the spectacle of the Red Cross men in military uniforms "that made them look like the lilies of the valley" gives
them "something to think about." Each spends a hundred dollars for a new uniform, "thinking with guilty horror how he
would break the news of that uniform bargain to his wife."
They are ordered to the front, but the new uniforms are not
ready. Each goes to his room after midnight to adorn himself
in his $17.93 habiliments. In ten minutes Henry appears
"caparisoned like a chocolate divinity!" But White's trousers
have a "net deficit of eight tragic inches" in the waist band.

Yet there we were. It was half past twelve. In six hours more we
must be on our way to the front—to the great adventure. Uniforms
were imperative. And there was the hiatus! Whereupon Henry
rose. He rang for the valet; no response. He rang for the tailor;
he was in bed. He rang for the waiter; he was off duty. There was
just one name left on the call card; so Henry hustled me into an
overcoat and rang for the chambermaid! And she appeared as innocent of English as we were of French. It was an awful moment!

But Henry slowly began making gestures and talking in clear-ly e-nun-ci-a-ted tones. . . . The maid became interested. Then he took the recalcitrant trousers, placed them gently but firmly against his friend's heart—or such a matter, showing how far from the ideal they came. Then he laid on the bed a brown woollen shirt, and in the tail of it marked out dramatically a "V" slice about the shape, of an old-fashioned slice of pumpkin pie—a segment ten or a dozen inches wide that would require two hands in feeding. Then he pointed from the shirt to the trousers and then to the ample bosom of his friend, indicating with emotion that the huge pie-slice was to go into the rear corsage of the breeches. It was won-derful to see intelligence dawn in the face of the chambermaid. . . . Suddenly she knew the truth, and it made her free, so she cried, "Wee wee!" . . . At two o'clock she returned with the pumpkin pie slice from the tail of the brown shirt, neatly, but hardly gaudily inserted in the rear waste line of the riding trousers, and we lay down to pleasant dreams; for we found that by stand-ing stiffly erect, by keeping one's tunic pulled down, and by care-fully avoiding a stooping posture, it was possible to conceal the facts of one's double life.[18]

Weeks pass and "Henry and Me" are still at the front. The major, their guide, insists that they go forward to Hill 304. Their moral cowardice overwhelms their physical cow-ardice, and their legs track ahead while their hearts track back.

Nearer and nearer we came to the open field, and by the same token, quicker and nearer and hotter came the German shells. We were continually on the duck. Our progress had an accordion rhythm that made distance come slow. We came to a dead mule in the road. He had been bombed recently, and was not ready for visitors. . . . As we passed the forward reaches of the mule, Henry began his kidding. . . . "Bill," he cried, "if we die we'll at least save our nice new hundred dollar uniforms down there in Paris!"
. . . So we slowly edged by that poor mule; he seemed to be the longest mule we had ever—well, he seemed to be a sort of trans-continental mule, but we finally got past him and came to the edge of the woods. It took about three ducks to twenty yards, and pass-ing the mule we had four downs and no gain. That gave the Ger-mans the ball. So when we got to the edge of the wood and were standing looking into the French trenches and at Hill 304 off at our right . . . the Germans came back with that ball. It came right out of Berlin, too. One could hear it howl as it crossed the Tier-garten and went over Wilhelm Strasse and scream as it whizzed

over Bavaria. There never was another such shell. And we ducked
—all of us. Henry said he never saw me make such a duck—it was
the duck of a life-time. And then that shell landed. It was a whole-
sale hardware store that hit—no retail affair. The sound was awful.
And then something inside of me or outside tore with an awful
rip. We had been reading Dr. Crile's book on the anesthesia of
fear, and suddenly it occurred to me that the shell had hit me and
torn a hole in me and that fear had deadened the pain. Slowly and
in terror my right hand groped back to the place of the wound,
expecting every moment to encounter blood and ragged flesh. We
were still crouched over, waiting for the fountain of junk to cease
spraying. Nearer and nearer came the shrinking fingers to the
wound. They felt no blood, but something more terrible! There,
dangling by its apex, hung that pie-shaped slice of shirt from those
cotton khaki trousers—ripped clear out! And Paris fifty miles
away! [19]

Out of this European trip came White's vision of a new
world. He talked little about fighting a war to end all wars,
little about making the world safe for democracy. But he did
see the triumph of the altruistic spirit. Provided the Allies won
the war, the important changes would be in men's social and
economic relations. The privileged classes, he believed, were
losing their perquisites. "Kings, overlords, potentates, politicians, capitalists, high priests—masters of various kinds" [20]
would find it difficult to regain their lost privileges once the
war was over. The autocracy that lived in Berlin was exactly
the same as the one that lived in Wall Street, in the "city" in
London, in the caste and class interests in France and Italy.
But in Germany alone Junkerdom rested on the divine right
of kings—"the last resort of privilege." In France and Italy
Junkerdom was a "motheaten relic"; in England the caste and
economic privileged classes were rapidly breaking up. In England, especially, he saw fundamental and lasting changes. Ballot reform had come to stay. He called attention to the English Labor Party's demand for the nationalization of railways,
mines, electricity, housing, and land tenure. In wages a new
principle was beginning to prevail. The cost of what seems to
be a decent standard of living, not supply and demand was determining the wage level. Labor was demanding a taxation on
the rich "to bring thir incomes and their holdings only to a
moderate rise above the common level—a rise in some relation

to the actual differences of mind and heart and soul and service
between men. . . ." All this was proof that a new order was
at hand.

In the Allied war organization, White saw the mobiliza-
tion of the spiritual forces. With the passing of the war, this
organization would pass; but democracy would always know
"that it can rise to a divine dignity of courage and sacrifice."
That knowledge of the latent power of men will mean "more
than written laws, more than justice established, more than
wrongs righted in any nation . . ." That organization was
the eternal evidence of the triumph of the spiritual over the
material. In America it represented the culmination of the
American spirit. His second novel, appearing some months
later, ended with the same thought.

. . . Men said: The old America is dead; America is money mad;
America is a charnel house of greed. Millions and millions of men
from all over the earth came to her shores. And the world said:
They have brought only their greed with them. And still the struggle went on. The continent was taken; man abolished the wilderness. A new civilization rose. And because it was strong, the
world said it was not of the old America, but of a new, soft,
wicked order, which wist not that God had departed from it.

Then the new epoch dawned; clear and strong came the call
to Americans to go forth and fight in the Great War—not for
themselves, not for their own glory, nor their own safety, but for
the soul of the world. And the old spirit of America rose and
responded. The long inward struggle, seen only by the wise, only
by those who knew how God's truth conquers in this earth, working beneath the surface, deep in the heart of things, the long inward struggle of the spirit of America for its own was won.[21]

The Martial Adventures appeared in April. Thereafter
White changed little in his point of view, save in his attitude
toward the German nation. By November he was ready to hang
the Crown Prince, Hindenburg, and Ludendorff. The German
nation must be made to suffer for sustaining "these swash-
buckling priests of Baal." [22] He did not mean that Germany
"should pay an eye for an eye." But he did mean "that whatever of physical restitution may be made, whatever of restoration of the wrecked and looted towns of France and Belgium
may be made, Germans should make, and we should have no
nonsense about it." [23]

On November 11, 1918, with Germany beaten and helpless, an armistice ended the war; and the memory of that day
still remains with everyone who lived through it. In Kansas
the news came about four o'clock in the morning, and within a
few minutes in every hamlet and village whistles were blowing,
bells were ringing, horns were going. Everyone was making
a noise with whatever he could lay his hands on. It was a time
of great rejoicing; men who for years had been passing without speaking suddenly found themselves talking like lifelong
friends. But that was but one side of the picture. Before the
morning was over the Kaiser was hanged in effigy and later
burned for good measure. Perhaps those who disposed of the
German Emperor had their tongues in their cheeks; nevertheless, vindicativeness burned in their hearts. William Allen
White differed little from his neighbors. For him the war spirit
had nursed German hatred and Messianic visions. Then suddenly, a strange thing happened. The hatred died, leaving only
the visions.

. . . In truth we have gained little but an opportunity. Men are
only as free as their hearts are kind. If this great war which has
overthrown the kings has also overthrown the selfishness and greed
in human hearts—high and low (for alas, greed is not an upper
class vice exclusively) then we shall be ready for the victory. But
if the war has not purified us, we are not ready. For to make the
world better we must conquer ourselves—our own greed, our own
selfishness, our own tyranny. . . .
    And unless the great war has made us all feel the pull of
brotherhood in our hearts, unless we all feel that we are willing to
compromise the vast differences which men must have living in
civilization, unless we are willing to submit to some injustices for
the larger justice to our neighbors, then we shall soon have the
same old world. But this is a season of almost Messianic hope.
That hope in the heart of humanity indicates a new vision in the
heart of humanity, which would seem to foretell a better day for
the world. And for this hope, even though it shall not be entirely
realized, for the hope that foretells a new heaven and a new earth,
which sooner or later shall come, we should give our thanks
today.[24]

Before Christmas White was on his way to Europe to see
if men had conquered selfishness and greed.

CHAPTER XVII

Has the Human Race Any Intelligence Left?

> Progress was twelve years flowing in. It will take two
> or three more years to run out. Then watch out for the
> backwash. Roll up your pants, O ye of little faith, and
> keep 'em up, even if the sun does burn a little while you
> wait.[1]

T HE SURGE of idealism that sent the United States troops
abroad to fight for the brotherhood of man was not long
in flowing out. America abandoned Europe to her fate
and resumed her policy of isolation. The party in power ignored social justice and followed the star of prosperity. Literature ceased to dramatize age-old ideals and denied the nobility
of man. Legislative councils refused the right of representation
to minorities and ignored industrial disputes. The Ku Klux
Klan arose to malign the Jews, the Negroes, the Catholics, and
the foreign-born. In the industrial turmoil both state and national governments concerned themselves little beyond exercis-
ing the police power, and the people themselves played host to
indifference, intolerance, and bigotry. Such were the years immediately following the armistice.

All this William Allen White militantly opposed. For him
the twenties were the dark years—a period in which he strove
with faith and hope for the old ideals. Buoyed by a robust
optimism, he never admitted defeat; sustained by sturdy faith,
he clutched every evidence of hope. Nontheless "something
awful" had happened in Christendom. It was more than "the
paralysis of commerce," more than "industrial debility," more
than "political reaction and apathy that chokes and poisons the
springs of progress." Man's faith in man was dying. It was
faith "that bellies the sails of commerce when the ship goes
out; faith that honest men will man her, that honest men will
take her cargo, that honest men will send back a decent

gain to the owners." It was faith "that makes men sweat in
industry; faith that their day's work will bring them a decent
living, that their day's planning will yield them a good profit."
It was faith "that holds men together in states . . . faith that
the word of rulers is dependable, faith that the common sense
of the people may be trusted to respond to humanity's decent
needs under government." It was faith "that holds the home
inviolate, and makes the social compact strong and wholesome." [2] This faith had departed from the people, and as he
beheld a wicked and indifferent generation he cried out.

> How long, O Lord, will starvation be met with in-
> difference, greed with complaisance, murder, robbery,
> and arson with cowardice, graft with a sneer, and ha-
> tred and avarice with fawning?
> How long, O Lord, how long before this weary
> world shall turn its face again to the Star? [3]

White saw the backwash begin in Paris. At no time in his
Versailles reports did he condemn the peace treaty so strongly
as he did in the years to come. During the Washington Disarmament Conference he said that the treaty was "so sown
with avarice and with intrigue and with commercial and political and imperial greed that . . . it is the very nest egg of
wars" which "from it even now are hatching hell upon earth
and bad will among men." [4] But though White did not adjudge
the treaty thus severely in its making, no sooner was he in
Paris than he realized that the victorious powers would ignore
the idealism that swept America into the war. In his first press
dispatch, before the treaty makers began, he reported that "on
the face of things, in Europe today, President Wilson's peace
program does not stand a dog's chance." He called attention to
the secret agreements to maintain England's position on the
seas, to guarantee to France the rich coal basin of the Saar, and
to prohibit German fortifications within thirty kilos east of the
Rhine. "The fourteen points of President Wilson," he concludes, "would seem to have merely an academic interest. Yet
they were the basis of the Armistice; but they are scraps of
paper as matters stand at the opening of the glad new year." [5]

Without international justice, he wrote, there can be no
world peace, a statement he was to reiterate in later years. The

conference was hardly well under way before he said that the nations seem to be treating the peace as "a grand grab-game." [6] Eleven days after his first article, he stated that "we haven't told our people the truth: That wars arise from economic causes."

We have not preached the partnership of society to our own people; we have not shown them the close relations between the Kansas hog-raiser and the Italian farmer who needs the Kansas meat; we have not taught our people to think in terms of world needs and world markets.

Without economic justice, he declared, "all the leagues in the world will fail that leave nations cramped beyond their will to stand cramping in economic fields." Peace, he believed, could be attained only by slowly working out "national economic adjustments," which would in turn "prevent war by removing the causes of war." [7] The last thought was the basis of his later support of the League and the World Court. White saw them as instruments for justice. They were an extension of his idea that governments existed to promote human welfare. The League with all its imperfections was a step in the right direction, and any step forward was better than no step at all. Never having believed that any organization would usher in the millennium, he, nevertheless, held that an imperfect organization would work for human betterment if mankind honestly used it.

White's reports are not without vindictiveness. In France "the white scar of ruins stretches like a leprous scale from the mountains to the sea," [8] and on a trip through Germany he saw "all their furnaces ablaze, all their big cities flashing with lights, all their great industries working day and night." The contrast was horrible "to the hours and hours of desolation that we had seen the day before, as we went through France." Then follow the most vengeful lines in his reports:

The peace should not be written until the delegates to the conference see not merely the devastation that is France, but the unpunished Rhineland. They are parts of the same picture.[9]

Of all he wrote of the Peace Conference, his own paper considered these lines most important. Whatever he said about the treaty being unjust, whatever he said about the conference being a grab bag, whatever he said about international peace being impossible without an equitable distribution of the world's resources—all was printed as routine matter. But these few vindictive lines, his paper boldly displayed. White, however, did not know what to do about punishing Germany. He said the Allies "seem to have lost the economic victory, the thing for which the war was fought." [10] Germany in some way would pay the bill for damages, then "start in the race for the world's markets abreast with England and ahead of France." [11] Of this he was sure. The equitable distribution of fats, oils, meats, and wheat, "rather than guns, will determine the peace of the world for the next hundred years." [12]

The disillusionment that began in Paris continued in America. At first White stood with Wilson in his fight with the Senate. The League of Nations was "not much of a league, but the best of its kind possible, and if it is a shadow of a league it is the shadow of a rising sun." [13] At the outset he saw partisan politics as the real danger to ratification. The Republicans, he wrote, cannot get together on a program of social, industrial, and economic reconstruction of the country, "so they are intent on discrediting the President," even though "they are jeopardizing the peace of the world." "It is small business," he asserted, "and what is more, it will wipe the Republican party off the map. For one more smashing defeat, and that defeat upon a fake issue, will start the daisies sprouting out of the toes of what was once a grand old party." [14] As the Senate fight wore on, White, believing that the Allies would accept America on her own terms, wanted Wilson to compromise. Not that he favored reservations. He saw no possibility of ratification on any other basis. But White never attacked Wilson in print. As the President's defeat became obvious, Wilson's tragedy became mankind's.

He, the first of all world statesmen at the end of a ghastly world catastrophe, tried to make a settlement based upon justice, not on force, upon what should be rather than what could be. Either the League of Nations will rise during this century and work for peace on earth and good will among men, or it will fail, and in its failure will herald in such an epoch of horror that humanity in its decay will look back to the glorious dream which this man dreamed as the beginning of the wreck of nations and crash of civilizations.

In either event, Wilson's name is safe. He aspired greatly; he strove with what strength he had, and with what weapons God gave him. He lost; his powers were not sufficient for his task. His hand was not as strong as his heart. He called the spirits from the vasty deep; but alas, they did not come. His loss is mankind's loss. But even if he lost, he lost, but losing won.

He is not the first Moses left in the wilderness, even though he stood by the burning bush; nor the first Isaiah to preach righteousness vainly to a wicked and perverse generation.[15]

White long held the delusion that America would go into the League. After the Republicans came into power he believed that the will of those Republicans who were for participation would prevail. He wrote many articles citing facts that indicated America was edging in by the back door. The net result of the Washington Disarmament Conference seemed to him to be the beginning of an association of nations, and the later Kellogg Pact appeared to have put the United States in for all practical purposes. As the issue faded, so faded the League editorials. He wrote finis to the question in a collection of his editorials appearing in 1937.

. . . I have a persistent feeling that maybe our entrance into the League with obvious reservations would have made a different world. But also only maybe. History is written in the indicative mood—never in the subjunctive.[16]

The World War gave White an international point of view, but this enlarged outlook never interfered with his interest in domestic problems. The last time he saw Roosevelt the ex-President was propped up in a hospital bed drafting a reconstruction program to submit to the Republican Party, and during the twenties White thought of himself as a Roosevelt Republican. Justice was "more important than prosperity; . . . our social and economic system is full of crass injustices which can be removed, but only by making those who take what they do not earn give it back to those who earn what they do not get." [17] He suggested a program for the Republicans. "Old issues are gone," he wrote, "and old leaders are passing and those who tarry are outworn." He did not want the campaign waged on the obvious mistakes of the Democrats. "War is waste, and when a nation goes to war, it goes to waste."

He outlined his policies under ten major heads. (1) Write the platform without reference to campaign pledges. (2) Solve the railroad question by establishing a unified system of transportation under private ownership through strict public control of stocks, rates, and services. (3) Give labor a larger part than it now has in industrial management, shortening the hours of labor, improving the conditions of labor, increasing the wages of labor, and deepening the responsibilities of labor for the out-put of our industries. (4) Put the tariff out of politics forever by increasing the authority of the tariff commission. (5) Put all manufacturers of food after it leaves the farm and all dealers of food under government license, regulating their profits and directing their necessary monopoly. (6) Demand a modification of the League of Nations so that our responsibility for the peace of the world will give us an effective control proportionate to our world power in maintaining the peace of the world. (7) Nationalize our natural resources, coal and oil and minerals, and operate them for the common good. (8) Make our government more responsible to the will of the people. "The spectacle of a President discredited at an election speaking for the American people for two years after his loss of confidence is as unthinkable as the spectacle of a discredited Congress sitting four months after it was defeated." (9) Reclaim millions of arid acres and give them to the soldiers, all watered or drained and ready for occupancy. (10) Look after the disabled soldier, seeing that he is re-educated, re-employed, and that his family is cared for.[18]

Will Hays, chairman of the Republican National Committee, made White chairman of the committee on social reforms and a member of the committee on labor, capital, and industrial relations. The tentative platform which White helped draw up was headed by Ogden Mills; when Senator James E. Watson defeated Mills for chairman of the resolutions committee, the platform was abortive. White, however, was a delegate to the convention and one of the twelve men on the subcommittee who drafted the convention platform.

The 1920 convention was the single time in White's life when he felt the occasion important enough to stand as a delegate. In announcing his candidacy, he told the voters he wanted to be a delegate—just that. When he was elected by a substantial margin, he paid his opponent a compliment as characteristic of its author as it was of its subject.

W. N. Smelser made a gallant but losing fight for delegate to the national Republican convention in the primaries in Lyon County. He played fair and was entitled to more votes than he got. His vote in his home ward certainly was complimentary, and he is not the kind of a man to forget it. It stood against the current running in the town and county toward his opponent. Smelser was greatly handicapped by the fact that he had no newspaper. The result would have been otherwise if he had owned a newspaper. For it is not the fact that a newspaper gets a man so much more or better publicity, that counts in an editor's favor. It is the fact that every day in the year a newspaper is doing something for someone, for the town, for the interests of a community, for various interests which are grateful. These assembled gratitudes make political majorities which go to editors.

Mr. Smelser need never fear the editor of the Gazette as a competitor again. This happens just once in a life time. It's like the man who had the baby! He wouldn't take a million for it nor have another for the national debt! And after that no other man ever did.[19]

In the platform drafting White advocated four planks, prohibition, the Kansas Industrial Court, anti-military training, and federal aid to maternity centers established by counties and states. On all four he lost. He supported planks favoring trade with Soviet Russia, collective bargaining, federal control of hours of women in intensive industry, machinery for free arbitration of labor disputes, old age pensions, social insurance, taking the tariff out of politics, and condemning the New York legislature for expelling its Socialist members. Had he had his way the nation would not have waited twelve to fifteen years before some of these policies were put into effect. During the Teapot Dome scandals he was writing that "the responsible leaders of both parties are out of touch with the people." They "are still fighting the windmills of a radicalism which the people generally accept."[20]

Harding's nomination was "an awful pill" for White, and Coolidge's little more palatable. He was to have given Coolidge official notification of his nomination. When the time arrived he begged to be excused. Once he voted with the Kansas delegation for Harding to break the deadlock. But he refused to march with the Kansans to deliver their banner to the Ohio delegation, and on the last ballot after Harding was nominated he broke away and voted for Herbert Hoover. Harding was "exactly the kind of a Republican who makes me see red." [21] A few weeks after the convention he stated in an address at the Emporia State Teachers College that he told his fellow delegates if Harding were elected he would disgrace the Republican Party. For once his prophet's license covered more than he suspected.

The 1920 political conventions left the Emporia editor in a dilemma. The "big senate bosses" named the candidate for the Republicans; the "big booze bosses" named the candidate for the Democrats.

The Republican issue cannot be prohibition; it cannot be social and industrial justice; nor can it be the promise of any new order. It will be "back to normal," the "return to the constitution," and the McKinley sort of thing, plus a rather meaningless "Americanism," which may mean deporting undesirable aliens, or twisting the lion's tail, or invading Mexico, or adding reservations to the covenant which sound well in school readers.[22]

As for the Democrats, the Wilson followers organized the convention, wrote the platform, but had been "unable to wring out of him the one word necessary to nominate McAdoo, and make the victory for the administration complete." The nomination of Cox and the Democratic platform "written in characteristically vague Wilsonesque, meaning all things to all men, and anything under any leader" completed the anti-Wilson victory.

Liberalism has departed from the Democratic party, and Murphy, Taggart, Nugent, the wets, the pre-Wilsonite democracy and the anti-Wilson bitter-enders are in control . . .[23]

Nor did the prospects for a third party offer any hope. "The American people are so party minded that a third party will poll only a respectable minority and that minority will be divided between Debs and the Forty-eighters." His final word on the conventions was that "the poor fish who really thought the war was to usher in a new era wherein the relations of men would move somewhat closer to justice, are permitted to go out and count the stars or vote for some pink party for pale people which promises the perpetual sunrise." [24]

The *Gazette's* editor, seeing nothing better, stayed with the Republicans. His paper endorsed their ticket, but almost avoided the national campaign. When Harding said something that seemed hopeful, he had his praise; but the old progressive enthusiasm was missing in White's editorials, not to return until the nomination of Hoover in 1928. White interpreted Harding's victory as "a barbaric yawp of enraged democracy at the incompetency of the Democratic party." Let us hope "he will face forward and forget old 'normalcy.' "

The American people have short memories. They will forget Wilson if Harding gives them something else disagreeable to kick about. In the laps of the gods lies the hot end of the poker. Harding must be careful not to touch it.[25]

After Harding's term began, the Administration almost convinced White that he had been mistaken about the President. Harding promised in his inaugural address to take the government out of business. Then he appointed a Secretary of Agriculture who supported the bill regulating the packers, and a Secretary of Interior who favored putting coal mines under federal control and regulation, and Harding himself endorsed a bill granting federal aid to hospitals taking maternity cases. Despite his appointment of Daugherty, White believed the President might fool his critics. By the end of his first year, however, Washington was not an edifying spectacle to the Emporia editor.

Here we have the power of the greatest government on earth, in the time of the world's mightiest crisis, dominated not by seers and philosophers, not by impassioned altruists, not even by practical students of affairs, but by more or less exalted ward heelers, county bosses, State leaders, and congressional directors of the Republican party.[26]

When a year and a half of the Harding administration had passed, White, on the basis of the President's record, made a personal appraisal. Harding was "a gentle, sincere, fair-minded man with courage and without pretense." His greatest drawback was lack of information and a limited background. "Roosevelt and Wilson knew or knew who knew books where they could find out the truth." But to Harding "the fundamentals that make big issues are new to him." [27] When the scandals broke after his death, White still believed that he was honest and courageous, but "didn't have the sabbe." [28]

America's aloofness in world affairs and the Administration's refusal to launch an aggressive social program were not so disturbing to White as the prevailing mood of the people both in the United States and abroad. At home, isolationism and do-nothingism were the negative side of the picture; rabid nationalism, disfranchisement of minorities, race riots, murder and death the positive. Organized murder in the South, massacre and civil war in Illinois, denial of representation to Socialists in New York, restriction of free speech in Kansas, and deportation of undesirable aliens by the government—all seemed to White a reversion to force where reason should prevail. In every instance he condemned force and pled for reason. In America, he wrote, "all that is left is doubt, negation, a passion to sit still and let things happen. And when bad things happen and keep happening, still we do not rouse." [29] Internationally the world presented an insane spectacle. Europe was "water-logged in suspicion and hate." Great Britain "tried to violate the decencies by inordinate demands for contributions from Germany, and now finds a bankrupt continent slowly lurching into anarchy." France "started in to make Germany helpless against France," and succeeded only in "justifying the French fear that Germany is implacable." America "sought to withdraw her moral support from the world and lost her moral sense at home." [30]

But two years had passed since the armistice ended the war that was to end all wars; and White, with his vision blasted of a world wherein reason reigned, was saying that "President Wilson had Billy Sundayed us into a millennial ecstasy." [31] Force had availed humanity nothing, but he never doubted the triumph of the altruistic spirit. Yet in the face of what had happened how could a nation with any sanity ever go to war again for the freedom of man? Had "the human race any intelligence left?" [32]

CHAPTER XVIII

The Other Side of Main Street

. . . We must not be sorry for the poor. We must not be sorry for any one. Pride under the new dispensation is bad enough; pride in the town, pride in the state, pride in the country, pride in the heroic patience of humanity; pride in the slow groping of mankind through the dark toward justice, toward that bungling institutionalized kindness called democracy—bah, that's the delusion of the cheerful idiot![1] But bad as pride is, wicked and weak as it may be, it is infinitely preferable to pity!

DURING the World War the progressive policies went into temporary eclipse. With the nation operating on a war basis, prices of farm products shot skyward. The farmer celebrated the new day by buying a Ford and mortgaging his home to make a down-payment on the quarter section across the road. For once his products bought more than the other fellow's; at last they had taken their rightful and permanent place in the scale of values. While he grumbled a bit at the government for setting the price of wheat, he, nevertheless, increased his acreage and stretched his credit to buy the new binder. Labor, too, was enjoying an undreamed affluence. Jobs went begging; jobs were to be had for the asking. The lowly farm hand, who a few years before had been glad to hire his services for a dollar and a quarter a day, now sniffed at anything less than five; if he knew the knack of stacking wheat, he could demand and get eight or ten. The village laborer drove his new car four blocks to work, then spent ten dollars of his weekly earnings for a striped silk shirt and eighteen for a pair of shiny yellow shoes. The "have nots" were now the "haves." He who did not work was an I. W. W. or something worse.

The so-called underprivileged classes had come into their own. The old order was gone; prosperity reigned in its stead. Even the old-fashioned progressive who clung to his theories that all was not yet right in the economic world could see great cause for rejoicing.

With the decline of progressivism passed also its reflection in literature. William Allen White's *In the Heart of a Fool* was a belated problem novel, appearing after the American people had lost their taste for political and economic reform. Except Upton Sinclair, American novelists in the post-war years shared the quiet complacency of the American people in ignoring the revelations of the Harding scandals, the concentration of wealth, and the orgy of speculation. Novelists left industrial, social, and economic reforms to the politicians and fell to berating middle-class life. Critics in and out of fiction ridiculed Victorianism, Puritanism, optimism, thrift, morality, industry, and conformity.

In one of its aspects, the novel of this period reflected and catered to the revolt of the younger generation. This was the era of flaming youth, of rolled hose, short skirts, bobbed hair, necking, hip flasks, and companionate marriages. Youth violated time-honored conventions; and, in reply to the fuming of the elder generation, said that the elders had got the world in a hell of a mess and so far as they were concerned they were going to live their own lives. Moralists moralized, editors editorialized, and parents grumbled, but youth traveled its own way. When the dean of women in the Emporia State Teachers College issued orders that all women students should wear dresses long enough to cover their knees when they sat down, the Kansas editors welcomed the decree with more commendatory comment than any other act of the school in that decade. Another Emporia college, seeking to increase its enrollment, circulated a placard bearing the picture of a lovely girl with a caption stating "She Will Be Safe at C. of E." However the advertising appealed to the parents, youth looked on and giggled, continued to worship at H. L. Mencken's shrine and to read *The Plastic Age, The Hard-Boiled Virgin, Flaming Youth,* and Shakespeare reprinted under the jazzy titles of a Kansas publisher.

This phase of the revolt the *Gazette's* editor beheld with twinkling and indulgent eyes. He knew the latest slang before most of the youngsters who thought it smart; and having been brought up in a country town familiar with the venery of the hayloft, the haystack, the livery stable, and the old-fashioned saloon, he could hardly be shocked by lascivious fiction. For twenty-five years he himself had sniped at Puritan prudery. Ten years before he had shuddered "to think of the state of mind of people who make the sex relations of plants or animals the subject of their modest blushes." His paper had never pretended "that the doctor brings the babies, that there is anything essentially nasty in recognizing the source of the old sow's pigs, the old cat's kittens, or the old hen's chickens." All facts of life were beautiful. Good morals were "not conserved by being nasty nice" [2] any more than by a particular mode of dress; and the Emporia editor refused to be startled even when writers hung their dirty linen out in the front yard for all the world to see. With certain other aspects of the literary revolt, White was not amused.

The post-war years brought into bold relief an assault on village life. Those who had written about the country town were said to have depicted it as "a place of idyllic felicities." Material happiness was matched "only by its depth of spiritual satisfaction." It knew "neither avaricious millionaire nor the lean and dispossessed proletariat." All its worthy citizens lived "in comfort; none in want, none in luxurious idleness." Its people dwelt together, "happy in the performance of the daily round of homely tasks." Religion was "a matter of simple faith, unspoiled by doubt and exemplified by good works"; and in their social and political life the villagers respected "the tenets and practices of primitive American democracy." [3] Such, it was said, had been the picture of the country town from time immemorial. So had its defenders, past and present, depicted it; and except for a few dissents from Mark Twain, two major protests from Ed. Howe and Edgar Lee Masters, all its delineators were in accord.

During the early twenties the attack on the country town grew into a major offensive. Critics denounced village thrift and industry as the cloak of avarice and cupidity. They pro-

claimed its friendliness the mere snooping of gossipy neighbors;
its optimism, the back-slapping and glad-handing of shallow-
minded Rotarians and narrow-minded Methodists. The villagers themselves were dull, hypocritical, ignorant, and intolerant. Village life instead of being noble, kind, beautiful, and
generous was narrow, provincial, unimaginative, and sordid.
So said the critics who essayed to inform the world of their
new discoveries.

If William Allen White is to be classified with either
school, he must be placed among the defenders; but his writings
embrace the thought of both. *The Court of Boyville* shows the
happy, democratic life in a pioneer Kansas village. *Boys—Then
and Now* portrays the sordid environment of the same period;
and according to Vernon Parrington, *In the Heart of a Fool*
suggests Sinclair Lewis. Some *In Our Town* sketches are
stories of idyllic beauty; others, suggesting later writers, de-
lineate the disintegration of character. White, to whom some
things are wholly white and others wholly black, never saw
all things wholly one or the other. What distinguishes him
from the realistic school is a belief in moral order in the universe—its violation brings its own retribution, its acceptance
its own spiritual rewards. For humanity in the large there is
hope; it may choose a more abundant way of life or it may
continue to live in baseness and vulgarity.

Those aspects of village life at which the Menckens,
Lewises, and Andersons directed their barbs, the Emporia
editor maintained were not peculiar to the country town. Merchants from Middletowns rush to New York, "throng the
great hotels, crowd the streets, dash around in taxis, maintain
the clearing house balance and furnish the raw material for
the great Rube skinning industry by which New York holds
first place among the cities of the earth." Then the country
man whose hide has been "gently but firmly peeled" takes his
experience home "and peels the hide off his fellows in the
county seat and they in turn skin and tan the villagers and the
farmers and the workers, who, in their innocence, pass the
skinning knife dexterously back over the rest of us and so
the balance of nature is maintained." [4] New York plays host to
the American Bankers Association, whirls its members about

to gawk at the points of interest, packs them into hotels, and stuffs them with bad food and dull speeches—even as Emporia entertains the Kansas bankers. New York's chamber of commerce clamors for new industries like a thousand Emporias. New York's tabloids and columnists peep, tattle, and gossip like the old village hags. Thus the Emporia editor answers the charges of the village beraters. The pot is calling the kettle black.

White's brief for the village hardly extends beyond asserting that what the villagers should be ashamed of is, unfortunately, characteristic of all American life. If Emporia with its fifteen thousand found itself unable to pay for four symphony concerts a year, New York with its millions stooped to begging the country yokels to send in their quarters to perpetuate the Metropolitan Opera Company. Though Emporia has, on the basis of population, more bookstores than New York,[5] still Emporia and the nation at large are illiterate compared to some European countries. Though Kansas with fewer than two million population has produced four notable books in a single year, still Kansans are an inarticulate people.

Nothing is more gorgeous in color and form than a Kansas sunset; yet it is hidden from us. The Kansas prairies are as mysterious and moody as the sea in their loveliness, yet we graze them and plow them and mark them with roads and do not see them. The wind in the cottonwoods lisps songs as full of meaning as those the tides sing, and we are deaf. The meadow lark, the red bird, the quail live with us and pipe to us all through the year, but our musicians have not returned the song. The wide skies at night present the age-old mystery of life, in splendor and baffling magnificence, yet only one Kansas poet, Eugene Ware, has ever worn Arcturus as a bosom pin. The human spirit—whatever it is in God's creation—here under these winds and droughts and wintry blasts, here under these drear and gloomy circumstances of life, has battled with ruthless fate as bravely and as tragically as Laocoon; yet the story is untold, and life no richer for the nobility that has passed untitled in marble or in bronze or in prose. Surely the righteousness which exalts a nation does not also blind its eyes and cramp its hands and make it dumb that beauty may slip past unscathed. Surely all joy, all happiness, all permanent delight that restores the soul of man, does not come from the wine, women, and song, which Kansas frowns upon.

Yet why—why is the golden bowl broken, the pitcher at the fountain broken, and in our art the wheel at the cistern still? This question is not peculiarly a Kansas question. It is tremendously American.[6]

Among the realistic writers of this decade Sinclair Lewis was White's favorite. His enthusiasm equalled that of Lewis's indiscriminate worshipers. When *Main Street* appeared, he bought forty copies to present to friends. He hailed it as "a most glorious book," said every American should read it, and ranked it with *A Hazard of New Fortunes, The Scarlet Letter,* and *The Breadwinners*—"the great novels of American life."

And especially should Emporia read it—and all the thousands of Emporias in this country; towns that because they have left "Main Street" and come into the country club status and the younger divorce set, and a community house, and organized charity and half a dozen community activities relative to music, the drama, playgrounds and civic beauty, think therefore that they have reason to rest and be proud. The journey is only well begun. Contentment is more wicked than red anarchy. And if reading "Main Street" will make us pick up our burden and go forward—and it surely will, we should vote bonds to distribute "Main Street" in every home in town, and compel its reading in the public schools.[7]

Nor did the subsequent squabble over whether or not Lewis had truthfully sketched midwestern life lessen his enthusiasm. Two years later, when *Babbitt* appeared, White said, "Most readers will hate the book. But the worse they hate it, the more they should read it."

It is not the truth any more than "Main Street" was the truth. But man! man!—it does assemble a lot of ugly essential and challenging facts about modern life. These facts are part of the truth about our times, big universal facts as true on the Avenue Victor Hugo or William-strasse or Picadilly Circus as they are of American life. Doubtless the Jews of Judea hated Jeremiah. But it was Jeremiah or a heathen conquest. He saved the Jews. Sinclair Lewis is one of the major prophets of our times, a Jeremiah probably, but Heaven sent. If we heed his lamentations, we are saved. If we ignore it, we are gone.[8]

Lewis leveled his attack on ways of life which White believed to be strangling America. Hence White's enthusiasm. Babbitt was "groping through a sordid wilderness of substantial things, luxuries, pomps, honors, fastness, to find his lost soul." His home, as homes had been made, failed him. His business, as business had been made, palled. His love for woman staled; and religion he found "as gross as his business and his mistresses." The tragedy of such an "agonized, stunted spirit searching pitifully for the image of its Maker . . . should make man, clattering futilely among the machinery of civilization stop, look and listen before proceeding upon his weary, useless way." [9] Babbitt's world had cramped and dwarfed his soul; John Barclay's way of life had warped and blunted his sense of justice. Both were a warning to a self-satisfied generation. Though their purpose differed, both men had attacked conditions leading to similar ends.

White rebelled when critics asserted that the realistic writers had told the truth about the country town; he maintained they had told but half the truth. The country town was not Utopia, "for Utopia is the hay on the end of the stick before the donkey's nose, moving forward as he strains under his load to get his heart's desire." [10] But the American country town was much like the Utopia of the mid-Victorian dream. White had beheld a miracle in his own state. Born in a poverty stricken pioneer village, he had seen this same village grow in material comforts where its inhabitants enjoyed luxuries unimagined by ancient kings. Born in an era that marked the end of Negro slavery, he had seen the spirit that threw off the shackles of slavery establish practices and institutions that made for human welfare. He marveled in the spirit and accomplishments of his people. He was unashamed of his fondness for his town, unashamed of his pride in his state. Needful and wholesome as the Lewises and Andersons and Dreisers were, they had given but a snapshot from a wapper-jawed camera. *Winesburg, Ohio* had caught the town dump and missed the park, *Main Street* had been "written in ignorance of the tremendous forces that make for righteousness in every American town," [11] *An American Tragedy* had transcribed the stenographic reports of a dirty murder trial.

The tiffs of White and Mencken were mostly a battle of words. When Mencken charged that the "Bible Belt" was "inhabited by stupid yokels, two-thirds of whom are benighted and miserable, uncivilized barbarians; preyed upon by two gangs of grafters, professional politicians of a peculiarly vicious type and crossroads ecclesiastics who are even worse," the Emporia editor answered in kind. He professed his fondness for "old Henry Mencken," then declared him to be "the top-sergeant of all the literary drill masters" whose job it was "to hang up his 'Bible-Belt' dummy and to snarl and show his teeth and roar while he jabs his bayonet into the dummy's belly for the instruction and edification of the recruits." [12] White enjoyed the pyrotechnics of Mencken, but rejected his philosophical credo. Mencken, Dreiser, and their colleagues reminded him of the antics of the little boy who wants to act bad. He thumbs his nose, writes naughty things on the sidewalks and fences, and says "yah, yah, yah" through his nose. These writers had represented a part of life, but they believed nothing and did it sadly. Their writings offered little beyond a moment of novelty—no purpose for being, no future for man. The whole group was the phenomenon of a period like Congreve's and his crowd who performed after the Restoration.

The fundamental weakness of the realists' attack on the country town was that they were seeing it from a car window, through the pages of a fundamentalist sectarian paper, or through personal experiences fifteen to twenty years earlier. When they were not giving a one-sided view of the small town, they were depicting a mode of life that had largely passed away. Take music, for example. Bernard DeVoto writing in *Harper's* in 1940 on the passing of main street was agreeably surprised to find high-school students in a drugstore at Council Grove, Kansas, talking about symphony records being distributed through a Kansas City firm. That the radio did much in the twenties to popularize good music is beyond dispute. But whether the tempo of appreciation speeded up or slowed down among high school students after 1920 is debatable. Had DeVoto been in Emporia in the spring of 1920 he would have found twenty-five hundred high school students participating in a week-long music festival. Students were playing solos and performing in groups numbering more than a hundred. Special trains had carried the young musicians in some cases more than a hundred and fifty miles. Emporia was then only one of a half

dozen such centers in Kansas, and so great had been the spread
of music in the schools that fifteen years earlier only in rare
cases could high schools furnish their own music at their commencement exercises.

For Emporia, which has the reputation of being a typical
country town, the radio and sound pictures have been a mixed
blessing. During the twenties world-famous artists made the
town. Anna Pavlowa, Ruth St. Dennis, Ted Shawn, Jane Cowl,
Ruth Chatterton, Ethel Barrymore, Otis Skinner, Harry
Lauder, Fritz Kreisler, the St. Louis and Minneapolis symphonies, dozens of choruses, bands, and musical comedies were
appearing. Fifteen years later the movie and radio had cut
down these attractions sixty per cent.

In the matter of observing Sunday, the realists were fond
of picturing midwestern communities dominated by preachers
and blue laws. Had one traveled across Kansas on a Sunday
afternoon in the twenties he would have seen groups of villagers and farmers every few miles playing baseball, but almost
wholly as an amateur game. In Emporia the picture houses
would have been closed, but that evening in two churches he
would have found, instead of a sermon, a movie, sometimes of
none too sacred a character. What the church people seemed
to object to was commercializing Sunday, not to games or
shows. For when Sunday was commercialized someone had to
work and they were against any unnecessary labor on Sunday.
The so-called Kansas blue law was one which forbade Sunday
labor.

The average realistic writer could have cut far deeper had
he been more observant of surface manifestations. Instead of
talking about cotton hose which disappeared with the war, the
merchant's wares which were being bought in New York by
department heads, and revival meetings which were then mainly
a thing of the past, he might have concentrated on growing
materialism. In that, Kansas was one with the rest of the
country. She was proud that she had a greater percentage of
farm boys and girls in high school than any other state. She
did not confess that the farmer sent his sons and daughters to
high school that they might make more money with less work;

she said nothing about merchants promoting new high schools to keep farmers from going to other towns to trade.

White's fundamental objection to the realists was that they denied the nobility of man. "About every other generation," he wrote, "along comes a group of bright young men in the writing game and discovers that beneath the clothes of men are the bodies of men."

Aha, they declare in joy upon their peaks in Darien: behold, man has intestines and means for reproducing his kind! This Jack Horner school of literature, which pulls out the preadamic plums from the puddings of humanity, and says What a big boy am I, is no new school. It is just ignorant. It can see nothing in man but his stomach and the caprices of his affections. Upon these things, but always above them, the whole journey of man from the crotch of the palm tree to the crumbling of the Saint-Mihiel sector has been made.[13]

The man of biology should not be forgotten, White contended, but "to ignore the social man is gross and fantastic ignorance." Among the men and women of Lewis' stories, "nobility is wanting." Babbitt would have been noble if he could, "but life penned him up and in his cage he paces like a wild thing, typical of humanity in our modern world, dreaming fatuously of a freedom that it can never know." [14] Human life was more than a "mechanical process."

Convince man it is and you rob him of his faith, hope, and love . . . One thing has persisted through all man's journey in this wilderness ever since he came down from the trees. That is his inextinguishable optimism, his unswerving hope, his unfailing faith. This faith and hope in the last period of his journey for two thousand brief years in the long millennial procession, have flowered into a slowly growing love of its kind, tolerance for its weaknesses, belief in its strength. By hooking up his growing social altruism man is building a civilization in which he is using more justice than ever was used on earth before. Man's growing belief in his own essential nobility in the last two thousand years is welding a chain of faith in the wise and benevolent purposes of his god. Some time as he sees farther into matter with the telescope and the microscope and with the cat eyes of science which peer into the dark places, man will throw that chain on to some great wheel of life and pull humanity out of its low estate into another and higher plane of life. To keep man's faith in his destiny alive through the creation of beauty, and so to urge man on to the Kingdom of God, is the purpose of art.[15]

White believed the popularity of the realistic writers to be a result of the World War. The western world "had gone through the Great War, killing, lying, murdering, stealing, and everything, greatly to its own discredit." It had "lost every sort of belief in the nobility of man." We saw that man "was a rattling good machine, that if you punched him here he would react there, and in a general way that accounted for everything that we could see in our philosophy." Ours, for the time being, "was the creed of the crapshooter." We "took a chance when we should have taken council." We "read the stars and wept;" and having nothing else to do "turned to Sherwood Anderson and psyched ourselves into his way of thinking, or perhaps, he, being an artist, took the color of his environment." [16]

About 1925 the popularity of the realists began to wane. While the vogue for their writings declined the appetite for biography increased. Perhaps the reading public, tired of stories about the futility of life, again craved romance and idealism; for every biography in a certain measure is a success story. Even the post-war debunkers had to have a subject worth writing about to justify their labors, and the more they studied their man the more they rationalized his conduct. The biography of this period did not subscribe to the story of the cherry tree and the hatchet; but, nevertheless, its subject emerged a hero. He did not turn out to be a bum and a stinker as did the men and women in fiction.

White's desertion of fiction for biography and history was natural and inevitable. His novels were a dramatization of the wisdom of the ages as reflected in the Ten Commandments, the Beatitudes, and the Golden Rule. Virtue was rewarded, not with material but with spiritual satisfaction. Vice was punished by death or remorse or spiritual atrophy. This type of fiction was as much outmoded in 1920 as the romances of Sir Walter Scott. By this time the editor of the *Gazette* who had embarked upon a literary career a quarter of a century earlier, was a national figure. Though his interest in literature had never lagged, a single editorial had sealed his fate. For twenty-five years he had observed and taken part in the national scene. Why should one trouble himself to write about a fictitious world when mankind's heroes stood at one's elbows? To him Theodore Roosevelt and Woodrow Wilson embodied the idealism which he had sought to convey in his fiction. With idealism in fiction gone, it was inevitable that his first two biographies should be lives of these two men.

CHAPTER XIX

Mary White

Probably if her father has any sort of lasting fame beyond the decade following his death, it will come from this editorial. I shall go as far as I go, which very likely is only a little distance, along the path where Mary's hand may lead me. That also is enough fame for me.[1]

MARY WHITE, the little khaki-clad girl with the flashing black eyes, the long pigtails, the red hair ribbon, and the red cotton handkerchief around her neck, was one of the most familiar figures in Emporia. Townspeople knew her in many situations. She would drive the family Dodge to Sixth and Commercial, stop in front of Charley O'Brien, traffic cop and friend of all children, and subject him to a good-natured harangue; she would walk down the street nodding to everyone and whistling like a thrush; she would play with Negro children and let them ride her pony as readily as the white; she would fill a fountain pen with skunk oil and barely escape getting expelled from school; she would carry some foul-smelling acid from the school laboratory into a department store and all but run everyone out; she would do her Sunday School exercise with obvious irreverence to her teacher and as obviously show her displeasure when someone spoke slightingly of religion; she would accept a dare at the drop of a hat, being a veritable daredevil.

The strongest blood in her veins was that of her mother's Kentucky ancestors. The Lindsays always had horses, and Mary had one from the time she was big enough to ride. Ultimately, her every interest ran to her horse. "Mother," her brother Bill once said, "you'll never be the grandmother of a child; you'll be the grandmother of a horse." But no amount of teasing from Bill, whom she idolized, could dampen her ardor for her horse. She started out with a burro, which was followed by a Shetland pony. The pony, like the burro, belonged to all the neighborhood children; and since the Whites lived next door to "nigger-town," Negro children were always riding the pony. When it came to choosing between getting to dinner on time and letting a youngster ride his turn, Mary was late and endured the punishment. Her parents were never able to devise any scheme to get Mary to her meals when a group of children were playing with her pony.

When Mary outgrew the pony, her parents got her a beautiful, black-satin horse. This was her reckless age; "Black Satin" was high spirited, and she narrowly escaped injury or death several times. Once as she was racing across the Santa Fe tracks on Exchange Street, she failed to see an approaching train. The horse whirled and ran with the train. Another time as she was racing with two companions, she came to a bridge so narrow that the three could not cross abreast. Mary's horse leaped the ravine. These escapes led her parents to get her a safer, quieter horse. Even then she escaped serious injury at least twice—when a car ran into her horse, and again when the horse slipped and fell on the street car tracks as she, on a dare, was riding it without a bridle down Commercial Street. With such a record it would be natural to assume that Mary met death in a reckless moment, but the assumption would be wrong; the daredevil period of her life was then in the past.

From the moment the fatal accident occurred, everyone feared Mary's injury grave. She was taken home and city officials stopped all traffic in the White neighborhood and telephone officials cut off calls to the home. Mrs. White was the only other immediate member of the family in Emporia; Bill was in Harvard and White was in the East on business. Neither was able to reach home before the end came, though the accident occurred on Tuesday evening and Mary lived until early Friday morning.

For some, the sudden death of a person near to them brings suffering so deep that their minds and body seem unequal to the shock. Of such is William Allen White, and perhaps it was this suffering linked to the reporter's iron will that produced his greatest editorial. On the morning following the funeral, for the first time in memory, the *Gazette* staff saw the doors closed that led into the editor's office. William Allen White had shut himself away from the world to write the simple story of his daughter's life.

The Associated Press reports carrying the news of Mary White's death declared that it came as the result of a fall from a horse. How she would have hooted at that! She never fell from a horse in her life. Horses have fallen on her and with her—"I'm always trying to hold 'em in my lap," she used to say. But she was proud of few things, and one of them was that she could ride anything that had four legs and hair. Her death resulted not from a fall but from a blow on the head which fractured her skull, and the blow came from the limb of an overhanging tree on the parking.

The last hour of her life was typical of its happiness. She came home from a day's work at school, topped off by a hard grind with the copy of the High School Annual, and felt that a ride would refresh her. She climbed into her khakis, chattering to her mother about the work she was doing, and hurried to get her horse and be out on the dirt roads for the country air and the radiant green fields of the spring. As she rode through the town on an easy gallop she kept waving at passers-by. She knew everyone in town. For a decade the little figure in the long pigtail and the red hair ribbon had been familiar on the streets of Emporia, and she got in the way of speaking to those who nodded at her. She passed the Kerrs, walking the horse, in front of the Normal Library, and waved at them; passed another friend a few hundred feet farther on, and waved at her. The horse was walking, and as she turned into North Merchant Street she took off her cowboy hat, and the horse swung into a lope. She passed the Tripletts and waved her cowboy hat at them, still moving gayly north on Merchant Street. A Gazette carrier passed—a High School boy friend—and she waved at him, but with her bridle hand; the horse veered quickly, plunged into the parking where the low-hanging limb faced her, and while she still looked back waving, the blow came. But she did not fall from the horse; she slipped off, dazed a bit, staggered, and fell in a faint. She never quite recovered consciousness.

But she did not fall from the horse, neither was she riding fast. A year or so ago she used to go like the wind. But that habit was broken, and she used the horse to get into the open, to get fresh, hard exercise, and to work off a certain surplus energy that welled up in her and needed a physical outlet. That need has been in her heart for years. It was back of the impulse that kept the dauntless little brown-clad figure on the streets and country roads of the community and built into a strong, muscular body what had been a frail and sickly frame during the first years of her life. But the riding gave her more than a body. It released a gay and hardy soul. She was the happiest thing in the world. And she was happy because she was enlarging her horizon. She came to know all sorts and conditions of men; Charley O'Brien, the traffic cop, was one of her best friends. W. L. Holtz, the Latin teacher, was another. Tom O'Connor, farmer-politician, and Rev. J. H. J. Rice, preacher and police judge, and Frank Beach, music master, were her special friends, and all the girls, black and white, above the track and below the track, in Pepville and Stringtown, were among her acquaintances. And she brought home riotous stories of her adventures. She loved to rollick; persiflage was her natural expression at home. Her humor was a continual bubble of joy. She seemed to think in hyperbole and metaphor. She was mischievous without malice, as full of faults as an old shoe. No angel was Mary White, but an easy girl to live with, for she never nursed a grouch five minutes in her life.

With all her eagerness for the out-of-doors, she loved books. On her table when she left her room were a book by Conrad, one by Galsworthy, Creative Chemistry by E. E. Slosson, and a Kipling book. She read Mark Twain, Dickens, and Kipling before she was ten—all of their writings. Wells and Arnold Bennett particularly amused and diverted her. She was entered as a student in Wellesley for 1922; was assistant editor of the High School Annual this year, and in line for election to the editorship next year. She was a member of the executive committee of the High School Y.W.C.A.

Within the last two years she had begun to be moved by an ambition to draw. She began as most children do by scribbling in her schoolbooks, funny pictures. She bought cartoon magazines and took a course—rather casually, naturally, for she was, after all, a child with no strong purposes—and this year she tasted the first fruits of success by having her pictures accepted by the High School Annual. But the thrill of delight she got when Mr. Ecord, of the Normal Annual, asked her to do the cartooning for that book this spring, was too beautiful for words. She fell to her work with all her enthusiastic heart. Her drawings were accepted, and her pride—always repressed by a lively sense of the ridiculous figure she was cutting—was a really gorgeous thing to see. No successful artist ever drank a deeper draft of satisfaction than she took from the little fame her work was getting among her schoolfellows. In her glory, she almost forgot her horse—but never her car.

For she used the car as a jitney bus. It was her social life. She never had a "party" in all her nearly seventeen years— wouldn't have one; but she never drove a block in her life that she didn't begin to fill the car with pick-ups! Everybody rode with

William Allen White on his seventieth birthday, February 10, 1938

William Allen White looks over the back page

Press Associa

Mary White—white and black, old and young, rich and poor, men and women. She liked nothing better than to fill the car with long-legged High School boys and an occasional girl, and parade the town. She never had a "date," nor went to a dance, except once with her brother, Bill, and the "boy proposition" didn't interest her—yet. But young people—great spring-breaking, varnish-cracking, fender-breaking, door-sagging, carloads of "kids"—gave her great pleasure. Her zests were keen. But the most fun she ever had in her life was acting as chairman of the committee that got up the turkey dinner for the poor folks at the county home; scores of pies, gallons of slaw, jam, cakes, preserves, oranges, and a wilderness of turkey were loaded into the car and taken to the county home. And, being of a practical turn of mind, she risked her own Christmas dinner to see that the poor folks actually got it all. Not that she was a cynic; she just disliked to tempt folks. While there she found a blind colored uncle, very old, who could do nothing but make rag rugs, and she rustled up from her school friends rags enough to keep him busy for a season. The last engagement she tried to make was to take the guests at the county home out for a car ride. And the last endeavor of her life was to try to get a rest room for colored girls in the High School. She found one girl reading in the toilet, because there was no better place for a colored girl to loaf, and it inflamed her sense of injustice and she became a nagging harpy to those who she thought could remedy the evil. The poor she always had with her and was glad of it. She hungered and thirsted for righteousness; and was the most impious creature in the world. She joined the Church without consulting her parents, not particularly for her soul's good. She never had a thrill of piety in her life, and would have hooted at a "testimony." But even as a little child she felt the church was an agency for helping people to more of life's abundance, and she wanted to help. She never wanted help for herself. Clothes meant little to her. It was a fight to get a new rig on her; but eventually a harder fight to get it off. She never wore a jewel and had no ring but her High School class ring and never asked for anything but a wrist watch. She refused to have her hair up, though she was nearly seventeen. "Mother," she protested, "you don't know how much I get by with, in my braided pigtails, that I could not with my hair up." Above every other passion of her life was her passion not to grow up, to be a child. The tomboy in her, which was big, seemed to loath to be put away forever in skirts. She was a Peter Pan, who refused to grow up.

Her funeral yesterday at the Congregational Church was as she would have wished it; no singing, no flowers except the big bunch of red roses from her brother Bill's Harvard classmen—heavens, how proud that would have made her!—and the red roses from The Gazette forces, in vases at her head and feet. A short prayer; Paul's beautiful essay on "Love" from the Thirteenth Chapter of First Corinthians; some remarks about her democratic spirit by her friend, John H. J. Rice, pastor and police judge, which she would have deprecated if she could; a prayer sent down for her by her friend, Carl Nau; and opening the service the slow, poignant movement from Beethoven's Moonlight Sonata, which she loved; and closing the service a cutting from the joyously melancholy first movement of Tschaikowski's Pathetic Symphony, which she liked to hear in certain moods, on the phonograph; then the Lord's Prayer by her friends in High School.

That was all.

For her pallbearers only her friends were chosen; her Latin teacher, W. L. Holtz; her High School principal, Rice Brown; her doctor, Frank Foncannon; her friend, W. W. Finney; her pal at The Gazette office, Walter Hughes, and her brother Bill. It would have made her smile to know that her friend, Charley O'Brien, the traffic cop, had been transferred from Sixth and Commercial to the corner near the church to direct her friends who came to bid her good-by.

A rift in the clouds in a gray day threw a shaft of sunlight upon her coffin as her nervous, energetic little body sank to its last sleep. But the soul of her, the glowing, gorgeous, fervent soul of her, surely was flaming in eager joy upon some other dawn.[2]

Whatever the appeal to others, "Mary White" communicated a far deeper feeling to the hearts of Emporia people. It was written for Mary's friends and abounds in local allusions. Yet despite the local references, the editorial had a universal appeal. In the month following its appearance, it was more widely reprinted than any other *Gazette* editorial, written before or since. Christopher Morley first recognized it as book material, and shortly after publication it became a standard selection for high school and college readings. To countless students William Allen White is known only as the author of "Mary White."

Peter Pan Park, the largest and most beautiful park in Emporia, stands as a memorial to Mary White. The White family presented it to the city with the stipulation that Mary's name should not be connected with it in any way and that the name White should never be entabled there in any form. It is Emporia's most popular recreational center.

The Roosevelt biography was almost ready for publication

Mary White 217

at the time of Mary's death. White had written an intimate biography; except for some notable incidents, like the split in the Republican Party in 1912, the life dealt not with matters of state but with personal relations, Roosevelt off the record in the White House, in his home, with his friends, with children, and the like. Mary was a part of the biography; and after her death, passages relating to her had to be revised. Since then, White has worked intermittently on the biography, but has never rewritten the parts about his daughter. Neither parent has ever recovered from Mary's tragic death. Never a day passes that Mrs. White does not speak of Mary; never does she hear the clatter of a horses' feet that tears do not come to her eyes. One of the most cherished memories of both parents is of a group of Negro children assembled on their lawn and calling to their comrades that Mary was dead while they stood sobbing with their faces turned toward the window in Mary's room.

CHAPTER XX

The Right of Free Speech

The right to a free utterance of honest opinions is
fundamentally right. . . . And to restrict any man from
the calm expression of an honest opinion merely because
there is a strike on in Kansas is unwise. Industrial
questions are not honestly settled by a suppression of
free utterance, either of speech or the press or of any
other kind, so long as the opinion is orderly and temperate and decent.[1]

THE NATION-WIDE coal strike of 1919 occasioned the
Kansas Industrial Act. For two or three years Alexander
Howat, president of the mine workers' union in the
Kansas coal district, had been antagonizing public opinion. He
or his subordinates had called strikes on such charges as the
gas man being late to work, the pit mule having a sore knee,
the wash house being too cold, the tipple scales out of order,
the light in the wash house turned on five minutes late, and
scores of similar causes. For the two years and nine months
ending December, 1918, records show three hundred and sixty-
four separate strikes at individual mines. The frequency of
these strikes and the pretexts for calling them prepared public
opinion for remedial legislation.

The general coal strike caught Kansas in zero weather.
In many places the coal supply was entirely shut off, and
wherever coal was burned the reserve was rapidly vanishing.
Governor Henry J. Allen asked the miners to produce enough
coal to prevent suffering; and when they refused, he obtained
a receivership and operated the mines under state control.
Eleven thousand Kansans answered his call for volunteer
miners; hundreds of men from surrounding states offered to

help; the governor of Nebraska offered fifteen hundred. Allen sent a regiment of the national guard to the mining district to prevent disturbances, and General Leonard Wood, of the national army, detailed six hundred men to act in case of an emergency. No friction developed, and the volunteers produced enough coal from strip mines to meet the temporary need.

Early in January, 1920, Allen convened the legislature in special session to enact laws to protect the public against the recurrence of such situations. W. L. Huggins, an Emporia attorney, had long studied the possibility of adjusting industrial disputes by court procedure, and a bill he drafted was introduced into the legislature. Both capital and labor objected from the moment they learned what was afoot. The two houses of the legislature individually or in joint session gave them and the public opportunities to express their views. Several labor representatives of national note opposed the legislation, W. L. Huggins, William Allen White, and others spoke for the public, and attorneys for various industrial associations represented capital.

Frank P. Walsh represented organized labor most ably. His address before the joint session and the discussion that followed lasted an entire day. Walsh vigorously denounced the proposed law as impossible, unconstitutional, state socialism in its most odious degree. He called it the most drastic measure ever proposed against union labor, asserting that it would make labor the slave of capital and encircle Kansas with a steel ring which organized labor could not penetrate. He maintained that it was unfair to capital, because it gave a bureaucratic board the right to fix wages and rules and regulations for the conduct of business. Capital, he said, backed the law because it would shackle labor and be the "cat o' nine tails" with which capital would scourge its back forever. He attacked the clauses that held certain lines of production essential, holding that every line of production was essential.

W. L. Huggins, the public's representative, defended the proposal. He said the bill offered a remedy better than the right to strike. The proposed court, he held, guaranteed the working man a fair wage, decent working conditions, and the right to an open and thorough investigation and adjudication of all disputes. To capital, he asserted, it guaranteed a fair return on investment; to the public, protection against the selfish quarrels of capital and labor. Huggins upheld the bill's constitutionality under the doctrine of public interest, and prophesied that within two years labor would be urging its adoption in other states. William Allen White appeared to lend moral support to the bill. White had a state-wide reputation as a friend of labor and was known to be an employer in his own right. White said that no attempt was being made "to throttle capital and labor in Kansas, but to emancipate them from their own stranglehold upon each other, and to establish an equitable and living relation between them." [2]

Capital's opposition, which charged state socialism, attracted no public attention; and after seventeen days of deliberation the Industrial Act passed almost without opposition. Only seven representatives and four senators voted no.

The Kansas Industrial Act was a document of thirty sections, some of which were subdivided. Its primary purpose was to protect the public against the evils of industrial warfare. In actual operation, it dealt in most cases with matters wherein the interests of capital and labor were at least more obvious than those of the public. Its most important provisions may be summarized under eleven headings. (1) It created a court of industrial relations composed of three judges. (2) This court had jurisdiction over certain industries defined as essential, the manufacturing of food products and clothing, the production of fuel for all purposes, the transportation of food, fuel, and substances entering into their making, and all public utilities. (Regulation of public utilities was later transferred to the public utilities commission.) (3) The court was empowered to operate specified industries wherever industrial disputes jeopardized public welfare. (4) It was given authority to regulate working hours and living conditions, and to establish a minimum wage or fix a standard of wages. (5) It could bring proceedings in the supreme court to compel obedience to its orders. (6) Persons and corporations affected by rulings were given thirty days to bring action to suspend the court's orders. (7) Collective bargaining was authorized for labor organizations. (8) Cessation of production was unlawful without the consent of the court. (9) Any person, firm, corporation, or association, including labor unions, who refused or failed to perform any act or duty enjoined by the industrial act, or who conspired to do so or to intimidate those who would, were subject to arrest and imprisonment. This provision made strikes illegal and was violently opposed by labor. (10) Ordinary persons who violated the act or any valid order of the court were guilty of a misdemeanor and subject to a fine not to exceed $1000 and imprisonment in a county jail for not more than one year. (11) Officers of a firm, corporation, labor union, or association who violated the act or any valid order of the court were guilty of a felony and subject to a fine not to exceed $5000 and imprisonment in the state penitentiary for not more than two years.

Most disinterested observers believe that the industrial court operated fairly well until the United States Supreme Court nullified its authority. But it had a stormy life. Organized labor refused to obey its edicts; and as a consequence, a number of labor leaders were sent to jail. But despite labor's opposition, it made greater use of the court than did industry. During the first eighteen months of its life, labor filed thirty-seven of the thirty-nine cases, and of these organized labor filed twenty-seven. Only low paid labor, however, used the court; and in every case the court's decisions were accepted as final. The court's eventual undoing was due to an industrial firm's refusal to accept its judgment. In the meantime, several incidents tended to discredit the court, and one of these involved William Allen White.

White's sympathies during the railroad strike in 1922 were about seventy-five per cent for the strikers. Before the strike began, he clearly indicated his position. To precipitate a strike at this time "is bad business," public opinion "will be fairly well lined up against" the strikers, and for the railway workers "to join with the coal strikers and tie up American industry is not particularly patriotic." But he also believed that the railroad "boys have a kick coming."

When they went to work for the railroad labor board two years ago they went to work with the explicit agreement that a living wage should be established upon which adjustments of all disputes should begin. The living wage was to be guaranteed to the men at the bottom of the industry, and for skill, risk, and length of apprenticeship higher than living wages were to be paid.

Now the railroad board declares that the living wage cannot be paid until profits and rehabilitation have been secured. That is to say railroad labor is only a commodity like other labor. It is to be paid without respect to the fact that it is necessary to the life of the nation, and the special guarantee of a living wage is to be scrapped.

That guarantee was a contract.

Perhaps it was an unwise contract for the labor board to make. But it was a contract and the men accepted it rather than strike when they accepted it, so America got value received, which was peace for two years. So now that the contract is to be incontinently junked, the boys have a kick coming.

Therefore, if they go out, and trouble occurs down in the railroad yards and freight cars are tipped over and burned and the troops are called out and we have a nasty little civil war called a strike, don't blame the boys and declare that they are led by reds and that they should be stood up against a wall and shot. They have their side. And when we talk so glibly about burying the hatchet in industry, don't forget that here is a case where we have buried the hatchet in the neck of labor.[3]

Public opinion in Kansas was unquestionably more than fifty per cent for the strikers. Kansas has many "railroad towns," and railway employees are active in community activities and enjoy the confidence and respect of their neighbors. The public, furthermore, believed that in this case the employees had had a raw deal. The strike had hardly begun when merchants and other businessmen began displaying placards stating their places of business were one hundred per cent for the strikers. Governor Allen in a telegram to the Arkansas City Chamber of Commerce ordered these cards out, stating that the industrial law "provides that any act is unlawful which to any extent interferes with the operation of railroads and such acts by merchants constitute conspiracy to interfere with and suspend efficient railway operation."[4] That day White took a hand in the matter.

The order is an infamous infraction of the right of free press and free speech. Certainly it has not come to such a pass in this country that a man may not say what he thinks about an industrial controversy without disobeying the law.

One of these cards went up in the Gazette window to-day. Instead of 100 per cent, we have started it at 49 per cent. If the strike lasts until to-morrow we shall change the per cent to 50, and move it up a little every day. As a matter of fact, the Gazette does not believe that any one—not even the Gazette—is 100 per cent right. But somewhere between 49 and 100 per cent the men are right. And if the Industrial Court desires to make a test case, here it is. This is not a question of whether the men are right or wrong, but a question of the right of an American citizen to say what he pleases about this strike. And if 49 per cent sympathy is permissible, in the next fifty days we shall all see where violation of the law begins. The Industrial Court which we have upheld from its conception, and still uphold, will have the nicest little chance to see just where it is lawful for a man to express his sympathy with his friends and neighbors, even if in his heart he believes they have made a mistake in the time of their strike.

Either we have free speech and a free press in this country, or we have not. Now is the time to find out.[5]

White's action brought the matter to an abrupt head, and he and Allen took the spotlight in the nation's headlines, partly because they had been personal friends for years, partly because of the issue involved, and partly because the industrial act had attracted wide attention as a social experiment. The enforcement of the act was up to the governor and the attorney general, and although White assumed that the cards had been ordered out by the industrial court, the court itself had taken no action in the matter. Attorney General Richard J. Hopkins took the position that the sympathy cards were illegal; and on the day after White posted his card, he said that "one who encourages lawlessness in Kansas by advocating it is himself violating the law and therefore is subject to arrest." W. L. Huggins, the presiding judge of the industrial court, said that White "is allowed to be either 49 per cent or 99 per cent in sympathy of the strikers." He advised against arresting White and told J. A. McDermott, an associate judge, that however the information was drawn it would be quashed. But McDermott held that White "is lending his moral support to an unlawful act, and thereby creating an atmosphere in favor of law violation." The governor said that "if White insists on being funny we will have to do something about it." [6] His arrest was thought to be imminent; but instead of arrest, Allen sent McDermott to Emporia to set White right in his thinking and persuade him to take down his card. McDermott failed in his mission, and White was arrested on the twenty-second. After his arrest he took down his card and asked all others to remove theirs. The next day the strikers took down all the cards in Emporia.

July twenty-fifth was "Governor's Day" at the Emporia State Teachers College, and Allen used the occasion to present his side of the controversy. He and White stood in the reviewer's stand while three thousand students marched before them, then went to the auditorium where White introduced Allen to an audience of four thousand, most of them in sympathy with White. Allen, in an eloquent and effective address, defended his action. "The industrial court law," he said, "forbids any intimidation or conspiracy or persuasion of men to keep them from work." By putting a striker's card in the window, White "was not violating what he thought was right but he was joining with the strikers in a way that might prove dangerous."

Bill White has the kindest heart in the world. He wouldn't hurt a flea. If we needed a posse in this town, Bill would be the brigadier general on the citizens' posse to preserve law and order, but when he sits down before a double action typewriter and writes out his emotions, he is a dangerous man.[7]

Two days later White answered Allen in an editorial addressed "To an Anxious Friend."

You tell me that law is above freedom of utterance. And I reply that you can have no wise laws nor free enforcement of wise laws unless there is free expression of the wisdom of the people— and, alas, their folly with it. But if there is freedom, folly will die of its own poison, and the wisdom will survive. That is the history of the race. It is the proof of man's kinship with God. You say that freedom of utterance is not for time of stress, and I reply with the sad truth that only in time of stress is freedom of utterance in danger. No one questions it in calm days, because it is not needed. And the reverse is true also; only when free utterance is suppressed is it needed, and when it is needed, it is most vital to justice. Peace is good. But if you are interested in peace through force and without free discussion, that is to say, free utterance

decently and in order—your interest in justice is slight. And peace
without justice is tyranny, no matter how you may sugar coat it
with expediency. This state today is in more danger from suppression than from violence, because in the end, suppression leads to
violence. Violence, indeed, is the child of suppression. Whoever
pleads for justice helps to keep the peace; and whoever tramples
upon the plea for justice, temperately made in the name of peace,
only outrages peace and kills something fine in the heart of man
which God put there when we got our manhood. When that is
killed, brute meets brute on each side of the line.

So, dear friend, put fear out of your heart. This nation will
survive, this state will prosper, the orderly business of life will go
forward if only men can speak in whatever way given them to
utter what their hearts hold—by voice, by posted card, by letter or
by press. Reason never has failed men. Only force and repression
have made the wrecks in the world.[8]

This editorial met with universal approval. Newspapers
and magazines spread it widely. The New York *World* called
it "a model of kindly and devastating criticism" and predicted
the world would give it "a place among historic public docu-
ments." [9] The Pulitzer Foundation awarded it the editorial
prize for 1922, the jury finding that it "excelled in clearness
of style, sound reasoning and in its power to influence public
opinion in the right direction." [10]

Some persons in Kansas believed ulterior motives lay behind White's arrest. One rumor held the whole affair a publicity stunt. It was charged that Allen and White planned the
arrest to further Allen's political ambitions by demonstrating
to the nation that he had the courage to arrest his best friend.
Another rumor called the arrest a deliberate frame-up to thwart
the strikers. The gist of this story was that White posted his
card, pretending that he was in sympathy with the strikers in
order that he might advise them to take theirs down and thereby
minimize their efforts. Both rumors were grounded in the
belief that two men could not seriously differ in their ideas and
continue their friendship. Proponents of both stories offered
their continued friendship as proof of their theories. To still
others, it seemed that a lot of pother was being made over
a mere placard. These persons granted to White and Allen
high and sincere motives, but held the issue at stake was not so
vital as either contended. Outside of Kansas no stigma attached

to the controversy. The press treated it with the utmost seriousness. Invariably, it upheld White, partly, no doubt, because censorship comes the nearest to being the newspaper man's bugaboo. White's defenders, however, were not confined to journalists. Five of the nation's leading constitutional lawyers, William E. Borah, John W. Atwood, Albert J. Beveridge, William G. McAdoo, and Herbert S. Hadley, were ready to submit briefs for White.

As soon as the air had cleared it became evident that the prosecution had no disposition to try White. White tried three times to get a trial but failed each time. On November 17, the attorney general's office ordered the case dismissed. Its aversion to prosecution, it said, was that the case did not present a thorough test case and that the office had on hand a large number of prosecutions considered more flagrant violations than the Emporia case.[11] Its disinclination to try White was natural: the office had advised Allen against arresting White in the first place. When the sympathy cards were put up, Attorney General Hopkins, a strong believer in the industrial act, took the position "that small or inconsequential but perhaps technical violations of the law should be passed unnoticed." Hopkins believed "that convictions in such small matters would likely be impossible, and that it would be more of a detriment to the Industrial Court law to suffer actual reversals in court or before juries than to let inconsequential matters go unnoticed." [12] White protested the move for dismissal, and Allen said that he had asked only for a continuance; but this Judge W. C. Harris refused to grant because the state administration would change before the case came to trial.

The move on the part of the state caused a flurry of comment. The Topeka *Capital* voiced editorially what may be regarded as representative newspaper opinion.

There is more to the case of W. A. White than stated in his plea that in dismissal without trial the case will be universally regarded as a fake from the beginning. There are issues to be settled which this case presents squarely and which ought not to be left up in the air. If men can be arrested, fined and committed to jail for doing what the Emporia Gazette editor did, it is important to know it. If his arrest was a mistake under the law, not only he but others in future similar circumstances of labor and capital strife in the state are entitled to know it, and this is what courts are for.

The White case raised an issue which must be settled at one time or another as to the rights of innocent bystanders in strikes within certain specified industries. Whether outsiders, including newspapers as well as merchants and others, in a strike in such industries, by expressing the opinions regarding rights and wrongs of the strike conflict become co-conspirators with strikers is a question which the courts have the opportunity to settle once for all in the White case, and which will remain a moot question if this case is dismissed without a trial. There can be no two sides to the issue raised by White, that having been arrested and accused of breaking the law, he is entitled to a trial in the courts.[13]

White was charged with "two offences against the industrial court law, one of conspiracy with others to hinder, delay, interfere with and suspend operation of the Santa Fe Railway, and one of picketing." [14] Material allegations in the complaint were all fictitious. Two men, William Pierce and Justin Morgan, whom White had never heard of, were named as co-conspirators. When the attorney general's office moved for dismissal, White asked Allen to amend the warrant in accordance with the undisputed facts so that they could get the state supreme court to decide on the fundamental question at issue; and newspaper reports at the time stated that Allen had agreed. Nothing, however, came of this move; and as the case was soon to come up in district court, Hopkins, who was to be out of the state on business, asked Allen to select some lawyer in whom he had confidence to try the case. Before going to Albany to attend a governors' conference, Allen made McDermott his representative. When the case was called on December 8 both Allen and Hopkins were in the East, and Charles Griffith, acting attorney general, had the case dismissed. The attorney general's office did not believe a prosecution could be successful and Allen had failed to provide a lawyer to prosecute. McDermott issued the following statement:

The question of law which is claimed to be involved here, in my judgment, can be raised only in one of two ways: first, by motion to quash the original information; or by trial, and the law submitted in the instructions of the court to the jury.

I understand that you have declined the first method, and the second is not possible at this time. I am, therefore, concurring in the recommendation of the attorney general's office that the case be dismissed when called December 8.[15]

The action of the prosecution brought a stinging rebuke from Judge W. C. Harris. He declared "the defendant in this case has not had fair treatment."

The court is forced to the conclusion, . . . by the conduct of the moving party, that this case was commenced maliciously, or recklessly, without investigation of the facts to ascertain whether a prosecution was justified, and in either event the action was equally reprehensible.[16]

Disappointment tempered Whites' reaction. He believed when Allen went East that the case would be submitted to the supreme court and he accused McDermott of overruling Allen. McDermott had been responsible for the warrant in the first place, and White said that he refused to try the case under any circumstances. He "has neither the common decency nor the manly courage to come down and try the case on its merits . . ." [17] Comment in the nation's liberal press fairly sizzled. *The New Republic* asserted, "The suit itself was one of the most gross, ugly and inexcusable assaults on freedom of speech which state intoxicated American politicians have yet perpetrated." [18]

The White case unquestionably weakened respect for the industrial court. The court was not responsible for filing the case, but was so closely associated with the proceedings that it had the blame. White's arrest was under the act that created the court. Enforcement of the act and the court's decisions were up to the administration that had sponsored the legislation. One of the court's members prepared the warrant for White's arrest and represented the Governor when the case was dismissed. White, himself, always wrote as if he were being prosecuted by the court, and in popular opinion this idea prevailed.

The state legislature abolished the court in 1925, without a dissenting vote in the senate and but three in the house. Two decisions by the United States Supreme Court had left it a mere labor-baiting agency. In the Wolff Packing Company decisions

such industries as coal mining, meat packing, and flour milling
were held to be private industries and not clothed with such
public interest as to permit a state to interfere with liberty of
contract between employer and employee. Its authority to fix a
temporary minimum wage and working conditions in these industries was declared unconstitutional. Without the authority
to define, enforce, and establish industrial justice by compelling
employers to pay fair wages, the court's power for preserving
peace in these industries diminished to imprisoning strikers.

CHAPTER XXI

The *Gazette* in Flower

Our papers, our little country papers, seem drab and miserably provincial to strangers; yet we who read them read in their lines the sweet, intimate story of life. And all these touches of nature make us wondrous kind. It is the country newspaper, bringing together daily the threads of the town's life, weaving them into something rich and strange, and setting the pattern as it weaves, directing the loom, and giving the cloth its color by mixing the lives of all the people in its color-pot—it is this country newspaper that reveals us to ourselves, and keeps our country hearts quick and our country minds open and our country faith strong.[1]

PROBABLY there never was a time from 1896 until 1929 that William Allen White could not have sold the *Gazette* at a handsome profit and made more money working for a magazine or city paper. His steadfast refusal to abandon the *Gazette* for political office or a better paying newspaper job arose not so much from his preference for country town life as from his passion for independence. He bought the *Gazette* that he might be free, financially and intellectually; its welfare became first his care and then his pride. Recognition of his paper has always delighted him. In 1938 when the Columbia Broadcasting Company put his paper on the "Americans at Work" program, his cup of happiness overflowed. The expense was past his understanding, but the honor was his unconcealed pride. Several months later when, after the first of a series of lectures at Harvard, he discovered that he had been talking to an international European audience, it "was a great day for Emporia," and he hoped to be forgiven for spreading

his "iridescent peacock feathers before the home folks." [2] Yet
the *Gazette* devoted less than half the space to the Harvard
lectures than to the "Americans at Work" broadcast and the
next month took no note whatever of White's commencement
address at the University of Indiana, though the speech was
worth more than two columns to the Kansas City *Star*.

The Emporia editor's aversion to office holding is
grounded in his desire to be his own fool in his own way. The
belief that he lacked the ability to administer the details of a
public office has made no difference in his public life. An elective or appointive political office would have necessitated entangling alliances, curtailed his independence, and injured his
paper editorially and financially. This attitude toward office
holding is not peculiar to him. The only difference was that
this side of office holding he was always in politics up to his
eyes. His conspicuously successful contemporary, Ed. Howe,
thought that "to get your opponent in politics is equal to getting him in jail," [3] and cites the example of his competitor
who after two terms as governor returned to find his paper
not paying expenses.

Yet White has gladly served in non-remunerative offices,
concerned with matters of policy rather than administrative
details, which did not take him away from his paper. Within
the Republican Party he has held offices from war chairman
to national committeeman. President Wilson made him a delegate to the Russian Conference at Prinkipo and President
Hoover sent him to Haiti with the President's Commission. In
his own state he was a regent of the state university from 1905
to 1912. When all state institutions of higher learning were
placed under a single board, he refused to serve longer because
one of the state schools was in Emporia; for he held that a
local regent would become the real head of the institution.
One governor, of an opposite political faith, failing to get
White to relent in his stand, facetiously remarked that he had
other good men he would like to appoint if it were not for
"Bill White's law." Since the creation of the all-inclusive board
in 1925, the "law" has been broken but once.

Least of all was White ever tempted by a political salary,
even when he was hard up and the local post office was the

country editor's legitimate prize for fighting his party's battles. Independence, honesty, courage, and intelligence, not a political subsidy, were the requisites of newspaper success. To be in politics below office holding was good newspaper business. An editor was the spokesman for a party. An independent country paper was either in bankruptcy or waiting for the sheriff. His first problem, therefore, was to maintain his editorial independence yet keep his paper in line for the county printing. The editor who got the county printing prospered and paid off the mortgage.

Undue publicity has been given to White's refusal to leave Emporia for metropolitan papers. Since "What's the Matter With Kansas?" and Sam McClure's failure to entice him to New York, writers have reiterated that he could have had the highest editorial jobs in the land. Usually the inference is that White stayed with the *Gazette* because he preferred a country town to a large city. White, himself, has fostered this belief. When the Chicago *Tribune* offered him $25,000 a year, his answer was that he "preferred to spend his life in a town where he could water his front lawn with thirty-five feet of hose." [4] Again, in the early twenties when it was rumored that he was going to New York to edit *Judge,* he wrote:

New York is a large town so far as population goes, and it has a lot of things going on every night. But man for man, Emporia is a better town, and though the night life of Emporia closes practically at 11 o'clock, one has to sleep some time and the sleeping arrangements in Emporia between midnight and 7 o'clock are far ahead of anything New York has to offer. And that is to be considered.[5]

The *Gazette's* editor unquestionably prefers Emporia, but his preference is not unusual. As he stood in line awaiting an honorary degree at Columbia University, a man behind him asked him who he was. "I probably don't belong here. I'm just a little country editor from Kansas," White replied. "That's all right," returned the speaker. "I'm just a little country doctor from Minnesota." [6] The questioner was the internationally famous surgeon, Dr. William J. Mayo. Many men as successful as White have preferred small towns to cities. Dr. Arthur C. Hertzler, Kansas' highest salaried citizen on the basis of the federal income tax reports, lives in a town of fewer than fifteen hundred people. Nationally known as a goiter specialist, author of many medical books and an autobiography which sold close to a half million copies, he pays taxes on an income well above $50,000 a year.

In private White contends that he had no talent for the New York scene—a seemingly preposterous statement when balanced against the combined judgment of the publishers who have sought to lure him away. Even though he were right about his talent, the excuse would not explain his refusal to write a daily syndicate column for the North American Newspaper Alliance. *Judge* once paid him $1,000 a month to write its editorials. Before the year ended he quit. There was a difference about editorial policies. Very early his earnings exceeded his needs, so that money was never a material consideration. What did matter was "the royal American privilege of living and dying in a country town, running a country newspaper, saying what we please when we please, how we please and to whom we please." [7]

The twenties unquestionably saw White's paper at its best. The millions of dollars the Santa Fe railroad put into its Emporia property, the increased enrollment in Emporia schools, the town's growing population, and the local and national prosperity resulted in thousands and thousands of inches of advertising which made possible a greater variety of news and features than ever before or since. During this period the *Gazette* installed a rotary press, stereotyping equipment, and the full leased-wire service of the Associated Press. Emporia for the first time had a paper produced in the same manner with the same press service as a city daily. The *Gazette* had its city editor, farm editor, society editor, telegraph editor, sports editor, and a half dozen reporters chasing news at the court house, city hall, undertaker shops, and schools. It was printing a mail edition in the afternoon for near-by towns; and with the coming of hard-surfaced roads, it further extended its territory and began delivering papers to farmers within a radius of forty to fifty miles.

Hard-surfaced roads, however, were as much of a boon to the *Gazette's* chief competitor as they were to the *Gazette*. The

Kansas City *Star* had never been able to get its evening paper into Emporia early enough for evening delivery. Once the *Star* tried printing an earlier, abbreviated edition which was distributed in Emporia each evening. When the *Star* gave the undertaking up as a bad job. White cackled back at them:

> Twinkle, twinkle little *Star*
> We can beat you where we are.

But he crowed too soon. Hard-surfaced roads and speedier automobiles put Emporia within two hours of Kansas City.

Before the twenties ended White was offered more than $400,000 for his paper. Though its profits then warranted the figures on the basis of an eight per cent investment, the offer reflected the current inflated prices. Proportionately, the $400,-000 was no more out of line than the $3,000 White paid in 1895. This remarkable appreciation in value was not exceptional to the *Gazette*. The story of the Emporia paper is the story of the average small town newspaper conducted with businesslike methods during the same period. As public schools made more readers, circulation grew from the hundreds to the thousands; as standards of living rose, advertising increased; as new methods of printing developed, newspapers enlarged and speeded up; as good roads and faster automobiles were built, trade territories expanded; so that the history of the country daily is that of adding a new machine to keep up with the procession. The inevitable end of this development was that newspaper publishing, even a country daily in a town of fifteen thousand, became big business. And always an ever guiding hand in the *Gazette's* expansion was that of Walter E. Hughes, its manager.

Hughes was a rare man. Large, moderately fleshy with a suggestion of flabbiness about the throat, glasses attached with a gold chain to his bosom so naturally that they seemed a part of him, he had the appearance, air, and poise of a successful professional man. His integrity, his loyalty to a trust, was the keynote of his character. Hughes seemed to think that when his judgment was sought the questioner wanted, not an echo of himself, but what Hughes thought. Thus it came about as he grew in experience and wisdom, he grew in the confidence of the Whites, the *Gazette* force, and the town. More and more, those about him relied on his judgment; and he gave to all the best that was in him. To the *Gazette* force he was counselor and friend. Most of the men under him had never known any other boss, and during his thirty-two years with the paper he discharged only three men who had worked under him for more than a year. To the town he was the link between the business interests and the paper, yet found time to take an active part in his lodges, his church, the Chamber of Commerce, and Rotary. To the Whites he was a loyal friend and faithful servant, who watched over their property with a painstaking care wholly foreign to White's nature. He knew where every penny came from, where every penny went, when and where every piece of equipment was bought and what it cost. He never asked an employee to do a task which he could not or had not done. He had grown from the *Gazette's* first delivery boy through every department to its manager.

In Walter Hughes the Whites had the utmost confidence. Year by year, little by little, he assumed greater responsibilities; and when Mrs. White became ill in the twenties, it was in the nature of things that "Walt" should thereafter look after their household bills. When extra expenses sent the bills up into four figures, Walt did the worrying; when White listened to the pleas of some worthy organization, Walt found the money. For all White's income went to Walt. If an advertiser tried to pay White, he said, "See Walt." When White brought home a syndicate check, he gave it to Walt, and the money went where Walt thought it would do the Whites the most good. To keep White's finances straight he carried a bank account in White's name on which White wrote checks. When the account was gone, the bank notified Hughes and he deposited another two thousand. "If I would let him write checks on the *Gazette*," he once said, "I would never know where we are. I could grow rich on what he gives away." [8] To persons who did not know the two men, White's reliance on Hughes seems incredible. When Mary and Bill were children and wanted money for candy or a show, White sent them to "Mr. Hughes." Walt decided whether or not they should have the money.

When Hughes died unexpectedly in 1932, the Whites lost

their best friend. The void he left in the *Gazette* was never filled; he had so built himself into the paper and the White family that he was irreplaceable. During his late years White paid him handsomely and carried a life insurance policy sufficiently large to keep his widow in comfortable circumstances.

Hughes was but one of the employees for whom the *Gazette* became his life's work. At his death, the average term of service was more than twelve years; today it stands at seventeen and a half. With its printers, employment was equivalent to a lifetime job. Conrad Jones, make-up man and oldest employee, started in 1900; and John Schottler, foreman, began in 1901. If an employee is kept on a year, he has made good; and thereafter if he leaves, he goes voluntarily. Because many young journalists use the *Gazette* for their apprenticeship training, length of service in the news and advertising departments averages under that in the mechanical. By 1920 its "graduates" numbered John Redmond, Burlington *Republican;* Roy F. Bailey, Salina *Journal;* R. A. Clymer, El Dorado *Republican* —all publishers of Kansas dailies; Oscar Stauffer, owner of a newspaper chain; Elbert Severance, Murdock Pemberton, and Brock Pemberton, who moved to the New York field; Burge McFall, Associated Press World War correspondent; and a score of others.

The Gazette's most conspicuous employee in the twenties was young Bill, who was getting his start in journalism. Bill, unlike his father, had had many advantages unknown to the average boy. He had gone through the Emporia High School, spent some time at the University of Kansas, and graduated from Harvard. Already he had been to Europe twice, the second time for six months with his father at the Versailles peace conference. Most of all he had profited from the thousands of books in the White home and the scores and scores of eminent men and women who visit the Whites.

His environment, however, had given him a certain handicap. He had gone Harvard in a big way, and the Bostonian accent of a native westerner sounds queer to Kansans' ears. Moreover, such stories as a petrified Indian being found in the new Emporia addition seemed not the subtlest of humor; and when he did set the town grinning with a story of some local group, those who were the brunt of the joke failed to see the humor. His lack of responsibility irritated his fellow workers, his want of discretion gave them gray hairs, and his impractical experiments kept them in an uproar. Through all Bill's vicissitudes, his father remained philosophical; and when asked how Bill was getting along, he replied, "I don't know whether or not Bill will ever have any sense."

Bill worked in every department on the paper; and not long after he started writing editorials, papers began copying and crediting them to his father. When Hughes died in 1932, he became manager. Later he cut loose from the paper, worked on eastern magazines and papers, and then wrote a novel. When the present war broke out, he became a foreign correspondent. By that time most Emporians were ready to concede that he had sense enough to run the *Gazette*. Bill had partially dispelled the shadow under which he had always worked—his father's fame.

At Christmas time the *Gazette* family, which includes the husbands, wives, and children, get together to eat their annual dinner, sing carols, and share in the paper's profits. The check which falls to each employee is the most important part of the evening, and its size depends upon years of service and individual earnings. At the end of his first year the employee is issued a $50 interest-bearing certificate; whose face increases $50 for each year of service. Certificates are not negotiable, nor is the "face" payable. For three years or less the interest rate is 6 per cent, and increases 1 per cent for each three years until the 12 per cent maximum is reached for nineteen years of service. In addition to the certificate check, each employee gets a 4 per cent bonus of his year's earnings. A printer who works fifty weeks for $40 a week receives an $80 bonus. The *Gazette* also carries a twenty-pay life insurance policy on each employee. The policy starts at $500 and increases with years of service to $3,000. At the end of twenty years' service the worker also receives a gift of $1,000. White pays himself $3,000 a year and gets what profits are left, if any.

White's profit-sharing plan, which drew from Theodore Roosevelt the statement that here is a man "who puts into practice the progressive principles he preaches," [9] remained in effect until 1938 when it was modified to comply with the social security laws. About the time the profit-sharing plan went into effect, White asked his printers to join the union. Some competitors were producing cut-rate printing at the expense of their employees' wages, and White wanted to force them to increase their wages or run non-union shops in a union town. His plan forced them out of business, and the *Gazette* continued a union shop, paying the union scale or better until the early 1920's. Then the employees, without consulting White, surrendered their charter because of the eastern strikes and consequent assessments. Two years later when an employee asked White for more money, he learned for the first time that he was operating an open shop.

The pivotal point in the *Gazette* is, and always has been, its editor. Among its employees there is a saying, "He's Bill White to the world but always Mr. White to us." The basis of this respect lies in no set policy of management, and a part of it reveals the hand of Mrs. White. She insists that a neat rest room with a comfortable cot be maintained for the women employees, she always sees that the young unmarried workers have dinner at the White home on Christmas, Thanksgiving, New Year's, and similar occasions, she presides over the *Gazette's* annual dinner as if she were entertaining visiting royalty, she has taken sick employees into her home and nursed them back to health. No one's pay check is ever docked because of illness. The *Gazette* pays the hospital bills when babies are born and does dozens of similar things for those who work there.

White makes a point of paying, in one way or another, for every service or favor. He will walk up to his telegraph editor and say, "Joe, I wish you would try your hand at editorials while I'm gone." Joe writes some editorials and when White returns he lays two ten-dollar bills on the telegraph desk. Joe starts to thank him and White says, "Aw, shut your mouth," and turns on his heel and walks away. All his workers say that they cannot thank him for anything. He will cut in with some such words as, "If you hadn't earned it I wouldn't have given it to you." He has been known to increase an advertising man's salary who had just lost an advertising con-

tract but who had written a five-line news local which he
thought exceptional. He is constantly doing people favors; and
because he is in so many activities, he is constantly asking
favors. He forgets about what he does for others, but not
about what they do for him. He will ask a former reporter who
is running his own paper to write an editorial on the death of
some Kansan whose life was noted for unselfish public service.
The old reporter complies and in a few days he receives a reward, but obliquely—perhaps a book, whose author the reporter knew, with White's statement that he knew the author
would like for him to have it.

He is always trying to uncover hidden talent, not only in
the *Gazette* but in the town. He encourages his reporters to
write editorials, he will hand a book to a student who happens
in and ask him to write a two-hundred word review, he will
pick up a copy of the Oxford Book of Verse and ask an English teacher if she has a student who she thinks should have the
book. One day in 1922 a student went into his office and laid
down some poems. White read them and told him he had never
read better from the hands of an amateur. He gave the student
a number of books to read, recommended that he take certain
college courses, and told him to keep on writing. For two years
the student wrote poetry and ate dinner in the White home
twice a month. Then one day he packed his books and went
home. Other men, he said, had made money raising wheat and
so could he. He had written thousands of lines, but had never
submitted one for publication.

Ask any reporter who worked for White in the twenties
what he remembers about him and he will invariably relate
little day to day incidents. The morning Lee Rich began work
White called him into the office to meet Charley Trapp, editor
of the *Pink Rag*. Five o'clock came and Rich could not find his
hat. White heard the commotion, came out with the hat and
said, "Lee, I've been hiring reporters for forty years and you
are the first one who ever hung his hat in the boss's office the
first day he was on the job." In the morning when he entered
the news room he called out, "What's going on in the darned
old world, anyhow?" [10] Much of the news he read as it came
off the wire. Every day he went through the exchanges, often

clipped out one, walked over to the managing editor's desk, pasted it on a scrap of paper, and wrote in an editorial comment "making a gem out of an ordinary piece of writing." He watched his reporter's work closely, giving them news angles they never dreamed of. Once a reporter worked hard on a story about the annual Santa Fe picnic—thought he had done a good job. The next day White made him write a story on the onions in the potato salad. The reporter "had forgotten to mention whether or not the salad was onionized." Another time a reporter wrote a story on a family of girls who had never been absent or tardy from school. White read the story, then sent the reporter to get one on the mother—told him she was, in his judgment, the one who should have had the write-up.

His essential humanity impressed his reporters even more than his sense of news values. They saw him hide out in the back office from a dim-witted old man who had been in the office several times and who was all wrought up because the city was running a sewer across his little tract of land. "I'm just too tired to face him tonight," White said. They saw a defeated candidate come in and start abusing him while he was reading exchanges. For a time he took the abuse, then "gave the politician a genuine character reading." As a big-fisted, long-armed reporter eased his way toward the politician, the disappointed office seeker turned and walked out; and White mumbled as he passed one of the desks, "I couldn't let him get away with it in front of everybody."

White's prejudices color his paper slightly. During the crossword puzzle craze, one subscriber asked him when the *Gazette* was going to print the puzzles. White described his own funeral procession to Maplewood cemetery and told him that evening but not before. He felt exactly the same way about the "funnies," but in matters of management and policy his employees have a part. White reserves the right to veto their recommendations; but if the employees are persistent, they get their way. When after three ballots the comic strips went into the *Gazette* in 1920, White's chagrin knew no end.

The boss is whipped . . . the force has beat him. He thinks they [comic strips] make a low appeal; that their humor is broad, and

their level of intelligence negligible. But the force maintains that
they sell papers. Why they should sell papers is beyond the boss;
except that the fact that people have low enough intelligence to
read the "funnies" do have money. . . . So with shame and
apology to the Gazette readers who have brains in their noodles
and not tripe or scrambled eggs, the Gazette begins its publication
of the "funnies." From which the good Lord deliver us.[11]

Though the *Gazette* receives the same press reports, it
cannot compete with the city daily in world news. Limited advertising necessitates limited space to press reports. Emporia's
proximity to larger towns puts the *Gazette* into competition
with larger papers, particularly the Kansas City *Star*. Later
press reports offset this competition partially. Though more
selective, the *Gazette's* may be two hours later than the *Star's,*
even though the delivery hour of both papers is the same. But
before the next issue of the *Gazette* arrives, the *Star* has a
morning paper on the Emporian's front porch, printed midway
between the two issues of the *Gazette*. The weekly cost of both
papers, with a Sunday edition thrown in for good measure, is
the same amount as that of his six copies of the home paper.
Such competition has to be met in other ways, and in one respect White's paper is among the nation's best.

An objective study of forty-four representative dailies
ranked the *Gazette* ninth. These papers were graded on twenty-
three lines of interests. Socialized news—stories of economic
and social problems, community welfare, and the like—carried
a positive score; sensationalism—stories of public violence,
murders, and sex—a negative. Nine papers received a negative
score; thirty-five positive. The *Gazette* stood ninth from the top
in the positive column, directly below the Atlanta *Constitution,*
New York *Times,* and New York *Herald-Tribune*. The Kansas
City *Times* (morning edition of the *Star*) stood twenty-
third.[12] The *Gazette* high rating was no accident. White's objective has always been to present unprejudiced and unbiased
news which appeals to the intellect rather than to the low instincts.

No treatment of state, national, or international news,
however, will hold the subscribers of a small town daily. Every
editor of a small daily knows that his front page is his parlor;

the other pages are the rooms wherein his subscribers live. Every piece of local news, though seemingly unimportant, interests some one. To report that Alfred Smith has repainted his house means more to Alfred for the moment than anything the President says. And the Alfred Smiths in the aggregate are the home town subscribers. These seemingly trivial items, moreover, reflect the spirit of the community. Thus the "Localettes" column has always been one of the *Gazette's* most popular features. There the reporters record the prosperity items, the jibes of neighboring editors, the number of transients to seek shelter in the local jail on cold winter nights, the return of Al Gufler's purple martins each spring. Mit Wilhite's first mess of roasting ears, Bert Rich's annual run-in with the officers—the pride and glory of the community, a little of its shame and dishonor.

The *Gazette,* attempting to reflect Emporia, opens its columns to whoever feels the urge to write. Preceeding every election the local Democrats have a column in which they are allowed to say whatever they wish, and throughout the year all comers are welcomed in the "Wailing Place" so long as they are willing to give the editor their names. The latter column, concerned largely with local matters, has occasionally attracted wide attention. In the weeks following Pavlowa's Emporia appearance in 1922, a controversy, partly in earnest and partly in fun, "spread a midwinter smile over a dreary land," "advertising Emporia, one way or another," and revealed "a number of complexes which were not wholesome, but which are being carried by their owners without suspicion that the world knows what is in their insides." The controversy centered about whether Pavlowa had given an artistic performance or a leg show. When the contributions grew wearisome, White shut the wailers off with one of his best epigrams: "To the pure all things are questionable; to others all things might be worse." [13] Three months later the Paris edition of the New York *Herald* and the London *Daily Mail* had White condemning the performance, and then it became "a terrible thing to live in a town with a paper which is read by exchange papers, and copied by people without a sense of humor." [14]

Partly because it is good journalistic practice for a personal editor and partly that the other side may be heard, White makes a practice of reprinting well-written articles lambasting him.

William Allen White is the most unique character in America.

One day he is the most lovable man in the nation, and the next day he is the most asinine, and it is all due to the fact that he has worms. . . . There are times when Mr. White writes in a manner scintillating and titillating, and with all wisdom. Then is when we love him.

Then comes the onrush of worms!

The hideous worms!

The worms that drive men crazy, and make them drivel, and leak at the nose and the mouth, and jibber and jabber childishly, idiotically and nonsensically.

And then is when William Allen White writes the stuff that breaks the hearts of communities. Then it is when he casts aside the graces, and becomes brutish. Then it is when we cannot love William Allen White.

But we do pity William when we cannot love him. And Atchison must assume the same attitude . . .

Atchison must drag out the mantle of charity in this case, and be kind to the fat old man who, on account of worms, does not know what he does.

Instead of kicking Bill White, Atchison should pray for him, for he is very much in need of prayer, for worms are as bad as devils. . . .

Poor Bill Allen White!

How his innards do rumble!

How distorted his face!

How distracted his mind!

Our great heart goes out to him!

Worms are hell!

They sure is! [15]

The *Gazette* has never grown so large that everyone is not a part of the news force. The sports editor turns in a society item as readily as the society editor, and a printer is as interested in news tips as job work. Mrs. White, too, sends or calls in news, and scarcely a day passes that White does not write some local and drop it in the basket on the city editor's desk. He writes few of the long stories, but those few reflect his personality. He talks to his readers directly, casually, informally. When in 1927 he gave a dinner for Kansas editors at which Herbert Hoover was guest of honor, the first paragraph of his story read:

To begin with, the neighbors brought in something. Mit Wilhite contributed a big basket of home-grown tomatoes and Maggie Ballweg contributed an Irish ham imported just before last Christmas and saved for this occasion. The ham baked, was sliced thin and served under fried chicken with a little smoked sausage beside it. Try it some day, the combination is not bad. Mrs. W. W. Finney and Mit Wilhite also furnished the zinnias, which were the only table decorations. The 25 chickens were especially dressed by Mrs. W. H. Caldwell and Mrs. Henry Williams who live west of town, who said they would not have dressed that many chickens even for pay for anybody but a man like Herbert Hoover. The Patterson Produce House sent out three dozen and a half grand Arkansas cantaloupes, the first on the market, which Hoover said were the best cantaloupes he had ever eaten. W. W. Finney grew the sweet corn on the cob. And Will Thomas of the Turkish, put an extra bait of peaches in the peach ice cream and worked Sunday to fix it, which he said he would not have done for anybody but Hoover. And Martha Klein, of the Gazette office, baked the biscuits, three square yards of them. And she and Bertha Colglazier, and Eva Knox fried the chicken and made enough cream gravy to float a ship, and the editors lapped it up. In answer to anxious inquiries from various editors, it may be said that the dope in the mashed potatoes which jazzed them up was chopped up onion and parsley.[16]

How White loves to dwell on details of a dinner! How he loves good food! On a late summer afternoon a member of the *Gazette* force often drives him home. On the way, he has the driver park, and the two go cantaloupe hunting. White subjects the melons to every test this side of an X-ray, and sometimes buys a single melon at as many as three grocery stores just to get the ones he knows he will like. He is very proud of his buying ability and frequently says to Miss Colglazier, their cook, "Bertha, I'm a good buyer, but I'm not worth a dime as a seller." Arrived home, he has first a large glass of mixed fruit juice, then the largest, reddest apple he can find. The apple disposed of he awaits dinner. Here is how Edna Ferber describes a dinner in the White home:

Platters of chicken, and always another platter of chicken. Vegetables of the bouncing Kansas kind. A great salad mixed honestly in a bowl, and turned and tossed until each jade-green leaf and scarlet tomato and blanched spear of endive glistened in its own coating of oil dressing. Home-made pie and home-made cake and ice cream.[17]

Credit for the White dinners belongs mainly to Mrs. White though White is no novice in planning a menu. Once he planned the Emporia Rotary dinners for more than a year without repeating a menu. When he is away reporting national or international conventions he invariably hunts up the city market and buys loads and loads of vegetables. Then he hires a good cook and puts on a dinner for old and new friends.

CHAPTER XXII

Baiting the Hundred Percenters

Before his nomination, Mr. Paulen denied that he belonged to the Ku Klux Klan. After his nomination he denied that he belonged to the Klan. Just a few days ago he again denied that he belonged to the Klan. He denied it thrice, and I listened for the cock to crow. It did not crow. And then I realized it couldn't crow because it was a Klucker.[1]

FOR approximately five years the Ku Klux Klan threatened to become the most powerful organization in Kansas. At the peak of its power it had intimidated professional and business men, wormed its way into Protestant churches, gained control of weekly newspapers, filled county and city offices with outright adherents, and was making a bid to dominate the state government. Its opposition to Jews, Negroes, and Catholics found a ready ear. Kansas Jews are so scarce as to be a curiosity, but they are invariably successful and the envy of lesser competitors. Negroes, though unorganized and uninfluential, are numerous and sometimes obnoxious. Catholics are in a strong minority, and to the Klan mind they take their orders direct from the Pope, store their church basements with arms to overthrow the national government, and countenance priests who debauch beautiful, screaming maidens. To those who imagined themselves sore and down-trodden, the Klan provided a temporary haven of rest; to those who had vainly aspired for public recognition, it guaranteed a means of relief; to those given to racial or religious bigotry, it furnished an outlet for their spleen; to those who were crooked or demagogic, it offered a new field for devious machinations. That organizers deluded the majority of its members into joining by high, yet false, ideals seems obvious. The Klan's rapid disintegration is difficult to explain except by its members' growing consciousness of its internal rottenness and duplicity.

To William Allen White the Klan was a pernicious and dangerous organization, compounded of hate, prejudice, intolerance, cowardice, ignorance, and foolishness. Making a case against a birthplace, a religion, or a race seemed to him to be downright un-American and cowardly; attempting to better conditions by substituting the findings of an irresponsible organization for the orderly processes of law proved the Klan to be composed of "moral idiots," who did not have enough faith in American institutions to trust them and who were too lazy to get out at the polls to evict incompetent officials. Its secrecy, its economic boycotts—all its methods of intimidation —constituted a menace to the peaceful neighborly living which he advocated. From its start in Kansas, he denounced its iniquitousness, but believed its sensible members either would redeem the organization or get out of it. Its boobs, he said, counted for nothing, "whether they had their shirt-tails in or out."

Organziation of the Emporia Klan began in late July, 1921. The *Gazette* reported that a group of Emporia men under the leadership of Dr. J. B. Brickell, after listening to the organizer's story, turned him down. White was greatly pleased at the agent's apparent failure.

It is to the everlasting credit of Emporia that the organizer found no suckers with $10 each to squander here. Whatever Emporia may be otherwise, it believes in law and order, and absolute freedom under the constitution for every man, no matter what birth or creed or race he may claim to speak and meet and talk and act as a free, law-abiding citizen. The picayunish cowardice of a man who would substitute clan rule and mob law for what our American fathers have died to establish and maintain, should prove what a cheap screw outfit the Klan is.[2]

White's faith was to be short lived. In a few days it was generally known that the Klan was organizing, and the *Gazette* carried one of its many editorials denouncing the organization. White said that if he found out who the Emporia Imperial

Wizard was, he would guy the life out of him. "He is a joke, you may be sure. But a poor joke at that." [3] Thereafter for a number of years the Klan was a lively topic in his editorials.

As late as March, 1924, White yet contended that patience and publicity afforded the most formidable weapons to fight the Klan.

. . . The fact that the mind of the Klansman is a child's mind does not make it necessarily different from other minds in its capacity to respond to sweet reasonableness and a neighborly patience. We who think we have grown-up minds have our own mental distempers. We are going through our own years of bitter disillusion. The great guns of the Western Front smashed so much more than the little French towns and the flesh and blood of the soldiers. They pounded on the faith of the world, the ideals of the world, the high hopes of the world, and amid the ruins we are all broken and sad. We should not be angry if the child minds about us show a strange perversity and a wicked bigotry which is bound to pass as humanity readjusts itself after the break-down of civilization.[4]

If White seems to reverse this stand a few months later, it should be remembered that he wanted to free weak-kneed politicians from Klan domination and to laugh the organization out of the state.

In 1924, the Republicans nominated Ben S. Paulen for governor of Kansas. When the Republican Party Council met in Topeka on August 27, it chose Congressman James G. Strong as its chairman and named Paulen chairman of the resolutions committee. This committee wrote the party platform, and Charles B. Griffith, one of its members, submitted a plank condemning the Klan by name. Griffith was attorney general and a candidate for re-election. He had already tried to oust the Klan from doing business in Kansas because it operated without a state charter. Griffith's plank got exactly one vote in the committee; and when Paulen read the party platform to the council, Griffith tried to bring out a minority report condemning the Klan. Strong refused to permit Griffith to speak, holding there was a previous question before the council. The council sustained his ruling and voted to accept the majority platform. Frank J. Ryan, secretary of state, a Catholic, and a candidate also for re-election, supported

Griffith, but neither got anywhere on the Klan issue. Both
Ryan and Griffith by virtue of their offices were members of
the state charter board. They constituted a majority on the
board and had refused to grant the Klan a charter, thus making it an illegal organization. The Klan, therefore, was out
to defeat them, as well as Jess W. Miley, state superintendent
of public instruction and candidate for re-election, who likewise had incurred its displeasure. In refusing to stand back of
Griffith and Ryan, the council demonstrated its attitude toward
the outlaw organization. The majority was either composed of
Klansmen, or its sympathizers, or men bidding for Klan support; and at the head of the Republican ticket stood Paulen,
who was credited with dominating the council's proceedings.

The Democratic Party put up Jonathan M. Davis, the
gubernatorial incumbent, for re-election. In his previous campaign Davis ran as a "dirt" farmer, and not a few impartial
observers believed that he succeeded only in bringing dirt into
state affairs. He was at outs with all other elective officers in
the state house, partly because not one of them was a member
of his party. But he had even more trouble with his legislature.
It sent him sixty-nine bills he had marked for defeat; and in
over-riding his vetoes, members of his own party joined the
Republicans. Politicians whom he appointed to office made
political footballs out of state institutions, including the schools.
Rumors of bribery were widespread; Davis himself was
eventually arrested, charged with conniving with his son in
seeking bribes in exchange for pardons and paroles. Irrespective of the merits of the rumors and charges, the best that can
be said for him is that he failed in his objectives and botched
his administration.

Davis was thought to be wobbly on the Klan. He was
accused of soliciting the support of both Catholics and Klansmen. Two of his appointees—a Klansman and a Catholic, so
it was charged—he switched as heads of state institutions to
silence the opposition in their immediate localities. When he
ran for re-election, his party platform carried an anti-Klan
plank. He was given credit for this plank; but his complete
silence on the issue until a few days before election, led some
observers to believe that his belated denunciation of the Klan

was a final gesture to stave off defeat. Many persons maintained that Davis was always governed by political expediency.

Many voters were convinced that a vote for either Davis or Paulen was a vote for the Klan. Before Paulen made his announcement, a movement was afoot to put an anti-Klan candidate in the field in the event he straddled the issue. White proposed to Joseph L. Bristow and W. R. Stubbs that one of them make the race, but both refused; and Victor Murdock and Henry J. Allen wanted White to run. White was attracted to the idea and took the matter up with Carles F. Scott, editor of the Iola *Register* and one of the strongest leaders of the conservative wing of the Republican Party. White wrote Scott that if Paulen's announcement "is mushy he oughtn't to be allowed to get by with it."

If I was dead sure that I wouldn't win I should be glad enough of the fun and to give a lot of fellows who want to vote for a man who is not a klansman a chance to vote. I don't want to be Governor of Kansas, it isn't in my line. I have four good books on the block. I am just turning out the Wilson book which I think is pretty fair and want to write more books and don't want to be bothered with administrative affairs which take a good deal of energy and attention.

But I am really attracted by the chance of getting out and talking a dozen or fifteen times in Kansas about the klan and about the decay of our state government due entirely, as I feel, to the fake cry of economy which has given us this high paid board of administrators of the educational, penal and charitable institutions. A more vicious and incompetent scheme for debasing and debauching government never was devised by man. It is the only state issue that I can see. And it is the perfect machine for the klan to operate in or any insidious minority controlling government. I would like mightily to see the primary law amended; *you* would say modified, cutting down the state wide vote on everything but Governor, Senator, Congressman and Attorney General. If the Attorney General could be appointed by the Governor, I should like to cut out the Attorney General from the primary. He shouldn't even be elected by the people as he should be the servant of the chief administrator. I should like to see a strong state convention in-augurated, with powers to nominate finally, all state officers excepting Governor, Congressman, Senator and Attorney General. And in the case of Governor, Attorney General and Senator to suggest one or two or three candidates for each office with the alternative that other candidates could be put on the ticket by somewhat larger

petitions than are now required. I should like to see a preferential
ballot on these four officers so that the minority could not win.
And I should like to see registration required for votes in the
primary, but I would not close the registration as proposed by the
legislature three years ago, so far in advance of the election.

The big thing, however, as I see it, is the Board of Administration. Someone ought to get out and talk to the people about
that devilish scheme. If I could get someone to serve as Governor
in the remote chance that I was elected, I might feel it my duty to
go out during October and make sentiment for a change in the
law. I should feel like promising the people to recommend just
these two bits of legislation: the reconstruction of the Board of
Administration by establishing honorary boards, and the modification of the primary law along the lines just suggested, and then
pledging the folks to go before the legislature every day, asking
them to pass the appropriation bills and adjourn with these two
things done. If it wasn't too much trouble and didn't add a third
complicated issue to the campaign, I would like to abolish the
Industrial Court and establish the old Department of Labor with
provision for an emergency court without punitive powers, merely
to gather data and make reports and so influence public sentiment.
But I fear this issue would start a wrangle and make a major issue
out of a minor matter. The major issue is the return of the old
Board system for the educational institutions retaining the state
purchasing agent and providing for an educational budget board
to be chosen from the three different educational boards, University, Normal and Agricultural College.

These things need agitation. I am willing to agitate, I suppose
I am a fairly good agitator, but I also fear for myself as administrator and the darn thing might run hog wild and elect me. Though
I think fear rather than vanity is at the base of my trepidation
which is honest.[5]

Scott replied after Paulen's announcement, sending
White his editorial comment "so shaped as to allow me to
jump either way." He assured him that he would not be elected,
"so you may dismiss that worry from your mind." He also
stated that he supported everything the Emporia editor advocated "long before you . . . and I wish to goodness somebody
would make a fight for them."

But the only practical result I can see from your candidacy
would be the election of Davis; and as between two evils I am inclined now—reserving the right to change my mind without previous notice at any time in the future—to think that Paulen would
be the least. He is going to make the Davis assault upon the

University and his playing-politics generally the crux of his campaign; and having done this he can hardly commit, himself, the sins for which he has crucified Davis. Paulen is weak and lacks courage, but he isn't vicious and he isn't eaten through with ambition.

So I really think you ought not to run, though to tell the truth I ain't carin' a lot if you do. The older I grow—and I'll be 64 tomorrow—the more I hate a rabbit. I don't want to be responsible for Paulen's defeat; but if it should happen in spite of me I wouldn't grieve a lot when I reminded him that I warned him.[6]

In spite of Scott's advise, White jumped into the race. To get his name on the ballot, he needed twenty-five hundred signatures. In a little more than a week, without asking anyone to solicit names for him, he had ten thousand. He formally filed his petitions and announced his candidacy on September 20.

I have filed my petition for governor and am in this race to win. It is the largest independent petition ever filed for an office in Kansas. Over three times more names were signed to these petitions for Carr Taylor and myself for lieutenant governor and governor than were needed. None of these petitions came from my home town or county. I wished honestly to test sentiment. The issue in Kansas this year is the Ku Klux Klan above everything. The Ku Klux Klan is found in nearly every county. It represents a small minority of the citizenship and it is organized for purposes of terror. Its terror is directed at honest, law-abiding citizens, Negroes, Jews and Catholics. These groups in Kansas comprise more than one-fourth of our population. They are entitled to their full constitutional rights; their rights to life, liberty and the pursuit of happiness. They menace no one. They are good citizens, law-abiding, God-fearing, prosperous, patriotic. Yet, because of their skin, their race, or their creed, the Ku Klux Klan in Kansas is subjecting them to economic boycott, to social ostracism, and to every form of harassment, annoyance and every terror that a bigoted minority can use.

And the leaders of two major parties in this state, lift no hand to defend these people. Ben Paulen, the Republican candidate for governor, accepted the Ku Klux Klan endorsement in the primary and owes his small plurality entirely to Ku Klux votes. Before the primary his party papers urged him to disclaim this un-American crew. After the primary before the party council again his fellow Republicans of all factions warned him that public sentiment would not stand for a minority nomination secured entirely by the Ku Klux Klan. In the Republican party council there was a strong element intent upon divorcing the Republican party from the Ku

Klux Klan. Ben Paulen, the Republican gubernatorial nominee, in the committee on resolutions defeated an anti-klan resolution. Then he went before the Republican party state council and with his prestige as party leader prevented even a debate upon the klan on the floor of the convention and by silence further tied the klan to him and disgraced his party in Kansas. Since then, in declaring that he was not a klansman, he has used the phrase "at this time," the one phrase that all klansmen use when denying their membership.

The Democratic gubernatorial nominee, Jonathan M. Davis, never, before the primary or since, has uttered one syllable which would offend the most ardent klansman. He had the klan endorsement in the primary. His party threw it over, but Davis has not disclaimed it.

So here are the two major parties in Kansas led in the race for governor by men who had klan support in the primary and who will not disavow that support today. A man who has not the courage nor does not rise in righteous indignation to denounce and defy the Ku Klux Klan in the primary and in the election, is not going to oppose it seriously in the governor's office.

I want to be governor to free Kansas from the disgrace of the Ku Klux Klan. And I want to offer Kansans afraid of the klan and ashamed of that disgrace, a candidate who shares their fear and shame. So I am in the race to stay and to win.

Kansas, with her intelligence and pure American blood, of all states should be free of this taint of bigotry and terror. I was born in Kansas and have lived my life in Kansas. I am proud of my state. And the thought that Kansas should have a government beholden to this hooded gang of masked fanatics, ignorant and tyrannical in their ruthless oppression, is what calls me out of the pleasant ways of my life into this distasteful but necessary task. I cannot sit idly and see Kansas become a byword among the states.

I call to my support least of all those who are oppressed by the Ku Klux Klan. We must have no class issue here. I call to my support rather all fair-minded citizens of every party, of every creed, to stop the oppression of this minority of our people. It is a nation-wide menace, this klan. It knows no party. It knows no country. It knows only bigotry, malice and terror. Our national government is founded on reason, and the Golden Rule. This klan is preaching and practicing terror and force. Its only prototype is the Soviet of Russia. So I feel that I am walking the path of duty in going into this race. I ask my fellow Kansans to come with me and to stand with me for free government and the righteous guarantees of our constitution, to all its citizens.[7]

White's candidacy attracted wide attention, but the national press expressed mixed views on the wisdom of his action.

The *Christian Science Monitor* thought he could have found "a more important question in both state and national politics than the Ku Klux Klan," and the New York *Evening Post* told its readers that "most Kansans stopped worrying about the Klan months ago" for it was dying in Kansas as it dies everywhere else after a time. The Boston *Post* prophesied that if citizens in other states could participate in the Kansas election, "Mr. White would walk away with the Governorship. In a secretive age, he thinks out loud. And he is human. That is why the rest of the country would like to see him elected governor." The New York *World* declared that he was doing a service, not only to Kansas, but to the whole country by coming out openly against the Klan.[8] In his own state, party considerations prevented the press from taking any but a partisan view of his motives.

Instead of making twelve or fifteen speeches, White spoke one hundred and four times to approximately 100,000 people. In the six weeks campaign, he traveled 2,783 miles in an old Dodge car driven by his son. He had no committees, no speakers' bureau, no publicity staff except the *Gazette,* no headquarters, and no literature. He himself comprised the grand total of his campaign. His expenses were confined to gasoline and oil and wear and tear on his car; friends and well-wishers furnished the meals and lodging. He opened his campaign in Cottonwood Falls and after his speech three men lit a fiery cross a block away, then drove as rapidly from the scene as a model T Ford would carry them. The Klan at this time enjoyed its peak strength in the Middle West; the very day he started his campaign thousands were gathering in Kansas City for the national Klan Klonvokation.

White's speeches were as serious as speeches could be which were intended to laugh the Klan out of the state. He avoided national and state questions except as they pertained to the Klan issue; wherever he went he put on a show marked by humor and picturesque language. The story that heads this chapter is typical of his humor, and the following paragraph is a sample of his play on the high sounding terminology of the Klan:

The gag rule first came into the Republican party last May. A flock of dragons, Kleagles, cyclops, and furies came up to Wichita from Oklahoma and held a meeting with some Kansas terrors, genii, and whangdoodles. . . . A few weeks later, the cyclops, Kleagles, wizards, and willopses-wallopuses began parading in the Kansas cow pastures, passing the word down to the shirt-tail rangers they were to go into the Kansas primaries and nominate Ben Paulen.[9]

When White bolted his ticket, he set the stage for lower political propaganda than usually prevails in Kansas. Public attention was largely centered on White and Paulen. Davis played a secondary role, partly because the Kansas press is overwhelmingly Republican. These Republican papers, like the party, split on the two; those that stayed with Paulen feared that White's defection would re-elect Davis. White's assertion that he was running as an independent Republican particularly irked the Paulen supporters. They accused him of bolting the party because he could not have his own way, of being a fanatic on the Klan, of making the race to advertise his forthcoming book, of seizing an opportunity to do a bit of self-advertising. No doubt all these accusations were legitimate tactics, but one by the Republican publicity committee could hardly be called square politics. Three weeks before the election, the committee made public a letter allegedly written by White to Fred Trigg of the Kansas City *Star*.

This is a rotten job you have wished on me. I had to hold a meeting yesterday on the sidewalk because so few people came out it would have looked silly to have held it in the hall. . . . If I can get out 75,000 votes, we will have Ben on the shelf. But if by any chance I am elected governor, I will have to put a cross on the state house dome, and wire the K.K.K. to keep the niggers away from the state house. Catholics, Jews and niggers are about all the support I have got . . .[10]

The publicity committee's purpose was to make White appear to be the tool of the Kansas City *Star*. Certain elements in both parties have always used the *Star* as the bloody shirt in Kansas politics. It is printed just over the state line in Missouri; therefore, it is a "Missouri paper" which, because of its tremendous Kansas circulation and interest in

Kansas affairs, "is forever trying to run the state house." Trigg was the *Star's* veteran Kansas correspondent, and the "Trigg letter," according to the publicity bureau, reflected White's classic style and characteristic thought. But instead of creating a sensation, it proved a dud. Paulen papers either ignored the letter or printed it inconspicuously.

The one indisputable fact about the outcome of the election is White ran third. The returns otherwise are open to various interpretations. White had approximately the same number of votes as the Democratic presidential nominee, but ran thirty thousand behind Davis. He and Davis polled ten thousand more than Paulen, but Paulen ran a hundred thousand behind his ticket. Democrats said that he split their vote; Republicans said it was obvious that his vote came from their party; White's supporters contended that he would have had more of Paulen's votes had not countless Republicans believed that a vote for him put Davis that much nearer re-election. All generally agreed that too many side issues in the race prevented it from being a clear-cut issue on the Klan. Griffith's, Ryan's, and Miley's candidacies seemed to afford a better test than did White's. These three were re-elected, but by slender majorities. In as much as the voting was heavy and the campaign dull except for the gubernatorial contest, a Catholic paper made a pertinent comment when it said that White chased the Klan out of the cow pastures into the polls.

The returns elated White. His campaign, he thought, had dragged the issue into the open and removed the curse of silence which the Klan had imposed on small towns. He believed that his 150,000 votes guaranteed that thereafter one or the other of the two parties would seek his followers. Whether he hastened the Klan's demise, whether he freed the Kansas parties from its domination, are matters that cannot be determined. Two years later the Klan was still to be reckoned with; but long before election, White was firing parting shots at the retreating organization.

Dr. Hiram Evans, the Imperial Wizard of the kluxers, is bringing his consecrated shirt-tail to Kansas this spring, and from five gloomy klaverns will make five Kansas speeches. We welcome him. Enter the wizard—sound the bull roarers, and hewgags. Beat

the tom-toms. He will see what once was a thriving and profitable
hate factory and bigotorium now laughed into a busted community;
where the cock-eyed he-dragon wails for its first born and the
nightshirts of a once salubrious pageantry sag in the spring breezes
and bag at the wobbly knees.

The kluxers in Kansas are as dejected and sad as a last year's
bird nest, afflicted with general debility, dizziness on going up
stairs, and general aversion to female society.[11]

Charles F. Scott lost most heavily in the anti-Klan contest. All his life he had undeviatingly supported the Republican
ticket; but this time, in spite of his advice to White to keep
out of the race, he announced for him and supported him vigorously. The day after the election a reporter for the Kansas
City *Star* asked Congressman U. S. Guyer to comment on
reports that a Kansan might be named Secretary of Agriculture. Guyer told the reporter that his district had two men
eminently qualified, Charles F. Scott and Samuel B. Haskins.
Washington papers published Guyer's remarks; and when
Chief Justice Taft read them, he called at the White House
and told Coolidge that had he been re-elected in 1912 Scott
would have been appointed to his cabinet. At that time Scott
had been in Congress ten years, four of which he had served
as chairman of the House Committee on Agriculture. Secretary of War Weeks, who had served with Scott, called on the
President and gave his endorsement, as did Frank Hitchcock
of New York. When Guyer later called on Charles Curtis, the
senior senator from Kansas, Curtis told him that Coolidge had
Scott in mind for the appointment, but said it would never do
politically because of Scott's support of an independent candidate for governor. Scott's defection evidently did not disturb
Coolidge, for he told Guyer that he "would gladly appoint Mr.
Scott if the Kansas delegation would request it," [12] and about
this time he wrote White that "I value your friendship very
much indeed, and greatly appreciate your service to your country." [13] When the Kansas delegation met, the will of Curtis
prevailed. Every member preferred Scott to all others; but
because of his refusal to support the Republican candidate for
governor, the delegation adopted a resolution endorsing William M. Jardine, whom Coolidge appointed.

White walloped one other organization over the prostrate

body of the Ku Klux Klan. In late July, 1927, a number of papers began making fun of the Daughters of the American Revolution for labeling certain Americans as reds and for circulating a folder called the "Common Enemy." The *Gazette* did not join in the merriment, but did call the charges ridiculous and the folder silly. "The bug under the chip," White said, "is that certain outfits like the Kansas Associated Industries . . . all over the country are trying to prevent the passage of social legislation, welfare legislation which will relieve injustices to women and children." He accused these groups of shaking the red flag of Bolshevism just as the "old time demagogues used to shake the bloody shirt in the seventies," and said that the D. A. R. "for the first time in its history has had to face a ribald public attitude without being able to reply." [14] White knew his name to be on the D. A. R. black list, but he did not care to make an issue of the matter. The ban against him had not yet been made public, and he was trying through personal correspondence to get his name removed from the black list.

On April 2, 1928, Associated Press papers carried a story about Mrs. Helen Tufts Bailie, a member of the D. A. R., who had denounced the organization for barring certain speakers from appearing before its chapters. She revealed that the Massachusetts chapters had black-listed Dean Roscoe Pound, of the Harvard Law School; President Mary E. Woolley, of Mount Holyoke College; Professor Felix Frankfurter, of Harvard; Federal Judge George W. Anderson, of Boston; W. E. Dubois, Negro novelist; the Reverend E. Tallmadge Root, executive secretary of the Massachusetts federation of churches: Clarence Darrow, Rabbi Stephen S. Wise, Norman Hapgood, Dr. David Starr Jordan, W. A. White, and Frank P. Walsh. These papers quoted Mrs. Bailie as saying that California and other states had "similar black-list factories." "They are all alike," she said, "in that none of them work in the open, but surreptitiously through patriotic and militarist societies, which readily become their dupes and circulate, privately, of course, lists of undesirables or doubtful speakers and organizations." [15]

Mrs. Bailie's attack inspired Mrs. Alfred Brosseau, president general of the D. A. R., to defend the Massachusetts

Top and bottom right—Two cartoons which appeared at the time of
William Allen White's attacks on Platt
Bottom Left—"A Real American Goes Hunting"; a cartoon by Rollin Kirby

Two old Sheepskin. Chaps who have been together for nigh onto forty years—
Coolie.

To Will White
with affectionate regard & hopes
Arthur Capper
Aug 2, 1932.

Press Association Inc.

William Allen White and Albert Einstein at Harvard
University in 1935, where they received honorary degrees

William Allen White and Senator Arthur Capper in 1932

daughters. In an interview approving their action, she stated that the "black-list was reported to include persons who have opposed the support given by the D. A. R. to the present navy building program." [16] This statement was White's cue to edge into the arena. He called the charge untrue, declaring that he had consistently supported President Coolidge's naval program. His name, he said, appeared on the black list before there was any question of armaments; and he accused the D. A. R. of being the tool of over-zealous military interests.

The whole D. A. R. hook-up with the superpatriot crowd seems to have come because of its foolish leadership that is developing a taste for those idle, apoplectic old gentlemen in red flannels and brass buttons who escape the boredom of their rich wives by sitting in club windows at Washington and bemoaning the decadence of a growing world. The nice old girls of the present D. A. R. administration have been hypnotised by the brass buttons of the retired army officers and lured into the red-baiting mania by the tea gladiators of Washington. These tea gladiators are keepers of the raw head and bloody bones of political conniptions, and they have certainly let the D. A. R. executives in for a lot of ridicule; which, by the way, the rank and file do not deserve. The idea of banning the Women's Federation of Clubs, the missionary boards, leaders in the Y.M.C.A. and Y.W.C.A., the League of Women Voters, and denouncing men like Dean Pound of the Harvard Law School and Federal Judge Anderson and President Woolley of Holyoke College, makes one wonder whether it is the Daughters of the American Revolution or the Daughters of the American Tories who are speaking.[17]

Mrs. Brosseau, confronted with White's comment, said that it was an "absolute misstatement of facts." She denied that she had "even by inference" labeled the organizations named as communistic, and maintained that she herself had given White "direct assurance of this fact last summer." Then Mrs. Brosseau made a fatal blunder. Regarding White's allusion to the D. A. R. being hypnotised by the brass buttons of the retired army officers, she said, "This is a personal matter between Mr. White and myself and I must consult him as to just what private census lists and records gave him his information as to our ages and susceptibility to hypnotisms." [18]

White lost no time in accepting the challenge; the evening papers carried his reply. "I have before me," he wrote, "the official list sent out by the D. A. R in a D. A. R. envelope, to the Regent of the Emporia chapter of the D. A. R., giving the list of subservient organizations which the D. A. R. has proscribed on account either of the organizations themselves, or 'the interlocking radical groups either through their directories or legislative programs.' " In disclaiming her personal responsibility for the list, he charged Mrs. Brosseau with "deft beating 'round the bush." He denied that he had ever charged her with stamping and mailing out the black lists herself, but charged her with putting the organizations under the ban of D. A. R. disapproval without consulting her national board of management. "I have before me her own official statement under the heading of April 16, 1927, in which she declares that she took the D. A. R. into the organization of tea-gladiators at Washington because she did not have time, she declared, to obtain 'a concensus of opinion from the national board of management of the D. A. R.' " "Mrs. Brosseau," he continued, "put the entire D. A. R. membership on the sucker-list of the super-patriots. That she cannot deny."

Then with one of his peculiar quirks, White gave his key to the list. "It particularly picks out organizations affecting colored people, Jews, and Catholics," he said. In proof of his contention, he named the banned organizations of these peoples and showed that many of the persons black-listed were either Catholics, Jews, or Negroes or were known as their defenders. "My guess," he says, "is that when the list was made up a kluxer sat in." It "goes out of its way in what Mrs. Brosseau calls her propaganda for peace to pick out and include the peculiar enemies of the Ku Klux Klan." He charged the D. A. R. had "yanked the Klan out of its cow pasture and set it down in the breakfast room of respectability, removing its hood and putting on a transformation." In one sentence he paid his respects to its president. "Mrs. Brosseau is a lovely lady with many beautiful qualities of heart and mind, but in her enthusiasm she has allowed several lengths of Ku Klux nightie to show under her red, white, and blue."

As for himself, White declared that a man who was a member of the small sub-committee that wrote the Republican platform a few years ago, who held a letter from the present

President thanking him for his Republicanism, and who was then a delegate at large selected by a conservative senator and leader of the Republican caucus in the Senate, "need hardly be put to the trouble to defend himself against the charge of Socialism." "But I cannot defend myself from having led the fight against the Ku Klux Klan four years ago, and that may be the reason why I am included along with the Jews, the colored people, and the Catholics, who Mrs. Brosseau's organization has so cruelly included in her unpatriotic list." [19]

White gave Mrs. Brosseau the "last say," and her statement was as short as his was long. "I thank Mr. White for his gallant offer of the 'last word,' and I hope it will be the last word in the entire matter. I emphatically disclaim all responsibility for the alleged list." [20] Beyond that she refused to comment.

It is axiomatic in Emporia that White once in a controversy, right or wrong, victor or vanquished, always wins. His unorthodox tactics, his unexpected turns, make him formidable. Once he was summoned before the legislature for hinting at corruption. When he admitted that he had no facts, the legislative body reprimanded him. White went home and wrote an apology praising the legislature so excessively that one who had been responsible for the questioning said that he made them all feel like skunks for what they had done. Another time an irate office seeker blamed White for his defeat. He went to the *Gazette* office and called White all the names he could think of. When he had finished White said, "Now, that we have that settled, what do we do next?" The disappointed politician never figured out the reply; but he repeated his story many times, always ending with the question, "what the ———— ———— can you do with a man like that?"

In bolting the Republican ticket in 1924, White was fighting for a principle. That was a joyful job. In stigmatizing the D. A. R. with the Klan, he had no fun. White was hurt to think that any group would brand him an enemy of America; when the D. A. R. leaders refused to heed his pleas, he gathered his information, carefully awaiting the time to make them rue the day they put his name on their black list.

CHAPTER XXIII

Prohibitionist

. . . I don't care for cocktails nor any kind of booze.
It means less than nothing to me, but if I thought a
hostess would be offended I would lap up a dishful. The
choice seems to be whether one would be considered a
hypocrite or proved a prig, personally I should prefer to
be considered a hypocrite.

An insisting hostess in Washington put me to sleep
for her dinner that way. A hostess in Honolulu who
pressed raw fish on me came very near having a tragedy
at her dinner, but I did take it. I have some dear friends
in California who have no marriage license in the family,
but I love to visit them.

These things, illegal booze, raw fish, marriage
licenses, all are matters of conscience in which I would
be the last to judge my neighbors and my friends. [1]

KANSAS was the second state to adopt state-wide prohibition. By an amendment to the state constitution in
1880, the electorate prohibited the manufacture and
sale of intoxicating liquors, except for medical, scientific, and
mechanical purposes. The majority was decisive, but did not
represent a wave of emotionalism. Temperance had long been
a lively topic. Even during territorial days legislative bodies
passed regulatory laws; and when state-wide prohibition became an actuality, it was but the culmination of an ever-
growing sentiment. Hard times, however, strengthened the dry
cause. In the middle seventies Kansas suffered a calamitous
grasshopper invasion. Thousands were destitute; so general
was the distress that other states had to aid the sufferers. Many
believed that liquor increased the economic burdens, and during the late seventies the prohibition movement speeded up.

In 1879, Governor St. John asked the legislature to enact prohibitory legislation. His legislative message reads in part:

Much has been said of late years about hard times and extravagant and useless expenditures of money; and in this connection, I desire to call your attention to the fact that here in Kansas, where our people are at least as sober and temperate as are found in any of the states of the West, the money spent annually for intoxicating liquors would defray the entire expenses of the State government, including the care and maintenance of all its charitable institutions, Agricultural College, Normal School, State University, and Penitentiary, and all this expenditure for something that, instead of making mankind nobler, purer, and better, has only left its dark trail of misery, poverty, and crime. Its direct effects, as shown by the official reports, have supplied our state prison with 105 of its present inmates.

Could we but dry up this one great evil that consumes annually so much wealth, and destroys the physical, moral and mental usefulness of its victims, we should hardly need prisons, poor houses or police.[2]

St. John's statement represents the characteristic Kansas attitude toward liquor control. Except to a small minority, the problem has ever been economic rather than moral. The dominant prohibitionists were not churchmen, preachers, or women; they were bankers, merchants, editors—men responsible for the commercial and industrial progress of their communities. Because liquor interfered with economic efficiency, they sought to banish it. To them prohibition guaranteed lower taxes, increased labor efficiency, larger saving accounts, and safer and saner living. Senator Arthur Capper is a typical Kansas dry. He publishes a group of papers whose combined circulation runs into the millions. Capper began work on his Topeka *Capital* as a part-time printer. Before he had a permanent job, he substituted for the printers who had not yet sobered up from the weekend orgy. Men like Capper preached the evils of liquor until they created the sentiment that made possible Kansas' drastic liquor laws.

State prohibition worked fairly well in Kansas. One who sought liquor could always find it, but the prohibitory laws worked as well as did the laws against gambling, prostitution, and murder. Liquor, like these other matters, ceased to be a state issue. As long as bordering states were wet, the dry forces waged an aggressive campaign. They utilized every possible means of keeping their cause before the public—newspapers, magazines, schoolbooks, the lecture platform. When national prohibition came, they lost their crusading zeal. The fight had been won, they believed, and in a few years the nation would accept prohibition as Kansas had. Their state had been dry for forty years. In that time they had strengthened the anti-liquor laws and reared a generation that had no taste for liquor. What national prohibition was to do for Kansas they could not foresee. The national press, the stage, and the screen made it a standard joke; Kansans along with the rest of the nation began to laugh. The violation of liquor laws appeared smart, especially to the country club set and youths in their late teens and early twenties. Places unfamiliar with liquor made its acquaintance; alcoholism, which had been declining before the national amendment, increased after 1920. Had the Kansas drys looked about them and consulted the statistics, they would have realized that national prohibition was no friend to the dry cause in their state.

Why prohibition worked better in Kansas than elsewhere, why Kansas retained it when most other states ratified repeal, are speculative questions. Some facts, however, seem significant. When Kansas was being settled, certain immigrants avoided the state because of its prohibitory laws, so that its people became somewhat selective. Kansas, which ranks first among the states in the percentage of American born citizens, has only four counties containing a large number of foreign born. There the anti-liquor laws gave trouble, and the prohibition situation was admittedly bad. Kansas is also largely agricultural. It has but two cities with more than 100,000 people. One of these is an overflow from a Missouri city, and Missouri has ever been regarded as wet. This fact makes impossible any conclusion on whether prohibition is more successful in an urban or a rural community. The other city, however, is situated in the interior. The situation there was likewise bad. The state attorney general was forever threatening ouster proceedings against local officials because they ignored prohibition violations. If Kansas is a fair illustration, its long experience with prohibition indicates that it works better among the native born and in rural communities.

William Allen White reflected the Kansas attitude. He was a dry because he believed that prohibition brought unquestioned economic benefits. He believed, also, that the nation once aware of these benefits would move toward prohibition as had his native state. Wanting the Eighteenth Amendment to have a fair trial, he opposed treating it as a joke. So thoroughly was he convinced of the justice of the dry cause that he resigned a twelve thousand dollar a year job with a humorous magazine because it insisted on making fun of prohibition. During the twenties his staunch friendship for the dries led him into a major political controversy.

Aside from its stand on prohibition, White had little in common with the dominant thought in the Republican Party during the twenties. One experience in bolting a national party was enough, though. When the Progressive Party faded, he concluded that if a liberal party under the leadership of Roosevelt could not compete, then to follow a third party headed by a man like La Follette was to throw one's vote away. He came to believe that a liberal could be most effective when working within one of the two major parties. The non-partisan farm bloc, which often held the balance of power during the Harding-Coolidge era, strengthened this belief. With such Republicans as Borah and Norris, he had much in common; and although they were not wielding great power within the Republican organization, they were to be reckoned with in the legislative halls.

White was a delegate to the Republican national convention in 1928. In his syndicate articles he left no doubt about what he thought of his party and its leading candidates.

When a great party like the Republican party resolves to keep business out of politics and politics out of business, when it abandons the purpose of its founders to make government an agency of human welfare the best minds of the country go into business and party conventions are conducted by a lot of animated rubber stamps debating solemnly whether to bow down in worship to an adding machine like Hoover or a cream separator like Lowden, or a back-firing tractor like Dawes.[3]

Though White was a member of the small sub-committee that drafted the platform, he treated the committee with no more respect than the candidates.

It was conservative to the point of reaction in its consideration of all social legislation excepting prohibition. The planks which the various women's organizations requested were ignored. Labor was treated with respect but not affection. And the plank of the Women's National Party demanding equality for women which would have wiped out the special industrial legislation for women, had no more courtesy than the planks presented by the League of Women Voters. Anything that looked like social change was rejected; any hark back to Rooseveltian progressivism was frowned upon.[4]

Prohibition was worth fighting for; and when the Democrats nominated Alfred E. Smith, White had his issue. For both Smith and Hoover he had profound respect. He believed that if Hoover were elected, he would be the most erudite man in the presidential chair since John Quincy Adams; and Smith's successful career exactly fitted White's idea of a political leader. There were, however, fundamental reasons for White's opposition to Smith: his Tammany connection, his wetness, his urban complexion. Basically, Smith's political strength in New York state had always been in New York City; and while White admitted that there was no good reason why the back alley should not produce as capable a leader as the backwoods, Smith's experience and habits of thought were provincial rather than national. White concurred with the Middle West in thinking that you could take Al Smith out of New York, but not New York out of Al Smith. Smith to many was a man earnestly striving to understand such national problems as agriculture, but thwarted by his limited experience and outlook. Smith's provincialism was sufficient reason for White to prefer Hoover; his attitude on prohibition justified militant opposition.

On July 7, White wrote an editorial on Smith's record that furnished the most sensational issue in the campaign. He testified to Smith's "unusual intelligence, splendid courage and rare political wisdom," but said that he had risen to power on "a curious political record." (1) Ten times in the New

York legislature he voted against allowing the people to vote on any sort of restriction of the sale of liquor. (2) Three times he voted against bills which would make it easy to convict the violators of liquor laws in the saloon days. (3) Three times he voted to repeal the law against keeping the saloons open on Sunday. (4) Four times he voted to remove zoning restrictions which would keep open saloons from churches and schools. (5) Three times he voted for laws favored by organized gambling and gamblers, and once he refused to go on record as voting for a bill against bribing labor union leaders. (6) Four times he voted against stopping gambling and prostitution in connection with saloons. Such a record, White concluded, "would have damned him deeper than the slag-pits of hell" in any other state; but in New York where he had never carried more than five counties, and those in the Tammany-controlled metropolitan area, he had risen to the governorship of a great state in the face of this record.

On July 12, when White officially opened the Republican campaign in Kansas, he repeated these charges. The next day Associated Press newspapers carried his speech, casting the die for a bit of sensationalism. Smith came back at White, charging that he had accepted the word of Reverend O. R. Miller, superintendent of the New York State Civic League, whom Smith said was circulating false information about his legislative record. "No one," Smith asserted, "places any stock in what Miller says, but Mr. White has brains and ought to know better." [5] Smith disclaimed any knowledge of ever voting against measures to stop gambling and prostitution in saloons and declared that he could remember no such proposals being before the legislature. White, in turn, denied he had ever heard of Miller, said that he got his information from the New York newspapers, and further pressed Smith by pointing out that he had not denied the "specific votes."

Smith's comments on the accusations ended the controversy temporarily, but when he injected Miller into the case, White had either to prove his charges or appear the victim of an alleged rascal. He was scheduled to do some writing in Europe; and going to New York early, he personally looked into

Smith's legislative record. On July 29 he released a statement reading in part:

> Governor Smith has been a busy man, a fine, useful American citizen since he left the New York assembly. . . . Two weeks ago he did me the honor to wallop me over a preacher's shoulders, calling the preacher, whom I never heard of, a liar and an 18-carat faker. In these two weeks I have employed two experts, working independently, and have gone into the New York assembly journal. I am now ready to present his assembly record to Governor Smith, not merely in broad, general terms, but to face him with his own votes on questions affecting the saloon and its two parasites—the gambler and the prostitute. . . .
>
> . . . If he questions any vote, a photostat of that page will be presented. . . .
>
> . . . These detailed record votes will show that he voted, or is so recorded, nearly a dozen times in the big controversial measures with the most notorious saloon men in the Tammany delegation. . . .
>
> No klansman in a boob legislature, cringing before a kleagle or a wizard, was more subservient to the crack of the whip than was Al Smith . . . in the legislature when it came to a vote to protect the saloon; to shield the tout, and to help the scarlet women of Babylon, whose tolls in those years always clinked regularly in the Tammany till. . . .
>
> This record is, of course, an old record of a young man. But the young man rose on this record. And today the issue is formed on the elements that made this old record—the return of the saloon, which Governor Smith as a young man defended so ably. But the Tammany system goes on today as it went on 100 years ago and, indeed, as it will go in all of our American cities unless Governor Smith and the sinister forces behind him are overthrown.[6]

The next day White made public his findings—a detailed statement of Smith's record running to two and one-half columns. He reprinted measures bearing out his contentions, showed how Smith had voted, and cited the bills by number and page, making it possible for any one who doubted to appeal directly to the record. Smith's answer, he said, "should not be an alibi, and lacking repudiation the record stands as a foreshadowing portent of what may be expected from Governor Smith in the White House." [7]

Then White did one of those things that make him the despair of party organizations. During the Roosevelt administration, when well-wishing Republicans were advising Roosevelt to curb his daughter's "shocking" activities, a member of the Kansas Republican Committtee once said to White, "Bill, every time I see you I know how the President feels when he thinks of Alice." Time and again White has furnished ammunition for the opposition because the two sides of a controversial question kept bobbing before his eyes; again and again he has thrown a wrench into a party organization when he undertook to play fair. This time Walter Lippmann, then of the New York *World,* told White that Smith was deeply aggrieved that he should charge him with protecting gambling and prostitution. Lippmann persuaded White to believe that Smith had cast his votes against those reform bills because he honestly believed that they were unconstitutional, or were not enforceable, or infringed upon personal liberty, or encouraged police blackmail. White granted to Smith "the purity of his motives which always should be granted in any political controversy," [8] and withdrew his charges on gambling and prostitution, letting those on the saloon stand.

When White issued his statement, Democratic newspapers in both their headlines and "leads" declared that White had retracted. Henry J. Allen, chairman of the Republican publicity committee then took a hand in the affair. White, now on his way to Europe, stated in answer to Allen's inquiry that he had retracted nothing. Without consulting White, Allen released his cablegram, further kindling the political fires. Then the Democratic publicity committee in a cleverly coined phrase asserted White had "retracted his retraction."

Smith, meanwhile, refused to comment. While White was in New York he was out of the state on a vacation. On August 6 he returned to Albany and began drafting his reply. On the twenty-first, the day before he made his official notification speech, he made public his answer. He denounced White's accusations as a slanderous attack upon him and his record, "unfair, unmanly, and un-American." Like the Democratic publicity committee, he attempted to turn the withdrawal charges into political capital, hinting that the Republican committee played an unseen part in the attempt to defame his character. "Mr. White," he said, "sailed for Europe with a happy and contented mind, I hope, and I would not disturb it by attempting to describe to him the heavy weight that he laid upon my family when he accused me of being a friend of prostitution." [9] In defense of his record, he advanced the same arguments as had Walter Lippmann. He maintained that the proposed laws were unconstitutional, unworkable, and unenforceable. With White's answer to his reply, the controversy disappeared from the front pages, though lesser Democratic candidates did not let the matter rest until after election.

White returned to America in early October; and except for his version of the controversy in the *Gazette,* he made no further comment on the gambling and prostitution charges. It was now his turn to feel unfairly treated. Smith and the Democratic committee had refused to believe, or at any rate would not acknowledge, that he had acted in good faith when he sought to withdraw the unsavory part of the record from discussion. Their interpretation that he had acted from weakness, he considered cowardly and cruel; their insistence that he had made numerous retractions he considered smart politics even though it had nothing to do with the facts. White was sent into the doubtful areas of the South and East as a campaign speaker, and though he refused to discuss the controversial points which he had sought to withdraw from the campaign, the Democrats continued to make the issue a part of their political strategy. Senator Joe Robinson, Democratic candidate for vice-president, said that White by one dishonorable act had destroyed a lifelong record of honorable dealing. When he campaigned in Kansas he read excerpts from one of White's *Collier's* articles extolling Smith; and White notified him through his paper that if he would look in his new book then on sale, he would not have to go back two years for such statements. Not until Smith's defeat was the last heard of gambling and prostitution.

Assuming that White's original accusations were beneath the dignity of a national campaign, the responsibility for the proportions which they assumed makes a nice problem. If White is to be blamed for injecting sensationalism into a presidential race, then Smith must be blamed for keeping it alive after White sought to squelch it. Had White known Smith's reasons for voting as he did, he never would have brought the charges. Had Smith taken the accusations up with White personally instead of publicly denouncing him as a political monger, the whole matter would have ended then and there. There were, however, no "if's"; and what the Emporia editor set in motion, the Democratic organization kept alive.

The election ended the controversy, but not White's part in the prohibition issue. For twenty years Easterners had considered him the spokesman for the dry West. Leading magazines sought his articles on prohibition; and during the life of the Eighteenth Amendment, newspapers printed interviews whenever he was in New York. Before Hoover had served half his term, he was viewing the issue with alarm. He saw the country getting into an emotional state where neither the wets nor the drys would admit the honesty or the intelligence of the other side. He prophesied that prohibition would be a leading issue in the 1932 campaign, possibly the only issue, and he feared that it might split both parties. We as a nation are playing with fire, he said, and in his judgment the country faced a crisis not unlike that brought about by slavery in the 1850's.

For more than two decades White had been advocating a change in the American constitution which would permit minorities an opportunity to take their case directly to the people, when they were sufficiently large to raise the question of whether they were minorities or majorities. He was more interested in the perpetuation of democratic institutions than in any other political or economic problem. Quite naturally then as opposition to the existing liquor laws increased, he took the stand that the wets had a just grievance. In his opinion, they were being denied an appeal to the people; and he had no sympathy for those drys who were making it impossible to get the question on the ballot. Consequently, he welcomed resubmission in 1932, holding that the sooner the voters acted the better the country would be and the safer the national government.

Kansas did not vote on repeal until 1934. A popular referendum had written prohibition into the state constitution, and the only method of getting it out was by a popular vote in a general election after a legislature voted to submit the issue to the people. From 1932 to 1934, 3.2 beer, which had been legalized by Congress, was openly sold in the state. Law enforcement officials attempted to prohibit its sale, but the state supreme court ruled in the absence of a specific law defining the intoxicating point of malt beverages the judge or jury trying each case should decide whether or not the beer was intoxicating. This ruling nullified attempts to prohibit its sale when numerous juries decided that the beer was not intoxicating. When the electorate voted on the amendment, they retained it by a large popular majority. The election returns, however, were open to conflicting interpretations. Drys believed the results meant the majority wanted to retain the existing liquor laws. Others maintained that they voted to retain the amendment because they did not want to see the liquor question thrown wide open. They said they cast their vote in the understanding that the laws would be liberalized.

The ballots were hardly counted before White came out for a modification of the "bone-dry" laws, "in the interests of common decency, in the effort to sustain neighborly relations, in the interests of the democratic principle of consideration for minorities." [10] He proposed a six point program. (1) 3.2 beer should not be prohibited, but should be subject to control by state, county, or city. (2) Possession of a small amount of liquor, however hard, should not be legal evidence of an intention to sell. (3) Manufacture of home brewed beer, of homemade cider, of homemade wine, should not be prohibited. Sale, however, should be. (4) Persons should be permitted to bring into the state small quantities, not to exceed a gallon of wine or a quart of hard liquor, for their personal use. (5) With the liberalization of the intent of the law should come more stringent legislation to enforce the liberalized laws. (6) New laws should be framed in the knowledge that prohibition was aimed at the organized liquor traffic and not at the personal use of liquor.

These rather mild proposals created a storm of criticism among the Kansas drys who were interpreting the election returns as a decisive victory. White was accused of being a traitor to their cause, a tool of the beer barons. He, nevertheless, held that if the drys "fantastically knocked around" the wet minority, prohibition would be just that much surer to be knocked out. During the next session of the legislature he opposed the bill that would have prohibited 3.2 beer. The senate and the house dead-locked, leaving the beer illegal yet openly sold in defiance of the laws. In 1937 the legislature finally legalized the beer, but left the other liquor laws untouched.

One is driven to the conclusion that White's attitude toward the liquor problem was the result of his environment. Certainly there is nothing in his thinking or habits suggestive of the crusader who believes that one drop of liquor imbibed is a passport to hell; and while he is a man of rather fixed habits, his prejudices are few and somewhat harmless. Yet it would be a mistake to assume that Kansas circumscribes his thinking, for no other reason than the fact that he is outside the state a good proportion of his time.

The Whites are not in Emporia as much as is generally believed. Every summer when they are not on a more distant trip, they spend a month or two in their Estes Park cabin in Colorado. In the fall or early winter they go to New York to see the shows, hear opera and symphonies, and look at pictures. Then in January or February they seek a warmer climate, California, Arizona, or New Mexico. In the spring White again goes East to attend meetings of various organizations of which he is a director or member, such as the Book-of-the-Month Club, the Rockefeller Foundation, the Pulitzer Foundation, and the American Society of Newspaper Editors. Mrs. White seldom accompanies him on this trip; she remains at home to put out her flowers. These trips are as much a part of their lives as their Emporia home, and White's trips to conventions, speaking engagements, and the like, added to them means that he is away fully half the time. During the year that this book was written, the Whites were away from Emporia seven months, counting only those absences of a week or more.

When he is in Emporia he follows a rather fixed routine. Every morning by eight Mrs. White or Miss Colglazier, their cook, companion, and friend, drives him to the *Gazette*. White does not drive. Bill once attempted to teach him; and just as he seemed to be making some progress, he waved and yelled proudly at a neighbor who was standing on his lawn and before

Bill could get the car under control White had it in his neighbor's front yard. After that incident the White family said "No" to the suggestion that he might learn to drive. Arrived at the *Gazette,* he climbs out head first, turns around and very elaborately bids the driver adieu, utterly unaware of the danger he puts himself in from passing cars. Once inside, he pads about saying "good morning" to every one, sometimes as many as four times within a half hour to the same employee. If he has been away, he calls on all; for, say the printers, "He thinks just as much of us as he does of those big guys back East."

When he is not busy, he gives the impression of never having had a perplexed moment. He has "the face of a cherub unsullied by sin," as one Emporian once put it, twinkling blue eyes, and impish smile. In his leisure moments, he potters about the office, unwrapping a book, opening a letter, or looking at an exchange. When he works, which is most of the time, he is all business. He dictates his editorials rapidly, reads the transcribed copy, and corrects the proofs. His office, whose walls are covered with letters, cartoons, and pictures of famous men, is about as conducive to work as a junk shop. His desk is littered with letters, papers, and books, to the depth of a foot. The privacy which he enjoys about equals what one would have on a busy street. The office has three entrances, and every person going back and forth between the news room and business office passes his desk. The third entrance is for outsiders who want to see the editor.

Despite the bedlam in which he works, he is not disturbed by persons running about or their noise. A caller may stand in the door for several minutes and turn and go away without White being conscious of his presence. This absorption in his work protects him from both the office force and visitors; for no one but a foolhardy person would break in on that concentration unannounced, and when one does White has a kindly but nonetheless effective way of getting rid of him when his business is finished. All visitors he meets with a friendly handshake, but woe unto that man who presumes on that friendliness. One newcomer to town once walked into his office, slapped him on the back, and called out, "Hello, Bill, how are you?" White slowly arose from his chair, looked at the caller, deliberately put on his glasses to look at him some more, then said, "Your name is—? You are from—, are you not? What can I do for you?"

Shortly before the noon hour, White calls home to say he is ready to come home for lunch. Lunch over, he takes an afternoon nap—a practice his doctor forced upon him. By three he is again at the *Gazette* where he works on books sometimes, magazine articles, and a correspondence which requires more than one stenographer. At five he quits work, goes home, drinks his big glass of fruit juice, eats his red apple, and awaits dinner. His recreation, which follows dinner, is the piano, phonograph, and books. He plays the piano for pleasure and to relieve his taut nerves. His repertoire includes the latest song hits and classics. All the numbers he plays by ear; and when he comes home from New York he sits down at the piano and plays the latest tunes, for the Whites never listen to the radio except for news and seldom go to the movies. Every evening he plays the phonograph for an hour, mostly symphonies from a large library of records containing the best money will buy. The remainder of the evening he and Mrs. White read.

Their home life is far from secluded; their hospitality is famous. Here is how Edna Ferber describes a visit:

The White family will call for you at the station, and return you to it. As you step off your train some one steps on it who is being farewelled by the Whites. As you board it twenty-four hours later there descends from it someone who is welcomed by the Whites. If you say, "Oh, I didn't know you had other guests, I hope I'm not inconveniencing you," you will find yourself addressing empty air because Will White, with one of your bags, and Young Bill, with the other, are already leading the way toward the family Dodge which is slightly swaybacked from much bearing of visitors and visitors' luggage . . . your twenty-four hours will be a mellow blend of roomy red brick house, flagged terrace, lily pond, fried chicken, books, ancient elms, four-poster beds, hot biscuits, front porch, old mahogany, deep-dish apple-pie, peace, friendliness, bath-rooms, Kansas sky, French peasant china, and the best conversation to be found east (or west) of the Rockies.[11]

The visit over, Miss Ferber could have said, White will say, "Come to see us whenever you are in Emporia, day or night." Nor do they have to be home; for a half dozen weekend guests during their absence has occurred more than once. Three or four times a week they have from two to a dozen for dinner. It may be a dinner to which they have invited Emporia friends to meet a visiting celebrity, it may be only Emporia friends or *Gazette* employees. On frequent occasions they throw their home open to organizations meeting in Emporia. The visitors are treated to good food and three storeys of beautiful furnishings—paintings, tapestries, vases, books, rugs, draperies, White's study with its autographed books, photographs, letters, and gifts from his contemporaries, Mary's room arranged and furnished almost the same as at the time of her death. The visitors explore the home from basement to attic, seeing all and enjoying all. And the Whites enjoy their pleasure.

Only once has their social life threatened to bring them trouble. It is not necessary or possible here to set forth the ramifications of the Finney scandals, ending in the son going to prison and the father taking his life; they have, however, been told in Bill's novel, *What People Said*. Warren Finney, local banker and telephone manager, had the hallmark of a gentleman. Tall, broad-shouldered, erect, proud—he appeared every inch a king; and when his rotten financial structure collapsed revealing his corrupt and perverted character, public scorn never touched his haughty figure. He and his wife wormed their way into the Whites' confidence. For years they were the Whites' closest friends socially; and despite warnings, the Whites, unsuspecting and blind, refused to believe that the Finneys were crooks. When Finney's son's financial bubble burst disclosing nearly a million dollars' worth of forged bonds, the father's machinations also came to light. Luckily for Will and Sallie White that they were in Europe when the law finally caught up with the elder Finney. Finney, who had depended on his and his friends' prestige to protect him, tried to incriminate White. Bill, then in charge of the *Gazette,* handled the situation with masterly finesse, and Walt Hughes had lived long enough to see that Finney never had an opportunity to get his hands on White money.

CHAPTER XXIV

The New Deal—Yes and No

We have, at times, said some harsh and maybe bitter things, even possibly untrue in hasty inadvertence, about our noble leader in the White House. At other times we have strung along with him. But always we have lifted our humble cry for tolerance. He may be goofy. He may smile too much. And he may always be playing the game with his eye on the ball—the same being the main chance for F.D.R.—but nevertheless he is about the only live President we have and in addition to that the man is honest and he is sincere, and our humble cry always has been and is:

"Don't shoot the pianist; he's doing his best!" And so affiant shall ever pray! [1]

DURING the Paris Peace Conference, George Creel said that White was for Wilson except at election time, and during the 1936 campaign Franklin D. Roosevelt boasted that White was for him three years and a half out of every four years. Theses have been written [2] showing that White has opposed the party that best represented his views, and social science teachers have accused him of turning his back on liberalism with the approach of each quadrennial election. All these accusations imply that irrespective of how independent, liberal, or non-partisan White may be, he accepts any candidate his party puts up and supports the Republican ticket when the test comes. Democrats have always brought the charges, sometimes to gain Democratic votes. The implication is that when there is no question of putting men in office, White supports Democratic policies. Ergo, the Democrat party is the liberal party. At election time, so the argument runs, he absurdly turns against the very men who champion his policies.

Notwithstanding its partisan purpose, the contention is not wholly false. Between the quadrennial elections, party considerations do not influence White's stand on issues. Having a strong liberal leaning, he often agrees with Democratic leaders like Wilson and Franklin Roosevelt. But in any presidential year, whether he agrees in the main with the Democrats or the Republicans or neither, he announces that the *Gazette* will support the Republican ticket. This is tantamount to announcing that until election, the *Gazette* is going to say whatever it can for the Republicans and nothing against them. The Democrats will either be ignored, or attacked where they are most vulnerable. Therefore, beware. The *Gazette* is now a partisan paper.

The accusations—whether brought by students, teachers, or politicians—may be reduced to a single sentence: White sometimes opposes a Democratic presidential nominee who better represents his views than does the Republican whom he supports. This fact admits of little argument. One might argue whether Harding or Cox best represented White's views. When the two were running White said that whenever he got to thinking about Harding, he would decide to vote for Cox, until he began to think about Cox, and then it seemed the only thing to do was to vote for Harding. One might argue about Davis and Coolidge, or Smith and Hoover, but not about Roosevelt and Hoover. The measures enacted during Roosevelt's first term in office better represented White's views than any other program after the Progressive period.

White's support of Hoover when he should have been supporting Roosevelt is explicable. Neither the Democratic nor the Republican Party is the sole guardian of liberalism or conservatism. In both parties these two forces wrestle for control and success goes first to the one and then to the other. As the complexion of parties changes, independent newspapers that confine themselves to making public opinion are free to cross party lines to support the party which best represents their cause. But the Emporia *Gazette* enjoys no such freedom. Its editor does not confine his efforts to molding public opinion. He is aligned with the Republican Party to bore from within. Sometimes his party represents his views fairly well; at other times, very badly. But irrespective of his views on his party's stand, he must support the ticket at election time if he is to maintain personal influence in party councils. Since 1912 White has been one of the half-dozen or dozen men who draft national platforms. He has helped write every Republican presidential platform, except one, when the party put a new man before the country. The exception was 1916, when he helped write the Progressive platform.

White is sometimes called an impractical visionary; he is sometimes accused of getting his facts crossed. For both accusations ample evidence exists; but despite his visions and his errors, he has a genius for knowing the political needs of the hour. Consider how President Roosevelt caught the imagination of the American people in the dark days of 1933 with action and ever more decisive, vigorous action, and then read White's address to President Hoover.

Surely the need of the hour is for strong, dramatic leadership, together with the drama of a cause. For ordinary times an ordinary President will do. But President Hoover, who has some sort of a shrinking horror of connecting his office with causes, should be told by his advisors that in extraordinary times, times of turmoil and panic, the Presidential office must take leadership in the country. If he contests with the Senate—and certainly he should—he must fight. If he fights he must appeal to the people, and to appeal to the people he must dramatize his cause or the cause loses, and with the cause his fortune falls.

Go to the people, Mr. President. They are dependable. Lincoln, Roosevelt and Wilson found the people a tower of refuge and of strength. Whoever is wise and honest and brave, they will follow to victory. But their leader must take them into his councils. They will repay candor with confidence.[3]

Through a friend White submitted a plan calling for the President to open relief offices in Cleveland and Chicago where Hoover would go on a part time basis to direct the work as he did in Belgium during the World War. But Hoover rejected the plan with the statement that he had to be President of the United States.

Again, White's comments on the 1933 elections reveal his political foresight. White warned his party of certain defeat unless it "gets right and gets right quick" with the people. The triumph of the progressives in both parties, he wrote, makes obvious that "liberal issues will defeat any man, or any party or any crowd or combination that tries to stop them." It "makes no difference what the reactionary Democrats think, . . . little difference what the reactionary Republicans try to do." Then he designated the issues for "must" legislation. (1) Something must be done about unemployment. (2) Something must be done for the farmer. (3) Something must be done to petrify lame duck congressmen. (4) The Muscle Shoals problem must be solved. (5) The tariff must be revised downward. (6) The right to enjoin labor in strikes must be abandoned so far as it effects picketing and lawful assemblage, and the right to solicit membership in the union. (7) Consideration must be made of old-age pensions, either in states or by the nation. (8) Public utilities must be controlled in the interest of the consumer of transportation, light, heat, and power. "Why are the party leaders blind to these things?" he asks. "They are as plain as a house afire and as dangerous." [4]

In other circumstances, White might have been a New Dealer, at least in the early part of Roosevelt's administration. But the circumstances that ushered in the New Deal left White cheering from the side lines while he watched another group enact a vast amount of social legislation which he had urged on an unwilling Republican Party. Nonetheless he enjoyed the show. He took malicious delight in some of Roosevelt's appointments—men who believed in what the *Gazette* had been "hammering away at" for thirty years. Roosevelt's policy, he wrote, "is plain as a barn door. . . . We are getting our revolution through the administrative arm of the government, without legislation." He hoped the conservative Democrats "who were lambasting Hoover a year and a half ago are enjoying what they got." As for himself, "the *Gazette* gets a great laugh out of this" in these "sad days of the depression." "In fact you may catch us grinning at any hour of the day or night to think of what has happened in this land of the free." [5]

The New Deal was nearly a year old when White wrote these words. What had been going on was "odd, most awful odd." The Constitution was "straining and cracking," but "after all the Constitution was made for the people and not the people for the Constitution." We "are toying gaily with billions as we once played cautiously with millions." We "are legerdemaining a huge national debt which is to be paid heaven knows when or how or where." The Emporia editor was bewildered. How much of "this New Deal . . . is false, how much is true, how much is an illusion of grandeur, a vast make believe, only time will tell." [6] Before Roosevelt took office, White started cheering on persistent rumors that he would recognize Russia and sign the Norris' Muscle Shoal bill. At the same time, he gave notice that he had not surrendered to the Roosevelt smile. "We have a shingle nail in our paddle to whack him a good sound sock in the spanker when he ties up with Tammany Hall in the matter of patronage," [7] he wrote. But White forgot to use this particular paddle. He knew the corruption of Boss Pendergast's political machine, as did thousands of others in the Middle West, though few suspected it of debauching Kansas City so thoroughly. He also knew the Roosevelt Administration accepted the support of this machine, and started to clean Kansas City up only after the votes had been safely delivered for a second term. Perhaps Roosevelt gave White so many other things to think about that he forgot patronage.

As a matter of fact, White supported Roosevelt's measures not wholly because he approved them. He called the NIRA "cock-eyed, pug-nosed, hump-backed, slather-mouthed and epileptic," but advised Little Business in Kansas "to get in and play ball." "She is no beauty, but gentlemen, she has a heart of gold and good intentions, which should count for something in this wicked world." [8] White believed that the failure of Roosevelt would mean Communism or Fascism. Between one or the other stood only the President, and Roosevelt in the White House was "our one fortress in this hour." His office was one of leadership, and he was "our only leader in this crisis." He had used his extraordinary powers "with moderation, courage and wisdom," and so long as there remained an immediate possibility of another slump in business, White supported Roosevelt whenever he asked for extraordinary authority. To Roosevelt the country could turn "in confidence, in faith, in hope" in the knowledge of his past achievements. [9]

As criticism of Roosevelt became more pronounced with

the approach of the 1936 election, White reported that Republicans were fooling themselves if they thought to destroy the laws Roosevelt had put on the books. Roosevelt, he said, may lose leadership, but his program is here to stay; when Republicans come to power they will administer it wisely and improve it sensibly. The last thought accounted for a part of White's warm support of Alfred Landon. White would never have agreed to the political argument that to put a Republican in the White House would have meant the repeal of the New Deal, and certainly he could never have imagined Landon making such an effort. Landon had been a member of the liberal Republican faction in Kansas, had cast his first vote for Theodore Roosevelt in 1912, had bolted the state ticket for White in 1924, and had "gone along" with the New Deal for four years.

A group of Kansas newspapermen were largely responsible for Landon's nomination, but White was not one of them. He was in the Orient when the Landon boom started; it was already sizeable proportions when he returned. In the national convention, however, White represented the governor. He was entrusted with bringing Senator Borah into line and with writing Landon's policies into the platform. How the various planks were written, how the platform emerged less liberal than Landon wished and less conservative than his eastern friends had hoped for, how he thanked the committee for their hard work and assured them that Landon would accept its decisions, how ten minutes after the committee disbanded he was shown a telegram from Landon amending three planks in the platform—all this White tells in detail in *What It's All About*.

While White was yet in the Orient, Kansas editors often hoped for his early return that he might strengthen the Landon cause. When White did write in Landon's behalf, many thought his old zest and sparkle missing. If this were true, it was to be expected. Whatever the political wisdom of choosing Landon, his nomination dulled the Republican campaign. In 1934 Landon was re-elected governor in a campaign where one of his major talking points was his support of the New Deal. During the presidential campaign the Republicans for obvious reasons never mentioned this fact and the Democrats ignored it. Had the Republicans opposed the New Deal outright, those militantly opposed to Roosevelt could have supported the nominee vigorously, and those of a liberal turn could have gone into the Roosevelt camp. But with Landon's nomination about all that was left for campaign thunder was that he knew the value of a dollar better than Roosevelt, had earned, not inherited, his wealth, and had proved that he could balance a budget. Hence, the people could expect less waste and more efficiency, more merit and less politics in governmental agencies. The attack had to center not on Roosevelt's measures, but on the way they were administered. It, therefore, took a lot of self-hypnotism to get a Republican liberal excited over the contest.

The fundamental difference between White's liberalism and the administration's became evident shortly after Roosevelt's re-election. Certain labor organizations, to force their claims, seized their employers' tools; and the nation beheld a new weapon in industrial warfare—the sit-down strike. These strikes immediately presented a major problem, and he who had been the leader in all other national problems kept silent. The White House had nothing to say, for publication at least. Whether Roosevelt approved the strong-arm methods, or was merely paying political debts is immaterial. He condoned the strikes by his silence; he consorted with labor leaders who employed the new techniques. The old methods for industrial reforms—those subscribed to by the Theodore Roosevelt and Woodrow Wilson progressives—were discarded.

The aim of the liberals during the first quarter of the nineteenth century, according to White, "was to cherish and deepen human self-respect." [10] As an incident to this problem, they sought to improve the environment in those social areas where class differences "were cruelly marked and wickedly depressed." There the immediate objectives were to provide better wages, better schools, better houses, and better recreational facilities. More specifically this meant a wider distribution of the gadgets of modern civilization—automobiles, bathtubs, parks, playgrounds, high schools, libraries, and the like—to those who labored to create the wealth of the country. But these rewards were not ends in themselves. What the liberals were trying to do was to brace up the human spirit in the underprivileged areas and arrange a social order in which the differences in social rewards were commensurate with the social and economic services to society.

In their struggle for social and economic reforms, the old liberals found the American middle class the greatest obstacle between them and their objectives. They could do something for the underprivileged by legislation, but no more than the middle class was willing to do. It was so property minded that it refused "to think politically in economic terms"; it would not vote "with any party with a real united front for social and industrial justice"; and it controlled both old parties. Moreover, it elected all the sheriffs, most of the mayors, and nine out of every ten governors. And it owned the guns. It could be "wheedled, coaxed, shamed, evangelized or scared into justice," but it could not "be bluffed or badgered." That being true any effort to force industrial justice immediately brought out the police clubs and the machine guns.

There were then two fundamental reasons why White had misgivings about what was going on in the ranks of labor. First, he thought the appeal for the vertical union was on the basis of class consciousness, and the old liberals had worked to eradicate class distinctions. Second, the objectives were sought by force, and to his mind force would not work. Roosevelt, or any other President, could go no faster than the middle class would let him. It dominated his party and controlled the arsenal. If he deviated too far from its thinking, he would lose control of his party, and therefore of Congress. If labor attempted strong-arm methods, his middle class followers would bring out the machine guns.

Roosevelt's interpretation of his first re-election returns as a mandate from the people White considered pure piffle. What he had assembled was twenty-seven million voters with no great common purpose, but a common fear—"the fear of adversity through the triumph of a government dominated by the plutocratic ideal." [11] In his majority were six "different, often divergent and sometimes entirely antagonistic minorities": old-time southern Democrats, northern urban Negroes, western farmers, militant middle-class liberals, a distinct labor group with proletarian consciousness, and the tammanies of

all the great cities. Such a heterogeneous majority needed but
an issue to start splitting up. Instead of having a monolithic
party, he had a majority heavily weighed down in the middle
by the middle class, which stood ready to prove who was running the country if its ideals were challenged.

Though believing the C.I.O. right in principle, White dis-
trusted the class conscious appeal by the "One Big Union" and
was a "bit white-livered" in seeing it established by coercion
and the labor racketeer. To White, who believed "in a step-at-
a-time inching toward Utopia by the evolutionary process all
under the orderly form of a democratic government," it seemed
that the devil was abroad whacking his ideals with a club.[12] But
if those who were championing the cause of labor appeared to
be walking a strange and treacherous path, even so were those
who were sponsoring legislation in the congressional halls.

However laudable the objective in enlarging the Supreme
Court, White opposed the bill because it would make a fundamental change in the American form of government. He had
two major objections to packing the court. First, in battering
down "the last weapon of defense which the people in another
day, returning to the sanity of orderly government, might need
to resume constitutional government," the President, "will
leave the club of his precedent for his successor." Already the
legislative branch of the American government had "ceased to
function as an independent political institution." To subordinate
the Supreme Court to the will of a Congress dominated by a
President would be to leave the United States, with Roosevelt's
passing, open to a less benevolent dictator.

The second major objection was that subjecting the
authority of the court to the will of a party would create a
government that functioned by impulse. The Supreme Court
was a vital factor in the stability of the American government.
It gave the people time to reconsider their demands, to revise
their impulses, and make sure their impulses were settled convictions. Nothing was truer, he said, than Mr. Dooley's statement that the court follows the election returns, "but it doesn't
always follow the first election, or the second, but after the
third or fourth election no court has ever been able to withstand
the lever of the public will when once that lever was per-

manently applied, when once was made manifest the final determined purpose of the American people." Nor should the
court follow immediately the election returns. Its traditional
function was to act as arbiter in clashing interests. To take
away that authority was to change the whole theory and system
of the court—to subject it to the control of a party whose majority may rest on irrelevant things, incompatible issues, and
immaterial prejudices.

White's opposition to the Supreme Court bill shows how
far he would follow Roosevelt. He was willing to go even
farther with the President in his economic program, but he was
not willing that the American form of government should be
changed to make these reforms possible. If one should have
said that the court was blocking reforms that the American
people were convinced they wanted, White would have pointed
to the judges' ages and asserted that Roosevelt's real grievance
was with the Death Angel. What he most needed was not the
power to pack the court but patience.

CHAPTER XXV

The Editor and His People

It is certain that the editor is not a preacher. If he preaches too much he is closed out by the sheriff. It is certain that the editor is not a teacher. If he teaches too much he is closed out by the mob. It is certain that the editor is not a giver of law, nor a ruler over the people. For if he sets himself up as an autocrat, there is an atmospheric uneasiness and places that knew him will know him no more. Yet in a measure the editor must be something of a preacher, something of a teacher, something of an autocrat. . . . The editor must be the judge of his news, of how it is told, what is recited and what omitted. He must interpret it. He must take a "slide" in everything. . . . The editor must be guide, philosopher, and friend to all—the rich as well as the poor. He must be executioner and undertaker, promoter and herald.[1]

KANSANS point proudly to their wheat, "the best in the world"; they like to think that their schools are among the nation's best, though their teachers are poorly paid and their certification requirements are shamefully low; they take honest pride in their approach to an equitable distribution of their wealth, being relatively free of the very poor and the very rich; they loudly acclaim their achievements, past and present, then cuss themselves and their state at home and abroad. Of one of their unique distinctions, they are totally unaware—their newspapermen.

Every state in the Union harbors newspapermen from Kansas. An editor of a big city daily, himself a Kansan, once asserted that excluding the native born, Kansas newspapermen outnumbered all others in every state outside of Kansas. The statement may exaggerate, but Kansans are found in every department of printing and publishing—from trade monthlies to sophisticated weeklies, from advertising agencies to book concerns, from press services and syndicates to columnists, from the editorship of America's most widely circulated magazine to the editorship of scores of obscure weeklies. In 1938, three editors of the Scripps-Howard Cleveland *Press* and three of the four columnists for the Scripps-Howard chain were Kansans. A list of Kansas newspapermen and their positions would include many of the highest offices in the land. But the list would be a mixed compliment to Kansas. These men left Kansas because other states offered greater opportunities.

Kansas has always had a powerful group of editors. Ed. Howe and William Allen White attained the greatest reputations, but among their contemporaries not far behind were Arthur Capper, Henry J. Allen, Victor Murdock, Clyde Reed, Charles F. Scott, and a score of others. And these editors did not happen by accident. Kansas was settled by a race of crusaders. With every group a newspaper immediately became its voice. When the territory opened, the pro-slavery people pushed across the Missouri line to Leavenworth. They set up their paper under an elm tree, and the first building finished housed the printing plant. The free-state people founded Lawrence, and the first paper printed on the town site was issued from an office having neither "floor, ceiling, or window sash." [2] Emporia printed its first paper in an unfinished room of the new hotel. With their rifles the Kansas settlers brought the printing press, and it was running before their rude homes were up.

In the fine arts the state is poor. Newspapermen wrote her best novels; a lawyer-journalist wrote her best poetry. In painting she gave birth to Henry Varnum Poor, John Noble, John Steuart Curry, and a home to Birger Sandzen, Sweden's greatest artist. In sculpture, architecture, and music, she lags behind. The state has been a testing ground for social, political, and economic theories, and her professional eminence lies in her newspaper men.

These same editors, ever alert to news, have contributed largely to the bad name of the state. When the hot wind seers, when the temperature boils, when the tornado strikes, when the dust blows, when ridiculous legislation gets on the statute books, when a fanatical reformer rises—the nation knows.

Easterners in Emporia have searched vainly for rooms where there were storm caves; yet "for any specific area or farm of one square mile the probability of being visited by a tornado is less than one sixteenth of one per cent per century." [3] One New England flood can destroy more lives and more property than all the tornadoes in the history of the state and be less sensational than a single Kansas tornado. Kansas editors have done their reporting so well that those who have never lived within her borders imagine her to be a land of perpetual drouths, dust storms, tornadoes, grasshoppers, and prohibitions.

These Kansas editors, living in a predominantly rural civilization, have carried on the Horace Greeley, Charles Dana, and Henry Watterson type of personal journalism. Leading two groups of lesser writers of opposing schools were Ed. Howe and William Allen White. Both men regarded each other more highly than their followers did. White's partisans usually dismissed the Sage of Potato Hill "with faint praise or loud damns." [4] He was a traitor to his environment; his idolators, debunkers and deflaters, "conservative in their political and economic leanings and scornful of the efforts of reformers." Howe's standard device for pleasing the average reader was to ridicule the brains and character of the average man. The average reader was expected to assume that the average man was some other fellow. When Jay House, a disciple of Howe who was later columnist for the Philadelphia *Public Ledger* and the New York *Evening Post,* succeeded in getting himself elected and re-elected mayor of Topeka against the opposition of the paper he was writing for, he was careful to antagonize the preachers and women's organizations, "on the theory that the unorganized women outnumbered the organized women and generally hate them."

Conversely, Howe's partisans thought little of White either as a personality or a literary technician. He was the arch-romanticist, "his bosom full of honey and love, enthusiastic over one cause after another designed to do good for the human race, always striving, uplifting, crusading, hoping and believing."

Embodied in the attitude of these two groups was the age-old struggle between romanticism and realism. Howe's grim account of the sad and brutal aspects of village life in *The Story of a Country Town* was the pioneer realistic novel in American literature, and according to the word of Edgar Lee Masters and Sinclair Lewis, gave birth to *Spoon River Anthology* and *Main Street*. White's emphasis on the pleasanter aspects of village life and his unceasing efforts toward its betterment earned him the reputation of being the voice of the prairies.

White, more tender-hearted and less brusque than Howe, reacted differently to the same situation. Once the two had identical subjects for an editorial. A sixteen-year-old boy killed a seventeen-year-old girl in what appeared to be a suicide pact. Howe's editorial follows:

Yesterday in a grove at Emporia, the dead bodies of two babies were found. The boy baby, aged 16, had shot and killed the girl baby, aged 17, and then killed himself. They "loved" each other with all the fervor of their calf hearts, and the crime is the result. In Hiawatha recently, the 14-year-old daughter of a very prominent man gave birth to twins; another result of calf love. In a country town near Atchison, at least six young men have disappeared in recent years to avoid arrest for the violation of the age of consent law. . . . These babies are allowed to associate together at all hours of the day and night and Society screams with horror at the result.[5]

White had every reason to see the case as impersonally as Howe. The girl came from another town and had no relatives on the town site. The boy had no near relatives in Emporia and had lately returned from a prolonged absence.

Last night here in Emporia a boy and a girl went out in the woods and the boy killed the girl; and then killed himself. The why of it all—Heaven knows but men can not understand. It was a pitiful tragedy and probably before the curtain rang down, all the human passions played their furious parts—love, jealousy, remorse, maybe hatred; and then the great blinding passion shame came and swept them to death, where passions cool in the eternity.

They were but children, and they lived, loved and doubtless suffered beyond their years. The way they went was a rough way, a down hill way, in some places doubtless a gay merry way. And we, who know but the meager details of their story, know only where the sad way led them; we see only the end—an end full of brambles and thorns. How they got to their journey's end, this man and this maid, the agony they felt in traveling their way, God, who is merciful and whose peace passeth understanding, surely He knows. But the world can only look at the puzzling way, the old, old way, the crooked way, they went, and say: Poor little man! Poor, poor little maid! [6]

Both men's writings are as marked in style as in tone. Howe's writings are terse and epigrammatic; White's loose and leisurely. Howe's effect comes from his economy of words; White's frequently, from piling up compound adjectives that increase in forcefulness much in the same manner as a rolling snowball increases in size. Each wrote with about the same facility, but only on rare occasions did White ever essay the style of Howe. When Woodrow Wilson died, he compressed his thought into four lines.

> God gave him a great vision.
> The devil gave him an imperious heart.
> The proud heart is still.
> The vision lives.[7]

Once again when a reporter brought him the notice that closed Emporia's leading bank, he scribbled these lines across its corner:

This scrap of paper appeared on the window of the First National Bank November 16, 1898. It was a good man's death warrant, a perpetual injunction against the plans of some bad men. It brought despair to hundreds of homes and joy to none. It is the last mute witness to the town's greatest tragedy.[8]

But these condensations are exceptional. Normally, an individual phraseology, a peculiar quirk of thought, stamp his writings.

. . . great spring-breaking, varnish-cracking, fender-bending, door-sagging carloads of "kids". . . .
It is hard to toot your own horn, but this snort is submitted herewith most respectfully.

A basic factor in White's editorial success is that he never writes unless he has something to say. In his apprenticeship he learned to avoid certain pitfalls. Two days after his first

Gazette, he wrote: "You will observe that there is no editorial in today's paper. It will be that way lots of times. When there is nothing to say there will be nothing said." [9] For four years he had got up daily editorials, sometimes as space fillers; and as his early interests were mainly political, he was unable to make his editorial column a permanent department for several years.

In 1923, an editorial writer on the Topeka *Capital* noted one of the secrets of White's editorial success. "William Allen White is the best loved writer in Kansas because he never looks in yesterday's file to see if what he proposes to write today is consistent." [10] The Topeka man wrote more truthfully than he suspected. White, as receptive to praise as any normal human being, never read "What's the Matter With Kansas?" in his own paper; he never took time to gloat. He prints his paper "without much thought of yesterday, with a keen interest in today, and a high hope for tomorrow." [11] *Gazette* readers have confidence in his opinions because he is more often right than wrong, but they know that he holds consistency to be "the never failing virtue of the jackass." [12] From the beginning he has preached that "facts change and with changing facts come changing conclusions," and "only the man who is wise enough to know this has a hold on truth." [13] The information at hand is the basis of his judgment; and if additional information seems to indicate another conclusion, he reverses himself. He wrote his editorials that way from the beginning. Two editorials on Carrie Nation are typical of what has appeared in the *Gazette* many times.

Carrie Nation is wrong—dead wrong. . . . She is crazy as a bedbug.[14]

She is all right. She is not crazy. She is doing a good, sensible work, and is doing it effectively and well.[15]

White has done his best writing for his own editorial column. There he reveals his many-sided character. The day by day recordings constitute what is going on in his mind and soul. Side by side stand the volcanic outbursts and the final kindly words over the death of a citizen. There he matches an acutely penetrating analysis of a perplexing problem with an equally erroneous conclusion based on inadequate information. There he manifests his neighborliness; his pride for his home town, its citizens, and its institutions, his thirst after righteousness, his burning indignation at intolerance, his understanding of Kansas in her frailty and strength, his humanitarianism, and his cosmopolitanism.

His passionate outbursts have made him known to the nation. On numerous occasions he has regretted that his writings on purely local matters attracted most attention. Once in righteous indignation at the stupidity and shamelessness of the city commission for offering boys twenty-five cents for stray dogs, he let out a blast that the Associated Press gave national circulation. For weeks after the episode the *Gazette* printed under "A Boy and His Dog" extracts from editorials and letters from every part of the country.

He has aimed his fighting editorials almost wholly against human folly. After 1900 few persons were singled out for unkind words. Frank Munsey was an exception. He "contributed to the journalism of his day the talent of a meat packer, the morals of a money changer and the manners of an undertaker. He and his kind have about succeeded in transforming a once-noble profession into an eight per cent security. May he rest in trust." [16] Again irked by H. L. Mencken's constant attacks on middle western life, White met him in the same literary arena.

With a pig's eyes that never look up, with a pig's snoot that loves muck, with a pig's brain that knows only the sty, and a pig's squeal that cries only when he is hurt, he sometimes opens his pig's mouth, fanged and ugly, and lets out the voice of God—railing at the whitewash that covers the manure about his habitat. [17]

Popular opinion to the contrary, White's fighting words are the exception, a mere fraction of the sparkle. What makes his editorials the glory of his paper is his many moods. His kindness, his unfailing good humor, his optimism, his traditional Irish wit, his clear and spritely style make his editorials readable. When he writes on national or international situations, Emporians listen because they feel that he speaks as one having authority. Nor does he further muddy the waters for the average reader; they know exactly what he is trying to say.

But his unceasing efforts toward maintaining peace and harmony in his community have done as much for his town and paper as any show of superior knowledge. Since 1900 his wit and humor, no less than his preaching of neighborliness, has been a foe of contention and strife.

. . . We have one humble request to make of our beloved and victorious candidate. We ask not that he fire Al Randolph; that is a matter he must settle with himself and his conscience. It is superfluous to ask that he get a new city attorney. That is a foregone conclusion. We desire not to dictate the administration's policy on the subway. But we do fervently pray that our beloved mayor will junk that statewide Stetson sunbonnet that has flapped in the breezes above his pink pellucid ears now for ten years, and get a new kind of hat. The occasion demands a change.[18]

The contest had been bitter, but not so bitter but that the new hat appeared within the week and the mayor had another editorial commending him for his exquisite taste in buying hats.

White has antagonized many people by his stand on local and national questions, but seldom in writing of individuals has he incurred their wrath. Senator Platt and Mrs. Meffert were notable exceptions. Yet sarcasm and persiflage are among his favorite devices. Possibly because he ridicules no one so much as himself or possibly because his sarcasm and persiflage are obvious, he escapes making enemies. Nevertheless, he sometimes demands too much of a reader's intelligence. His appeal to Governor Arthur Capper to retain Harrison Parkman, a Democratic hold-over and an Emporia editor, is characteristic. But scores of Emporians saw no humor in the editorial, thought that White had maliciously attacked Parkman, and six subscribers discontinued the *Gazette*.

Now we have no reason to shed crocodile tears over Harrison Parkman. He is the human hyena and moral leper who runs the scurrilous, venal, unspeakable rag around on Fifth Avenue, a creature whose base, degraded nature has made him a portable plague spot wherever he goes. But nevertheless, in spite of these infamous graces of mind and heart he has made a good fire marshall, and he might very well be retained by the administration.[19]

Editors of small-town Kansas dailies frequently indulge in good-natured banter. Once every county had a county seat war; stealing the court house at the point of a gun was a common practice. Editors in rival towns were advocates for their communities, and their principal duty was to slander and abuse the other town. As town quarrels subsided, repartee replaced enmity; editors adept at retort periodically matched wits. The *Gazette's* traditional enemies are the Ottawa *Herald* and the Lyons *News*. White is at his best with the Lyons paper.

> Paul Jones, the doughty admiral of the Little Arkansas, from his tall turret in the Lyons News, scanning the Kansas skies, notes the Gazette's complaint that we had fireworks on the Sunday before the Fourth, gambling and a strip-tease act in the carnival here recently, and that nobody complained. Nobody is not exactly right. Two Emporia preachers pointed the accusing finger of scorn at the county and city officers. However, be that as it may. Paul Jones says that the reason for this moral and political lassitude on behalf of the sovereign squat is "simply this: This is a new age with a new standard of morals."
>
> What do you mean "new age"? Nearly 50 years ago, Rudyard Kipling, the poet laureate of world imperialism, clanged out a rhythmic line which recalled the time when "the monkeys were walking together, holding each other's tails."
>
> New age the cat's foot. Same old devil! But hell no longer's a-popin'! Some one in shaking down the clinkers has put out the fire![20]

This good-natured kidding takes many forms. Once White asked Topeka "to elect some hospitable and popular person to invite the editor of the *Gazette* and family" to Topeka to hear the Minneapolis Symphony Orchestra. When the invitation "extended in the generosity of an ardent heart" was neglected, he threatened to move the capital.

> . . . McPherson once was seriously considered as an excellent place for the state capital. We have thought there was some merit in the McPherson proposition, and the longer we think, the more merit seems to be in the proposition. But in hearing good music we do not think. We just enjoy the concord of sweet songs, and gradually become amenable to reason.[21]

White, in his lighter vein, is at his best when Kansas is his subject. Then his aptness for phrase, his flashes of wit, his love for his state find full expression.

Lawrence is a city on a hill. And its light shines afar. Topeka is the giver of laws. Wichita has been famed for 50 years for her sex appeal, which in the early days was one of her major industries. Hutchinson gives salt and savor to a sometimes sad, drab Kansas life. Pittsburg may be depended upon in times of crisis to burst into internecine strife with all the rockets' red glare, all the bombs bursting in air thereunto appertaining. Leavenworth, moss-covered and hoary, is the "Miss Haversham" of the Kansas cities. Atchison, once a perennial fountain of vitriol, is a crumbling reminiscence of her former days of glory and of hate, Dodge City, where murder and sudden death once flowered in exuberance, to-day is a pillar of sweetness and light. But Abilene, fairest village of the plain for two happy months in August and September, sends forth the beneficences and bellyaches of a magnificent watermeloncholia. Which is counteracted by a joyous cantalouping from the Solomon to the Smoky. All of which brings a super three star, triple X gallupousness to a period of fried chicken, sweet corn and jumbo tomatoes. These viands combined make Kansas a place of pure delight.

In these glad days the Kansas death rate falls. For we hesitate in Kansas to go forward in ordinary procession to our crown and harp and robe, lingering wistfully the while thinking of Abilene. We forget the pearly gates and jasper paving, hesitating to stick our toes in the waters for a final plunge in the glassy sea. Abilene cantaloupes and watermelons hold us to the earth earthy.[22]

White's editorials are as varied as life itself, from which they well up. They mirror the life of a "prosperous prairie town, its joys and griefs, its hopes and disillusions, its pawpaws and pancakes, its fight against red rum, its yearly miracle of spring and autumn, its views of the nation and the world." [23] Two collections have been published; a dozen volumes equal in quality could have been compiled, for his editorials are characterized by evenness in quality rather than by sporadic flashes of wit and wisdom. Daily, year in and year out, White has contributed from one to two columns of original material to his paper, except on those occasions when he was away from Emporia for extended periods. During his years of editorship the editorial column has remained essentially the product of his own personality. Only once did it ever bear the impress of another person. For several years after 1907, Walt Mason contributed editorials. The two men were wholly unlike in temperament, and the column reflected the personalities of the

two. Both men in unconscious competition and in the vigor
of middle life turned out reams of editorial matter. The column
grew and grew until it completely filled two pages.

White has now been writing editorials for more than fifty
years. He began as a student at Lawrence where, in reporting
local incidents, he made editorial comments. From that time,
when his domain was a little country town, he has traveled
a long journey, but never getting out of touch with the common
man. In an unusually busy life, the ordinary relations of people
have continued as much his concern as affairs of state. Almost
any issue of the *Gazette* will prove this fact; its editorials are
a running commentary on what appears important, the piano
recital of Percy Grainger the night before, the Congressional
investigation of un-American activities, the Utopian pension
plans, the 1940 campaign with Roosevelt running for a third
term, and, in keeping with the season, the New York *Sun's*
famous answer to the little girl who wanted to know the truth
about Santa Claus.[24]

Essentially, White is the same man today he was fifty
years ago. Then, as today, his major interests were literature,
writing, politics, and people; but the spiritual and intellectual
growth that accompanied the developement of these interests
changed his point of view completely. Therein lies the chief
difference between White at twenty and White after fifty, not
in sitting in a county convention at twenty and a national convention at fifty. At twenty he was an arrogant preacher; in his
seventies he is a preacher still, but with a strong philosophical
bent. His increasing years brought a broadening of vision, a
deepening of knowledge, and a mellowing of attitude. His
changed attitude on national questions is generally known; his
changed attitude toward people is not, though it is no less
apparent. Two editorials written nearly a half century apart
show how far White has moved from his earlier position.

In the earlier one he contends that "a large number of
languid, lazy, ugly Ethiopian loafers who never did a lick of
work and whose worthless carcasses only block the sidewalks
and disfigure the appearance of the town" should, "if they
cannot be put on the stone pile, . . . be given notice to leave."
"The fact that their mothers take in washing to keep them,"

he says, "does not relieve them from being without visible means of support." [25] The later editorial is like the earlier in style—both have the long series of descriptive adjectives, even two identical phrases, "lick of work," and "visible means of support"—yet in point of view they are entirely unlike. No one can read the later one without realizing its author had a passion for folks and had thought deeply about the meaning of life. It is the "final words" which, when he wrote his salutatory editorial, he hoped to say over the middle-aged Emporians; but utterly different from anything he could have written then. It equals many of his better known editorials, though it was never reprinted in another paper; it is William Allen White at his best, which is saying that it is William Allen White. "Tom Williams" is more than two columns in length, but the three paragraphs reprinted here show that it portrays White quite as much as the old Negro.

Tom Williams, who died yesterday afternoon, was my friend. He was black, coal black. Probably his Ethiopian ancestry went straight back to Africa without a white cross to mark the journey. I was about to say he had never done a lick of honest work in his life. That would hardly be true. I can remember when he used to do housecleaning. But it irked him—not the work, but the regular hours of commercial employment. Occasionally he would do chores for a friend but even then he would rather have the service established on anything than a money basis; an old suit of clothes, say, or a place to sleep or best of all a cup of coffee now and then, or the right to a chat in the kitchen and a sandwich. He was almost exactly my age and I have known him for more than 40 years about as well as I have known many a white man in town. He claims to have been in the penitentiary three times. I think he was bragging. I can only remember twice, both times for arson. Publicly he claimed to be innocent. He never told me that. The tale of his innocence was for casual acquaintances and strangers.

He was not a thief in the strict sense of the word. He wouldn't take anything that he thought anyone wanted or could use. But he picked up trifles around that were out of use and either used them or traded them off—preferring barter to sale. Other colored folks said that he stole dogs. He told me the dogs just naturally followed him. I think—with certain reservations—this is true, more or less! But you could always go to Tom when you wanted a dog of any particular age or breed and give him a month or two and Tom would show up with it. He would not lie much about the breed unless he thought you were the sort of a

man he had to lie to in a trade. Many white men have the same
sort of virtue. They don't lie unless their fellow bargainers force
them into it. . . .

Thinking it all over—that 40 years and more of acquaintance
which became a sort of friendship—I suppose the basis of my
affection for Tom Williams was the fact that he came to me in
trouble and always showed me his best side. One of God's major
blessings upon me, I see now in the declining years of a long life,
probably comes from the fact that men who are full of flaws and
weaknesses and who visit upon others the curse of their weaknesses turn to me only their good side, never victimize me. Most
likely this unfortunate trait which blinds my eyes to faults that
others see and shun, furnishes the clue and key to my regard for
Tom Williams. . . . To the town he was just old black Tom
Williams, shiftless, idle, crooked and at times half mad—just one
of the town "characters." To me he was a man of some parts and
consequences despite his failings and despite the complete and
abject inconsequence of his life. What more than "town characters"
are most of the town's best known citizens. Their wealth and fame
have sifted away after death as Tom Williams's dogs have gone.
Some of us a little queer in one spot, others soft in another—out
of plumb a bit here and there—sagging in secret moral decay or
bulging with a facade of rococo rectitude. We are known by our
neighbors as much for our odd streaks as our good ones—famed
here on earth only as "town characters," and "town characters"
all of us stand before the Good God's throne of grace—in 50 years
forgotten of men! The tremendous handicap of his race, of course,
weighted Tom heavily. Yet I have known so many other men with
fewer virtues and with many of Tom's defects who have gone
much further without even Tom's brains! [26]

An editor has more than a dollar and cents relationship
to his community, and it is the quality of this other relationship
that marks him in his profession. White's remaining in a small
town when he could have gone up caught the imagination of his
colleagues quite as much as his notable activities. To them,
"His crowning achievement among the many to be credited
to him has been remaining first, last, and always the editor of
the Emporia *Gazette*." [27] It is true that had he not been a
national citizen he could never have had a national reputation;
it is true also that White as a local and as a national citizen is
one and inseparable. When newspaper editors say, therefore,
that his "newspaper service represents the highest example of
the influence and leadership that may be exercised by an Amer-

ican writer and editor," [28] they are thinking of both the local
editor and the national figure.

The newspapermen hold most of the publicity tools, and
they have used them effectively to advertise White. Presidential
election years, he averages being on the pages of the New York
Times once a week, an average about one half higher than that
of other years. For the most part, these entries are not there
because he is an editor. When his colleagues, however, begin to
write about him as an editor who used his ten talents, the sentiment that underlies the hard exterior of the newspaper profession begins to show—they grow lyrical: He is an oracle, a
sage, a philosopher, an American institution. Sometimes they
are right, sometimes wrong; yet to be thought an approximation of the ideal by one's fellows is no mean honor.

CHAPTER XXVI

The Voice of the Prairies

So, first of all, let us thank God for our freedom. That is well. Then let us lift up some other prayer than the Pharisee's complacent cant. Let us with our genuine Thanksgiving raise from our hearts a humble cry for some wisdom, for guidance and for leadership that will give us direction and power to use this freedom that we cherish to make men really free.

With all our gratitude for the blessings that we have—and they are real, generously bestowed, even if we have earned them well—let us hope and pray that the tools of democracy hanging in our halls of state and of commerce, of agriculture and of industry, may not grow dull and rusty because we are too dumb or too callous to use these democratic tools to widen "the blessings of liberty to ourselves and our posterity." [1]

T HE INHABITANTS of the Atlantic seaboard often think of Ohio as the West, and those of the Rocky Mountain regions frequently speak of Kansas as the East. Both West and East are purely relative terms, and to call William Allen White the spokesman for the Middle West is to say little more than that for a generation he has been the one person in his section of the country who has commanded a national hearing. Certainly no one who knows anything about his state has ever contended that he unfailingly represents Kansas thought; for in Kansas, had the state no other industry than agriculture, conditions under which men farm differ so greatly as to create wholly different problems. In eastern Kansas, where the altitude is around a thousand feet and the annual rainfall around forty inches, the farmer grows diversified crops, which, on the whole, he feeds to his own livestock; in western Kansas, where the altitude is around four thousand feet and the rainfall around fifteen inches, the farmer can grow only wheat, which must be shipped east as grain or flour. The westerner, unlike the easterner who lives on the farm and tends an eighty to a half section, may live in town and farm from a hundred to ten thousand acres. He plows his land with a tractor in August, plants his wheat with a tractor in September, then, nine months later if he has a crop, reaps and threshes his grain in one operation with a tractor-drawn combine. For him the uncertainty of rain makes farming a precarious business, but it is a business; whereas farming for the easterner is not a business at all but a way of life. Because wheat farming differs so greatly from barnyard farming, the western farmer faces problems quite unlike those the easterner faces; and to a lesser degree the dairy farmer, the irrigation farmer, and the cattle raiser face individual problems. Evidence of this fact is reflected among Kansas congressmen, who in representing the interests of their constituents, split on agricultural measures. In periods of distress, these distinctive and sometimes conflicting interests have resulted also in the state choosing a Democratic President and a Republican governor, or a Democratic governor and a Republican legislature, or sending two Republicans to the United States Senate, one to be the party whip for a conservative administration and the other to be the head of the nonpartisan farm bloc. In such a situation no man could speak for all Kansas. White, who probably best understands and best embodies the Kansas spirit, has never spoken for more than a faction. Sometimes that faction represents the dominant thought in the Middle West; on rarer occasions it represents the dominant thought in the nation. But as a representative of majority opinion in Kansas, White does not compare with Senator Arthur Capper. In prosperity, depression, and recession, Capper has always polled a majority on election day. He has always known which way the political winds were blowing and made hay accordingly. White as often as not pitches against the wind.

Being in the minority never disturbs White. As a citizen he burns with convictions, and not infrequently champions a

William L. White broadcasting on Christmas Day, 1939, in a dugout on the Mannerheim Line in the presence of a Finnish censor. Picked up by short wave, this broadcast inspired Robert Sherwood to write *There Shall Be No Night*

Mr. and Mrs. White on their return from their trip to the Orient in 1936

minority issue from which, when it becomes popular or a lost cause, he turns to another minority issue. As a writer—particularly the journalist in syndicate articles, magazines, and books—he has the faculty of being able to analyze objectively the opinions of himself and others. Probably this fact explains in a measure why he has been thought of as the spokesman for the Middle West, for White's writings are all concerned with his own times and with subjects where he has intimate, first-hand information. Since he knows more about the Middle West than he does about the East, the South, the Southwest or the Far West, the Middle West is usually his subject.

When White bought the *Gazette,* he had literary aspirations; and in his forty-five years in Emporia he has averaged a full-length book every three years. In the early twenties, he turned definitely from fiction to non-fiction, his last short stories appearing in 1921. In structure and style these stories are in marked contrast to those of his early years. Well developed and closely knit in plot, they indicate that he could have conformed to the exigencies of the later date had popular tastes in subject matter been congenial to his thinking. His non-fiction books fall roughly into two types, biographies and essays. The biographies are written from the point of view of a western progressive, but hold no brief for progressive principles. No one has ever accused White of writing partisan biographies; the moralizing of his novels is missing. They have the objectivity of a political analyst; in them White is the reporter. The essays are the work of the editor, written, however, with a regard to historical movements and with the leisure and contemplation impossible in the daily editorial. They, like the editorials, interpret what White considers important. Thus the essays reflect his more settled convictions rising from his observations.

White's first popular non-fiction book was a life of Woodrow Wilson, published in 1924. In part, its popularity may be attributed to the rising interest in biography and to the curiosity about the perplexing personality of the war President. In telling the story White takes a middle position, aligning himself with neither the idolaters nor the detractors. When the biography appeared, the controversy about Wilson was still raging, so that some reviewers accused White of being entirely out of sympathy with Wilson's aims and ideals while others said that he worshiped the war President. A later estimate of the biography states that it is "the best short account of Wilson that has yet appeared." [2] Were White to write a biography of Wilson today, he would produce a much better book. Not that later source material has invalidated his thesis—White is a better biographer.

White's best biography is his second book on Calvin Coolidge, *A Puritan in Babylon*. Apparently Coolidge fascinated White, but it was the sort of attraction that exists between opposites. In habits of thought, temperament, political faith, and environment, Coolidge represented everything White was not and much that he condemned. He was the product of a New England environment differing from White's West quite as much as Emporia from Boston. To the end of his life he believed in invested capital, in the virtues of the rich, the wise, and good. The growing industrialism, the selfishness and short-sightedness of many industrial captains, the role of immense wealth, the problems of reaction and reform never troubled him. Coolidge preached the gospel of work and practiced "masterly inactivity"; White preached shorter hours, higher wages, and more leisure—for the other fellow. Coolidge could not see "any moral obliquity in a man sitting in a case in which he was interested"; [3] White crusaded under the progressive banner to get business out of government. Coolidge differed only with his subordinates, accumulated political capital through favors, acted in a crisis when Coolidge would be saved, never admitted being wrong, never lost a friend, and never bolted a party.

That for five years White should have devoted his spare hours to writing the biography of a political leader who, when he was President, appeared to him to be a "museum piece" would be natural had White set out to debunk Coolidge; but the man who emerges, despite his limitations, is neither knave nor fool. Wise according to his lights, honest, upright, and loyal, he is portrayed kindly, sympathetically, and generously. White's purpose was, of course, to depict the career of the President who subscribed to an antique political philosophy (really a personal philosophy that grew from an environment barely touched by the mechanical changes of the past hundred years), which, applied to the national state, proved inadequate. In telling his story White is concerned with what happened, not his own political theories; and his success in the biography is due chiefly to his intimate knowledge of politics and politicians, his peculiar aptitude for understanding the New England environment and mind, and his ability to submerge his own political beliefs and see his hero in the larger whole. To diagnose Coolidge "with a physician's objective thoroughness," [4] or as another writer puts it, to bring him alive and at the same time perform an autopsy,[5] to write a biography which Charles Beard found to be among the twelve most interesting histories written in the thirties [6] proves that White can write without being a spokesman for his party or his community. In short, he is a reporter as well as an editor.

The essays are White's thought on contemporary problems. His last volume, *The Changing West*—the territory west of Buffalo and Pittsburgh, north of the Ohio River, onward to the Pacific Coast from Los Angeles to Seattle—bears the subtitle, "An Economic Theory About Our Golden Age." In this territory, White holds, the constantly moving frontier made a civilization of its own kind. This civilization was not built by supermen sifted from other regions or by hardships of the frontier welding men from dross to steel; but rather by men, morally and intellectually literate, living in an environment where a vast increment of wealth from rising land values created a reservoir of fluid capital, which, distributed economically and digested socially, financed the development and led to a golden age of prosperity and individual freedom. This economic theory is interwoven with spiritual values, which for White are of prime importance. Stripped of its spiritual aspects his thesis is this:

Basic in the West's material development were ever-rising land values. So long as there was cheap land to be improved, the farmer could improve his farm out of the credit from its increasing value, or sell a part of his high-priced land to buy cheaper land farther west for his sons, who in turn repeated the process. Thus for one hundred and fifty years the westward-rolling wave of prosperity continued until there was no more cheap land. The wealth "that came from the land and the rise in the price of land, the farms, the forests, the mines, created a base of fluid capital." [7] That capital structure became the basis for an enormous expansion of credit, and with that expanded credit, "investments were possible which produced labor-saving machines, increased man's output and further enlarged man's wealth and still further made credit expansion wise and stable." [8] Two inventions, the steam engine and the unlimited corporation, accelerated the development, enabling the West to make use of the fluid capital to build an industrial and commercial empire which was and is today, except in spots, rural. The golden age ended when land values became static. Valuations began to equal or exceed capitalized earning power, and the farmer discovered that his dollar was not going so far as the other fellow's. Because he was not willing to submit to a peasant's subsistence, the nation found itself facing a perpetual, and so far insolvable, farm problem.

How static land values, end of immigration, decline in birth rate, affected conditions in the West—these are problems for the economists. White believes that rising land values were the cause, rather than the result, of the West's prosperity; but he does not insist that his economic theory be accepted. He is far more interested in the spiritual qualities creating and leavening this prosperity, for they played the major role in making the West a peculiar civilization. The spiritual part of the theory is this:

What marked the western pioneers from other pioneers "was the thing called liberty and the definite love of it." Abraham, who trekked out of the land of Ur three thousand years before, could have understood, with a little tinkering, every material thing, except the gun and the book, that White's own grandfather had when he crossed the mountains into Ohio. But spiritually, the difference between the attitude of mind and heart of John White and his tribe and Abraham and his tribe "represented the progress of three thousand years.

It was the spiritual environment of the men in those two great treks—the one led by Abraham out of the land of Ur and the other of which John White was a part, coming from New England

and the Atlantic coastal states into the new lands of the West—
that defines the essential differences between the two civilizations
which grew up in the Valley of the Euphrates and in the Valley
of the Mississippi. John and Fear had attained in a large measure
something which Abraham and Sarah felt only as a vague yearning. It was the thing called liberty and a definite love of it.[9]

The American westerners, he continues, were free men,
free bodies, free spirits. No king could tax them, no tyrant
could compel them to bear arms, no church could force them
to worship God against the dictates of their own conscience.
"They could establish their own form of government without
let or hindrance. They had the right of trial by jury and carried
with them the writ of habeas corpus. They had their personal
freedoms, of speech, of conscience, of the press, and the right
of assembly." [10] They fought with the forces of the wilderness
not for freedom but for security, and "each pioneer family
fared well or ill somewhat according to its own application of
courage, intelligence, and industry." [11]

Out of their spiritual and economic freedom grew the little
white church and the little red schoolhouse, "two deeply sym-
bolical institutions." The church "stripped of its gaudy theo-
logical trappings," stood for the morals of the community, out
of which grew "a yearning for justice, the striving of men
toward an ideal of human relations." Their God was a spirit,
"as unreal and as unapproachable as justice, peace, love, liberty,
mercy, judgment, or wisdom," a god "who impersonated their
pioneer ethical ideals." Their religion "contained an ethic and
plan for human relations based essentially on a hazy vision of
liberty" and embodied a "profound faith in others that implied the acceptance of the Golden Rule." [12] The schoolhouse
"represented the pioneer's contact with reality." It challenged
"moral, political, and economic stagnation." It became the basis
of material progress; for out of it "rose the college and its
laboratory and the private and public bureaus of research." [13]
On the church and on the school, "two basic free institutions,"
the West was built, "a unique civilization in the earth, a new
thing for mankind." [14]

White is by no means ignorant of the dark side of the
picture, for the development of the West exemplified the "two

forces in the heart of men—his yearning to be neighborly and his instinct to grab and to hold." [15] The church had its adulterers, murderers, hypocrites, and liars; at every point were thieves, swindlers, grabbers, and gougers. White is drawing a balance; and, in the main, he finds it good. The wealth of the West, which in other times would have become the hoardings of the few, which would have been exploited without any gain to human freedom, relieved men of the fear of hunger and gave them a chance to be kindly. The altruistic spirit had an opportunity to grow—and it did grow. Moral progress was reflected in the rise of institutions that protected the weak: "manhood suffrage, the abolition of slavery, the right to hold the homestead against debt, free state universities for the common people, commissions and courts for the redress of economic wrongs such as rebates and trade discriminations of various sorts." [16] Political progress was reflected in "honest ballot laws, primary elections, the direct election of United States Senators, the initiative and referendum." [17] Economic progress was reflected in the dissemination of material things, which gave us a brand new world, both wonderful and mysterious.

. . . I want to show you a strange and, to me, save for the spirit of our democracy, an inexplicable thing. It's the town of Emporia —population around 13,000—typifying American semiurban life, and Lyon County, Kansas, symbolizing our rural life. Twenty-seven thousand people lived in our town and county a quarter of a century ago, and the census shows almost exactly the same number of people living here now. But a survey of life at the end of this quarter of a century indicates an amazing change. It is the change in the standard of living. Our town depends almost entirely upon the surrounding county; certainly upon trade conditions in the environing state. The production of wealth in this county and state has not greatly increased in these twenty-five years. The number of acres under cultivation is about the same. The amount of brains and brawn fertilizing those acres is today what it was when Taft was President. Yet, for some reason, the vastly increased number and kinds of things we are using now in our daily lives to make them brighter and happier cost us two or three times as much as the few things we used a quarter of a century ago. In spite of this, for all our excess spending, our bank deposits have more than doubled, which shows that, with our prodigality, some way we are saving.[18]

Today, White continues, there is in Lyon County a car for
every family; twenty-five years ago there were fewer than two
hundred. In the same twenty-five years the number of telephones tripled, so that the county now has as many telephones
as houses. Radios are still expensive toys; but they are beginning to crowd the telephone, "for eight houses in ten in Emporia, and seven in ten in the county contain radios." The automobile, the telephone, the radio are not the whole story,
however. Emporia's clothing stores carry styles a week after
they are first "splashed on Fifth Avenue in New York"; and
the year round its grocery stores display cauliflower, fresh peas,
green beans, lettuce, and carrots, "and great luscious citrus
fruits of kinds undreamed of by our fathers." Lyon County,
he says, is better housed, better fed, and better dressed than
at any time "after the twentieth century's turn." Yet this
higher standard of living has appeared even though Lyon
County has not increased its population, its tillable acres or
their productiveness since 1900. Nevertheless, with the county
depending upon agriculture primarily and farm purchasing
power below the 1914 parity for years, its people have doubled
their bank deposits while they spent more for goods and
services. "It's crazy as a bedbug," he says, "but there it is!" [19]

To White, the increased physical comforts do not constitute the most important part of the gain. In any consideration of social progress he ultimately assesses the change in
terms of spiritual values. The test "is found in the expanding
spirit of man," and "only where man's environment affects his
spirit, is a change of environment worth while." The hired
girl of twenty-five years ago, a symbol of those who earned
their bread by the sweat of their brow, is no longer condemned
to the menial drudgery that branded her in the social scale.
Now she is happier, because "she feels that she has more social
status, more self-respect, and an eight-hour day." "Shorter
working hours and less physical grime and grind have dignified
labor . . . and with that dignity has come the chief end of it
all: the growth of self-respect." And the struggle in the contest
for social change is worth while only "in so far as shorter
hours, better wages, a wider participation in the civilization that

rises from man's toil make the man a happier, kindlier, wiser, more self-respecting man." [20]

White is aware that many Kansas counties fall short of Lyon's prosperity. Three hours' motor journey westward some counties are more prosperous than Lyon, but another three or four hours onward some counties have lost a third of their population in recent years because of droughts and dust storms. Even Lyon, for all its gain in the last twenty-five years, has farm problems to face; and its problems, like those in other parts of the West, add up to "mounting farm tenancy, growing farm debt, and, in the last few years, . . . increasing . . . mortgage foreclosures." [21] The West, he says, established national prosperity with an "approximation of justice in human relations" [22] unequalled in any other nation, and upon some solution of these farm problems "rests the stability of our American institutions and the continuance of life on this continent under American ideals." [23]

The basis of the farm problem, White believes, is that in the nineteenth century the farmers "set up a scale of living under which, because they had votes, they created schools, built roads, established governmental services, and levied taxes far in advance of the living standards and government services enjoyed by other rural people in other lands." [24] They paid for this high standard of living out of the increment from the land. In the first decade of the twentieth century they were doing fairly well. Then the World War raised the price of farm produce and ruined them. They laid by no surplus "after the manner of industrialists," and "went in for a lot of luxuries which became comforts—the telephone, the motorcar, the movies, good roads, processed foods." Moreover, these comfortable luxuries "created wants, and wants created habits, and habits created an American way of rural life . . . which again greatly lifted the farmer's standard of living" and "incidentally . . . changed his cast of thought." [25] Spiritually, they were "stepping out, high, wide, and handsome, from the old way of farm life into a new way of thinking," but all the while they were building a huge debt. They mortgaged their future in the hope of everlasting profits figured on the basis of those which came to them "out of the unique and terrible economy of the war." The early 1920's brought deflation, a national farm problem, and the "Sunset for the Golden Age." [26]

Although White admits frankly that he does not know the answer to the farm problem, he doubts that the solution lies in a government subsidy. During the last two decades, billions of dollars "have been diverted directly or indirectly from their natural trend and course to relief for the farmer." But obviously the diversion of wealth to a special purpose "does not produce the same results, does not answer the purpose which the natural diversion of an economic surplus produced in the pioneer economy of the nineteenth century." [27] Neither does he condemn the farmer for asking for a standard of living which the business and professional interests in the country town take for granted. Of one thing he is sure: The American farmer will not accept a peasant's status.

He has a ballot. He can read and write. He has gone to an eight-month school. Young farmers and their wives have been through high school and have known something of college. They will not be declassed. They have learned to organize politically. They have power of life and death over our politicians. More than that, in the farmer's hands, who has a balance of power between the parties, lies the decision of the way our country shall go, the economic and social course it will take during this century. This balance of power in the West is an actual majority in most western states. And as the West has half of the Senators of the United States and a dominant minority of the members of the House of Representatives, the farmer holds a national balance of power.[28]

To solve our national economy, White thinks that we will have to produce "more wealth, more goods, more substantial things to be digested naturally through social organisms of parliamentary government"; [29] and to get this increased productivity, we must "get more power out of fuel." [30] His solution, then, is based on the "mysterious" rise in Lyon County's standard of living after 1900. The distribution of material things in Lyon County—a symbol of life in the West—was due to the democratic process. Of that he is sure. But the rise in the standard of living—as reflected in more automobiles, telephones, radios, and better houses, clothes, and food—in the face of a static population, static land values, and decreased purchasing power of agricultural products, leaves him puzzled.

He is a country editor, not an economist; but he cannot help forming an opinion about how this could be. His explanation is that we extended the physical power from fuel. After 1900, he says, rising land values were not dependable, prices rose sporadically; but we "improved and cheapened the process of making gasoline," we learned how to "extract the heat from coal and oil much more competently," we increased the profitable carrying capacity of one electric wire "in practical use both in distance and in the extended usefulness of a single wire." This extension of physical power from fuel was "responsible for the rise of mass production." Mass production "required mass distribution," and under the evolutionary processes of democracy it "brought myriads of new things to myriads of people." [31] If we could further increase the power of fuel even a few per cent, he continues, we "would add a considerable mass to our production, a mass quite comparable to the annual increase in the increment of the land of the nineteenth century." [32]

But the little red schoolhouse holds but a part of the answer. The whole answer "will come only if the little white church holds the fort of its faith in God and men, in the fellowship of mutual aid, faith in some kind of democratic equality of opportunity." [33] Under our social philosophy, "a phase of the Christian religion," we did erect for one hundred and fifty years "a standard of living and an ideal of justice under liberty that was the envy of mankind;" [34] and may we not expect that as the laboratories yield their secrets, "the increment of increased power will produce tolerable justice under a philosophy which has worked, not perfectly, but humanly well?" [35] He thinks it will. He puts his trust in free enterprise under the democratic process—"that type of human structure in which men of good will may have most freedom, and men who are obviously selfish must reason their way to have their will." [36] "The trouble with tyranny, with despotism, with the totalitarian order is that, whether the dictatorship be of the proletariat, or of the plutocracy, or of the military arm of the state, any tyrant makes the man of ten talents the slave of the dumb tyrant who holds his job by reason of his arrogance, his ruthlessness, and his cunning." For this reason, he believes the totalitarian state is doomed, not because it enslaves the man of one talent and regiments the man of five, but because it "hampers, checks, tries to guide and control the man who under the free democratic process, by reason of his talents and powers, may assume leadership and give direction to the life about him." [37]

Industry, White thinks, is the immediate American domestic problem. The establishment of industry upon an equitable basis would distribute the benefits and blessings from the growth of fuel power, give labor a new status as a consumer of goods and chattels, and, incidentally, do all that we can do for the farmer. An equitable basis "presumes that labor shall no longer be sold in the open market as a commodity," that collective bargaining "must be firmly established"; for the day is past when man alone can bargain "on anything like equality, justice, or fraternity, with a buyer of labor who represents a great corporate industry." Collective bargaining will give labor self-respect, but that power is not enough. Labor must have "an increased share in the products of labor."

Then the self-respecting workingman may consume up to his capacity to earn the things that shall come pouring out of the mills and factories as well as the products of the American farm.[38]

The short-sightedness of certain blind owners of the tools of industry, he says, impedes industrial progress. Yet labor is asking very little. When a man elects to live by his hands, he decides "not to go after money and the power of money as his life's first aim." He will be happy with a middle-class status:

A decent house equipped with modern comforts and a few luxuries, good food, respectable clothes, an education for his children which shall include high school and, if the son or daughter desires it, a college education. In addition to these decencies workingmen require and are beginning to demand security against sickness, old age, and unemployment.[39]

The fear of employers that deny to labor the realization of this ideal, "is a phantom," the greed "a curse." He calls on the owners of industry "in the new pioneering age of the machine" to have faith in their country and their fellow man—the faith that "turned the wilderness of the West into a fairly civilized land." In that faith they "may go on to the next evolutionary stage of democratic progress," but they "must cut loose from the Stone Age economic theory that the metes and bounds of certain funds, wages, interest, profits, and the like can be gauged in advance by known laws and prophetic rules."

Pragmatic experience, and that alone, will point out the boundaries of the possible and the impossible in all institutions, all aspirations and ways of life, all progress in government, in business, in human associations. That, men of five and ten talents must realize. In the faith of that realization they must walk like Shadrach, Meshach, and Abednego into the fiery furnace of the tomorrow.[40]

John Chamberlain, in reviewing *The Changing West,* said the book "is filled with gleams of insight which will provide the impetus for other books" which may or may not refute White.[41] Similar statements about his writing have been made before, and there is some evidence that the gleams of light have had their following. How else may the editorials on the *Gazette* editorials be explained, or that rather generous sprinkling of out-of-state *Gazette* readers, ranging in cast of thought from J. P. Morgan to Big Bill Haywood?

CHAPTER XXVII

Mobilizing Public Opinion

It is not a question of form of government between Great Britain and the European dictators. It is a way of thinking, a way of life, a social order, a slave economy that menaces the world. And this world cannot live half slave and half free. For our high standards of living, the product of free men, free enterprise, and that precious initiative and genius that rises out of a free conscience, a free press and a free government, cannot stand the strain of competition with starving men, the competition of industrial production manned by conquered slaves, and peasants ground in poverty, indentured upon the soil.[1]

ONE NOVEMBER morning in 1937 a student laid a copy of the Emporia *Gazette* on a historian's desk in an eastern university. A few days later the teacher said to the student: "That Armistice Day editorial of White's is the best statement of the European situation I have seen. What he says is borne out by what I saw in Germany last summer. If you are through with this paper, I would like to show it to some of my friends. There are some things here they need to know." Three years later almost to the day White was in Washington conferring with the President, the heads of the Navy and War Departments and Defense Commission. Generals and admirals, politicians and industrial magnates, were opening their doors to him; and not a few were saying how strange that a small-town Kansas editor should be the leading force in the movement to aid Britain.

Yet there was nothing unnatural in the fact—a crisis arose, and White saw the truth, or what he thought was the truth, and had the courage to follow it. That formula he had followed for years, so that in a world crisis it was perfectly natural for White, who had been growing in wisdom, honor, and prestige for nearly a half century, to come forward and organize American opinion on a vital foreign policy.

From the outbreak of the European conflict to January, 1941, when he resigned as chairman of the Committee to Defend America by Aiding the Allies, White's primary objective in his public activity was the preservation of American institutions and the American way of life by keeping America out of the war. To keep America at peace, he organized a nonpartisan committee to make sentiment for repeal of the embargo law which forbade the sale of munitions to nations at war; hoping to keep America at peace, he organized a nonpartisan committee to make sentiment for repeal of the embargo law which forbade the sale of munitions to nations at war; hoping to keep the country out of conflict, he brought into existence the Committee to Defend America by Aiding the Allies, with its chief objective the supplying of Allies with materials to defeat, or at least hold off, the totalitarian powers until America could defend herself. At no time did he feel that America ever had more than a gambler's chance of keeping out of the war; but as long as a remote possibility remained, the chance was worth the gamble.

When the conflict began, White said there were two roads to war. At that time he obviously believed the Allies were much better prepared than they were. If, he says, we continue to stop shipment of actual munitions of war to them, about all they will miss is our airplanes; but these they need so badly that the war will "drag on two or three years, in which case the Allies will need food." Then the Germans will put meat, grains, and butterfats on the contraband list; and our ships, in attempting to carry those things to the Allies under our present law, will be torpedoed. Indignation will rise at the loss of life, and "we are in the war." Getting in at this time may be too late to help the Allies; and with "an undecisive victory, our turn will be next to the totalitarian states in the 1950's."

The other road, he says, lay in the cash and carry plan. If we ban all our ships from belligerent waters and agree to sell munitions of war to whoever can come and get them, our trade "with the Allies in airplanes and guns and all sorts of steel products will speed up." Our ships will lie at anchor, but the Allies' ships will come for our products and boom industry. Millions of men "will go into the destructive business of making things for war," and foodstuffs will increase in price, whether or not we demand cash for them. We shall be where we were when we were selling to the Allies in 1914, 1915, and 1916. If they pay cash, they "will start a tremendous American boom"; and if we insist on their paying cash, we will have to stop selling or give them credit when their cash runs out. If we stop selling, "millions of men will be thrown out of work." Our whole economic set-up, being based on war industry, will collapse; and we shall see idle men in the streets the second time, not hitch-hiking but raising barricades. These men "will damn the government that stopped sending supplies to the Allies because the Allies couldn't pay for them" and they "will begin to shoot." "So," he concludes, "maybe we shall lend them money to buy our goods." And if we do that we "shall be right back where we were in 1917. We shall have to get into the war now as we got into it then, partly to save our economic structure from panic." [2]

The cash and carry plan, though fraught with dangers, seemed safer to White. Under the existing law he believed America could not escape the war, long or short; under the cash and carry law, with America backing up the Allies, we might be able to escape in a short, decisive conflict.

While Congress was debating the cash and carry measure, Clark Eichelberger, director of the League of Nations Association, called White and asked him to head a committee to advocate repeal of the embargo. White refused but after a number of other friends, at the request of Eichelberger, had pressed him, he consented. He telegraphed a number of prominent Americans asking them to join him "in a national nonpartisan committee for peace through revision of the Neutrality Law." To revise the law, he said, "goes as far as human ingenuity can to lessen the danger of American involvement," adding that "by repealing the arms embargo our country is no longer aiding Hitler to the disadvantage of the democracies who are resisting the spread of dictatorship." [3] On October 2 he announced the formation of "The Nonpartisan Committee for Peace Through the Revision of the Neutrality Law," with Eichelberger as director and himself as chairman. During the week more than two hundred joined, and White went to New York to direct the organization. The committee sent out an appeal for money, then "got out a ton of circulars in favor of repeal, signed by the leading American clergymen, and bishops of the United States." [4] On the radio, a number of Catholic clergymen and laymen answered Father Coughlin, who was dramatically opposing any change in the neutrality law; and the committee shipped these transcriptions, with others favoring repeal, to local broadcasting stations in the West. The disc that carried White's speech carried one on its opposite side by Al Smith, thus emphasizing the nonpartisan, nonsectarian, nonsectional aspect of the campaign. Mayor Fiorello H. La-Guardia of New York went to Boston where he pleaded for revision before one of the largest crowds ever assembled there. Such were some of the committee's activities which unquestionably affected the legislative halls. But in face of the decisive congressional vote they were not necessary to guarantee repeal. Nevertheless, Washington correspondents said that the administration was grateful for its work; and when passage of the new bill was assured, White had a two-word telegram from President Roosevelt: "Thanks, Bill."

The committee's technique, like that employed later by the Committee to Defend America by Aiding the Allies, followed a familiar White pattern. It consisted in attracting to its membership an impressive number of national figures of unquestioned integrity and respected intelligence who represented subdivisions of American life, such as education, business, public affairs, religion, and journalism. Then through the printed and spoken word, it forced public attention on the issue, trying at the same time, to counteract the influence of the opposition's leadership. Thus a distinguished Catholic layman, Alfred E. Smith, took up the cudgels against Father Coughlin; and Mrs. Dwight Morrow, author and acting president of Smith College, disapproved of the isolationism of her famous son-in-law, Charles Lindbergh. And finally, and always, it sought to give the average American citizen a realizing sense of his own dignity and power by showing him that public opinion was but crystallized private sentiment which would guide the President and Congress to act accordingly once they were aware of its existence.

White was never in doubt about the principle that should guide American foreign policy. The war was our war, meaning the Allies were not merely fighting our battles. The hate and arrogance and national greed motivating the totalitarian states was the "reverse side of the shield where the victors at Versailles hammered out revenge, shame and economic tyranny." Neither side in Europe had clean hands, and America had "some share of guilt for conditions that made this second war inevitable." But the time had passed "to try the old case and look back upon past wrongs." Americans had to face a world of fact, not the world "as we might have made it." [5] So long as Germany, Russia, Italy, and Japan could make men "go out and die for a day's rations, America, the British dominions, the Netherlands, France, and the Scandinavian countries were in great danger of destruction." [6] Our interest and safety, therefore, lay in throwing America's moral and economic weight back of the Allies.

Thinking of the average middle-class American in terms of a world dominated by Nazism, White pictured what would happen to American ways of life. The business man would lose his free market and free enterprise. He would be unable to "send his ships and his salesmen over the world in a competitive world market." The loss of world markets would compel the government "to restrict his output, to allot his sales, to allocate his quantity of raw materials and to fix his prices." The laboring man would have to go where government sent him "in response to the dire need of a restricted, throttled industry" that would "follow the closing of a thousand ports where the laborer's finished product once found open markets." In a world dominated by force, the preacher when he taught humility, when he advocated kindness, when he pointed to the golden rule "as the great spiritual element that is slowly solidifying Christian civilization," would be shocked when told "to keep his mouth shut" by those powers whose authority he threatened by his altruistic statements. The scientist would "turn his endeavors and point his researches toward those "special objects" which would "increase the power of the state to spread the doctrine of national jealousy, arrogance and malice." No longer could he "indulge himself in an inquiry into pure science"; no longer could he hope that what he found, correlated with the discoveries of others, would, some day, "lead to healing and . . . give strength to men all around the earth in their battle with the untoward circumstances which hamper their lives." The lawyer could not "be sure of a fair trial for his client in open court, with the ancient democratic weapons of justice always at his hand." The teacher would realize that in a controlled economy he "must not teach the subversive doctrine that man is a free agent and that the spirit of man has inalienable rights which no state should check or strangle." [7]

The totalitarian philosophy of force, then, being a denial of sacred American principles, America's interest was in an Allied victory. White thought, furthermore, American sentiment pro-Ally; and with American welfare in mind he was finally persuaded to see what he could do about molding this sentiment into an effective weapon of defense. In the spring he went to New York to confer with a group of Republicans about the 1940 platform. He did not want his party to commit itself to a foreign plank that "might make it look silly" in the midst of a campaign.[8] Party interest and national interest, he thought, demanded that there be no isolation plank. Meanwhile, Germany had invaded Norway and pro-Ally feeling had hit a new high. White, in New York, was turning over in his mind ways and means by which this sympathy could be translated into Allied aid. On May 6, he drafted a brief memorandum, left it on Clark Eichelberger's desk, and returned to Emporia. Events were moving extremely rapidly; and with the Nazi blitzkrieg under way in Western Europe, White telephoned Eichelberger on the 19th, "I think it is about time to act," and his telegram urging the formation of a committee to carry the idea of throwing America's moral and economic weight on the side of the Allies went out to several hundred national leaders:

As one democracy after another crumbles under the mechanized columns of the dictators, it becomes evident that the future of western civilization is being decided upon the battlefield of Europe.

Here is a life and death struggle for every principle we cherish in America, for freedom of speech, of religion, of the ballot and of every freedom that upholds the dignity of the human spirit.

Here all the rights that the common man has fought for during a thousand years are menaced.

Terrible as it may seem, the people of our country cannot avoid the consequence of Hitler's victory and of those who are or may be allied with him. A totalitarian victory would wipe out hope for a just and lasting peace.

The time has come when the United States should throw its economic and moral weight on the side of the nations of Western Europe, great and small, that are struggling, in battle for a civilized way of life, that constitute our first line of defense.

It would be folly to hold this nation chained to a neutrality policy determined in the light of last year's facts. The new situation requires a new attitude.

From this day on, America must spend every ounce of energy to keep the war away from the western hemisphere by preparing to defend herself and by aiding with our supplies and wealth the nations now fighting to stem the tide of aggression.

This is no time for leaders to consider party or factional advantage. All men and all creeds and clans may well call upon our President to confer with leaders of all parties looking to a foreign policy providing for an increase in armaments to defend ourselves and for every economic effort to help the Allies.

In foreign affairs we must present an unbroken, nonpartisan front to the world, it is for us to show the people of England, of France, of Belgium and Scandinavia that the richest country on earth is not too blind or too timid to help those who are fighting tyranny abroad.

If they fail, we shall not have time to prepare to face their conquerors alone.[9]

The response was immediate. The next day the Emporia Western Union kept open after working hours to handle the business of the Committee to Defend America by Aiding the Allies, and the names of those joining ran to a half column in the *Gazette*. Within a week, in addition to the national committee, thirty local chapters in densely populated centers had been organized or were preparing to organize. During the months that White headed the organization, local chapters were set up in seven hundred centers.

The purpose of the committee, according to White, was "to build up sentiment which will back the President and warrant congress in giving every legal economic aid possible to the Allies in the sale of material and munitions to help in the conflict." [10] European conditions, he said, called for a "revision of our neutrality stand so that the country can keep the war away from this hemisphere by preparations for defense and by aiding the victim countries with supplies and wealth." [11] Its first objective would be "to get a list of men and women whose names and careers stand high in the nation and whose judgment will impress Congress with the wisdom of this committee." Then when a measure which represented the committee's views came before Congress, the committee would, after discussing its legal and economic soundness, "by all open and honorable means" do what it could "to make sentiment in favor of that measure." [12]

The history of the Committee to Defend America by Aiding the Allies—its part in determining American foreign policy, its methods of mobilizing public opinion—is a research topic for some future historian after the committee's work has been finished and the lapse of time permits the historical perspective. Though such a task is impossible at the present time, a sketch of it during its first months is necessary here because it largely reflected White's policies.

The Committee to Defend America by Aiding the Allies, which was soon known as the White Committee, did not wait for measures to come before Congress to support. In July White stated its objectives under four heads. It was, first of all committed to the policy of extending "all moral and material aid which may be given to maintain England as our first line of defense." To implement this policy it advocated: (1) Supplying Great Britain "with such planes, guns and ships as she may legally purchase from our armed forces as soon as possible and in the greatest possible quantities without injuring our national defense." (2) Making available to Great Britain "our surplus food supplies." (3) Immediate effective expansion of our preparedness program "so that we may safely aid Great

Britain in every legal way possible and quickly, as the by-product of that expansion." (4) Assistance in bringing mothers, children, and old people from the British Isles to the Western Hemisphere "when or if it becomes necessary." (5) Crystallizing public opinion which "would encourage Congress to give the President whatever legal authority necessary to accomplish these ends, or to amend to whatever extent necessary existing legislation that interferes with giving such aid to the Allies." (6) Removing difficulties "prohibiting Americans from volunteering in the Allied armies." (7) Establishing, if necessary, with the approval of other members of the Western Hemisphere, "a trusteeship over French and Dutch possessions until the full independence of those countries is restored and they are able to exercise free sovereignty over those territories." (8) Guarding against war materials "reaching aggressor nations either directly or through neutral powers." [13] Its three other objectives—preparedness at home and in the other parts of the Western Hemisphere for our national defense, maintenance of the democratic process in all its forms in dealing with enemies within our borders, and education of democracy for the preservation of liberty—never had the committee's emphasis like aid to Britain. Actually the committee's propaganda was directed toward holding Britain up as America's first line of defense, her peril, and the consequences in case she fell, and in making sentiment for some specific aid to Britain.

As the fortunes of war changed so changed the objectives of the committee; but as long as White remained at its head, it held that America's peace, way of life, and institutions, depended upon aid to Britain. "No one can guarantee that the United States can avoid military involvement," it stated, "but one thing is certain; the only chance of avoiding war is by giving all material assistance to Great Britain and her allies immediately." In a statement of policy issued in November, it urged: (1) Greatly increased arm production, and pledged its support to the President "in the use of his full legal powers under a state of national emergency if necessary, to mobilize at once all the industrial resources of the nation for maximum production." (2) Production of merchant vessels at the World War rate "for lease or rent to the British," and formation of a shipping pool "so that American ships could operate in the Indian and Pacific oceans and thus release Britain's shipping for service in the Atlantic." (3) Assumption by Congress of "a larger share of responsibility, with the President, for the policy of aid to the Allies." In this connection it wanted Congress to revise our international policy by repealing or modifying "restrictive statutes which hamper this nation in its freedom of action when it would co-operate with nations defending themselves from attack by nations at war in violation of treaties with the United States." At the same time, because Japan had joined the Rome-Berlin alliance, it recommended a "firm" policy in the Pacific: (1) Giving "all material and financial help to China that is possible without lessening our aid to Great Britain." (2) Extension of American "embargoes upon exportation of all war materials to Japan." (3) Announcement that the United States and Great Britain had made "their naval bases in the Pacific open to each other's fleets." (4) Establishing "a clear naval understanding with Great Britain" which would permit the British and American fleets "to be placed in the most advantageous position to protect the Atlantic for the democracies and to stop the spread of war in the Pacific." In addition to these matters, it wanted the President "to call a conference of all peoples who cherish freedom, including the governments in exile, for a reaffirmation of faith in a world of peace based upon justice and the security of nations." [14]

From its beginning the committee admitted frankly that it was a propaganda organization. To effect its ends it combined the skill of a public relations committee with the experience of life-long party workers in a country town. It flooded newspaper offices with printed material, distributed hundreds of thousands of circulars through local chapters, sponsored radio talks over national chains and local stations, got out a book, *Defense for America,* under White's editorship, ran page advertisements in metropolitan newspapers, and induced friends of the Allied cause to send Congress millions of telegrams supporting Allied measures. At the Democratic and Republican national conventions, it lobbied to keep isolation planks out of both party platforms and tried "to nominate a man for president in the Republican party who would advocate aid to Great Britain boldly, consistently, wisely and continuously." During the Presidential race it attempted "to keep the issue of aid to Britain out of the campaign by making it unanimous as the pledge of both candidates." [15] To carry on these activities it raised approximately a quarter million dollars in small sums from twelve thousand citizens.

In the midst of the presidential campaign, White wrote a magazine article which, though in line with British aid, is a curious revelation of his own character. Millions of citizens of the United States, he says, believe that if Great Britain should fall we would have no force with which we could stop Hitler if he desired to establish military bases in the Western Hemisphere. Yet, we as a nation are more interested in preparedness "as a stimulant to business than we are in preparedness as a symbol of our prowess in the great international game of root hog or die." This complacency, he says, arises from the very nature of democracy itself; French powerlessness and English tardiness were of the same cloth:

For democracy is a social, economic and political organism founded and surviving upon the theory of mutual help. Democracy was born two or three thousand years ago when credit became international. Credit is founded on the belief that on the whole the average man will do as he says, will pay his debts, act like a gentleman and play the game of business to his own hurt if his honor is at stake. . . .

The democratic belief in the wisdom of the majority is rooted in the conviction that in considerable masses of men no one is mean enough, greedy enough, or cruel enough deliberately, maliciously to go out to wreck the good-will of the majority. So it happens that a democracy faced with the threat of war denies the danger, refuses to believe other men, nations or races are really as bad as they are painted.[16]

The strange part about this theory is not that it satisfactorily or unsatisfactorily explains British blunders and French decay, but that White's analysis of democracy is an analysis of his own personality. White finds it hard to believe that men are wilfully cruel or greedy. That connivers and sharpers would use him and his reputation to attain their own selfish ends is for him hardly more than a fact in the abstract. For a long,

long time, the glasses through which he sees mankind have been slightly rose-tinted.

No yardstick can be devised to measure White's value to the committee. He was fond of referring to himself as "only the rooster on the cowcatcher, crowing lustily sometimes at the crossroads." [17] Time and again, he spoke of himself as a stuffed-shirt, getting the credit for the work of other men and women. But understatement is his usual method of referring to his achievements; and this much is true: he worked prodigiously in committee matters. Specifically, in two important committee objectives he played an influential role. In keeping sentiment alive to send World War destroyers to Britain, the committee played an important, perhaps even the decisive, part. The President had been for aiding the Allies from the outbreak of the war, but could make no move committing the United States to such a policy until he was certain he had the support of the American people. He, therefore, relied chiefly on White and his colleagues to make the sentiment enabling him to exchange fifty destroyers for military bases in the Western Hemisphere. Again, during the presidential campaign White was peculiarly fitted to serve the committee, which wanted both candidates pledged to aid the Allies. White enjoyed the confidence of both President Roosevelt and Wendell Willkie, the Republican nominee; and when Willkie opened his campaign, he announced that White was one of the three men who had helped him formulate his foreign policy.

Unquestionably, White's name helped the committee immeasurably. Because of the widespread public confidence he had enjoyed so long, because his opposition to war had been public knowledge for a quarter century, a formidable array of national leadership aligned with the group, and the public took its stated objectives at face value. For an avowed propaganda organization, it was singularly free of outside criticism; and almost no criticism was directed at White. He was, indeed, called a warmonger by Mussolini's Fascist editor Virginio Gayda and West Virginia's Senator Rush Holt—the American public accepting the charges of each at equal or no value. Beyond a few newspaper and magazine articles showing that the committee was the natural haven of war advocates, almost no

criticism of it appeared before December, 1940; and this in a
large measure was due to the name of the man who stood at
its head.

During the last ten days of 1940, public opinion in the
United States reached what Mark Sullivan called "a case of
split personality-mass schizophrenia." [18] Everybody, almost,
wanted to help Britain, and was, at the same time, afraid that
further aid would involve the country in war. Because Britain's
purchasing power was supposed to be nearing its end, the
Johnson Act barring loans to nations in default on war debt
payments was up for heated argument. Revision of the Neutrality Law to permit American vessels to carry war contraband
to the war zones or the sending of American convoys to Britain
was, likewise, a touchy topic. Proponents and opponents hurled
names at each other carelessly and recklessly. Those favoring
greater aid were "interventionists" and "warmongers"; those
in opposition were "appeasers" and "isolationists." Verne Marshall, in a brief bid for fame, announced his No Foreign War
Committee to offset the propaganda of White's committee
which he said had developed "the same public psychology as
that which was carefully created during the war period preceding our declaration of hostilities in April, 1917." [19] General
Robert E. Wood was, so he later testified before the Senate
Foreign Relations Committee, running his America First Committee "essentially . . . to counteract the so-called W. A.
White Committee." [20] A bad case of nerves was clearly in the
saddle; and when the President announced a forthcoming fire-
side chat, all three committees with other groups who did not
bother to find a name for themselves began to bombard the
President with telegrams telling him what to say. Obviously,
the public temper was as much the result of the approaching
Congress as it was of the situation abroad. Everyone knew that
the Administration would have to declare its foreign policy
in a few days, and the public mind had reached a state similar
to that just before the end of a bitter election campaign.

During this period White created a furor at the committee's headquarters by stating his and the committee's position
in a story for the Scripps-Howard Newspaper Alliance. "The
only reason in God's world I am in this organization," he said,

"is to keep this country out of war." He denied that he or his group was in favor of sending convoys with British or American ships—"for convoys, unless you shoot, are confetti and it's not time to shoot now or ever"; he asserted that the committee was not in favor of repealing the Johnson Act, for "there are half a dozen other good legal ways to get aid to Great Britain"; and he said it was not even "remotely" true that they favored "repealing that portion of the neutrality law which forbids American ships to carry contraband of war into the war zone." If he were making a short motto for the committee, he said, it would be "The Yanks Are Not Coming."

For we could not equip them, transport them and feed them if they went. We have less than 200,000 ready and we need them worse at home on the assembly belt than we need them in Europe. War would defeat the first and last end for which our committee is organized, to defend America by aiding Great Britain, and would bring on a 30-year conflict.

Concluding, he said, he had "no doubt that some members who are not officially representing us are martial-minded," but "not one official utterance of our organization has anything remotely suggestive that we feel the only alternative for American defense through aid to Great Britain is war," and in all their executive councils, in all their policy making committees, he had "never heard war as an alternative objective seriously discussed by any official group of our organization at any time." [21]

White's statement brought a short but violent reaction from a number of eastern members. Major General John F. O'Ryan, U.S.A. retired, in an open letter to White termed the committee's present policy "pallid and ineffective" and said that if the Scripps-Howard story was authentic "consider this letter my resignation." The New York chapter issued a strong statement announcing that it would not be "intimidated by the word 'warmonger.'" [22] From New York's Mayor La Guardia, however, came the strongest blast. In a letter addressed to White at the committee's headquarters he said in part:

Strange, when the going was good for the Allies, you and others were strong in saying what you would do. Now that the going is bad, you are doing a typical Laval.

It occurred to me that the committee had better divide. You could continue as chairman of the "Committee to Defend America by Aiding the Allies with Words" and the rest of us would join a "Committee to Defend America by Aiding the Allies with Deeds." [23]

La Guardia did not then or later show where White had misrepresented the committee, say on what policies he differed with him, or explain what he meant by a typical Laval although he did tell the Senate Foreign Relations Committee the "surprise element" in White's statement led him to refer to the Kansan as a Laval.[24]

The controversy was not out of the public press before White's resignation was in the hands of the executive committee. Every reason he gave for resigning may be taken as a contributing factor, the job "was too big a one" for him, he had his "own life to live" and he wanted to celebrate his seventy-third birthday in peace and devote the year or two or three left to him "to writing some books and helping with some chores around the house here in Emporia and in Kansas," he "had a definite sense that the war fever was rising" which "set a lot of perfectly good men to ghost dancing, whooping it up for war, demanding convoys," and the like, he could not run the job properly without going to New York, and "the need for hard, concentrated, intelligent work on the chairman job" was "too much for a man who has to earn a living running a country newspaper" and who had other obligations he could "not lightly lay aside." The resignation coming hard on the controversy led many to assume that White got out because of its war-minded members. A letter from White to John Temple Graves II of the Birmingham *Age-Herald* would seem to bear out this assumption. White says, "In two of our chapters, New York and Washington, we have a bunch of warmongers and under our organization we have no way to oust them and I just can't remain at the head of an organization which is being used by those chapters to ghost dance for war." [25]

Conclusive as the letter sounds, it states the occasion rather than the underlying cause. White's objective from first to last was to mobilize public opinion for aid to the Allies. When that had been accomplished, his task was done; and it is significant that he first considered getting out after the presidential campaign had ended without either candidate wavering on British aid. Being persuaded to remain, he stayed until the President announced his "arsenal-of-democracy" and "all-out aid" policies. Then his task was finished, for White has always been one to crystallize public sentiment on issues and leave the administration of details to others.

While the storm was raging over the Scripps-Howard interview and White was thinking about resigning, he wrote an editorial which bespeaks one side of his personality. It reflects his usual buoyant optimism, but more than that, it demonstrates his ability to cut loose from the vexations of the day, personal or national, and see his fellowmen in terms of passing centuries.

Looking back from the next century, historians will be amazed that men today did not know definitely why they were fighting. They were caught in a trap. The multiplication of machines had thrown millions of men out of work. As little nations grew up, they found themselves starved when the machines threw their own millions out of work. The machines kept on multiplying. The unemployed kept on trudging the streets hunting jobs. Society was not able to solve the problem of mass production because it had no way to establish mass distribution.

The human mind in 1939 had not conceived the justice that was necessary to socialize the machinery of the Twentieth century. For certainly we have not set up political institutions that will do the job. The reason why we have not set up political institutions to do the job is that we have not grown in moral intelligence, in a sense of the dire need of neighborly equity. We have not become Christian enough to establish a Christian civilization. That we could resort to war, a horrible, bestial war, a vast organized idiocy, indicates that the injustices that made the baffled, frustrated peace of Versailles impossible, produced twenty years afterward the hell that is the new world war. . . .

But of this much be sure: that in the end, no matter what happens the resilient spirit of man will rise again. The instincts of neighborly decency will organize themselves into equitable government. That government will develop institutions which must bring justice out of those new toys, the machines, that man has made from the devices of his mind and heart. We shall learn to live with

the machine after this war and it will be a new relation, a happier
world, an era of widening justice. So ring out the old and ring in
the new! [26]

Such editorials as these, no doubt, leads papers like the
New York *Times* to speak of the *Gazette* as "a sane, kindly
breath of the Kansas prairie"; [27] such editorials, doubtlessly,
are responsible for White being known as a seer. But White
would be the last person to think of himself as a seer. The thing
that has happened to him is as wonderful as a dream and sometimes, he thinks, as unreal. Through it all he sees himself as a
country editor, often cutting a ridiculous figure. And one of
his major delights in life is to come back to Emporia and tell
a group of friends some comical story where the joke was on
William Allen White. Here is an incident that happened while
he was defending America by aiding the Allies.

Because he was chairman of the committee, White ordered
a telephone installed in his Estes Park cabin, before he and
Mrs. White made their annual summer pilgrimage to Colorado.
No sooner had they stepped inside the cabin door than the
telephone rang. Mrs. White answered and informed her husband that the President wanted to talk to him. As White was
going over to pick up the receiver, Mrs. White bustled around
and made sure that the driver, maid, and secretary were out of
the way and could not hear the confidential conversation. Later
the same day, Wendell Willkie called and Mrs. White again
acted to insure privacy. That week, White talked again to
Willkie, once to Secretary of State Hull, once to Secretary of
War Stimson and once to Secretary of Navy Knox. Mrs.
White, each time the telephone rang, made sure that nobody
was listening. Some time passed and the Whites went to Denver to attend a chapter meeting of the committee, there the
toastmaster introduced the committee chairman with what
White called a "double-dip introduction." In the course of his
rather lengthy introduction, the toastmaster mentioned the
prominent persons who had called White at Estes. Both White
and his wife were astounded at the man's exact knowledge about
the calls. After the meeting, White made for a telephone official

and asked: "How in the devil did that fellow know about those calls?"

"Why, Mr. White, didn't you know?" the official replied. "You're on a party line!"

Footnotes

CHAPTER I

[1] William Allen White, "Kansas—A Dream State," Kansas City *Times*, January 29, 1921.
[2] Lyman B. Kellogg, "Early Days at the Emporia Normal," Emporia *Gazette*, June 11, 1927.
[3] *Ibid.*, June 13, 1927.
[4] *Ibid.*, June 13, 1927.
[5] Emporia *News*, January 21, 1865.
[6] Laura M. French, "A Biography by 'L.M.F.,'" Emporia *Gazette*, May 7, 1924.
[7] *Ibid.*, May 7, 1924.
[8] *Ibid.*, May 7, 1924.
[9] *Ibid.*, May 7, 1924.
[10] White, "Memoirs of a Three-Fingered Pianist," *Woman's Home Companion*, LIV (September, 1927), 12.
[11] Emporia *Gazette*, May 7, 1924.
[12] Emporia *News*, April 19, 1867.
[13] *Ibid.*, May 3, 1867.
[14] Emporia *Gazette*, May 7, 1924.
[15] The family tradition is that he came to America in the 1630's. He was a freeman from England. Between 1653 and 1655 he moved to Taunton, later Raynham, Mass.
[16] Personal information from Mr. White.
[17] Bent Murdock, "Some Kansas Sayings," Emporia *Gazette*, June 15, 1903.
[18] Douglass *Tribune*, February 15, 1935.
[19] *Ibid.*, February 15, 1935.
[20] Jessie Perry Stratford, *Butler County's Eighty Years*, 1855-1935, 16.
[21] Douglass *Tribune*, February 15, 1935.
[22] Emporia *Gazette*, February 20, 1935.
[23] *Ibid.*, May 7, 1924.
[24] Emporia *Gazette*, May 7, 1924.

CHAPTER II

[1] White, *Boys Then and Now*, 5-6.
[2] Oscar Eugene Olin, "Will White—Boy and Man," *Western Homes*, October, 1897, 12.
[3] White, "Memoirs of a Three-Fingered Pianist," *Woman's Home Companion*, LIV (September, 1927), 13.
[4] White, *Boys—Then and Now*, 19-20.
[5] *Ibid.*, 18-19.
[6] El Dorado *Republican*, June 20, 1887.
[7] White, "Memoirs of a Three-Fingered Pianist," *Woman's Home Companion*, LIV (September, 1927), 13.
[8] *Ibid.*, 13.
[9] *Ibid.*, 80.
[10] *Ibid.*, 80.

[11] White, "It's Been a Great Show," *Collier's,* CI (February 12, 1938), 16.
[12] White, *Boys—Then and Now,* 20.
[13] *Ibid.,* 22.
[14] *Ibid.,* 8.
[15] *Ibid.,* 12-15.
[16] *Ibid.,* 13-16.
[17] Emporia *Gazette,* July 4, 1907.
[18] White, "It's Been a Great Show," *Collier's,* CI (February 12, 1938), 63.
[19] *Proceedings,* American Society of Newspaper Editors, 1929, 79.
[20] Olin, "Will White—Boy and Man," *Western Homes,* October, 1897, 12.
[21] Emporia *Gazette,* May 7, 1924.
[22] White, "Memoirs of a Three-Fingered Pianist," *Woman's Home Companion,* LIV (September, 1927), 13.
[23] Emporia *Gazette,* July 4, 1907.
[24] *Ibid.,* June 10, 1902.

CHAPTER III

[1] From the diary of Robert L. Jones, November 9, 1884.
[2] Emporia *Gazette,* November 12, 1914.
[3] Olin, "Will White—Boy and Man," *Western Homes,* October, 1897, 12.
[4] White, "Memoirs of a Three-Fingered Pianist," *Woman's Home Companion,* LIV (September, 1927), 84.
[5] Personal information from Mr. White.
[6] Emporia *Gazette,* May 31, 1935.
[7] White, "Story of a Friend," Brown County *World,* March 2, 1894.
[8] *Proceedings,* American Society of Newspaper Editors, 1929, 80.
[9] Emporia *Gazette,* July 26, 1917.
[10] *Ibid.,* July 26, 1917.
[11] A piece of printer's copy to be set in a type approximately the size of that now used in the wanted sections of the large, daily newspapers. Because of its demands on the eyesight and because of the tediousness involved in its composition, printers avoided nonpareil copy.
[12] *Proceedings,* American Society of Newspaper Editors, 1929, 81-82.
[13] White, "Story of a Friend," Brown County *World,* March 2, 1894.
[14] Nine years later White sent Herbert on a secret mission to Emporia to find how Major Calvin Hood, the banker, felt about White acquiring the Emporia *Gazette.* Herbert put on the same bold front that had characterized their student days, telling the banker that if necessary he would lend White $3,000 to buy the paper. When Herbert was ready to leave, the Major took him by the arm and asked him if the newspaper business was so lucrative that one could make $3,000 in the few years that Herbert had been editing his paper. Herbert replied that it was not—that he expected to borrow the $3,000 from him to lend to White. Whereupon the Major was moved to make a confession. He told Herbert that when the two were students, he had given his cashier orders to turn their checks to him when they overdrew their accounts that he might be personally responsible for the checks until they had deposited sufficient money to cover them.
[15] Personal information from Mr. White.
[16] Ewing Herbert, "William Allen White," *Kansas Newspaperdom,* April, 1894, 2.
[17] Personal information from Mr. White.
[18] *Proceedings,* American Society of Newspaper Editors, 1929, 82.
[19] Emporia *Gazette,* October 23, 1925.

[20] *Ibid.*, July 26, 1917.
[21] El Dorado *Democrat*, August 5, 1886.
[22] Emporia *Gazette*, November 5, 1909.

CHAPTER IV

[1] Extant records at the University of Kansas show that White made a straight "B," except for one failure. He made "C" in three courses, two mathematics and one Latin, and "A" in three courses, two rhetoric and one history. In all other courses he made "B," except in Solid Geometry.
[2] White, "My K.U.—A Lovely and Glamorous Life," *Graduate Magazine*, XXVI (May, 1938), 5.
[3] Twentieth Annual Catalogue, 86.
[4] Personal information from Mr. White.
[5] Thornton Cooke, "And When I Came to K.U.," *Graduate Magazine*, XXXVII (September, 1938), 6.
[6] Edwin E. Slosson, address before the Kansas State Teachers' Association, Emporia, Kansas, November 5, 1928.
[7] *Dictionary of American Biography*, XVII, 221.
[8] Personal information from Mr. White.
[9] White, "Memoirs of a Three-Fingered Pianist," *Woman's Home Companion*, LIV (October, 1927), 8.
[10] *University Review*, IX (December, 1888), 120.
[11] *Ibid.*, IX (February, 1888), 148.
[12] General Frederick Funston, "Reminiscences of Kansas University," *Kansas Magazine*, I (April, 1909), 13.
[13] The University of Kansas is situated on a high hill, called Mount Oread.
[14] Cooke, *Opus Cit.*, 6.
[15] Burton Rascoe, "Contemporary Reminiscences," *Arts and Decoration*, XXX (November, 1928), 100.
[16] Emporia *Gazette*, June 1, 1926.
[17] *Sunflowers*, 6.
[18] Albert Bigelow Paine and William Allen White, *Rhymes by Two Friends*, 161-63.
[19] Conversation with W. D. Ross.
[20] This and the following anecdote are from Fred Funston's reminiscences of Kansas University, *Opus Cit.*, 12-15.
[21] Chester Woodward, *Alumni Achievement Report of 1936*, 96.
[22] Ellis B. Stouffer, "Development of Scholarship at the University of Kansas," *Graduate Magazine*, XXXIX (January, 1941), 8.
[23] *University Courier*, February 15, 1887.
[24] Topeka *Capital*, August 11, 1887.
[25] Quotations relating to this incident are from a letter by Thomas F. Doran, January 16, 1939.
[26] *University Review*, IX (October, 1887), 50.
[27] Lawrence *Journal*, August 3, 1888.
[28] *Ibid.*, August 19, 1888.
[29] *Ibid.*, August 3, 1888.
[30] *Ibid.*, July 31, 1888.
[31] Emporia *Gazette*, July 26, 1917.
[32] Personal information from Mr. White.
[33] *Weekly Journal*, October 17, 1889.
[34] Emporia *Republican*, June 11, 1882.
[35] A well-known Kansas editor and author of that period.
[36] Lawrence *Journal*, August 18, 1888.
[37] CLXXVI (December 26, 1903), 18.

CHAPTER V

[1] Emporia *Gazette,* January 8, 1930.
[2] *Ibid.,* September 18, 1901.
[3] *Ibid.,* March 6, 1939.
[4] See *The Autobiography of Lincoln Steffens,* 502 ff.
[5] Emporia *Gazette,* October 12, 1901.
[6] El Dorado *Republican,* August 22, 1890.
[7] *Ibid.,* May 30, 1890.
[8] Emporia *Gazette,* November 5, 1909.
[9] *Proceedings,* American Society of Newspaper Editors, 1929, 84.
[10] Emporia *Gazette,* November 5, 1909.
[11] *Ibid.,* November 5, 1909.
[12] Reprinted in *The Real Issue,* 168.
[13] *Proceedings,* American Society of Newspaper Editors, 1929, 84.

CHAPTER VI

[1] White, "The Man Who Made the 'Star,'" *Collier's,* LV (June 26, 1915), 25.
[2] Carl Van Doren, *Contemporary American Novelists, 1900-1920,* 135.
[3] The story is two and one-fourth columns in length. It appears on page 7 of the June 16, 1892, edition under the title "Broke the Slate."
[4] *Proceedings,* American Society of Newspaper Editors, 1929, 85.
[5] W. G. Bleyer, *Main Currents in the History of American Journalism,* 318.
[6] *William Rockhill Nelson,* 50.
[7] Bleyer, *Ibid.,* 319.
[8] Nelson was called Colonel by his friends; Baron by his enemies.
[9] White, "How I Wonder What You Are," Kansas City *Star,* September 18, 1930.
[10] *Proceedings,* American Society of Newspaper Editors, 1929, 85-86.
[11] White: "I stole them from him." See also White's "The Man Who Made the 'Star,'" *Collier's,* LV (June 26, 1915), 13.
[12] White, "How I Wonder What You are," Kansas City *Star,* September 18, 1930.
[13] April 21, 1894.
[14] "How the Story of Aqua Pura Grew," Kansas City *Star,* August 18, 1930.

CHAPTER VII

[1] Emporia *Daily Republican,* May 21, 1895.
[2] Kansas City *Star,* February 18, 1932.
[3] Emporia *Gazette,* June 1, 1895.
[4] *Ibid.,* September 6, 1932.
[5] White, *Forty Years on Main Street,* 4-5.
[6] Emporia *Gazette,* July 26, 1898.
[7] *Ibid.,* June 8, 1895.
[8] *Ibid.,* February 12, 1896.
[9] *Ibid.,* June 3, 1896.
[10] July 19, 1895.
[11] Emporia *Daily Republican,* July 31, 1895.
[12] Emporia *Daily Republican,* August 20, 1895.
[13] Emporia *Gazette,* April 6, 1899.
[14] *Ibid.,* April 8, 1899.
[15] Emporia *Daily Republican,* April 7, 1899.
[16] Emporia *Gazette,* October 10, 1900.
[17] *Ibid.,* January 20, 1897.

[18] *Ibid.*, February 18, 1898.
[19] *Ibid.*, May 5, 1897.
[20] *Ibid.*, November 8, 1897.
[21] *Ibid.*, November 8, 1897.
[22] *Ibid.*, June 16, 1896.
[23] In an international broadcast from London in 1932, White discussed the London telephone exchange and the prevailing styles in men's footwear, in addition to the problems facing the World Economic Conference.
[24] Emporia *Gazette*, June 17, 1896.
[25] *Ibid.*, June 16, 1896.

CHAPTER VIII

[1] Emporia *Gazette*, August 16, 1926.
[2] Statistics are from William E. Connelley, *History of Kansas*, II, 1135 ff.
[3] White, *The Editor and His People*, 5.
[4] Victor Murdock, *Folks*, 103. Sometime before Murdock had tried unsuccessfully to dub an Oklahoma reformer, named Daniels, as a sockless statesmen. Daniels was not wearing socks when Murdock saw him, but Simpson was.
[5] Connelley, *Ibid.*, 1168.
[6] All quotations on this and the following page are from "The Sweep of It," Emporia *Gazette*, August 11, 1896.
[7] The Populists and the Democrats had endorsed the same roster of candidates.
[8] Emporia *Gazette*, August 16, 1926.
[9] *Harper's Weekly*, XLVI (February 1, 1902), 155.
[10] Emporia *Gazette*, August 15, 1896.
[11] Mark Sullivan, *Our Times*, I, 138.
[12] Emporia *Gazette*, August 27, 1896.
[13] *Ibid.*, September 25, 1896.
[14] *Ibid.*, August 15, 1904.
[15] *Ibid.*, August 15, 1904.
[16] *Ibid.*, August 16, 1926.
[17] *Ibid.*, September 25, 1896.
[18] *Ibid.*, November 19, 1896.
[19] Charles W. Thomas, Belleville, Illinois, in the Emporia *Gazette*, September 25, 1896.
[20] Cleveland *Leader*, February 13, 1897.
[21] *Ibid.*, February 13, 1897.
[22] [Cleveland] *Weekly Herald and Leader*, February 20, 1897.
[23] White later had to go to Washington at his own expense to prevent McKinley from naming him as a compromise postmaster.
[24] *Sunday Voice and Clevelander*, February 21, 1897.
[25] From the correspondence of Paul Lemperly.
[26] Emporia *Gazette*, February 22, 1897.

CHAPTER IX

[1] Emporia *Gazette*, February 11, 1933.
[2] *The Court of Boyville*, xxiii.
[3] *Ibid.*, xxi.
[4] W. D. Howells, "Psychological Counter-Current in Recent American Fiction," *North American Review*, CLXXIII (December, 1901), 876.
[5] Claude G. Bowers, *Beveridge and the Progressive Era*, 175.
[6] *Stratagems and Spoils*, 214.
[7] Howells, *Op. Cit.*, 877.
[8] Emporia *Gazette*, March 3, 1937.

[9] Charles C. Baldwin, *The Men Who Make Our Novels*, 556-57.

[10] "The Bolton Girl's 'Position,'" 62.

[11] Emporia *Gazette*, January 24, 1901.

[12] Russell Blankenship, *American Literature as an Expression of the National Mind*, 651.

[13] Albert Shaw, *The Golden Book*, XI (April, 1930), 94.

[14] These and the following quotations are from Washington press dispatches of December, 1901.

[15] White, "Platt," *McClure's Magazine*, XVIII (December, 1901), 151.

[16] It lies in my mind that "the Someone" was George Harvey. He not only wanted to protect Platt, but his own financial patron, Thomas Ryan et al. It would have made a very jolly and sensational piece for the judicial theatre.—Letter from John S. Phillips, July 15, 1939.

[17] Emporia *Gazette*, February 11, 1937.

CHAPTER X

[1] Emporia *Gazette*, October 1, 1901.

[2] *Ibid.*, December 27, 1902.

[3] *Ibid.*, January 5, 1903.

[4] *Ibid.*, May 23, 1921.

[5] *Ibid.*, June 2, 1911.

[6] *Ibid.*, February 9, 1903.

[7] Mark Sullivan, *The Education of An American*, 189.

[8] Emporia *Gazette*, November 18, 1904.

[9] Conversations with their neighbors.

[10] Emporia *Gazette*, April 3, 1906.

[11] F. L. Pinet, "William Allen White—Kansas," *Kansas Magazine*, II (July, 1909), 2.

[12] Burton Rascoe, "Contemporary Reminiscences," *Arts and Decoration*, XXX (November, 1928), 63 ff.

CHAPTER XI

[1] Emporia *Gazette*, February 6, 1899.

[2] White, *What It's All About*, 5.

[3] Emporia *Gazette*, September 6, 1901.

[4] *Ibid.*, April 15, 1899.

[5] *Ibid.*, April 15, 1899.

[6] *Ibid.*, March 5, 1938.

[7] *Ibid.*, January 10, 1898.

[8] *Ibid.*, January 10, 1898.

[9] *Ibid.*, December 26, 1895.

[10] *Ibid.*, January 28, 1903.

[11] *Ibid.*, April 27, 1898.

[12] Emporia's quota of volunteers was filled within four hours after the call was issued.

[13] Emporia *Gazette*, June 29, 1898.

[14] *Ibid.*, July 8, 1898.

[15] *Ibid.*, February 16, 1899.

[16] *Ibid.*, January, 17, 1901.

[17] *Ibid.*, March 20, 1899.

[18] *Ibid.*, January 10, 1902.

[19] *Ibid.*, May 30, 1899.

[20] *Ibid.*, December 30, 1901.

[21] *Ibid.*, January 2, 1902.

[22] *Ibid.*, April 14, 1900.

CHAPTER XII

[1] Emporia *Gazette,* December 14, 1906.
[2] *Ibid.,* November 3, 1896.
[3] *Ibid.,* December 28, 1906.
[4] *Ibid.,* March 3, 1908.
[5] *Ibid.,* July 27, 1922.
[6] White, *Forty Years on Main Street,* 83.
[7] *Ibid.,* March 4, 1909.
[8] *Ibid.,* November 30, 1903.
[9] Kansas City *Times,* April 20, 1929.
[10] White, *Masks in a Pageant,* vi.
[11] Emporia *Gazette,* September 7, 1901.
[12] *Ibid.,* December 7, 1903.
[13] *Ibid.,* April 13, 1903.
[14] White, "A Page of National History," *Saturday Review of Literature,* VII (October 25, 1930), 261.
[15] Emporia *Gazette,* March 15, 1904.
[16] *Ibid.,* July 5, 1904.
[17] *Ibid.,* October 4, 1904.
[18] *Ibid.,* November 25, 1904.
[19] Since the election of Edward Hoch in 1904, every Republican governor, except one, has been the liberal faction's candidate. Kansas has had only five Democratic governors, none of whom was re-elected to a second term.
[20] Emporia *Gazette,* March 29, 1906.
[21] Topeka *Capital,* July 5, 1906.
[22] *Collier's,* XLI (July 11, 1908), 8.

CHAPTER XIII

[1] White, *A Certain Rich Man,* 248.
[2] *Main Currents of American Thought,* III, 346.
[3] Figures are for cities over 8,000.
[4] *The Autobiography of Lincoln Steffens,* 368.
[5] White, *A Certain Rich Man,* 403.
[6] *Ibid.,* 209 ff.
[7] Emporia *Gazette,* June 11, 1919.
[8] *Ibid.,* June 27, 1938.
[9] *Ibid.,* August 4, 1909.
[10] *Ibid.,* December 12, 1928.
[11] White returned to Kansas to find a well-developed movement to make him lieutenant governor.
[12] The White home is built of red stone from the Garden of the Gods in Colorado.
[13] Emporia *Gazette,* August 27, 1909.

CHAPTER XIV

[1] White, "Why I Am a Progressive," *Saturday Evening Post,* CXCIII (April 23, 1921), 3.
[2] This summary of governmental change is from Chapter II, *The Old Order Changeth.*
[3] *The Old Order Changeth,* 50-51.
[4] White, "When the World Busts Through," *American Magazine,* LXXI (April, 1911), 747.
[5] White, "Insurgence of Insurgency," *American Magazine,* LXXI (December, 1910), 170-171.

[6] White, "Why I Am a Progressive," *Saturday Evening Post,* CXCIII (April 23, 1921), 4.

[7] White, "Government of the People, by the People, for the People," *Independent,* LXXXV (February, 1916), 190.

[8] "William Allen White on Mr. Steffens' Book. 'The Shame of the Cities,'" *McClure's Magazine,* XXIII (June, 1904), 221.

[9] *The Old Order Changeth,* 189.

[10] White, "A Democratic View of Education," *Craftsman,* XXI (November, 1911), 130.

[11] *The Old Order Changeth,* 228-229.

[12] White, "Free Kansas," *The Outlook,* C (February 24, 1912), 407.

[13] Emporia *Gazette,* April 21, 1904.

[14] White, "The Partnership of Society," *American Magazine,* LXIII (October, 1906), 583.

[15] *Ibid.,* 580-81.

[16] White, "What Democracy Means to Me," *Scholastic,* XXXI (October 23, 1937), 9.

CHAPTER XV

[1] Emporia *Gazette,* November 5, 1913.

[2] *Ibid.,* November 11, 1907.

[3] Topeka *Capital,* June 17, 1908.

[4] Emporia *Gazette,* November 9, 1910.

[5] *Ibid.,* December 7, 1909.

[6] *Ibid.,* January 14, 1910.

[7] *Ibid.,* June 30, 1910.

[8] Quotations are from the Topeka *Capital,* September 1, 1910.

[9] Henry F. Pringle, *Theodore Roosevelt,* 544.

[10] White, "The Progressive Hen and the Insurgent Ducklings," *American Magazine,* LXXI (January, 1911), 394.

[11] January 8, 1912. It is easy to believe that when White made this statement he thought Roosevelt would not be a candidate.

[12] White, "Should Old Acquaintances Be Forgot," *American Magazine,* LXXIV (May, 1912), 13-18.

[13] *Ibid.,* 18.

[14] For a discussion of this point see Pringle's *Theodore Roosevelt,* Chapter VII; Lincoln Steffens' *Autobiography,* Chapter XXI; and Pringle's *The Life and Times of William Howard Taft,* Chapter XXXIX.

[15] Emporia *Gazette,* April 6, 1912.

[16] *Ibid.,* January 1, 1917.

[17] *Ibid.,* June 24, 1912.

[18] *Ibid.,* June 24, 1912.

[19] *Ibid.,* August 10, 1912.

[20] *Ibid.,* April 18, 1911.

[21] *Ibid.,* July 2, 1912.

[22] *Ibid.,* July 3, 1912.

[23] All actual charges at one time or another.

[24] Emporia *Gazette,* January 13, 1914.

[25] *Ibid.,* September 3, 1912.

[26] *Ibid.,* November 4, 1912.

[27] Charles Vernon, "A Panegyric on Emporia," Emporia *Gazette,* May 14, 1927.

[28] Emporia *Gazette,* October 21, 1913.

[29] *Ibid.,* March 4, 1914.

[30] *Ibid.,* September 20, 1913.

[31] *Ibid.,* September 9, 1912.

[32] *Ibid.,* September 27, 1915.

[33] All quotations are from White's syndicated articles in the Topeka *State Journal,* June 5-12.
[34] The 1916 Progressive nominee for the vice-presidency.
[35] Emporia *Gazette,* October 6, 1916.

CHAPTER XVI

[1] Emporia *Gazette,* April 20, 1914.
[2] See "What Readers of the Outlook Think of the War," *Outlook,* CVIII (September 2, 1914), 44-47.
[3] Theodore Roosevelt, "The World War: Its Tragedies and Its Lessons," *Outlook,* CVIII (September 23, 1914), 173.
[4] Emporia *Gazette,* August 29, 1914.
[5] *Ibid.,* September 10, 1914.
[6] *Ibid.,* May 11, 1915.
[7] *Ibid.,* May 10, 1915.
[8] *Ibid.,* May 15, 1915.
[9] *Ibid.,* September 8, 1915.
[10] *Ibid.,* October 27, 1915.
[11] *Ibid.,* December 30, 1916.
[12] *Ibid.,* March 21, 1917.
[13] *Ibid.,* March 24, 1917.
[14] *Ibid.,* April 25, 1923.
[15] *Ibid.,* May 1, 1917.
[16] *Ibid.,* April 3, 1917.
[17] *Ibid.,* April 12, 1918.
[18] White, *Martial Adventures of Henry and Me,* 66 ff.
[19] *Ibid.,* 114 ff.
[20] All quotations are from Chapter VII of the *Martial Adventures.*
[21] *In The Heart of a Fool,* 613-14.
[22] Emporia *Gazette,* November 9, 1918.
[23] *Ibid.,* November 13, 1918.
[24] *Ibid.,* November 28, 1918.

CHAPTER XVII

[1] Emporia *Gazette,* May 18, 1916.
[2] White, "Will They Fool Us Twice," *Collier's,* LXVIII (October 15, 1921), 5.
[3] Emporia *Gazette,* December 17, 1920.
[4] *Collier's, opus cit.,* 6.
[5] Emporia *Gazette,* February 1, 1919. (Dated January 10).
[6] *Ibid.,* March 8, 1919. (Dated February 14).
[7] *Ibid.,* February 15, 1919. (Dated January 21).
[8] *Ibid.,* March 15, 1919. (Dated February 19).
[9] *Ibid.,* March 6, 1919. (Dated January 25).
[10] *Ibid.,* May 17, 1919. (Dated April 24).
[11] *Ibid.,* March 15, 1919. (Dated February 19).
[12] *Ibid.,* April 5, 1919.
[13] *Ibid.,* July 16, 1919.
[14] *Ibid.,* July 11, 1919.
[15] *Ibid.,* November 10, 1920.
[16] White, *Forty Years on Main Street,* 179.
[17] Emporia *Gazette,* July 23, 1919.
[18] *Ibid.,* July 24, 1919.
[19] *Ibid.,* March 10, 1920.
[20] *Ibid.,* April 28, 1924.
[21] *Ibid.,* June 14, 1920.

[22] *Ibid.*, July 7, 1920.
[23] *Ibid.*, July 7, 1920.
[24] *Ibid.*, July 7, 1920.
[25] *Ibid.*, November 3, 1920.
[26] White, "The Best Minds, Incorporated," *Collier's*, LXIX (March 4, 1922), 19.
[27] Emporia *Gazette*, October 5, 1922.
[28] *Ibid.*, April 28, 1924.
[29] *Ibid.*, July 24, 1922.
[30] *Ibid.*, August 16, 1922.
[31] White, "Why I am a Progressive," *Saturday Evening Post*, CXCIII (April 23, 1921), 4.
[32] Emporia *Gazette*, January 17, 1923.

CHAPTER XVIII

[1] White, "We Who Are About to Die," *New Republic*, XXVI (March 9, 1921), 37-38.
[2] Emporia *Gazette*, February 6, 1911.
[3] Russell Blankenship, *American Literature*, 650-51.
[4] Emporia *Gazette*, October 5, 1922.
[5] *Publisher's Weekly*, C (November 26, 1921), 1793.
[6] White, "These United States; Kansas," *Nation*, CXIX (April 19, 1922), 462.
[7] Emporia *Gazette*, November 23, 1920.
[8] *Ibid.*, October 2, 1922.
[9] *Ibid.*, October 2, 1922.
[10] White, "The Other Side of Main Street," *Collier's*, LXVIII (July 30, 1921), 7.
[11] *Ibid.*, 8.
[12] "Savory Sage," *Literary Digest*, CXXIII (April 24, 1937), 31.
[13] *Opus Cit.*, 8.
[14] Emporia *Gazette*, October 2, 1922.
[15] White, "This Business of Writing," *Saturday Review of Literature*, III (December 4, 1926), 355-56.
[16] White, "The Country Editor Speaks," *Nation*, CXXVIII (June 12, 1929), 714.

CHAPTER XIX

[1] White, *Forty Years on Main Street*, 24.
[2] Emporia *Gazette*, May 17, 1921.

CHAPTER XX

[1] Emporia *Gazette*, July 20, 1922.
[2] William E. Connelley, *History of Kansas*, II, 769.
[3] Emporia *Gazette*, June 22, 1922.
[4] *Ibid.*, July 19, 1922.
[5] *Ibid.*, July 19, 1922.
[6] *Ibid.*, July 20, 1922.
[7] *Ibid.*, July 25, 1922.
[8] *Ibid.*, July 27, 1922.
[9] "A Document on Liberty," *Literary Digest*, LXXIV (August 19, 1922), 32.
[10] Emporia *Gazette*, May 14, 1923.
[11] Topeka *Capital*, November 18, 1922.
[12] Governor Allen was so intensely in earnest in his endeavors to uphold

the law that he asked the Attorney General to prosecute Mr. White. I was of the opinion that while there might be a technical violation of the law by Mr. White that a prosecution would not be successful, and therefore, the best way to handle the matter was not to proceed against Mr. White. The matter was delayed for a number of days [after White put up the card] during which I avoided further conference with Governor Allen. However, he finally sent for me and rather vehemently demanded that Mr. White be prosecuted. Thereupon being under the Governor's direction, I authorized such prosecution.—Letter from Judge Richard J. Hopkins, November 29, 1939.

[13] Topeka *Capital*, November 19, 1922.
[14] Emporia *Gazette*, December 9, 1922.
[15] Topeka *Capital*, December 8, 1922.
[16] *Ibid.*, December 9, 1922.
[17] *Ibid.*, December 9, 1923.
[18] *The New Republic*, XXXIII (December 27, 1922), 106.

CHAPTER XXI

[1] White, "The Country Newspaper," *Harper's Magazine*, CXXXII (May, 1916), 891.
[2] Emporia *Gazette*, May 9, 1939.
[3] E. W. Howe, *Plain People*, 131.
[4] Mark Sullivan, *The Education of an American*, 116.
[5] Emporia *Gazette*, December 12, 1921.
[6] *Ibid.*, June 20, 1935.
[7] *Ibid.*, December 6, 1911.
[8] Conversation with Hughes in 1924.
[9] Kansas City *Star*, February 10, 1928.
[10] Conversation with Lee Rich.
[11] *Ibid.*, October 4, 1920.
[12] Susan M. Kingsbury, *Newspapers and the News*, 24-25.
[13] Emporia *Gazette*, February 15, 1922.
[14] *Ibid.*, April 26, 1922.
[15] *Ibid.*, August 16, 1932.
[16] *Ibid.*, July 19, 1927.
[17] "Kansas, Too, Has Its 'White' House," *Literary Digest*, LXXXVI (July 25, 1925), 47.

CHAPTER XXII

[1] From William Allen White's Campaign Speech.
[2] Emporia *Gazette*, July 28, 1921.
[3] *Ibid.*, August 2, 1921.
[4] White, "Patience and Publicity," *World Tomorrow*, VII (March, 1924), 87.
[5] September 2, 1924.
[6] September 6, 1924.
[7] Emporia *Gazette*, September 20, 1924.
[8] "William Allen White's War on the Klan," *Literary Digest*, LXXXIII (October 11, 1924), 16.
[9] Kansas City *Times*, September 23, 1924.
[10] Topeka *Capital*, October 15, 1924.
[11] Emporia *Gazette*, May 5, 1925.
[12] All statements in this story are based on a speech by U. S. Guyer, *Congressional Record*, Vol. LXXXIV, No. 749, 13937-38.
[13] December 31, 1924.
[14] Emporia *Gazette*, July 27, 1927.

[15] *Ibid.*, April 2, 1928.
[16] New York *Times*, April 3, 1928.
[17] Emporia *Gazette*, April 3, 1928.
[18] Topeka *Capital*, April 5, 1928.
[19] Emporia *Gazette*, April 5, 1928.
[20] Topeka *Capital*, April 5, 1928.

CHAPTER XXIII

[1] New York *Herald-Tribune Magazine*, December 11, 1927, 8.
[2] Noble L. Prentis, *A History of Kansas*, 202-03.
[3] Emporia *Gazette*, June 11, 1928.
[4] *Ibid.*, June 14, 1928.
[5] *Ibid.*, July 14, 1928.
[6] *Ibid.*, July 30, 1928.
[7] *Ibid.*, July 31, 1928.
[8] *Ibid.*, July 31, 1928.
[9] *Ibid.*, August 21, 1928.
[10] *Ibid.*, November 9, 1934.
[11] "Kansas, Too, Has Its 'White' House," *Literary Digest*, LXXXVI (July 25, 1925), 46-47.

CHAPTER XXIV

[1] Emporia *Gazette*, September 27, 1939.
[2] Charles E. Wager, "William Allen White's Editorial Writings," Kansas State Teachers College, Emporia, 1935.
[3] Emporia *Gazette*, December 13, 1930.
[4] *Ibid.*, November 18, 1930.
[5] *Ibid.*, January 18, 1934.
[6] *Ibid.*, April 6, 1933.
[7] *Ibid.*, January 5, 1933.
[8] *Ibid.*, July 18, 1933.
[9] *Ibid.*, January 3, 1934.
[10] Quotations in this and the following paragraph are from "A Yip from the Doghouse," *New Republic*, XCIII (December 15, 1937), 160 ff.
[11] This quotation and those that follow unless otherwise noted are from "Supreme Court—or 'Rule by Impulse,'" New York *Times Magazine*, April 25, 1937.
[12] *Opus Cit.*, 160.

CHAPTER XXV

[1] Emporia *Gazette*, January 26, 1901.
[2] Richard Cordley, *History of Lawrence, Kansas*, 24.
[3] Government figures quoted in *Kansas Facts*, IV (1933), 171.
[4] Quotations contrasting Howe's and White's personalities are from an article by A. T. Burch in the Cleveland *Press*, October 9, 1937.
[5] Emporia *Gazette*, July 9, 1898.
[6] *Ibid.*, July 7, 1898.
[7] *Ibid.*, February 4, 1924.
[8] *Ibid.*, May 29, 1899.
[9] *Ibid.*, June 5, 1895.
[10] Topeka *Capital*, November 16, 1923. The next day White made this paragraph the subject of an editorial on consistency, but changed it to read: "The Emporia Gazette is the best loved paper in Kansas because its editor" etc. The word "loved" was not well chosen. White has never had to live down "Emporia's best loved citizen," not even "the town's most valuable citizen." Everybody in Emporia does not call him "Bill," despite feature

writers. To perhaps a dozen he is Bill; to boyhood friends he is Will; to all others he is Mr. White.

[11] Emporia *Gazette*, June 1, 1925.
[12] *Ibid.*, July 11, 1906.
[13] *Ibid.*, November 17, 1923.
[14] *Ibid.*, January 28, 1901.
[15] *Ibid.*, February 11, 1901.
[16] *Ibid.*, December 23, 1925.
[17] *Ibid.*, December 12, 1922.
[18] *Ibid.*, April 8, 1914.
[19] *Ibid.*, November 28, 1914.
[20] *Ibid.*, July 14, 1937.
[21] *Ibid.*, April 19, 1924.
[22] *Ibid.*, August 15, 1935.
[23] Webb Waldron, "The Voice of the Prairie," *Collier's*, LXXIV (August 9, 1924), 8.
[24] December 9, 1939, issue.
[25] Lawrence *Journal*, August 11, 1888.
[26] Emporia *Gazette*, December 1, 1926.
[27] Ida M. Tarbell, *All in the Day's Work*, 259-60.
[28] *Proceedings*, American Society of Newspaper Editors, 1938, 12.

CHAPTER XXVI

[1] White, "Thoughts Amid Thanks," New York *Times Magazine*, November 19, 1939, 23.
[2] Edward H. O'Neill, *A History of American Biography, 1880-1935*, 335.
[3] White, *A Puritan in Babylon*, 280.
[4] R. L. Duffus, "The Character of Coolidge," New York *Times Book Review*, November 20, 1938, 1.
[5] Joseph G. Dinneen, "Coolidge Without Legend," *Saturday Review of Literature*, XIX (November 19, 1938), 7.
[6] "Books of the Decade," *Yale Review*, XXIX (December, 1939), 422.
[7] *The Changing West*, 16.
[8] *Ibid.*, 16.
[9] *Ibid.*, 4-5.
[10] *Ibid.*, 7-8.
[11] *Ibid.*, 8.
[12] *Ibid.*, 9-10.
[13] *Ibid.*, 11.
[14] *Ibid.*, 13.
[15] *Ibid.*, 41.
[16] *Ibid.*, 21.
[17] *Ibid.*, 22.
[18] *Ibid.*, 83-84.
[19] *Ibid.*, 83-88.
[20] *Ibid.*, 88-89.
[21] *Ibid.*, 73.
[22] *Ibid.*, 112.
[23] *Ibid.*, 59.
[24] *Ibid.*, 60.
[25] *Ibid.*, 62.
[26] *Ibid.*, 63.
[27] *Ibid.*, 78.
[28] *Ibid.*, 77.
[29] *Ibid.*, 79.
[30] *Ibid.*, 111.

[31] *Ibid.*, 80-81.
[32] *Ibid.*, 112.
[33] *Ibid.*, 110.
[34] *Ibid.*, 112.
[35] *Ibid.*, 113.
[36] *Ibid.*, 116.
[37] *Ibid.*, 125.
[38] *Ibid.*, 126.
[39] *Ibid.*, 127.
[40] *Ibid.*, 128-129.
[41] "The New Books," *Harper's Magazine,* CLXXX (December, 1939).

CHAPTER XXVII

[1] From White's radio broadcast, August 22, 1940.
[2] Emporia *Gazette,* September 26, 1939.
[3] *Ibid.*, October 3, 1939.
[4] *Ibid.*, November 6, 1939.
[5] White, *Defense for America,* "Introduction," XI-XII.
[6] Emporia *Gazette,* September 26, 1939.
[7] White, *Defense for America,* "Introduction," VI-VII.
[8] White's address before the Emporia State Teachers College Republican Club, May 14, 1940.
[9] Kansas City *Star,* May 19, 1940.
[10] Emporia *Gazette,* May 20, 1940.
[11] New York *Times,* May 20, 1940.
[12] *Ibid.*, May 26, 1940.
[13] White, "Objectives of the Committee to Defend America by Aiding the Allies," July, 1940.
[14] Statement of Policy, November 26, 1940.
[15] Emporia *Gazette,* January 3, 1941.
[16] New York *Times Magazine,* September 8, 1940, 1.
[17] Radio address, August 23, 1940, but repeated many times.
[18] *Time,* XXXVII (January 6, 1941), 11.
[19] New York *Times,* December 18, 1940.
[20] Emporia *Gazette,* February 4, 1940. Wood's testimony, like that of La Guardia's referred to later, was in connection with the hearings on the "lease-lend" bill.
[21] *Ibid.*, December 23, 1940.
[22] New York *Times,* December 28, 1940.
[23] *Ibid.*, December 29, 1940.
[24] Emporia *Gazette,* February 11, 1941.
[25] *Christian Century,* LVIII (January 15, 1941), 76.
[26] Emporia *Gazette,* January 1, 1941.
[27] New York *Times,* January 4, 1941.

Bibliography

WILLIAM ALLEN WHITE'S WRITINGS

BOOKS

Boys—Then and Now, New York: Macmillan, 1926.
Calvin Coolidge, New York: Macmillan, 1925.
A Certain Rich Man, New York: Macmillan, 1909.
The Changing West, New York: Macmillan, 1939.
Conflicts in American Public Opinion, (With Walter E. Myer), Chicago: American Library Association, 1925.
The Court of Boyville, New York: Doubleday and McClure, 1899.
Defense for America, (Editor), New York: Macmillan, 1940.
The Editor and His People, (Editorials Selected by Helen Ogden Mahin), New York: Macmillan, 1924.
Forty Years on Main Street, (Editorials Selected by Russell H. Fitzgibbon), New York and Toronto: Farrar and Rinehart, 1937.
God's Puppets, New York: Macmillan, 1916.
In The Heart of a Fool, New York: Macmillan, 1918.
In Our Town, New York: McClure, Phillips, 1906.
The Martial Adventures of Henry and Me, New York: Macmillan, 1918.
Masks in a Pageant, New York: Macmillan, 1928.
The Old Order Changeth, New York: Macmillan, 1910.
Politics: The Citizen's Business, New York: Macmillan, 1924.
A Puritan in Babylon, New York: Macmillan, 1938.
The Real Issue, Chicago: Way and Williams, 1896.
Rhymes by Two Friends, (With Albert Bigelow Paine), Fort Scott: M. L. Izor and Son, 1893.
Some Cycles of Cathay, Chapel Hill: University of North Carolina Press, 1925.
Stratagems and Spoils, New York: Charles Scribner's Sons, 1901.
A Theory of Spiritual Progress, Emporia: Emporia *Gazette,* 1910.
What It's All About, New York: Macmillan, 1936.
Woodrow Wilson—The Man, His Times and His Task, Boston and New York: Houghton, Mifflin, 1924.

PERIODICALS AND PUBLICATIONS[1]

"The Abuse of the Direct Primary," *Independent,* CXIII (July 5, 1924), 18.

[1] A selected list of magazine articles. Poems, collected short stories, newspaper articles, and all but a few book reviews have been omitted.

"Address of the President," *Kansas State Historical Quarterly,* VIII (February, 1939), 72-82.

"Al Smith, City Feller," *Collier's,* LXXVIII (August 21, 1926), 8 ff.

"And the West Is West," (Story), *Saturday Evening Post,* CXCIII (June 18, 1921), 10 ff.

"Annihilate the Klan," *Nation,* CXX (January 7, 1925), 7.

"The Anti-Saloon League," *Saturday Review of Literature,* IV (June 16, 1928), 961-62.

"An Appreciation of the West," *McClure's Magazine,* XI (October, 1898), 575-80.

"Are Human Movements Independent of Wars?" *Journal of Social Forces,* III (May, 1925), 393-95.

"Are the Movies a Mess or a Menace?" *Collier's,* LXXVII (January 16, 1926), 5 ff.

"As Kansas Sees Prohibition," *Collier's,* LXXVIII (July 3, 1926), 23.

"The Average American," New York *Times Magazine,* January 4, 1931, 1-2.

"The Balance Sheet of the Nation," *Saturday Evening Post,* CLXXV (March 28, 1903), 8 ff.

"Battle Hum of the Republic," *Collier's,* LXXXII (August 18, 1928), 8 ff.

"Beefsteak As I Prepare It," *Better Homes and Gardens,* XII (April, 1934), 97.

"The Best Minds, Incorporated," *Collier's,* LXIX (March 4, 1922), 5 ff.

"Bill's School and Mine," *Journal of Education,* LXXV (March 7, 1912), 257-58.

"Blood of the Conquerors," *Collier's,* LXXI (March 10, 1923), 5 ff.

"Books of the Decade," *Yale Review,* XXIX (December, 1939), 419-20.

"Books of the Fall," *Saturday Review of Literature,* XIV (October 10, 1936), 16 ff.

"The Boom in the Northwest," *Saturday Evening Post,* CLXXVI (May 21, 1904), 1-3; (May 28, 1904), 1-2.

"Boys—Then and Now," *American Magazine,* CI (March, 1926), 7 ff.

"The Brain Trust," *Saturday Evening Post,* CLXXV (March 21, 1903), 1-3.

"A Brief for the Defendant," *Collier's,* XLI (July 4, 1908), 9-10.

"Bryan," *McClure's Magazine,* XV (July, 1900), 232-37.

"Building Up of the Prairie West," *Collier's,* XXIX (May 10, 1902), 10.

"The Business of a Wheat Farm," *Scribner's Magazine,* XXII (November, 1897), 531-48.

"Calvin Coolidge," *Collier's,* LXXV (March 7, 1925), 5 ff.; (March 21, 1925), 13 ff.; (April 4, 1925), 9 ff.; (April 18, 1925), 9 ff.

"Candidates in the Spring," *Yale Review*, XXIX (March, 1940), 433-43.

"Captain Henry King—the First Kansas Story Teller," *Kansas Magazine*, 1935, 25-28.

"Caring in a Nightmare," *Survey Graphic*, XXVII (August, 1938), 405.

"Carrie Nation and Kansas," *Saturday Evening Post*, CLXXIII (April 6, 1901), 2-3.

"Certain Voices in the Wilderness," *Kansas Magazine*, I (January, 1909), 1-5.

"The Challenge to Democracy," *Vital Speeches*, IV (June 1, 1938), 494-96.

"The Challenge to the Middle Class," *Atlantic Monthly*, CLX (August, 1937), 196-201.

"Cheer Up, America," *Harper's Magazine*, CLIV (March, 1927), 405-11.

"Cleveland," *McClure's Magazine*, XVIII (February, 1902), 322-30.

"Concerning 'Art for Art's Sake'," *Agora*, III (April, 1894), 290.

"The Confederate Colonel as a Political Issue," *Agora*, II (July, 1892), 27-31.

"The Conflict Between the Important and the Interesting in Newspapers," *Proceedings*, American Society of Newspaper Editors, April, 1935, 34-36.

"The Country Boy," *Saturday Evening Post*, CLXXVI (December 19, 1903), 18.

"The Country Editor Speaks," *Nation*, CXXVIII (June 12, 1929), 714.

"The Country Newspaper," *Harper's Magazine*, CXXXII (May, 1916), 887-91.

"Croker," *McClure's Magazine*, XVI (February, 1901), 317-26.

"Cuban Reciprocity—a Moral Issue," *McClure's Magazine*, XIX (September, 1902), 387-94.

"The Dawn of a Great Tomorrow," *Collier's*, LXXI (March 17, 1923), 11 ff.

"The Democratic Revival," *Saturday Evening Post*, CLXXVII (August 13, 1904), 6-7.

"A Democratic View of Education," *Craftsman*, XXI (November, 1911), 119-30.

"The Dollar in Politics," *Saturday Evening Post*, CLXXVII (July 2, 1904), 8-9.

"Don't Indulge in Name-Calling With Press Critics," *Editor and Publisher*, LXXII (April 22, 1939), 14 ff.

"A Dry West Warns the Thirsty East," *Collier's*, LXX (September 2, 1922), 3 ff.

"An Earlier Cycle of American Development," *Social Forces*, IV (December, 1925), 281-85.

"The Ebb Tide," *Saturday Evening Post*, CLXXXVII (December 19, 1914), 3 ff.

"Edna Ferber," *World's Work*, LIX (June, 1930), 36 ff.

"The Education of Herbert Hoover," *Collier's*, LXXXI (June 9, 1928), 8 ff.

"The Educational Service of the Library," *School and Society*, XVIII (November 10, 1923), 554-55.

"Emporia and New York," *American Magazine*, LXIII (January, 1907), 258-64.

"The End of an Epoch," *Scribner's Magazine*, LXXIX (June, 1926), 561-70.

"England in Transition," *Collier's*, LXIV (September 27, 1919), 9 ff.

"Esther, The Gentle," *University Review*, IX (March, 1888), 161-63.

"The Eternal Bounce in Man," *Vital Speeches*, III (July 15, 1937), 606-8.

"The Ethics of Advertising," *Atlantic Monthly*, CLXIV (November, 1939), 665-71.

"A Eulogy of the Santa Fe and Santa Fe men," *Santa Fe Employes' Magazine*, VI (May, 1912), 45.

"Ever Been in Emporia?" *New Republic*, XXII (May 12, 1920), 348-49.

"The Fair-Play Department," *Saturday Evening Post*, CLXXV (May 2, 1903), 1-2.

"The Farmer—and His Plight," *Survey*, LXII (June 1, 1929), 281-83.

"Farmer John and the Sirens," *Saturday Evening Post*, CXCIV (November 12, 1921), 10 ff.

"The Farmer Takes His Holiday," *Saturday Evening Post*, CCV (November 26, 1932), 6-ff.

"The Farmer's Votes and Problems," *Yale Review*, XXVIII (March, 1939), 433-48.

"Farmington," *Saturday Evening Post*, CLXXVII (January 21, 1905), 20.

"Fifty Years of Kansas," *World's Work*, VIII (June, 1904), 4870-72.

"First Shot in a New Battle," *Collier's*, LXIV (November 22, 1919), 5 ff.

"Folk," *McClure's Magazine*, XXVI (December, 1905), 115-32.

"40 Years: New Men, Old Issues," *New York Times Magazine*, August 9, 1936, 1 ff.

"Four Cornered Fight for Statehood," *Collier's*, XXXII (January 16, 1904), 7-8.

"The Freedom that Has Made America Great," *Vital Speeches*, VI (August 15, 1940), 642-44.

"Free Kansas," *Outlook,* c (February 24, 1912), 407-14.

"From Harrison II to Roosevelt II," *Saturday Review of Literature,* xi (September 22, 1934), 121 ff.

"From One Country Editor to Another," *Saturday Review of Literature,* xvii (January 29, 1938), 5.

"Funston—the Man From Kansas," *Saturday Evening Post,* clxxiii (May 18, 1901), 2 ff.

"The Futility of Reports," *Review of Reviews,* lxxxiii (March, 1931), 46.

"The Gentle Art of Knocking," *Kansas Knocker,* i (April, 1900), 23-24.

"The Glory of the States: Kansas," *American Magazine,* lxxxi (January, 1916), 41 ff.

"God Only Knows," *Homiletic Review,* cvii (April, 1934), 303-5.

"The Golden Rule," *Atlantic Monthly,* xcvi (October, 1905), 433-41.

"Good Newspapers and Bad," *Atlantic Monthly,* cliii (May, 1934), 581-86.

"Government of the People, by the People, for the People," *Independent,* lxxxv (February 7, 1916), 187-90.

"Governor Smith and Myself," *Commonweal,* ix (February 6, 1929), 402.

"Grafting and Things," *Saturday Evening Post,* clxxvi (May 7, 1904), 4.

"The Great Political Drama at St. Louis," *Collier's* (St. Louis Convention Extra, July 12, 1904), 2 ff.

"Greatheart," *World Review,* vii (October 22, 1928), 85-86.

"Haitian Experience," *Proceedings,* American Society of Newspaper Editors, April, 1930, 103-8.

"Hanna," *McClure's Magazine,* xvi (November, 1900), 56-64.

Harper's Weekly, xlvi (February 1, 1902), 155.

"Harrison," *Cosmopolitan,* xxxii (March, 1902), 489-96.

"The Helpful Career of Abijah P. Jenks" (Story), *Judge,* lxxxii (July 15, 1922), 3-5.

"Herbert Hoover—The Last of the Old Presidents or the First of the New?" *Saturday Evening Post,* ccv (March 4, 1933), 6 ff.

"Here Was A Man," *Saturday Review of Literature,* viii (November 7, 1931), 257 ff.

"The Highbrow Doughboy," *Red Cross Magazine,* xiv (August, 1919), 19-24.

"Hot From the Griddle," *Saturday Review of Literature,* ix (September 3, 1932), 73-74.

"How Far Have We Come?" *Survey Graphic,* xxvi (December, 1937), 669-72.

"How Free Is Our Press?" *Nation,* cxlvi (June 18, 1938), 693-95.

"How Free Is the Press?" *Collier's,* ciii (April 8, 1939), 16 ff.

"How Kansas Boarded the Water Wagon," *Saturday Evening Post*, CLXXXVII (July 11, 1914), 3 ff.

"How May the West Survive?" *Christian Science Monitor Magazine* (May 20, 1939), 1 ff.

"How May the West Survive?" *North American Review*, CCXLVIII (Autumn, 1939), 7-17.

"How the Rain Came" (Story), *Push*, 1 (September, 1902), 4-5.

"How to Stay Out of War," *Forum and Century*, XCVII (February, 1937), 91.

"How We Buried Him," *Graduate Magazine*, VII (August, 1909), 260-61.

"I Cover the Pacific Waterfront," *Proceedings*, American Society of Newspaper Editors, April, 1936, 39-44.

"If I Were Dictator," *Nation*, CXXXIII (December 2, 1931), 596-98.

"In Kansas, the Landon Home State," *Review of Reviews*, XCIII (April, 1936), 55.

"Insurgence of Insurgency," *American Magazine*, LXXI (December, 1910), 170-74.

"Is Our Way of Life Doomed?" New York *Times Magazine*, September 8, 1940, 3 ff.

"It's Been a Great Show," *Collier's*, CI (February 12, 1938), 16.

"Journalism—Its Good and Its Gray Side," *World Review*, VIII (March 18, 1929), 104.

Judge, Editorials from November 26, 1921, to August 12, 1922, inclusive.

"Just Wondering," *Kansas Magazine*, 1934, 86-88.

"Kansas and Prohibition," *Kansas Magazine*, 1937, 50-52.

"The Kansas Conscience," *Reader Magazine*, VI (October, 1905), 488-93.

"The Kansas Fight," *La Follette's Weekly Magazine*, 1 (January 16, 1909), 5 ff.

"Kansas: Its Present and Future," *Forum*, XXIII (March, 1897), 75-83.

"The Kansas Red Scare," *Kansas Magazine*, 1938, 130-31.

"Landon: I Knew Him When," *Saturday Evening Post*, CCIX (July 18, 1936), 5 ff.

"The Larger Cycle of American Development," *Social Forces*, IV (September, 1925), 1-5.

"The Last of the Magic Isles," *Survey*, LVI (May 1, 1926), 176 ff.

"Lawton—The Metropolis of the Wilderness," *Saturday Evening Post*, CLXXIV (September 7, 1901), 3 ff.

"The Leaven of the Pharisees," *Saturday Evening Post*, CXCII (May 29, 1920), 20 ff.

"Liberalism for Republicans," *Review of Reviews*, LXXXVII (January, 1933), 27.

"The Librarian, A Community Engineer," *Libraries,* XXXII (April, 1927), 183-84.

"Lincoln and Our Democracy," *Collier's,* XL (February 15, 1908), 10-11.

"Litmus Papers of the Acid Test," *Survey,* XLIV (June 5, 1920), 343-46.

"The Lone Lion of Idaho," *Collier's,* LXXVI (September 12, 1925), 6 ff.

"McKinley and Hanna," *Saturday Evening Post,* CLXXVI (March 12, 1904), 1-2.

"A Man of Courage," *Saturday Review of Literature,* IX (October 22, 1932), 185-86.

"The Man Who Made the 'Star,' " *Collier's,* LV (June 26, 1915), 12 ff.

"The Man Who Rules the Senate," *Collier's,* LXXVI (October 3, 1925), 10 ff.

"Mary Elizabeth McCabe," *Kansas Newspaperdom,* I (May, 1894), 2.

"Memoirs of a Three-Fingered Pianist," *Woman's Home Companion,* LIV (September, 1927), 12 ff; (October, 1927), 8 ff.

"The Migratory Executive," *Saturday Evening Post,* CCII (March 15, 1930), 10 ff.

"The Mind of Coolidge," *Collier's,* LXXVI (December 26, 1925), 6 ff.

"Moscow and Emporia," *New Republic,* XCVI (September 21, 1938), 177-80; XCVII (December 7, 1938), 193.

"Mr. Howe's New Novel," *University Review,* X (December, 1888), 111-13.

"Mr. White Comes Back," *Saturday Evening Post,* CLXXXVII (November 14, 1914), 25-27.

"Mr. White Interviews Himself," *Proceedings,* American Society Newspaper Editors, April, 1929, 79-91.

"My K. U.—A Lovely and Glamorous Life," *Graduate Magazine,* XXXVI (May, 1938), 5.

"The Natural History of a Gentleman," *Saturday Evening Post,* CLXXVII (July 30, 1904), 13-15.

"The New Congress," *Saturday Evening Post,* CLXXIV (January 2, 1902), 5-6.

"Now We Eat It 'n' Like It," *Rotarian,* LIV (February, 1939), 10-11.

"The Odds Against the U-boat," *Collier's,* LX (December 8, 1917), 4-6.

"The Old Order Changeth," *American Magazine,* LXVII (January, 1909), 218-25; (February, 1909), 407-14; (March, 1909), 506-13; (April, 1909), 603-10; LXVIII (May, 1909), 63-70; August, 1909), 376-83.

"The Old Problem of the Dog and the Engine," *American Magazine,* LXXI (February, 1911), 517-20.

"Old Slugs," *Newspaper West,* II (July, 1899), 93.

"On Bright Angel Trail," *McClure's Magazine,* XXV (September, 1905), 502-15.

"On Our Way—But Where Are We Going?" *Saturday Review of Literature,* X (April 14, 1934), 625 ff.

"One Year of Roosevelt," *Saturday Evening Post,* CLXXV (October 4, 1902), 3-4.

"The Other Side," *Sunflower Magazine,* III (September, 1905), 8.

"The Other Side of Main Street," *Collier's,* LXVIII (July 30, 1921), 7 ff.

"A Page of National History," *Saturday Review of Literature,* VII (October 25, 1930), 261-63.

"The Partnership of Society," *American Magazine,* LXII (October, 1906), 576-85.

"The Passing of Reuben," *World Review,* VII (September 24, 1928), 21 ff.

"The Passing of the Free Editor," *American Mercury,* VIII (May, 1926), 110-12.

"Patience and Publicity," *World Tomorrow,* VII (March, 1924), 87.

"Pay Day in Politics," *Saturday Review of Literature,* XVII (April 9, 1938), 10-11.

"The Peace and President Wilson," *Saturday Evening Post,* CXCII (August 16, 1919), 15 ff.

"Platt," *McClure's Magazine,* XVIII (December, 1901), 145-53.

"A Poet Comes Out of Tailholt," *Collier's,* LVI (December 25, 1915), 3 ff.

"Political Signs of Promise," *Outlook,* LXXX (July 15, 1905), 667-70.

"The Politicians," *Saturday Evening Post,* CLXXV (March 14, 1903), 1-3.

"The President," *Saturday Evening Post,* CLXXV (April 4, 1903), 4 ff.

Proceedings, American Society of Newspaper Editors, April, 1938, 131-35.

"The Progressive Hen and the Insurgent Ducklings," *American Magazine,* LXXI (January, 1911), 394-99.

"Progressive Leader," *Saturday Review of Literature,* XVI (July 10, 1937), 5-6.

"A Reader in the Eighties and Nineties," *Bookman,* LXXII (November, 1930), 229-34.

"Ready Made Homes Out West," *Saturday Evening Post,* CLXXXV (April 26, 1902), 12.

"The Reorganization of the Republican Party," *Saturday Evening Post,* CLXXVII (December 3, 1904), 1-2.

"Rights of a Columnist,"*Nation,* cvxxi (May, 1928), 607.
"Roosevelt, A Force for Righteousness, *McClure's Magazine,* xxviii (February, 1907), 386-94.
"Roosevelt and the Postal Frauds," *McClure's Magazine,* xxiii (September, 1904), 506-20.
"The Santa Fe Magazine," *Santa Fe Magazine,* xxi (December, 1926), 39.
"Science, St. Skinflint and Santa Claus," *American Magazine,* lxiii (December, 1906), 182-84.
"Seconding the Motion," *Saturday Evening Post,* clxxvii (July 23, 1904), 4-5.
"The Sheriff and the Chaperon," *Saturday Evening Post,* clxxiii (March 30, 1901), 14.
"Shock Troops of Reform," *Saturday Review of Literature,* xix (April 8, 1939), 3-4.
"Should Old Acquaintance Be Forgot," *American Magazine,* lxxiv (May, 1912), 13-18.
"Simplifying the Business of Politics," *Woman's Home Companion,* li (November, 1924), 21 ff.
"The Solid West—Free and Proud of It," *Collier's,* lxx (December 30, 1922), 5 ff.
"Some Notes on the Evolution of the Girl from Greensburg" (Story), *University Review,* xiv (April, 1893), 225-28.
"Some Personal Glimpses of Early Kansas Editors," *Kansas Editor,* xviii (March, 1933), 1.
"Speaking for the Consumer," *Vital Speeches,* v (November 1, 1938), 47-49.
"Splitting Fiction Three Ways," *New Republic,* xxx (April 12, 1922), 22-26.
"The State Administration—A Weak Man in a Strong Situation," *Agora,* iv (October, 1894), 90-95.
"Storming the Citadel," *American Magazine,* lxxii (September, 1911), 570-75.
"Sullivan I and Roosevelt I," *Saturday Review of Literature,* xix (November 19, 1938), 3-4.
"Summer on a Cattle Ranch," *University Review,* x (September, 1888), 13.
"The Supremacy of Beefsteak," *Nation,* cxvii (December 26, 1923), 731.
"Supreme Court—or 'Rule by Impulse'," New York *Times Magazine* (April 25, 1937), 3 ff.
"Swinging Around the Circle," *Saturday Evening Post,* clxxv (June 27, 1903), 1-2.
"Taft, A Hewer of Wood," *American Magazine,* lxvi (May, 1908), 19-32.
"Taft, T. R., and the G. O. P.," *Saturday Review of Literature,* xxi (October 28, 1939), 3-4.

"Tale That Is Told," *Saturday Evening Post*, CXCII (October 4, 1919), 19 ff.

"Teaching Perkins to Play" (Story), *Saturday Evening Post*, CXCIV (August 6, 1921), 12 ff.

"A Tenderfoot on Thunder Mountain," *Saturday Evening Post*, CLXXV (The Trail, November 8, 1902), 1 ff; (The Foot of the Rainbow, November 15, 1902), 3-5; (The Foot of the Rainbow, November 22, 1902), 15-16; (The Pot of Gold, November 29, 1902), 3 ff.

"Theodore Roosevelt," *McClure's Magazine*, XVIII (November, 1901), 40-47.

"A Theory of Social Progress," *Columbia University Quarterly*, XII (September, 1910), 408-20.

"These United States; Kansas—A Puritan Survival," *Nation*, CXIV (April 19, 1922), 460-62.

"They Can't Beat My Big Boy," *Collier's*, LXXIX (June 18, 1927), 8 ff.

"This Business of Writing," *Saturday Review of Literature*, III (December 4, 1926), 355-56.

"Those Heartbreaks in Washington," *Collier's*, LXVIII (December 31, 1921), 7 ff.

"A Thought for a Great Occasion," *American Legion Monthly*, I (July, 1926), 8.

"Thoughts After the Election," *Yale Review*, XXX (December, 1940), 217-27.

"Thoughts and Thanks," New York *Times Magazine* (November 19, 1938), 4 ff.

"Three Years of Progress," *Saturday Evening Post*, CLXXXIV (February 24, 1912), 3 ff.

"Tinting the Cold Gray Dawn," *Collier's*, LXVIII (December 17, 1921), 5 ff.

"Turning Knowledge into Votes," *National Municipal Review*, XXIII (February, 1934), 85-86.

"Twelve Years of Mr. Bryan," *Collier's*, XLII (October 17, 1908), 12-13.

"Two Recent Kansas Books," *University Review*, X (March, 1889), 199-202.

"Uncommercial Traveling," *Saturday Evening Post*, CLXXIV (May 3, 1902), 12.

"The Unknown Soldier," *Collier's*, LXVIII (November 12, 1921), 13.

"W. A. White on the Kansas Court," *Nation*, CXV (December 27, 1922), 718.

"We Who Are About to Die," *New Republic*, XXVI (March 9, 1921), 36-38.

"Wendell Willkie," *New Republic*, CII (June 17, 1940), 818-19.

"What About Our Courts," *American Magazine,* LXIX (February, 1910), 499-505.

"What Democracy Means to Me," *Scholastic,* XXXI (October 23, 1937), 9.

"What Happened to Walt Mason," *American Magazine,* LXXXVI (September, 1918), 19.

"What Music Has Done for Me," *Etude,* LVI (December, 1938), 779-80.

"What 1920 Holds for Us All," *Collier's,* LXV (January 3, 1920), 7.

"What the War Did for Brewer," *Yale Review,* VIII (January, 1919), 243-251.

"What the West Thinks of Wall Street Now," *Collier's,* XXXII (November 28, 1903), 9-10.

"What's the Matter With America?" *Collier's,* XXXVIII (October 20, 1906), 18 ff; (November 10, 1906), 16 ff; (December 1, 1906), 16 ff.

"What's the Matter With America?" *Collier's,* LXX (July 1, 1922), 3 ff.

"What's the Matter with American Cooking?" *Pictorial Review,* XXVII (July, 1926), 4 ff.

"When Club Women Are News," *Clubwoman,* XIII (May, 1933), 5.

"When Johnny Went Marching Out," *McClure's Magazine,* XI (June, 1898), 198-205.

"When the World Busts Through," *American Magazine,* LXXI (April, 1911), 746-47.

"Where Are the Pre-War Radicals?" *Survey,* LV (February 1, 1926), 556.

"Who Killed Cock Robin?" *Collier's,* LVIII (December 16, 1916), 5 ff.

"Why All the Rumpus?" *Collier's,* LXXII (August 25, 1923), 5 ff.

"Why I Am a Progressive," *Saturday Evening Post,* CXCIII (April 23, 1921), 3 ff.

"Why the Nation Will Endure," *Saturday Evening Post,* CLXXVII (March 4, 1905), 12.

"Will America's Dream Come True?" *Collier's,* LXIX (February 18, 1922), 9 ff.

"Will They Fool Us Twice?" *Collier's,* LXVIII (October 15, 1921), 5 ff.

"William Allen White on Mr. Steffens' Book, 'The Shame of the Cities,'" *McClure's,* XXIII (June, 1904), 220-21.

"William Allen White Sizes 'Em Up," *Collier's,* LXXIV (August 9, 1924), 7 ff.

"William Allen White to F. H.," *New Republic,* XIX (May 17, 1919), 88.

"A Woman of Genius," *Saturday Review of Literature,* IX (November 12, 1932), 235-36.
"Woodrow Wilson," *Liberty,* 1 (November 15, 1924), 19-23; (November 22, 1924), 22-26.
"The Worthy Rich," *Saturday Evening Post,* CLXXVIII (January 13, 1906), 12.
"A Yip from the Doghouse," *New Republic,* XCIII (December 15, 1937), 160-62.
"The Y. M. C. A. Huts 'Safety Valves' for Our Boys in France," *Touchstone,* II (January, 1918), 344-50.

ITEMS OF GENERAL REFERENCE

BOOKS

ABBOT, WILLIS J., *Watching The World Go By,* Boston: Little Brown, 1934.
BALDWIN, CHARLES C., *The Men Who Make Our Novels,* rev. ed., New York: Dodd, Mead, 1924.
BLANKENSHIP, RUSSELL, *American Literature as an Expression of the National Mind,* New York: Henry Holt, 1931.
BLEYER, WILLARD GROSVENOR, *Main Currents in the History of American Journalism,* New York: Houghton Mifflin, 1927.
BOWERS, CLAUDE G., *Beveridge and the Progressive Era,* New York: The Literary Guild, 1932.
BUCK, SOLON J., *The Agrarian Crusade,* New Haven: Yale University Press, 1920.
CONNELLEY, WILLIAM E., *History of Kansas,* 5 vols., Chicago and New York: American Historical Society, 1928.
CORDLEY, RICHARD, *History of Lawrence, Kansas,* Lawrence: E. F. Caldwell, 1895.
Dictionary of American Biography, 20 vols.
FERBER, EDNA, *A Peculiar Treasure,* New York: Literary Guild, 1939.
FRENCH, LAURA M., *History of Emporia and Lyon County,* Emporia: Emporia *Gazette,* 1929.
HICKS, GRANVILLE, *The Great Tradition,* New York: Macmillan, 1933.
HOWE, E. W., *Plain People,* New York: Dodd, Mead, 1929.
KINGSBURY, SUSAN M., HORNELL HART, and ASSOCIATES, *Newspapers and the News,* New York: G. P. Putnam's Sons, 1937.
MARBLE, ANNIE RUSSELL, *A Study of the Modern Novel,* New York: D. Appleton, 1928.
MENCKEN, H. L., *Prejudices* (First Series), New York: Alfred A. Knopf, 1919.
MOONEY, VOL. P., *History of Butler County,* Kansas, Lawrence: Standard Publishing Co., 1916.

Bibliography 359

MURDOCK, VICTOR, *Folks,* New York: Macmillan, 1921.

O'NEILL, ELWARD H., *A History of American Biography,* 1800-1935, Philadelphia: University of Pennsylvania Press, 1935.

PARRINGTON, VERNON LOUIS, *Main Currents of American Thought,* 3 vols., New York: Harcourt, Brace, 1930.

PRENTIS, NOBLE L., *A History of Kansas,* Topeka: Caroline Prentis, 1909.

PRINGLE, HENRY F., *Theodore Roosevelt,* New York: Harcourt, Brace, 1931.

QUINN, ARTHUR HOBSON, *American Fiction, An Historical and Critical Survey,* New York: D. Appleton-Century, 1936.

SERGEANT, ELIZABETH SHIPLEY, *Fire Under the Andes,* New York: Alfred A. Knopf, 1927.

STEFFENS, LINCOLN, *The Autobiography of Lincoln Steffens,* New York: Harcourt, Brace, 1931.

STRATFORD, JESSIE PERRY, *Butler's County's Eighty Years, 1855-1935,* (El Dorado): Butler County *News,* 1934.

SULLIVAN, MARK, *The Education of an American,* New York: Doubleday, Doran, 1938.

——, *Our Times,* 6 vols., New York and London: Charles Scribner's Sons, 1931.

Sunflowers, edited by T. F. Doran and W. A. White, Lawrence: Journal Publishing Co., 1888.

TARBELL, IDA M., *All in the Day's Work,* New York: Macmillan, 1939.

VAN DOREN, CARL, *Contemporary American Novelists, 1900-1920,* New York: Macmillan, 1922.

WILDER, DANIEL W., *Annals of Kansas,* Topeka: George W. Martin, 1875.

William Rockhill Nelson, by members of the Staff of the Kansas City *Star,* Cambridge: The Riverside Press, 1915.

PERIODICALS AND PUBLICATIONS

ABBOTT, JOHN M. K., "Bill White and the Shirt-Tail Rangers," *Outlook,* CXXXVIII (November 5, 1924), 360-61.

" 'Bill' White's Start," *Literary Digest,* XLVIII (March 21, 1914), 642 ff.

BLYTHE, SAMUEL G., "Great Men and Their Neighbors," *Saturday Evening Post,* CLXXIX (June 15, 1907), 20-22.

BROUN, HEYWOOD, "What's the Matter With White?" *Collier's,* LXX (July 1, 1922), 18.

CANHAN, ERWIN D., "The Patient Liberal," *Christian Science Monitor Magazine* (April 15, 1939), 6.

CHAMBERLAIN, JOHN, "The New Books," *Harper's Magazine,* CLXXX (December, 1939).

CHENERY, WILLIAM L., "The Sage of Emporia," *Collier's*, LXXXI (June 9, 1928), 33.

CLESS, G. H., JR., "William Allen White Reign of Terror," *Scribner's Commentator*, IX (December, 1940), 38-43.

CLUGSTON, W. G., "Sage of Emporia," *Midwest*, I (January, 1937), 6 ff.

COOKE, THORNTON, "And When I Came to K.U.," *Graduate Magazine*, XXXVII (September, 1938), 6.

"Country Editor," *Time*, XXIX (April 26, 1937), 84 ff.

DEVOTO, BERNARD, "Main Street Twenty Years After," *Harper's Magazine*, MLXXXVI (November, 1940), 580-87.

DE YOUNG, DIRK P., "Interview With William Allen White," *Dearborn Independent*, January 24, 1925.

DINNEEN, JOSFPH G., "Coolidge Without Legend," *Saturday Review of Literature*, XIX (November 19, 1938), 7.

"A Document on Liberty," *Literary Digest*, LXXIV (August 19, 1922), 32.

DUFFUS, R. L., "The Character of Coolidge," New York *Times Book Review*, November 30, 1938, 1.

FERBER, EDNA, "Kansas, Too, Has Its 'White' House," *Literary Digest*, LXXXVI (July 25, 1925), 45-47.

FUNSTON, FREDERICK, "Reminiscences of Kansas University," *Kansas Magazine*, I (April, 1909), 12-15.

"A Great American Reaches Seventy," *Christian Century*, LV (February 16, 1938), 197.

HASKELL, H. J., "Further Martial Adventures of Henry and Me," *Outlook*, CXXXI (August 2, 1922), 559-60.

HAUSAM, CLARICE L., "Romance of American Journalism: William Allen White," *Editor and Publisher*, LX (February 11, 1928), 12.

HERBERT, EWING, "William Allen White," *Kansas Newspaperdom*, I (April, 1894), 2.

HINSHAW, AUGUSTA W., "William Allen White and the Evolution of the Emporia *Gazette*," *World's Work*, LIX (August, 1930), 64-67.

HOWELLS, W. D., "Psychological Counter-Current in Recent Fiction," *North American Review*, CLXXIII (December, 1901), 876-78.

"In Germany With William Allen White," *Literary Digest*, LXI (April 26, 1919), 64-66.

"The Kansas Cut-Ups," *Collier's*, LXXX (August 10, 1929), 49.

Kansas Facts, IV (1933).

"New Martial Adventures of 'Henry and Me,'" *Literary Digest*, LXXIV (August 5, 1922), 17-18.

New York *Herald-Tribune Magazine*, December 11, 1927, 8.

OLIN, OSCAR EUGENE, "Will White—Boy and Man," *Western Homes*, October, 1897, 12.

PAINE, ALBERT BIGELOW, "Rhymes by Two Friends," *Kansas Magazine,* II (September, 1909), 65-66.
PINET, F. L., "William Allen White—Kansan," *Kansas Magazine,* II (July, 1909), 1-7.
"Plowing the Soul in Kansas," *Collier's,* LIV (February 13, 1915), 15.
"A Progressive Republican at San Francisco," *Review of Reviews,* LXII (August, 1920), 198-99.
"A Protean Editor," *Saturday Evening Post,* CLXXVI (December 26, 1903), 18.
Publisher's Weekly, C (November 26, 1921), 1793.
RASCOE, BURTON, "Contemporary Reminiscences," *Arts and Decoration,* XXX (November, 1928), 63 ff.
ROOSEVELT, THEODORE, "The World War: Its Tragedies and Its Lessons," *Outlook,* CVIII (September 23, 1914), 169-178.
"A Sage Looks at Swing," *Time,* XXXV (May 20, 1940), 41.
"Savory Sage," *Literary Digest,* CXXIII (April 24, 1937), 29-32.
SERGEANT, ELIZABETH SHEPLEY, "The Citizen from Emporia," *Century Magazine,* CXIII (January, 1927), 308-16.
SHAW, ALBERT, "William Allen White Talks to His Neighbors," *Golden Book,* XI (April, 1930), 94.
"Story of a Tide," *Time,* XXXVI (August 19, 1940), 12-15.
STOUFFER, ELLIS B., "Development of Scholarship at the University of Kansas," *Graduate Magazine,* XXXIX (January, 1941), 6-9.
Tattler, "William Allen White," *Nation,* CIV (February 1, 1917), 139-40.
TITTLE, WALTER, "Glimpses of Interesting Americans," *Century Magazine,* CX (July, 1925), 305-8.
WALDRON, WEBB, "The Voice of the Prairie," *Collier's,* LXXIV (August 9, 1924), 8.
"What Readers of the Outlook Think of the War," *Outlook,* CVIII (September 2, 1914), 44-47.
"What's the Matter With White?" *Outlook,* CXLIX (August 15, 1928), 611.
"William Allen White," *Current Opinion,* LXXVII (December, 1924), 700-2.
"William Allen White," *Everybody's Magazine,* XXXIV (March, 1916), 354.
"William Allen White of Emporia: An American Institution Is Seventy," *Life,* IV (February 28, 1938), 9-13.
"William Allen White: The Sage of Emporia," *Look,* February 15, 1938, 9-11.
"William Allen White; Reformer and Optimist," *Craftsman,* XVIII (September, 1910), 680-81.
"William Allen White's War on the Klan," *Literary Digest,* LXXXIII (October 11, 1924), 16.

Index

Index

of 1922, 223; reunion of the Rough Riders, 130; split into two factions, 116; suicide pact of a boy and girl, 290; readers' appreciation of Wm. A. White's editorials, 293; Wm. A. White about himself, 113-14; Wm. A. White's home, 115; Wm. A. White's return from Europe (1909), 148

Emporia, College of, 25-26, 29, 30

Emporia State Teachers College, 196, 200, 224

England, *see* Great Britain

Estes Park, 67, 273, 331

Europe, 198, 203, 319, 320; difference of governments, 315; European rulers, 181-82

European War, 1914-18, 177-188; *see also* World War

Evans, Hiram, 256

Evening Post, Chicago, 91, 92

Evening Post, New York, 254

Evening Star, Kansas City, *see Star,* Kansas City

Farmers' Alliance, 53-54

Fascism, 281; *see also* Totalitarian states

Ferber, Edna, 117, 244, 275

Field, R. M., 94

Fields, Roswell, 61

Finney, W. W., 216, 276

Fisher, Dorothy Canfield, 35

Flaming Youth, 200

Foley, Peter, 48

Folk, Joseph W., 104, 134

Foncannon, Frank, 216

Food, manufacturers and dealers of, 194, 197-98

France, 177, 179, 183, 187, 198, 319, 321, 325; Allied war organization, 187; caste and class interests, 186; *see also* Versailles, Treaty of

Frankfurter, Felix, 258

Franklin, Edward C., 36, 43

Franklin, William L., 36, 43

French, Laura, 144

Friedburg, Cass, 26

Fulton, T. P., 26, 28, 29

Funston, F., 36, 37, 43, 97, 124-25

Fusion Party, 87

"Gaiety of War, The," 125

Garland, Hamlin, 93, 94

Gayda, Virginio, 326

Gazette, Emporia, 42, 51-53, 63, 78, 79, 80, 81, 82, 87, 93, 94, 100, 102, 103, 104, 112, 113, 114, 115 117,

121-23, 136, 137, 230, 232, 292, 303, 321; appearance between the 90's and 1900's, 108-11; Armistice Day editorial, 315; bought by Wm. A. White, 70-71; reviews of *A Certain Rich Man,* 147-49; Christmas dinner, 237-38; circulation by 1903, 110; closed shop, 237-38; conservative attitude, 127; Daughters of the American Revolution, 258; editorial staff, 144, 232-33, 243; election (1920), 195-96; average term of service of employees, 236; employees and profit-sharing plan, 237-38; employees' welfare, 237-38; traditional enemies, 295; improvement of equipment, 144, 233; funny section, 240; high rating among 24 dailies, 241; position of Walter E. Hughes, 235; indebtedness, 70-71, 93-94, 110, 117; training for journalists, 236; denouncing the Ku Klux Klan, 247-48, 252, 256-57; Robert M. La Follette, 121, 136; local column, 241-42; joined by Walt Mason, 145-46; on the New Deal, 280; news to be excluded, 113; during the nineteen twenties, 233; Harrison Parkman, 308; purchase offers, 230, 234; puzzle section, 240; advocacy of railroad legislation, 133; railroad strike of 1922, 221; attitude of readers, 292; out-of-state readers, 129, 314; aligned with the Republican Party, 278-79; split in the Republican Party, 163; ignorance of Th. Roosevelt's foreign policy, 132; Th. Roosevelt's headquarters in the 1912 campaign, 170; Th. Roosevelt a regular reader, 130; reunion of the Rough Riders, 130; Spanish-American War, 125; competition of the Kansas City *Star,* 241; printing of telegraphic news, 75; "Wailing Place," 242; Wm. A. White's editorship, 299-300; Wm. A. White's editorials express his honest opinion, 182; Wm. A. White's campaign for governorship, 254; Wm. A. White's refusal to run for governor, 169-72; Wm. A. White's story about himself, 113-14; development under Wm. A. White's management, 73-74; in memory of Mary White, 213-16; Wm. A. White's refusal to work for metropolitan papers, 230, 232;

Index

Index